M000286271

Women, Their Names, & The Stories They Tell

Where We've Been...Where We Are...
Where We Are Going

Elisabeth P. Waugaman, Ph.D.

Women, Their Names, & The Stories They Tell

Where We've Been...Where We Are...Where We Are Going

Elisabeth P. Waugaman, Ph.D.

Vox Femina Press, LLC
Rockville, MD

ISBN 978-0-615-38226-5

Copyright © 2010 Elisabeth P. Waugaman, Ph.D.

All rights reserved.

FIRST EDITION

Cover Design and Interior Page Layout by Michele Craig,
Snapdragon Graphics LLC (www.mysnapdragon.com)

TABLE OF CONTENTS

– PART TWO –
THE NAME FROM THE OUTSIDE IN:
HOW WE GET OUR NAMES AND WHAT THEY MEAN TO US
111–332

PREFACE

During a conversation with Joy, I realized we could learn a lot about female identity by listening to women discuss their given names. Shakespeare questions the importance of names when Juliet ponders, "What's in a name? That which we call a rose/ By any other name would smell as sweet" (Romeo and Juliet, II.ii.44-45). When asked the same question, women had a lot to say. In writing about their given names, they reveal what is most important to their sense of identity. They offer us new ways of thinking about the self—new psychological and spiritual insights drawn from ancient traditions, different religions, cultures, races, and age groups. The younger generations provide insight into how our culture is changing. I did not realize how much women's diversity would teach me and how it would inspire me. My understanding of self, family, and even spirituality has changed. I am not the same person I was when I started this quest. Reading their stories, you will find the keys to treasure chests full of gems set in ancient, contemporary, and even futuristic settings—knowledge of the past, present, and future that will enrich your understanding of who you are and what it is to be a human being.

Part I, The Name from the Inside Out, centers on how women feel about and adapt to their names. Each section asks questions that invite you to ponder your own psychological development. Native Americans describe our oldest and most complex naming tradition. How can their ancient naming traditions help us enrich our identity? How do we first learn about identity through names? What are the ramifications of nicknames, common names, and unusual names in the formation of the self? How can we overcome name ambivalence? How is identity affected by compound names? Why do so many women discuss middle names? Do women with many different names have a different sense of self? What about women's liberation and its name aftermath? How do women feel about their titles? Why do some women choose a new name? Do our names limit how we think about ourselves? How can our names help us enrich our identity? By comparing your experiences to those of the essayists, you will gain a better understanding of how your own sense of self was formed.

Part II, The Name from the Outside In, considers external influences on names. Ancient African naming traditions describe a very different concept of time and ancestry from that of the West, which prompts a consideration of time, family, race, and new genetic discoveries. Essays on the religious significance of names end with a discussion of the latest findings concerning the development of the world's religions. Black American Muslim naming traditions introduce the topic of slavery. The latest information from recently published books and websites provides little known history about this ancient and contemporary plague. Names drawn from the performing arts, the fine arts, and mythology lead the reader through history and diverse cultures. Because women also address the esoteric, music and color are considered as well as numbers which lead to a discussion of the numerical structure of the universe and the individual as understood by both the ancients and contemporary science. Younger generations discuss changes in the sense of self as a result of the Computer Age. What are the consequences of multiple screen names, passwords, daemons, and avatars for our sense of identity? How can we orient ourselves in this new world of multiple identities that seem to threaten the very essence of the self? Our ancient naming traditions can serve as our guide in this brave new world that holds enormous promise and danger. References to books and websites are included so that you can pursue whatever interests you.

Many essayists told me they made discoveries about themselves writing their essays. I hope that after reading this book, you will write your own name essay. Among other things, you will reconnect with the past and think more creatively about the present and the future. Rewriting your essay from time to time helps to assess and renew your ongoing personal evolution.

ACKNOWLEDGMENTS

Peggy O. Heller, MSW, Ph.D., *(Portrait of the Artist as Poet, Word Arts Collage)*, provided generous and gracious editing and commentary, as did Drs. Richard Waugaman and Randi Finger. Special thanks also go to Michele Craig for her editing and formatting of this book.

I am deeply grateful to the many women who wrote essays about their names for the wonderful trip they have taken me on, for the discoveries I have made from their wisdom, and for the new, more creative understanding of self they have given me. I hope that you too, dear reader, will finish this identity quest with the same sense of wonder. Readers who would like to post their name essays, or share links or stories about women's names, can do so by googling: womens-names.com (http://www.womens-names.com/). This site can become a valuable resource for anyone who wants to learn more about identity based on personal stories and lessons learned from life. Mathew Tinsley (tinsley@tinsology.net) is to be recommended for his design of the website.

Part One

Given Names and the Evolution of Identity: Names from the Inside Out

How women feel about their names—the internal, psychological dimensions of names—is one of the most striking themes in the essays. In the U.S., our oldest and most complex naming tradition is that of the Native Americans. How do they feel about their names? Can their ancient naming traditions enlighten us in the 21st century? Do they reveal truths we have forgotten? Do they have keys to identity we do not?

Chapter 1
NATIVE AMERICAN WOMEN:
THE MANY DIMENSIONS OF A NAME

The following essay was submitted by Brooke W.S. Helman, a member of the Mohegan tribe, one of the Algonquin speaking tribes originally from the Thames Valley in Connecticut. Despite the fact the Mohegans fought with the British against other Indian tribes and despite British court rulings recognizing their landholdings, the Mohegans were dispossessed. There are now fewer than 2,000 Mohegans.

– A –
NAMES AND STORIES

• • •

Seeking Ethnic Unity
Brooke W.S. Helman
(Native American, Mohegan)

My mother intentionally gave all of her children a name that either a male or female could have knowing that it was harder for women to find jobs then. I am the youngest of 3 sisters, and as such, she got the last of the naming out of her system. My oldest sister is named conventionally—she's Stacy Renée. My middle sister is Shannon Rebecca Hespera. I am Meghan Branwynne Gwynetthe Brooke, and I spell it differently than my mother did. I am superstitious and wouldn't want the name of that goddess upon me. My mother never liked Meghan as much as the other names, so I've always been called Brooke. This sat well with me; there were mean children in school called Meghan, and I didn't want to be seen the same way.

When I applied for my last job, I was very impressed by the Board of Trustees. I have a deep voice, so it is hard for some people to tell what gender I am over the phone. My Board had no idea until I showed up whether I was a man or a woman. When this was related to me later, I asked which they would have preferred. I was told very candidly that they were looking for the most qualified applicant and they didn't give a wit if I were male or female or something else.

The ethnic name that I am highly honored to have is Wompsi'kuk' Skeesucks. You earn an American Indian name. It is fluid. It changes as you change. Mine is an unusual name for many reasons. Out East, the names are generally not animal names. Most are attitude or natural event names. This is particularly so for women. I fully expected an attitude name like Dances Like a Boy, and joke about this often. I was given my name, Eagle Eye, for noticing little things far in advance. It's almost a long-range planning name, if you will. But there is also much medicine behind Eagle. Eagle is the messenger between the Earth and Creator, and so is very honored. Just as the eyes relay the message from your heart to the rest of the world. People that are wise can look at someone's eyes and see the truth or lies there. When I am most comfortable and generally among Natives, I go by 'Kuk'. That keeps my attitude in check, but it honors my name and lets others pronounce it quickly and with no problem.

When I was married, I knew what my Indian name would be, and I had decided to take my husband's name. I was so excited because I would finally be able to change my name to what everyone called me. My full legal name would not even fit on the marriage license. So, I explained to the clerk what happened and requested that she abbreviate it to Brooke and my Indian name. She refused to do that. I argued here, knowing how not arguing with my driving instructor had me carry the burden of Meghan around for so many years. She would not let me change it, even to just Brooke, despite the form being unable to accommodate what she admitted is my full legal name. I received the same treatment from the DMV and the Social Security folks.

Professionally, I use BWS Johnson. It honors my American Indian name. It's doubly good, because if people were trying to find me and just used "Brooke Johnson" for their search, they wouldn't meet with much success. I also like that it is a natural conversation starter. Many people ask "What does the WS stand for?" The letters serve to separate out the people that are genuine in their compassion from the ones that are too busy to bother. The busy people will be satisfied with "They stand for my Indian name." Compassionate people will ask another time. "Yes, but what is your Indian name?" Very caring people, and these are few and far between, will take the time to learn the Algonquian and painstakingly repeat it after me until they learn it. A small handful of these will ask what it means. Fewer still will ask after the significance. Questions are terribly important in my line of work, but we get caught up in answers too often. I was very touched when a colleague corrected a committee on my behalf. She had noticed that I always wrote and signed BWS Johnson. When they went to publish the report with Brooke Johnson, she noted the difference and asked my opinion. I was so very grateful.

———

One of the striking aspects of Brooke's essay is that of the many stories she has for her names—stories that go back in time to embrace long lost

legends and spirits, stories about nature, personality, and culture.
I asked her to explain to me in greater detail what she meant when she said
a Native America name "(…) is fluid. It changes as you change," and she
provided the following response.

– B –
THE EVOLVING NAME

• • •

A Name is Fluid
Brooke W.S. Hellman

*Realize that what I say is only what I know, which is much, much smaller than
what Grandmother Shi would say by a lot. Even if you asked Grandmother Shi,
she might know what many Nations know, but maybe she wouldn't know every
Nation's traditions. Only Chief can speak for the Mohegan people, too. It would be
like asking an Italian what the Indo-Europeans meant by something.*

*When a child is young, they might get a name. But they are very small.
And there are very few who can see what the child will be in time. We can all be
anything. So like personality, this name may not be settled. Children are flexible
still. Then, when you are a teen, you might be given a name that is closer, or maybe
the younger one will still suit you. When you're an adult, even though things are
settled, you might do something terrible, or something great, or something terrible
might happen to you. I knew a man from another nation that was Bear. He served
in Viet Nam and when he came back and had ceremony, he was Wounded Bear.
There are so many Bears: it's a very common name like John.*

*Suppose the wheel keeps turning. As you age, or when you are honored to
become an Elder (not all old people are Elders), your name might change or be
totally different as you change. Some people are like lakes. They change very little as
they age. Lakes fill in, but it takes a very long time for that to happen. Some people
are like rivers. When you trace the Mississippi, or any other river, it can be very
small at its source. Later on, it can be wide and strong. When it meets the ocean,
it spreads out. If you asked someone which river they were looking at [along] those
different points—if you asked if they were all the same and they hadn't followed
along with you—would they know?*

*I knew a Dancing Wind once who was a Cheyenne Elder. She would say her
name, and it was perfect for her. I smiled when I met her. But most people hear
that and they don't know what it means. They think it's a wispy cheerleader kind of
name. Dancing Wind is a tornado. She is named for her temper.*

– C –
THE MANY DIMENSIONS OF A NAME

. . .

Environmental, Social, and Spiritual Dimensions
Shiakoda Qkalokqua Saunders

(…) My Chief named me "Autumn Wolf Moon" which I wear proudly! Autumn is my season, Wolf is for my people, and Moon is for the mother. I have now reached Grandmother status and I am very proud of this. I have been teaching young ones what I have learned—this is what it is all about. I also help people trace their roots by giving them information on where to look and what to do next. So I also have the name of "Grandmother."

. . .

A Spiritual Name
Charlie Toledo, Director:
Suscol Intertribal Council

Charlie Toledo is my birth name. Toledo is a Native American surname native to New Mexico. My first name is Charlene. I'm a second to a twin brother Charles. My mother was going to name us Jess & Jessica after my father's anglicized forename Jess, from the Hispanic Jesus.

I don't know why she chose Charles & Charlene. It sounds like redneck cowgirl's slang...Charleen. I received the nickname Charlie in 5th grade Catholic elementary school when we were studying Charlemagne in ancient history. All my girlfriends started calling me Charlemagne—that made us all laugh. Me too! I liked being called after an ancient king.

Late that same year it got shortened to Charlie. In high school my subsequent attempts "to grow up" to the full name of Charlene were thwarted at my first attempt. I was leaving 1st period English class on the first day of freshman year in high school when a new classmate asked me, "What is your name?" I answered with "Charlene," just to have a former elementary school pal reply very loudly, "Whatever! We all call her 'Charlie.'" That was that for the rest of my life really.

I like the name Charlie it has a nice happy sound to it and then in college and high school my twin bro changed his name from Charlie to Chuck. So that is how we went through the rest of our lives Chuck & Charlie. With my surname folks always remember my name usually with a smile.

I do have a spiritual name that is used only in ceremony but has the same sound as Charlie. When speaking or doing presentations I just use the name Charlie. At 57 it is my name, and it always brings a smile, "Oh a girl named Charlie?"

Because my name is unusual I do tell that story or some story about my name.

The spiritual name is private but just to acknowledge it is there. Many tribes have different traditions about naming. Some wait and have a baby name for two years, then a name at puberty, then a name that is given as they pass to adulthood. Currently it is a habit to give many nicknames to a child or person. It is always funny to see which ones stick...Fatty, Nosy, Tubby, Guy-Guy, Sissie or Cissie, or brother, uncle.

The Lakota and Eastern tribes have clan names and given names that tell a story of the family—like Fast Horse, Walking Man, Big Bear, Turtle, Yellow Hawk, Grey Hawk, Mankiller. California names are more nicknames and more diminutive due to all the forced re-locations and torture that really dismantled the Indian communities. In the old days Native Americans had one name, then their clan of family lineage; but colonization forced last name changes. Often the name was given by the priest baptizing the baby or by the rancher that owned them. That devastation was greater on the California coast than in the Midwest or south and northwest. Now many folks are giving their children names in their traditional languages, and then a more typical Christian name as was done in my family.

Growing up with a man's name has always been funny. I used to often hear, "Charlie! That is a man's name." My immediate response to gales of laughter, "No it's not: I am a woman; can't you see?" People don't react like that very often anymore because using a man's nickname for a woman is more common now. Charlie was more accepted after the "Charlie" perfume appeared back in the '70s, which my friends thought was named after me ... a free spirit traveling the world, etc.

So I think having an unusual name has a positive effect as it gives you something to talk about to new people and they remember you and your name. The advantage of being a public person is it clears out folks who pretend to know me. Before my gender became well known locally and it was my name that was in newspaper articles sometimes, even I would hear folks say, "Charlie, yes he is a very well respected man." That still lets me know if I am dealing with someone I know or a stranger as in you wrote Mr. Toledo ... just a little heads up about who really knows me or about me.

Brooke W.S. explains that Native Americans do not consider a name a fixed label. On the contrary, names should change as the individual changes. Children are given a name with the understanding that their name may change at adolescence. As people change with time, their names may be changed to reflect their development. Brooke W.S. points out that in her culture, you earn your name.

This flexibility with given names provides constant opportunity and inspiration for growth throughout life by reinforcing the individual's relationship with society, which bestows new names. This naming tradition is acutely sensitive to the individual. When Bear's name is changed to *Wounded Bear*, the new name is not only a badge of honor, since he was wounded fighting for his country, but also a signal of the need to be considerate of an injured spirit/body. The same is true for the woman named *Dancing Wind*, which is not only a beautiful image, but also a warning about her temper. Native American names mirror the character of their owner and serve as a guide for how the individual should be treated. By not hesitating to expose shortcomings, the Native American naming tradition provides a powerful incentive for the individual to overcome them. Names communicate skills, needs, even shortcomings, and place individuals forthrightly in society. Names serve as both psychological and social mirrors: the name does not provide a mask—a hiding place.

In addition to a name that reflects the individual's character, Native Americans also have tribal names, which are like our surnames. Shiakoda explains that *Wolf* is for her tribe. Today, most Americans usually have fairly restricted contact with or even awareness of distant relatives. A few non-Native American families have gatherings in which members come from far and wide, but this is a relatively rare phenomenon. With the exception of tribal and clan names, the concept of a family tribe is almost totally absent in the U.S. and most of Western culture, which conceives of families in a much more linear pattern. To most Westerners, the word *family* usually calls to mind first the nuclear family, then the linear family. Native American tribal names have a social dimension that has been largely lost in the Western world as families have been separated geographically and have grown much smaller than in the past. The meaning of family has grown more and more restricted in the West with the passage of time.

Native Americans names also link them to nature. Brooke W.S. sees her name *Eagle* as a link to both nature and spirituality—the Eagle links heaven and earth. Shiakoda explains that the *Moon* in her name links her to the Mother. Names drawn from nature have a spiritual dimension because Native Americans believe all of creation is sacred. Names drawn from nature are also symbolic. When Native Americans hear their full names, they are reminded of the psychological, social, and natural dimensions of their identity—of their personal and social selves as well as their bond with Nature. Most Western women no longer have these dimensions in their names. The U.S. Census Bureau reveals that there are still a few women's names overtly drawn from nature: names like *Lily, Rose, Jasmine, Dawn,* and *Amber.* These names became old-fashioned and were considered insubstantial. The loss of the link between names and nature suggests why Western culture has been so destructive to the environment: Western names and identity lost their ties to nature. I hope there will come a time when Western women will once again feel free to have names that link them to nature and to the feminine, without fear of discrimination. When that day comes, we will know that men and women are truly equal; and nature will be recognized as being as important as business or science. Recent name studies indicate that names from nature are making a comeback in the United Kingdom with names like *Olivia, Ruby,* and *Lily* in the top ten in 2008.[1] The trend is also starting in the U.S., which had one name, *Ashley*, drawn from nature in the top ten in 2000; two, *Ashley* and *Olivia* in 2001-2007; and three, *Ava, Olivia,* and *Chloe* in 2008 and 2009.[2] *Ava* comes from *Eve, Olivia* from the olive, and *Ashley* from the ash tree. *Chloe* means "budding," or "green shoot" and has ties to the fertility goddess Demeter.[3] It is no longer immediately apparent that these names are drawn from nature: the tie is very muted, a mere whisper, compared to the Native American naming tradition or the British names, *Ruby* and *Lily*. The move towards names drawn from nature is just beginning in the U.S.; it will be interesting to see how the trend develops as we continue to grow more aware of the impact of human activity on the earth's environment.

Charlie reveals that Native Americans have a spiritual name that is kept secret and is known only to the individual and the Medicine Man. Having a secret spiritual name provides the individual with a pure, immutable core identity. The spiritual name represents the inviolable divine essence of the individual. The admonition not to speak the sacred name reflects the same admonition found in Judaism not to speak or write the sacred name of God. By not revealing the sacred name, it is spared any exposure that would sully it. No matter what happens to the individual, her secret, sacred name will remain untainted. The sacred name provides a pure nucleus, a powerful source for healing should the individual suffer harm: the secret name protects the innermost, spiritual self.

We find echoes of the Native American spiritual name in the Catholic sacrament of confirmation (associated primarily with English speaking countries, Germany, Poland, and Lithuania) when adolescents pick a middle name from the list of saints and also in the ancient Jewish tradition of giving a Hebrew name in addition to the child's social (e.g., American) given name. (Contemporary Jewish women may have very different ideas of what the Hebrew name means to them as either a spiritual or a cultural identity or both.) The Native Americans and the Old Testament have ancient traditions for bestowing a new name to represent a changed individual. The number of Catholic countries that follow this tradition suggests that it may also be derived from an ancient naming tradition. A sacred name identifies—gives reality to—the spiritual essence of the individual and serves as a reminder of the divine spirit within us: when named, the sacred within us is no longer an abstraction. The sacred name becomes a named, identifiable part of the self that can be called upon to help avoid spiritual pitfalls as well as to heal from trauma.

Native Americans still face name discrimination for driver's licenses and social security numbers. Forbidding the use of Native American names destroys their culture. For many years in the U.S., Canada, and Australia, indigenous children were taken away from their parents. They were placed in schools where they were not allowed to speak their native languages or keep their native names. As a result, many indigenous cultures have been lost. This is not only a loss for the world's languages, each of which imparts its particular understanding of the world through its unique vocabulary, but also a loss for the world's social and spiritual cultures. Considering the Native American tradition of the given name as a guidepost, we can well understand Brooke W.S.'s consideration of individuals according to their sensitivity to her name.

The Native American naming tradition is the most psychologically complex described in the essays. Native American names provide an evolving sense of the self and link the individual to four dimensions—the psychological, social, natural, and spiritual realms. With their names, Native Americans can immediately summon all these diverse aspects of the self. Most contemporary Western women cannot summon up diverse aspects of the self with their given names, which serve primarily to identify a unique individual, a self-apart. With the exception of names passed on for generations, Western naming traditions celebrate primarily the singularity of the individual. Without the Native American naming traditions that invoke the psychological, social, environmental, and spiritual aspects of the self, how can we access these dimensions of ourselves with our given names?

We can embark on an identity quest using our names for inspiration. In a quest, like in life, it is what we discover on our trip that measures our success. The key element is adventure—what happens along the way.

You can begin your quest by delving more into Native American traditions, which will enrich your own: *The Native Americans* by C. Taylor, *Dancing Colors: Paths of the Native American Woman* by L. Thorn, *The Spirit of Native America* by A. Walters, *The Ways of My Grandmothers* by B. Wolf, *From the Heart of Crow Country* by J. Crow, and *The Mystic Warriors of the Plains* by T. Malis are possibilities. On the web, you can check out *Native American Spirituality* (http://www.religioustolerance.org/nataspir.htm) and *Seeking Native American Spirituality and Traditional Religion*, which provide caveats and a substantial list of books about Native Americans written by Native Americans (http://www.native-languages.org/books.htm).

Chapter 2
NICKNAMES

The following essays illustrate that most American nicknames do not develop linearly like those of Native Americans. A few essayists have a surprising number of variations on a name, and a few have nicknames that are bestowed on the individual for something they did just as we see in the Native American tradition; however, most of the nicknames the essayists discuss are diminutives of the given name. Participants acknowledge that there is a subset of nicknames that they refuse to reveal because they are "too childish" or "too personal"—because they make the participant feel too vulnerable. The nicknames women are the most willing to discuss are those given by the family or those women pick for themselves. More rarely they discuss nicknames given by others. The essays reveal that nicknames are the closest most Americans come to the Native American concept of the evolving self.

Nicknames actually played a role in the creation of surnames. Surnames were gradually adopted to distinguish one individual from another and derive from a variety of sources—places, occupations, and traits, which include nicknames. *The Oxford English Dictionary* (OED) states that the Normans brought hereditary surnames to England in 1066. A surname (*surnom*) in French was originally an additional name, a nickname, like King Richard the Lionheart or Catherine the Great. In French *surnom* still refers to a nickname—a name added to the given name—rather than a family name (*nom de famille*). In English, however, surname has gradually come to mean *family name*. The two languages remind us of the historical transformation of some nicknames into family surnames.

This transition is also documented among common folk with the use of "tee names" (nicknames) in the fishing villages of Scotland. Scottish tee names were used to distinguish between individuals who shared both given and surname. The OED's etymology of *tee* suggests that tee means too—i.e., a name added to another name. Tee names were so essential for distinguishing individuals that they were recorded in official records, which led to confusion with the tee name sometimes replacing the surname. Tee names could describe family relationships (e.g., "Kitty's Jamsey" meaning James the son of Katherine); characteristics, which could be positive or negative (e.g., James McKee "the Short" could become James Short); or the tee names could have unknown origins if the story behind them was forgotten (e.g., James McKee "the Prince" could become James Prince). The last two examples illustrate how tee names sometimes replaced the actual surname. According to specialists, tee names spread throughout England and were at first called "to-names" (because they were added to the name: 10th century) and only later referred to as nicknames (15th century).[4] According to the OED, *nickname* derives from Old Norse. This complicated written history indicates that nicknames can play an important role in the creation of an individual's identity.

What do the essayists tell us about how nicknames develop and what they mean to them? For most of us, the first nicknames we hear and say are *Mommy* and *Daddy*.

– A –
MOTHER'S NAMES

• • •

You Are Not Elisabeth. You're Mommy.
Adele
(as recollected by her mother)

I will never forget the day my three-year-old heard my given name and realized for the first time that I was somebody else besides Mommy. She looked at me and frowned, "You're not Elisabeth. You're Mommy." When I explained that Elisabeth was my given name just like Adele was her given name, the frown did not go away. I continued in an effort to erase the frown. Since she was our only child at that point, I said, "You're the only one who can call me 'Mommy.'" That seemed to help. It was startling to see my three-year-old trying to fit together different pieces of her mother's identity. At age three, she was beginning to learn that identity is not singular but multidimensional.

Does this essay stir up any memories for you?

Women's earliest sense of identity comes from their mothers. Children have numerous diminutives for *Mother: Ma, Mama, Mommy, and Mom,* usually in that developmental order. Because diminutives are used for the mother and father, it follows that diminutives are often used for children, who receive nicknames that are usually based on their given name. Our earliest associations are to nicknames (the familiar and sometimes private names our families use); these associations help explain why nicknames are so powerfully emotive for all of us.

Elisabeth tries to reassure Adele that although she has another identity in addition to that of Mommy, Adele is still the only one who can call her Mommy—the mother's identity is still unique, intact. Adele's fear of an unknown identity (that of Elisabeth, an identity that might threaten

Mommy's identity) is assuaged: the two identities can coexist simultaneously. Through her mother's different names, the child learns that identity is multifaceted as opposed to singular.

I can remember hearing my mother addressed as "Betsy" and thinking that I didn't know that part of her: for me as a child, the world of Betsy was an unknowable, unpossessable aspect of my mother. I remember that this mysterious aspect of my mother forced me to wonder how much I really knew or could know my mother. As a child, this comes as a surprise—that we cannot know other people completely, not even our own mothers. Underlying this awareness is, of course, our childhood desire to be in total possession of our beloved. Understanding that we cannot totally possess our mothers helps children develop healthy relationships with others in which they realize they can never totally possess another individual. Parts of our friends and loved ones will always be unknowable and unattainable. One of the ways we first learn these lessons is through understanding our mother's different identities through her different names.

• • •

We Called Our Mother "Dear"
Anonymous

One of our aunts told us we had "a dear mother." So we dropped the mother and called her "Dear." One day my brother called up to the floor (we lived in a tenement) and he didn't want to be called a sissy. So he called, "Rose, Rose!" (her given name); and she was furious.

———————

This episode had such an impact that the essayist chose to write about it rather than her given name. The essay expresses the same sense of unhappiness Adele feels when she first hears that her mother has other identities besides that of Mommy; however, here it is the mother who is unhappy that her child calls her by her given name rather than *Mommy* or *Mom*. Just as Adele resisted her mother's given name, her social identity, here the mother resists the child's use of *Rose*, her social name, rather than *Mom*, her family name. The social name puts the mother and the child outside of the family context; and the mother rightfully feels this as a breach of family relationships.

———————

This essay introduces the important social element in the mother-child relationship. Changes in the nicknames for mother can serve as guideposts for the development of the child—as the child's name for the mother evolves, so may the child's name. When *Mommy* becomes *Mom*, the child's name may follow a similar evolution—*Jenny* may become *Jennifer*—although this

13

process may take longer, or the nickname may never be abandoned. At a certain age, *Mommy* has to be dropped for a more socially acceptable name: *Mom*. Children are forced to grow up by society, sometimes prematurely, as suggested by this essay. The social pressures here are so intense that the children feel forced to abandon even *Mom*. They find a way to express their affection for their mother without being attacked as sissies by calling her "Dear." *Dear* can be interpreted as either loving or sarcastic. By its very ambiguity, *Dear* protects them.

These social experiences with mother's nicknames are among the first in which the child learns about the complexities of social identity. Many of us still have memories of this transition, which may be painful and awkward if it entails admonitions to drop *Mommy*—a harsh awakening to the fact that childhood is being left behind. Do you remember transitioning from *Mommy* to *Mom?*

– B –
THE GIVEN NAME AND SELF-IDENTITY

• • •

I Always Remember Feeling Funny When....
Stephanie Monahan

My name is Stephanie. I always remember feeling funny if there was someone else in my class with the same name. There weren't many other Stephanies. So I guess I felt special that my name didn't belong to lots of other people. Professionally, I always sign my name Stephanie. But when I consider someone a friend, I close emails with Steph. And I always feel more comfortable with people who call me the shortened version. When picking a name for my daughter, it was important to me that her name not be on the most common list. I wanted her to know that we picked a special name just for her. So we chose a unique spelling: Emilia. And we called her Emmy for short. I sometimes wonder if it is confusing for her (she's two) to have two names. Now she is learning to spell her name and sometimes she's not sure which one to use.

The first time a child hears her name used by someone else, there may be an odd feeling that her identity is no longer uniquely hers. "That's my name, not yours!" a child may think to herself. In our early development, our names are a crucial part of our sense of self. As we develop, we outgrow this unique identity with our names; but it remains in our subconscious and explains why women can be very adamant about the pronunciation and the spelling of their names. If either is incorrect, the identity is incorrect—even if, rationally, we know the person addressing us knows who we are. The error triggers a very deep-seated sense of the self, which explains why these mistakes can be so surprisingly irritating: they challenge our innermost sense of who we are. Do you remember the first time you heard your name used to address someone else? How do you react now when you meet someone with your name? I have noticed very mixed reactions. Sometimes my namesake smiles, sometimes she looks away. Namesakes may avidly, or tepidly discuss, or may avoid conversation about our shared given name. Reactions can be very different and may briefly reveal our earliest sense of self as centered in the name. What have you noticed?

Stephanie notes how confusing it is for a young child to have two names—a given name and a nickname. The youngster has to gradually figure out which one to use. At an early age, children with nicknames are beginning to learn about the complexities of identity. Children without nicknames can only learn this from others. One wonders if children who grow up without nicknames have a different, perhaps more singular, sense of self because they have not experienced the multifaceted dimensions of identity experienced by children with nicknames.

– C –
AM I ADOPTED?
THE FOUNDLING FANTASY

The following essay describes what I call the Foundling Fantasy. At some point, children may wonder if their parents are really their true parents. I distinctly remember questioning if my parents were, indeed, my "real" parents. I remember the doubts made me feel both inspired (perhaps my real parents were like characters out of a story book) and uncomfortable (perhaps I didn't know as much as I thought I did). Do you remember this fantasy?

Freud calls these extended childhood fantasies "Family Romances" and maintains that this is one way in which the child acquires "the right to doubt."[5] Doubt leads to questioning our identity, which is essential for developing our sense of who we are. Fantasy about our identity is crucial for inventing new ways of seeing ourselves—for enriching our creativity.

• • •

Growing Into a Name
Kathleen Landis Rauhauser

I am told that my parents chose between Jacqueline and Kathleen for my first name. As a child in the '50s, I didn't see myself as a Jacqueline and was pleased they chose Kathleen. One of my darling nieces is named Jacqueline and it suits her just fine. (While there is no known Irish in our family, we are Pennsylvania Dutch, of Palatine German and Scandinavian descent. One might say I got the gift of the Blarney from my first name. :)

My middle name is my mother's maiden name, Landis. So Kathleen Landis Rauhauser says who I really am. Kathleen was I. Landis was my mother's contribution. Unfortunately I have gotten her arthritis instead of her saintly nature. Rauhauser was my father's family name. I wish I had gotten his brilliance rather than his temper. :)

I think having this name was a good thing in my case. As a child I felt distanced, and I guess a lot of us felt that way. But I didn't know that. In our circle of friends many of the children were adopted, and there was something in me that said maybe so was I. As years went on people would say I looked liked my Dad. In false disgust, I'd say, "But I'm not bald and I don't have a mustache!" In the '60s and '70s when many people wore wigs, my mother and I went to the same hair salon. We wore the same style wigs and really did resemble each other. Both of these experiences pleased me and helped confirm I really am Kathleen Landis Rauhauser.

Early on I was nicknamed Kathy. At one point there were three Kathys in my class at school. This served me well. When the teacher called on Kathy, I could either act like she meant one of the others, and one was quite bright, or I could blurt out the answer if I thought I knew it. However, upon changing school districts, I decided to become Kathleen at school. So when I meet people from my past, I generally can figure out when I knew them from how they address me. My family, of course, continues to call me Kathy. When my mother was alive I knew I was in trouble if she called me Kathleen. And, of course, I liked it when my father would call me Kathleen the Queen. Was there ever a Queen Kathleen?

Now I generally go as Kathy but professionally use my given name, Kathleen.

– D –
FAMILY NICKNAMES

Nicknames that become dominant and sometimes replace the given name are often nicknames given by the family.

• • •

Before I Was Born
Bonnie Perkins

My parents picked out the name Bonnie Burk before I was born. If the baby were to be a girl, they knew exactly which girl she was to be and exactly whom it was that they were waiting for! The only problem with the name "Bonnie" is that there

is no Saint Bonnie, so they had to pick a saint's name that could fit with "Bonnie."
The only one they could find was Saint Bonaventura. So my official given name
is "Bonita." In Catholic grade school in those days, no nicknames were allowed, so
I was "Bonita" all through elementary school. "Bonnie" was the name my family
used. When I went to a public high school, however, it seemed like everybody had
a nickname, so I was called "Bonnie." Ironically, I didn't like it at first because I
thought it sounded too cutsie after being called "Bonita" all through elementary
school. I did adapt to "Bonnie," however: the name fits me, and it has a nicer ring to
it. "Bonnie" is a better fit for my size and personality. I am small, and people tell me
I have a lively, sunny personality.

Bonnie's essay presents the interesting twist of someone who grows into her nickname, which is the opposite of what usually happens: most people grow out of their nicknames. Her parents' certitude about her name—that she was "Bonnie" before she was "Bonita"—must have helped her adapt to her nickname as "a better fit" than her given name.

• • •

From the Beginning
Windy

When we were in school, I used my nickname Windy, but my full first names are
Margaret Winslow (….) My parents nicknamed me Windy from the beginning,
but they must have called me Winslow sometimes. My younger sister couldn't say
Winslow when she was learning to talk so she called me Dodo. That nickname lasted
until I was old enough to learn about the dodo bird (about the third grade, I think),
but my sisters and aunt still call me Doe sometimes. I don't remember that my
mother regularly called me Winslow unless she was angry with me and then it was
always a sharp "Margaret Winslow."

When we were growing up and later when I went to college in our part of
the country, I knew several Wendys, but I could never hear any difference in the
pronunciation of their names and mine. It wasn't until I went to the Northeast
to graduate school that I could hear a difference in Wendy and Windy. I still pay
attention when I hear either pronunciation—just in case someone is talking to me.
It is especially interesting right now because I have a colleague named Wendy and
we frequently joke about our names.

My first job was as a day counselor at a playground when I was in the eighth
grade. I had to get my Social Security card then and I used my full name on it. That
usage has been the source of confusion to others and an occasional frustration to me.

I prefer to use M. Winslow professionally, but Social Security has influenced
the way I am known to the IRS and to employers and insurers. Other accounts

I have more control over. I could change my name legally to drop the Margaret, but I have never done so. It is much too interesting to see all the variations that have occurred over the years. I have heard of two other women with the first name Winslow, one of whom has the nickname Windy, but I have never met either of them (...)

· · ·

Ever Since I Can Remember
Cathy Trauernicht

Ever since I can remember, I've been called "Cathy" ... except, at times, when my parents were trying to get my attention and, I suppose, I wasn't responding...then I would hear, "Catharine!" I do like Catharine, but never insisted people call me that name. Over the years, friends have given me other nicknames, so Catharine always seemed a bit formal.

· · ·

Judy Suits Me Fine
Judy Gottlieb Herman

I am Judith (Judy) Gottlieb Herman. I was named after my great-grandmother. Her name was Judith Frieda and that became my name. I was always just Judy growing up. Except when my parents were angry, then I became Judith and I knew I had better watch out (....)

I have a relatively informal style and so the Judy suits me fine... Judith is a bit too formal for me.

Kathleen, Windy, Cathy, and Judy mention that their parents used their given names when they were angry. Parental usage of the given name to express displeasure may explain why some women never grow into their given names, which become associated subconsciously with failure and shame. The association of the given name with parental disapproval may also help explain why some children never want to grow up—they associate their grown-up names with trouble.

Parental usage of the given name to express anger allows the parent to express anger toward a more formal, and therefore more distant—a partially disassociated—representation of the child. The angry parent is subconsciously separating the child from the family unit and putting her in an externalized social framework in much the same way the children did when they called their mother "Dear." This usage creates the illusion of placing the anger outside the family unit—the parent's anger is directed at Margaret Winslow, not at Windy; at Judith, not Judy. The parent's use of the

18

grown-up name as opposed to the nickname may also make it easier for the parent to feel anger if it is not directed at the nickname, which personifies the innocence of childhood.

The use of the more formal given name directs the child's attention to a more social, more grown-up self. The objective of this parental use of the grown-up name is to appeal to the child's more mature self, but ironically this parental practice can create the unpleasant association of the grown-up name with shortcomings—thereby giving the grown-up name a bad name, so to speak. Do you have memories like these?

• • •

A World of Culture
Nina V.

I have long believed that one's name and its associations have far-reaching effects on one's personality. Nina's email below proves it. She is my beloved niece and when she was born I lobbied for a name that would reflect her Italian heritage and our family tradition so she was named Nina in honor of my grandmother and, as a side benefit, after me. The two of us joke about who is the real Nina since when I came to America at the age of ten my ethnic name, Mariantonina, was shortened to Maria. Maria is a name to which I have never related. It is a name given to me by school officials who were ignorant of my culture and didn't want to bother learning about a strange name. And so, in my professional life I am Maria: it is a stage name for my professional life as a lawyer and executive.

In my personal life—with my immediate family and with my extended Italian family—I am Nina. In addition, I do have a nickname I adore, it is Wia, a short version of Maria, given to me by my infant first nephew 38 yrs. ago. He could not pronounce Maria and so he called me Wia. It is a name used by all my nieces and nephews and something I enjoy very much. Going back to my niece Nina, you may draw your own conclusions from her essay about how her ethnic name has influenced her, but I would like to add that I am a lawyer and so is she. I have had a wonderfully rewarding career in the public sector in state and federal service: Nina is also in federal service. Both of us served in our law school law review and have had very similar interests and successes in a variety of academic areas. What's in a name? A world of culture, hopes, dreams, aspirations!

Having answered to more than one name, including a married name, I would say that one's birth name is the foundation that defines who one thinks one truly is—nicknames and other changes are merely cosmetic, an attempt to redefine ourselves in evolving roles. My favorite name is Nina, it is what my beloved parents called me and with the name came responsibility: I understood that as I lived my life I needed to live up to the principles and values of my grandmother, who, in her 100 years of life, truly owned that name. I am very proud that my niece owns her name and has magically understood how special she, and it, truly are.

Like Brooke W.S., Nina loses part of her name because of a functionary. Nina is unable to identify with *Maria* not only because it is only part of her given name, *Mariantonina,* but also because *Maria* does not represent her ethnic origins. Nina describes the sense of formality many essayists feel concerning their given names with the image of her given name as "a stage name." The given name is a front: it is not the *real* individual. For many of these essayists, their given name is merely a formality—a dressy version of the name to be worn when necessary for formal and professional occasions. This distinction suggests that these essayists have a sense of a personal and a social self, which they recognize with different names. What about you?

• • •

A Common Italian Nickname
Nina B.

I am Italian-American, and first generation on my mother's side. I have a brief story that I'd like to share with you about my name.

I was named Nina after my great-grandmother, Maria Antonina. Nina is a diminutive version of the name Antonina, so it is not a common Italian name, on its own, but is a common nickname. This is mainly because traditionally, most Italians were named after a saint. There is no Saint Nina, but there is certainly a Saint Antonina. Nina could also be the diminutive of another name: for example, Giovanna as a diminutive could be Giovannina so the nickname could be Nina for this too. I was named Nina despite the fact that my immigrant mother, Silvana, wanted to call me a "popular American name," like Brooke, Lauren, or Heather. The rest of my family protested, especially my mother's sister, Maria Antonina, known as either Maria or Nina. My Aunt Maria calls me Ninetta usually, yet another diminutive built on the first!

Being called Nina could have played a role in who I am today. I feel very connected to my Italian heritage, and grew up with a multicultural awareness, always intrigued by other cultural traditions. Because of my heritage, I resonate more deeply with other first generation children or immigrants rather than Caucasian Americans from families here for many generations.

Nina's fascination with nicknames is not surprising since her given name is a nickname. Her aunt makes her nickname-given-name into yet another nickname—*Ninetta,* a double diminutive. Diminutives add playfulness and affection to names, which can be further enhanced with double diminutives.

Everyone Knows
Beth

I was given the name Elizabeth. Everyone knows me as Beth. My Italian father and Irish-English mother named me after Saint Elizabeth. I was Bethy when I was young, but I have grown out of it. My older brother is the only one who can still call me Bethy and get away with it.

There are some recent acquaintances who have taken to calling me Bethy and I don't mind all that much. Maybe because they are 10+ years older than I am. I guess from elders, it's endearing. From peers and others younger than myself, it's ... I don't know ... patronizing? At least, unpleasant.

Elizabeth may have more different diminutives than any other given name. *The Baby Name Network* lists one hundred and twenty-five variants for *Elizabeth,* which may help explain the name's continued popularity in the U.S. since 1800, as well as associations with well-known figures like the mother of John the Baptist, the historical Queen Elizabeth I, literary associations with authors liker Elizabeth Barrett Browning, characters like Elizabeth in *Pride and Prejudice* and Beth in *Little Women*, pioneers like Elizabeth Cady Stanton and Elizabeth Blackwell, and a series of actresses.

Any nickname to which *-i, -ie,* or *-y* can be added becomes a double diminutive: ex., *Deborah>Deb>Debby, Jane>Jan>Janie,* or *Susan>Sue>Susie.* Names with double diminutives provide the child with the interesting opportunity for growing out of a nickname while retaining one. If you want to provide your child with the possibility of retaining a nickname as a grown-up after giving up her childhood nickname, consider names that have double diminutives.

• • •
My Parents Always Intended
Tricia Larkin

My name is Patricia but my parents always intended to call me Tricia. I could never understand why they didn't just name me Tricia and save me all the hassle. For example, I was always called Pat on the first day of school before I corrected the teacher. But I have no more connection with the name Pat than I do with Susan or Adrienne. It doesn't suit me and I do not identify with it at all. My mother claims that she intended to name me Tricia but the nurse in the Navy hospital where I was born in the '60s told her that she couldn't do that. She told her that Tricia is just a nickname and that I had to have a full name. I have always wanted it to be just Tricia.

I thought Tricia was an easy name until a few years ago when I moved to Switzerland. When I introduce myself as Tricia to a German speaker they inevitably say "Wie bitte?" (What?) I repeat my name clearly... Tricia. Then they say "Wie bitte?" and I repeat it again. I get another confused look then I say "Patricia" and they say, "Ohhh, Patricia," as if to say why didn't you just say that in the first place? So after all these years my full name is coming in handy!

Possibly because of my life long annoyance with my name, I took choosing my daughter's name very seriously. My husband and I had a list of about 20 names to consider. I wrote each one on an index card with first and last name. Then I wrote any information I could find about the name on the other side (origin, meaning, popularity, etc.). Then we each ranked the names and came up with the top 10. We negotiated down to 5 and kept thinking about the names for the last week or so before the birth. We finally had it down to two names, Lucie or Camille. When the baby was born, we still hadn't decided. We asked a few people what they thought of the names. My sister liked them both. My husband's brother liked Lucie because he thought it was cuter and Camille was too serious. My husband's parents liked both but preferred Lucie because my mother-in-law had a grandmother in Brazil named Lucie (or Lucy).

Tricia's essay makes us aware that America's love affair with the nickname is not universal. Europeans do not immediately use nicknames like we do here in the U.S. A nickname sheds formality for informality, invites rather than distances. This informality is often surprising to other cultures, which may maintain more of a distinction between the social and the familial-private self. Nabokov, a great Russian novelist, describes the European malaise with the instant use of nicknames in his novel *Pnin*: "In the beginning Pnin was greatly embarrassed by the ease with which first names were bandied about in America: after a single party (...) you were supposed to call a gray templed stranger 'Jim,' while he called you 'Tim' for ever and ever. If you forgot and called him next morning Professor Everett (his real name to you) it was (for him) a horrible insult."[6] Older cultures created hierarchies over the centuries with complicated naming traditions that maintained status and distance. The American tendency to dispose of these formalities can appear as overly assertive or even presumptuous. Using the name given upon introduction until a more informal name is offered avoids risking effrontery.

Like Brooke W.S., and Maria, Tricia discusses the loss of her name due to a functionary, a theme throughout the essays. Tricia also discusses international ramifications of names, which are becoming more and more important as we move into the constantly shrinking world of the 21st century. Her essay serves as a possible role model for how to choose a child's name by doing careful research and by asking friends and family for their reactions, thus giving everybody the feeling of participating in the process and discovering what associations people have to the name.

• • •

It Fits Me Perfectly
Molly Hart

I was born a preemie baby and had to stay in the hospital for a month. My parents didn't name me for a while so the nurses called me SuzieQ. My parents thought it was so cute and almost named me that! I have always been called Molly but my real name is Mary Ellen. My parents intended to call me Molly from the day I was named. Back in the olden days you had to have a saint's name in order to be baptized in the Catholic Church. I was only called Mary Ellen when I was in trouble and on the first day of school. The teacher never called me Mary Ellen after the first day. I made sure of that. My driver's license, passport, and checking account all use the name Molly. I never had it legally changed. The SS# is still in Mary Ellen though! I thought Molly was short for Mary. I also thought it was very Irish. My maiden name is O'Connell so a name like Molly O'Connell told people a lot about me before they even met me! Once I had a family tree made, and the woman told me Molly was Hebrew in origin. When Barry and I were first married, we lived in an area in Georgetown with three Mollys within a block! Me, Molly O'Day, and Molly Donahue.

I have always, always loved my name ... it fits me perfectly. It seems so perky, sporty, upbeat, and fun. Only a very, very few people have ever called me Moll. One aunt has always called me Mollykins. I kinda liked it. People remember my name. It sounds like music to my ears when I hear someone calling me, a friend, a child, etc. I've never met a Molly who was depressed, boring, or lazy. I love reading about characters named Molly, hearing about pets named Molly (there are a lot of dogs named Molly) and I think Molly the American Girl Doll is wonderful. I take it as a great honor when a friend names their child Molly. The name never seems to go out of style. The couple of professional articles that I have published in my field use the name Molly. I think it might look a little informal but that is OK.

Molly even uses her nickname for signing articles and official documents. *Molly* was originally an Irish nickname for *Mary*, which means bitterness. American society has totally changed the associations with *Molly* and *Mary*, perhaps due to the American spirit of creating its own cultural traditions like "the unsinkable Molly Brown." In addition *Mary* was the most popular American name for girls for most of U.S. history. *Mary* is associated with sweetness, innocence, and purity rather than the biblical meaning of bitterness.

Because *Molly* is a nickname, it is even further removed from the biblical meaning. *Molly* signifies exactly the opposite of its original meaning, not only for Molly, but also for most Americans who hear the name. Molly has created her own meaning for her name. Have you done this for your name?

American culture has always had a reputation for changing and remaking things; so it is not surprising the same has happened with names. Molly has made her name a reflection of who she feels she is: she has filled her name with a multitude of upbeat, happy associations that will always serve to uplift her spirit. All of us can do this for our names.

– E –
CHOOSING ONE'S OWN NICKNAME

The previous essays concern nicknames given to the child by the family. The following women choose their own nicknames.

• • •

I Picked a Nickname
Beth Cady

My name is Elizabeth Cady, although I go by Beth in everything except my professional publications/presentations. I went by Elizabeth until the 5th grade, which is when I decided that it was a really long name to write on all the school papers I had to do, so I picked a nickname. I tell everyone to call me Beth, and I think I picked Beth in part because it doesn't end in a long e sound like my last name. My mother, whose name is Katie, argued forcefully for not having two people in my family with similar-sounding first and last names.

I was named after first and middle names of women on both sides of my family. However, I was born in New Zealand and Queen Elizabeth was in town the day I was born, so I tell everyone that I was named for her. I've been asked many times if I was named for or am related to Elizabeth Cady Stanton, but as far as I can tell I'm not.

I think my name suits me, especially going by Beth. To me Elizabeth is a more formal name, and I don't consider myself to be a very formal person, although I do use it in my professional life.

• • •

Then I Decided
Janie Steuart

My name is Janie. It is a nickname for Jane. I was named after my mother who was named after her mother. I was called Janie Dee as a child as not to be confused

24

with my mother. I used that name until I was thirteen, and then decided I liked only Janie. When I see people from my childhood they still address me as Janie Dee. People confuse my name with Jamie, Jean, Janine, and Jeannie. I am constantly saying it is spelled JAN-(as in Nancy)-IE. They often spell it Janey. I cannot imagine being called Jane. That would be like calling me a completely different name. I am Janie. A friend of mine kids around with me and calls me jane-knee.

• • •

But Then I Decided...
Elizabeth K. Cadell

I've always been delighted with the names I was given because I was named after both of my grandmothers (Elizabeth Katherine) - and I especially like the name, Elizabeth, so much so that I named my daughter Anne EliSabeth. I use my baptismal name for professional use, simply because it is proper. Until I was 25 my family and friends called me "Betty," a result of the era in which I was born. But then I decided that it sure would sound silly to be called "Betty" when I was 40 so I asked everyone to call me "Liz," which I chose because my beloved French grandmother was always called "Lizzie." Now that is what is on my license plates—and you'd be surprised how many truck drivers see those plates and then honk and holler, "Hi, Lizzie!" I am very much a traditionalist and classicist so I wish more people would name their sprouts some of the good, "old" names, not these silly and even nonsensical ones that their children will have to change for their career worlds.

• • •

I Picked My Own Nickname
Marty

When somebody calls me by name, I can tell when he or she knew me from the name they use. I was Martha, like my mom, until my two brothers nicknamed me Matt, after Matty Mattel.[7] Matt was a boyish sounding name, which fit better with their unfulfilled wish for another brother. By the time I was in elementary school, I was called Matt in the family and Martha outside the family. When I went to college, I decided I wasn't happy with either "Martha" or "Matt": I decided on "Marty." That's the name I've used ever since. Picking it myself was important to me for creating my own sense of who I was and who I wanted to be.

I Preferred Tricia
Patricia Joyce Yandle

My name is Patricia Joyce; I was named after my father's sister who died as an infant. Most of my life with those outside my family and with most significant others, I have used Tricia. I preferred Tricia to Pat which everyone else assumes must be your name if you have such a long name as Patricia. My family members still call me Patricia.

At what age do women pick nicknames for themselves? Beth does so precociously at age ten. Janie changes her name at adolescence when name changes are frequently made to mark the transition from childhood. Marty changes her name in college, which usually marks a transition to an independent identity outside the family. Liz changes her name as an adult, which is more unusual. These essayists illustrate that name changes can be made at any time throughout life.

Why do these essayists pick their own nicknames? Beth picks her nickname as a child not only to differentiate her name from her mother's, as Janie does, but also to make life easier with a shorter signature—for practical reasons and to establish her own identity. In college, Marty picks a new nickname to better suit the image she wants to project. Marty feels the new nickname will help her transition into "who (she) wanted to be." As an adult, Liz picks a new nickname because she does not think *Betty* will age well: she wants to adjust to changing times. Tricia picks a nickname for its originality—to be different. These women pick their nicknames to assert or to reflect their personal sense of identity, to facilitate changes at different points throughout life, and to keep up with the times. They recognize their personal evolution with their name changes: their new names reflect a new sense of identity.

All of these essays are an inspiration for anyone who dreams of changing her name: it can be done.

– F –
NICKNAME COMFORT

In the previous essays, women with nicknames given by their families or with nicknames they choose themselves, center their identity on their nicknames. The following excerpts highlight the comfort that nicknames give and why women would choose to have a nickname, even if the family does not give them one.

• • •

Intimate and Loving
Sue Martin

The various nicknames I've had—Suzie, L. Sue, Suzella—I have enjoyed because I believe they are intimate and loving. A nickname usually comes from a deep connection and familiarity that is very comfortable. Those are the people who know and understand me best and with whom I can truly be myself, no matter what they call me!

• • •

More Comfortable
Stephanie Monahan

...when I consider someone a friend, I close emails with Steph. And I always feel more comfortable with people who call me the shortened version.

• • •

An Endearment
Julie

I love my name, Julia Elaine. I was named for my paternal grandfather Julius. My twin brother's name is William Julius. My name suits me very well. When I go to a business setting or now as a 54-year-old, I try to go by Julia, but before I know it I am saying my name is Julie. I like both names very well. Also interestingly enough, in Hebrew the "y" sound is added to indicate "my," so for example, my friend's husband's name is Sam; and she calls him Sammy, or "my Sam." So for me Julie sounds like an endearment. Julia sounds more formal.

• • •

Keeping a Lost Nickname
Judy McGowan

None of us had much of a nickname though my siblings tend to call me Jude. I would never dream of introducing myself as Jude, but when I talk to myself (!), I find that I call myself Jude!

Nicknames are described as "intimate," "loving," "comfortable," "an endearment." The sound of the nickname evokes all these soothing emotions, even when strangers use it. Nicknames constantly rekindle our childhood feelings of love and security. There are psychological advantages to going through life with a name that evokes these subliminal feelings of being totally loved and cared for. Judy increases her ability to access these emotions by using her nickname to address herself. Nicknames can be a sustaining oasis that allows us to tap into our happiest, carefree memories.

Nicknames are not always a source of strength and comfort, however. Few women are willing to reveal childhood nicknames that seem silly or childish as opposed to endearing. Ella Frances bravely shares her frustrations with her nicknames, which have doggedly followed her throughout life. She is not alone in her frustration with the indomitable nickname. Her story bids us consider how others feel about the names we use to address them.

• • •

All is Lost
Ella Frances

I was named for my mother, Ella Frances Bard Brown, who was in turn named after her maternal grandparents, Ella Cannon McCullough and Francis Marion McCullough. (He was apparently named after the Revolutionary War guerilla, the South Carolina "Swamp Fox.") My mother was always called "Ella Frances," except by her in-laws, who unintentionally annoyed her by calling her "Ella." I, on the other hand, was addressed as "Titter" by my older brother, who was trying to say "Sister" and missed. The family of course found this cute and so called me "Titter," which was soon shortened to "Tis." Tis I remained until college when I renamed myself "Tes" in a moment of foolishness. The only people who ever called me "Ella Frances" were the teachers at the private schools I attended, where nicknames were wisely outlawed. I have since tried to be called Ella Frances when introducing myself to various groups, but the minute anyone familiar calls me "Tes," all is lost.

As a girl, I didn't mind the nickname because I hated my real name. No one else was an "Ella" much less an "Ella Frances," and I disliked the whiney voice my grandmother used when addressing my mother. Now, of course, I like the idea of an unusual name and have not allowed any of my three children to be addressed by a nickname.

• • •

My Dad Nicknamed Me
Clicker Morgan

(…) when I was in a crib I made clicking noises with my mouth. So, my Dad nicknamed me "Clicker." It wasn't supposed to stick. The neighborhood kids picked it up. In elementary school and on through high school, I went to school with a girl named Frances Hixon. It was quite confusing for teachers and for us with our names so close. When my 4th grade teacher learned about my nickname, she asked to use it at school. From that point on, my nickname fate was sealed, despite my series of other names! To this day, I've never met another "Clicker."

As we have seen, women keep their nicknames for a variety of reasons. They may associate their given names with trouble because of the parental tendency to use the given name when angry or they may keep their nicknames because of the subconscious, emotional oasis nicknames allow women to tap into. Ella Frances provides another reason nicknames persist—American culture.

Although we may find the nicknames *Tis* and *Tes* charming, Ella Frances does not. Given her desire to use her given name, the dominance of her nicknames is frustrating. By refusing to use her given name, society is in a sense refusing to let Ella Frances grow up. There is always the possibility that a nickname will stay with the individual throughout life. To free her children from the same destiny, Ella Frances does not allow her children to have any nicknames—a stipulation we will find in other essays. Two essayists, Sophy and Elvira, describe successful name changes after the husband announces that his wife is to have a new name.

Trying to stop the use of a nickname puts the individual in the awkward position of both correcting someone and asserting a more formal, seemingly distant identity. Perhaps the solution to this thorny problem is that old adage of just telling the truth: "I use my given name because it carries on the memory of my mother and my grandmother. I feel closer to them when I hear it. My nickname separates me from family: that's why I prefer not to use it." When people understand why the individual wants the given name used, they should respond positively.

Clicker has no problems with her indomitable nickname, perhaps because she has such sweet stories about it. Stories play a crucial role in how we relate to our names.

Chapter 3
GROWING INTO THE GIVEN NAME:
A CIRCULAR EVOLUTION

In the first chapter, we discovered the Native American emphasis on the evolution of the name to reflect changes in life, which Brooke W.S. Helman describes as "a flowing river." The following essayists remind us of this Native American concept because they describe a linear evolution that allows them to use their names as time markers. They also describe a circular evolution as they grow into the names they were given at birth.

– A –
THE NICKNAME AS A TIME MARKER

As the following excerpts indicate, the evolution into the given name can provide time markers in life.

• • •

I Can Generally Figure Out
Kathleen Landis Rauhauser

(...) When I meet people from my past, I can generally figure out when I knew them from how they address me.

• • •

I Can Tell
Helen Jo

(...) I can tell when in my life people knew me by what they call me.

• • •

I am at Least 95% Sure
Barbara Mattson

Since I was the first grandchild on both sides, my parents didn't want to use any of my relatives' names for fear of hurting someone's feelings. So they named me "Barbara Ann" because they liked the name.

When I was growing up, everyone called me "Barbie." Among the explanations for this was that there was already a "Barbara" in the school for the blind dorm. When I was in jr. high I wanted people to call me "Barbara Ann." There was one boy who was eager to win my heart, so he complied. Now I can't listen to the Beach Boys' song with the lyrics, "Ba ba ba, ba Barbara Ann" without thinking about this.

When I started Spartanburg Junior College, I wanted people to call me "Barbara" because I wanted to discard what I felt was a childish name. However, "Barbie" stayed with me among my new friends since Sister Lynne taught us at the college. When I went to Columbia College, even though a grade school friend roomed with me, very few knew me as "Barbie," and this has continued. Some pen pals and amateur radio operators have learned about my nickname, and some have called me "Barbie." This is OK if I consider them family or a friend. When someone calls me "Barbie", and I don't recognize them, I am at least 95% sure it's a family member or someone from the Junior College or grade school.

• • •

Now That I'm Older
Lynn Weatherby

I was named Lynn Marie, and all my relatives called me Lynn Marie because my mother didn't want anyone nicknaming me Lynnie. When I went to school, I dropped my middle name. Mostly everyone from that time on called me by my first name, which I loved. Only a couple of people whom I have treasured as special friends have affectionately called me Lynnie. My relatives still call me Lynn Marie, but now that I'm older, I love that too.

– B –
CLOSING THE CIRCLE

• • •

When I Took My First Job
Christine Reynolds Arnold

I was born Christine Reynolds Arnold. I'm not sure why my parents picked Christine, but my middle name was after my great uncle John Reynolds who never had children (and supposedly because he gave my financially struggling parents a $1000 check!). I went by Christie through my childhood and am still called that by my family and childhood friends. In middle school, I started going by "Chris" because I thought it sounded more "cool" and not so girly. "Chris" stuck through high school and college so all my high school and college friends call me that. When I took my first job and from thereafter, I went with "Christine' because it seemed more professional. Everyone who met me after the age of 22 calls me "Christine," including my husband. I recently went to my 20th high school reunion and had to get used to everyone calling me "Chris." The following day, I went to a reunion with all of these childhood friends and my family so it was "Christie." I had to keep checking my nametag!

Christine's use of her given name marks multiple transitions—from childhood to adolescence, from college to a job and marriage. Do you fit this pattern?

• • •

To Find My Own Voice
Rebecca J. Snow

I love my name, Rebecca. Growing up my family called me Becca, and in second grade my best friend was also called Becca. My second grade teacher decided that I would be called Becky since we both had the same name, and I did not object. All through high school and college my friends called me Becky and my family called me "Baca." I remember getting married in 1998 and everyone was calling me different names at my wedding. Around the same time, I discovered my life's calling as an herbalist and I started taking herb classes at the Dreamtime Center for Herbal Studies in Virginia. Through this process of finding my passion for plants, I also started to find my own voice. I realized how much I loved my birth name, Rebecca, so poetic and powerful. I remember reading how the Rebecca of the Old Testament, who married Isaac, wore a nose ring, which to me, represents a bit of sassiness! I decided to claim the name that I love, so from then on I have introduced myself as Rebecca.

As Rebecca explains, some girls find a friend or a role model who also shares their name—a member of their "name tribe." These namesakes can become like sisters and may play an important role in the other girl's development. Did you have a namesake friend or know someone who did?

– C –
THE DOUBLE CIRCLE

• • •

A Double Loop
Sophy

When I was born, I was named after my mother, Sophy, who herself was named after her grandmother, Sophia (or Sophy). However, from the beginning my parents agreed they didn't want a child with the same name as her mother, due to the confusion of two people being called: "Sophy." (This is a silly argument, since only my father called my mother by her first name. The rest of us called her, quite properly, Mummy.)

I was nicknamed Penny, after the Pennsylvania Railroad Company, because my lawyer father was in trial on behalf of the company when I was being born, and the judge excused the proceedings so that he could go see my mother in the hospital. If he had won the case, he would have earned a million dollars. As it happened he lost. So that was a joke in our family.

"Pennies from heaven," my parents teased me; and my sister, "You can never get rid of a bad penny." Why did I always cringe at my parents' affectionate saying? Why did I think they must mean the very reverse of their words? Why did I accept on the other hand—and fight fiercely against—my sister's witty teasing?

The fact is that by the time I was twelve I was ready to take on my own true name. I wanted to be Sophy. Even at that age I thought (looking ahead to my long life) how absurd it would be, to be called "Penny" when I was fifty: a diminishing nickname, too "small" for the person I intended to become. I rolled the word "Sophy" on my tongue—"Sophy," meaning Wisdom. I wanted Wisdom.

There was another and exotic reason that I wanted the name "Sophy." I felt a guilty and exciting bond with my great-grandmother Sophy Tayloe (who died before I was born). She had married just before the Civil War, had three sons, and on the death of her husband, she never remarried—she was independent!—though she had a "friend" who took her every afternoon for a carriage ride in Rock Creek Park and who took naps in the large house with stables on the corner of 31st and N Street in Georgetown. ("Be quiet," Cousin Phyllis was told as a young child. "Don't wake up the Major.") It was thrilling and a little wicked to think of my free-spirited great-grandmother, especially since every woman I knew as a child was married, domestic. I'm writing of a time before the Women's Movement, when being "married" meant a subtle loss of independence, a sort of unspoken (albeit happy) bondage to house and husband. I could not have articulated all these things, especially since my mother was happy in her marriage; but I knew deep inside that I didn't want that life: I wanted adventure. I wanted to be a boy—or, rather, a girl with all the rights and privileges of a boy. And "Penny" wasn't going to do it. (For the faithful wife, think, Penelope, when I was closer to Clytemnestra.)

At fourteen I went away to boarding school and tried for the first time to change my name. But the minute my schoolmates heard the nickname "Penny" (my sister was in the same school) the name stuck to me like burrs.

At seventeen, off to Smith College. I tried again to become "Sophy," with the same result, and again when I took my Junior Year Abroad in Italy, where Sophia is, after all, an Italian name. However, the Italians would no sooner light on the nickname "Penny" and instantly they'd pick it up in delight: "Panny," they pronounced it.

I was engaged to be married when my future husband first heard my name. It was David who changed my name for me, simply by insisting that I was not Penny but Sophy. Of course my parents never switched, or my aunts. But eventually it became my name, and even my sister and brother started using it.

33

Now I am close to seventy, and only a handful of people still use the nickname, yet now I treasure the diminutive "Penny." Today I hear in it all its overtones of intimate affection. My parents have died, my aunts. Only my nieces (daughters of my sister) and a few schoolmates still call me Penny. Usually I'm called Sophy, and now I miss the nickname, too.

Sophy makes a double circle, returning first to her given name and then to her nickname, which evokes memories of lost friends and family. She describes the Proustian power of the nickname to recapture the feelings of the past. Louisa May Alcott depicts the same phenomenon in *Good Wives* (cf. p.321); and Willa Cather captures the evocative emotions called forth by a name in *My Antonia* (p.319).

• • •

Back to the Very Beginning:
The Abandoned Chosen Name and Multiple Time Markers
Heather Frances Perram Frank

My father is a Roman Catholic of French and Irish descent and my mother is a converted Roman Catholic of English and Scottish descent who was raised in the Anglican Church of Canada. I was born at Georgetown Hospital and raised in the Washington, D.C. area. I was baptized and raised as a Catholic, but converted to Judaism as a student at Newcomb College.

My parents named me Jane Frances, after my father's aunt (his mother's sister) and his mother. In those days, women stayed in the hospital for several days even after an uncomplicated birth, which gave my maternal grandmother time to fly in from Winnipeg, Manitoba and visit us at Georgetown.

My grandmother, Elva (I was always told her she was named for England's queens Elizabeth and Victoria), told my mother that Jane was a "boring" name and suggested giving me a Scottish name, Heather. My parents liked the name (and my grandmother was bossy), so they changed the birth certificate. Since we were still in the hospital, apparently it was easy to do.

I don't know if my great aunt Jane, or my grandmother knew that my parents had named me Jane and then changed my name to Heather. My grandmother's given name was Mary Frances Patricia Doyle, but to her parents and sisters, she was always Frankie. Her husband called her Pat, however. My grandfather died when I was 3, and after that my grandmother was always called Frankie and introduced herself that way. My mother's maiden name was Franklin, so I think it's kind of nice that I now have the surname Frank.

I have never had a nickname that stuck, though a few people tried to call me Heath (pronounced like the first syllable in my name). When they were mad at me

34

as little kids, my three younger sisters referred to me as Foodoo Montor (my sister Noel came up with that—we think she was trying to say Voodoo Monster). As adults, when they're jealous of the way my mother makes a fuss over me, they refer to me as Princess Caraboo (who was a fake princess about whom a movie was made). My first husband called me Hen, after the anxious, organized and self-reliant little red hen in the folk tale. My dear friend Chris calls me The Little Madam, because I like everything just so.

When I worked in programming at AOL, I found out accidentally that colleagues in the newsroom called me Smurfette. Someone sent an IM that was about me, to me by mistake. As such nicknames go, I guess it could have been worse—there was something affectionate about it. And it kind of made sense: I was the lone female exec in a chain of male bosses, I can be insufferably cheerful and part of my job was to try to get people to work collaboratively with each other.

My conversion to Judaism meant, among weightier things, choosing a Hebrew name. I didn't really like any of names that started with the letter H, so I chose a Hebrew flower name, Shoshannah. I never really use it, but it was part of our marriage vows when I married my present husband and it's on our kettuba. I always like hearing it or reading it—it's like a secret/sacred person inside of me.

I like my name and I think it suits me, but I am a little concerned that it will be weird to be an old Heather. It seems like such a young name. I sometimes say I will go back to being Jane when I am a dignified old lady.

––––––––––––––

Heather's essay contrasts with the others because she has so many different nicknames. Her Hebrew name, *Shoshannah* (lily), mirrors her English flower name. The lily is celebrated for its beauty and hardiness; it symbolizes faith and trust. Her reference to her Hebrew name, as "a secret/sacred person inside me," is a startling echo of the Native American concept of a secret, sacred name. In Heather's case, closing the circle is especially striking since by returning to *Jane*, she would be returning to the first name chosen for her but abandoned—the name with a family history.

Chapter 4
MULTIPLE NICKNAMES:
THE COMPLEXITIES OF IDENTITY

In the previous essays, women listed as many as three variations on their given name. Heather was unusual with five: most of them mirror her personality traits. In considering her proliferation of names, Christine (p.31) humorously said she found herself constantly checking her nametag on a multiple reunion visit back home. What are the implications of many, diverse nicknames?

• • •

The Dragon of True Self Names
Bonita Winer

Maybe the entire problem is that I don't have a name that I can dependably remember when I'm stressed. My biological parents found unity on very few subjects but one was their fondness for that nursery tale of love and loss—Little Bo-Peep has lost her sheep and can't tell where to find them. Leave them alone and they'll come home wagging their tails behind them. Mama embroidered Bo-Peep at the center of my first blanket while Papa went in search of a name that could logically be shortened to Bo.

Coincidentally, he had just discovered that he was, like most of his family, a diabetic, and couldn't bring himself to reveal this news to my mother who would be both terrified for him and furious that their baby might develop the same ravaging disease. To postpone the day of revelations he went for long walks in depressing places and eventually discovered the name "Bonita" carved into the gravestone of a sixteen-year-old girl who had been buried in an Oregon cemetery. The first sheep I lost was he. The second was my mother. Eventually she came home again but he never did. So much for plots taken from nursery rhymes.

Next my grandparents took possession of naming me and, being Scotch-Irish, they called me Bonnie. Clyde, my granddad, loved to sing when he worked; and long after he had died, I could tilt my head at just the right angle and still hear his raspy baritone doing a chorus of "My Bonnie lies over the ocean, my Bonnie lies over the sea. / My Bonnie lies over the ocean. Please bring back my Bonnie to me." I loved that song until one day Grandma Blanche indulged herself in a dour Scot's moment and described how she hadn't been very upset when, sometime before my third birthday, I had been taken from them to live with my mother and her new husband, but Grandpa had cried like his heart was broken.

Now when I tilt my head in that familiar way I can only hear the second stanza to the song: "My Bonnie ate a poison mushrooms. Now she lies under the sea. / My Bonnie ate a poison mushrooms. Oh, bring back my Bonnie to me." Scotch ballads have such a way with reaming the joy out of any sentiment.

To this day there are a few men who call me Beep: my dad, uncle Dwight and my brother Joe. As a child I never liked being referred to as the short blast of a car horn but just this last year I came to realize that the name hadn't rolled off a line in Detroit but had originally been a contraction for Bo-Peep. This simple explanation suddenly transformed an ugly name into a cute name. It wasn't me, I mean it wasn't a name I would ever call myself, or expect the Dragon of True-Self-Names to whisper as an enchantment key but it was a name which expressed the pleasure that a shy, twenty-six-year-old Dalton Holland must have taken in his new girlfriend's baby daughter. And Dad's continued use of that single syllable, Beep, now revives for me that moment when I was nothing but a tiny head upon his chest, a present experience of that simple phrase "The Quaker Way." From Uncle Oscar's first steps upon the sidewalk in Harper he was complete and named but in his presence I came to think of myself as three different girls: Bitsy Bo, the subservient child who struggled to live up to Oscar's daily plans for my self-improvement; B., who rebelled at Oscar's rigid authoritarianism; and Me, the secret self who prized nothing so much as invisibility.

When my son was about ten we visited my grade school in Harper during a reunion weekend. He needed to go to the bathroom and took off after I gave him directions. Several minutes later he sidled up to me and whispered, "What's a proper noun?" I smiled and whispered back, "A name of a person, place or thing. They're the nouns you have to capitalize. Like New York, or Michael Jackson, or Sony." He answered with his usual pat phrase, "I know that." So then I asked, "What made you want to know about proper nouns right now?" "There was an old lady who saw me in the hall. She said, "You must be Bonnie Holland's little boy. You look just like her." She asked if I could remember proper nouns. I can. I told her so. She said, "That's good because your mother never could." Then he pointed across the room at my fourth grade teacher, Mrs. Mayberry. "That's her, the really, really, old lady."

My secret weakness, the one I had kept from even Uncle Oscar hadn't ever actually been a secret. All fifteen hundred people in Harper, Kansas must have thought of me as Willmetta Holland's little girl who couldn't remember proper nouns. A neurologist once explained my struggle to retrieve proper nouns from what seemed like a rubber cement zone in my memory was due to the same brain damage that treats me to a blockbuster migraine every 7 to 8 days. According to his theory, I have no difficulty with common nouns because they're stored in a different area of the brain. My favorite psychoanalyst has another theory that the unconscious does funny things to avoid hurt. If, for instance, all your all siblings have biblical names like Joseph, Sarah, Rebecca, John and your name was something decidedly exotic like Bonita your unconscious might try to ignore the whole naming thing. Or if an uncle named William Carl made a special mention of you in his will then you might come to trust and even marry a man named Carl William.

• • •

Indifference and Transience
Deborah Silverton Rosenfelt

My first name is "Deborah." I was named after my father's mother, D'vorah, whom I never met. She died in the great influenza epidemic of 1919, when my father was six years old. According to custom, his father then married her still-single sister, Rivka. I know little about my father's mother, my namesake. My father barely remembers her, though he yearned for her all his life.

My mother tells me early in my growing years that "D'vorah," in Hebrew, means "bee." "It's a good name for you," says my mother. "You keep busy like a bee. You also buzz around and make noise." "What about the honey?" I ask. "Yes, and what about the sting?" she replies. Then she laughs and gives me a hug. (This may not be a true memory. Maybe this is more what my mother is like now. At 96.)

My mother's mother, my Bubbe, called me "D'voraleh." I loved the way her lips and tongue shaped the soft Yiddish diminutive. "Eat, D'voraleh, you're as skinny as a bird." When I particularly like myself, I still address myself this way. Last week, I ran a diagnostic on my computer and figured out on my own how to fix my dysfunctional printer. "Good job, D'voraleh," I complimented myself out loud.

To my sister, I am Deb. She is a Margery, called Marge. I'm not sure when or why we opted for these monosyllabic designations. "Hey, Deb, it's Marge," says the message on my answering system. Her voice, the inflection almost always the same, always reassures me. I am here, it says. I am thinking about you. I have an invitation for you, a question, a concern about Mom. When anyone else calls me Deb, I flush with friendly feelings, by association.

*When I reprimand myself, I am Deborah. Procrastinating? "Come ON, Deb'ra, get to work." Watching TV or reading too late at night? "Come ON, Deb'ra, go to bed." Avoiding the pile of bills? "Come ON, Deb'ra, they won't pay themselves." Finding the pint of Haagen Das low-fat extra-rich vanilla-bean ice cream melted to lukewarm milkishness on top of the refrigerator? "**DEBORAH!**" Other friends of mine, even those who, like me, live mostly alone, tell me that they don't talk out loud to themselves like this. This surprises me. How do they keep themselves in line, how do they keep themselves company?*

Professionally, too, I am sometimes Deborah, especially when formally introduced. Most of the time, though, among friends and colleagues, I am Debby. I spell it with a y, but I don't mind when people misspell it with an "i.e.," as they often do. I have sometimes wondered why others make such a fuss over a letter or two, though I have also wondered if my indifference on this point indicates something missing in my character. I liked the sound of "Debby" best when it came over a loudspeaker at a horse trial: "and Debby Rosenfelt has made it through the water and is heading for Jump 13." So what if I had already been disqualified in dressage? The speaker heralded a triumph, a perfect cross-country ride.

My family loved language, every one of us, my mother the English and Latin teacher most of all. But that love did not really extend to our names: there was no inclination to play with them, to see them as infused with significance. I think we were all unconscious materialists, convinced that our bodies, our experiences, our emotions existed quite independently of any discursive formation. Or maybe my parents carried too heavy a knowledge about how both bodies and words could go up in smoke to invest much passion in the meaning of names.

My mother tells me that I used to say, "I'm Debby Beth Sivverton and a good girl." Now I'm Deborah Silverton Rosenfelt, and, I like to think, a pretty good woman. "Beth" has atrophied from lack of use, displaced by my maiden name, which I want to retain even though it IS only one generation old, changed by my father from "Silverstein" when he was trying to get into medical schools inhospitable to Jews. "Rosenfelt" belongs to my long-ago-ex husband. Why didn't I change back to my maiden name? The indifference again, compounded by my father's comment: "Why bother? A Rosenfelt by any other name would smell so sweet." He was an awful punster.

• • •

Suggestive, but Not Definitive
Martha LaBare

In my teens I minded that my name was Martha. Once I had some context for words and meanings and names as words with meanings, I was not happy. I looked it up: "Lady." Okay. But the dumpy wife next door to Dennis the Menace was Martha. George Washington's wife, who didn't seem terribly interesting, was Martha.

Then: Albee's "Who's Afraid of Virginia Wolf." Not who I wanted to be. But I LOVE the play, and know the Martha role with Uta Hagen, Colleen Dewhurst, and Kathleen Turner. And of course Liz in the movie, so good and yet a pale copy of Hagen. They expertly gave the name a bad name.

I had never known another Martha in school. Then I landed on a hall of early admission women students at a Southern university, and of us fifty, three were named Martha. I took the opportunity to change to Martie.

In my teens, our next-door neighbor was a gorgeous (blonde, lacquered nails, graceful, kind) woman whose name was Martha, but she was called Martie, spelled that way. I adopted it in my freshman college year. It was younger, more casual, more suited to my teen sense of new and separate self.

And has been misspelled ever since. Even my husband preferred the more masculine Marty. I published poems with "M." and my last name. That solved it—Martha, Marty, Martie, even Marti—which I never used. (Give me a break.)

An aside: I've helped friends with their books, and in acknowledgments, often!, the first or last name has been misspelled.

But Martha: So middle-aged. But now "I are one." It fits. It's as serious as am I, as logical, as settled into scanning the meaning of life.

I did find out that a few generations back on my mother's side was a Martha Lucinda. I like the music of that, much more than Martha Jane. The Jane, or both names, were used only by my dad (as Janie) and an aunt who shared the middle name.

I no longer know automatically who calls me Martha or Martie. People switch-hit. Nicknames abound, and my married name and professional titles are used seriously and playfully. "Martha" now seems one of many names, suggestive but not definitive.

Martha/Martie/Mighty Mitts/Dean-lette/Mrs. McEvoy/Marty The Bear/Prof/Etc.

• • •

I Answer to Most "J" Names
Jennifer Duncan

So my name is Jennifer Lynn (Johnson) Duncan. I had no idea when I was younger that I had one of the most popular names of the '70s. I was born in 1971. The only real story I know as to how my parents named me was that my mom loved the name Jennifer. (So did a lot of other people I guess.) I am glad I was a girl because if I was a boy—I would have been Paul Everett Johnson 3rd. Not that I don't like my dad and grandfather's name but I like having "my own." I think it was 6th grade when I realized there were a lot of us out there. There were 6 Jennifers in 2 classes of 6th graders. 6 out of 40 kids were Jennifer. It was then my first nickname from friends (rather than family) came to be. I was JJ. I loved it.

I do love the fact that I have so many options for my name. (Jen, Jenny, Jennifer—even the spellings can be different—Jenn, Jennie etc.) My parents and I still battle (in the written word)—I prefer and sign my name Jen—they use Jenn. HMPF! :)

I never ever liked Jenny. I thought it was too girly and frufru. Except for the fact that my mom's parents—my Meema and Peepa Whelan called me Jenny J. I allowed that and as the years passed came to love that they called me something different. And they were the only ones who used that name. I remember in college my junior year roommate heard my grandparents call me Jenny J and she picked it up. It—again—became a special name only for her to use. Since my grandparents on my mom's side have died, I find it a fond and often emotional memory. When the few people who know that name (cousins and sister)—Jenny J and they use it—I feel my heart tug. No other name really has that much "meaning" so to speak.

Again as the years went on—having Jennifer Johnson—kind of an original name—gave many folks cause to create nicknames. I became JJ again in college when going thru rush (for sorority pledging). There were tons of Jennifers and I wanted to be remembered. I became JJ thru my college years and that even morphed to Jage, Jager, JMaster Flash (because of a dance move HAHA).

It is interesting when I think about it—I answer to most J names. I can tell who/where many of my friendships stem from by what name they call me:

Jen—high school, JJ—college.

A few friends from college have now known me in my hometown or have hung out with high school friends or my parents enough that they switch to Jen when the situation is appropriate. Some high school friends have remarked that they will not use JJ even though they hear college friends use this name because "that is not how they know me". It is funny to think—that even though Jennifer and all its various forms is my name- others feel "ownership" too.

My last thought is in answer to "does my name suit me?" You know even though I may have grumbled over the years at times that I had a less than original name. I love it. I am a Gemini and have many personas or should I say a broad and energetic personality. These nicknames in a way help me encapsulate my memories, experiences and relationships throughout my life. I am very much about the people that are a part of my life—I value my relationships. And I feel my name has become one aspect for reflection of these experiences/memories.

The previous essayists have a surprising number of nicknames, including names the women give themselves as well as nicknames family and friends give them. Bonita has seven, Deborah has five, Martha has seven, followed by "etc.," and Jennifer has eight. All have intriguing explanations as to why they feel a lack of attachment to any one name. Bonita speaks of physiological reasons, but she also gives psychological reasons: her name does not fit in with the biblical names given to her other siblings. Deborah says that the lack of significance for her name may be due to the fact that her family members were materialists or that they knew everything, including people, can suddenly vanish in a holocaust. In the latter case, a proliferation of names would help fill the losses by literally multiplying one individual through her many names. Martha finds her given name, which she has grown into, as "suggestive but not definitive." Jennifer answers to most *J* names. These essayists remind us that names are transient and changing, depending on who is addressing us and what aspect of ourselves we may be thinking about.

Bonita notes that different names may represent different aspects of the self. She discovers this precociously as a child: "I came to think of myself as three different girls." Deborah addresses herself by her different names depending on the mood she is in. Misspelling her name *Debby* as *Debbie* does not bother her because Deborah doesn't have the same attachment to the name as women with only one or two names. Because her different names reflect so many different aspects of her life, Martha explains, one name alone cannot be complete. For Jennifer, "These nicknames (...) help me encapsulate my memories, experiences and relationships throughout my life." These women manifest a complex understanding of both themselves and their relationships with others through their multiple names: nicknames mirror not only the self but also others.

From these essays, it appears that multiple names facilitate self-awareness and self-understanding. Multiple names reflect different parts of the personality, which provide different perspectives. Different names also provide insight into others: Jennifer says her many nicknames make her aware of how other people relate to her. Bonita and Deborah describe wonderful coping mechanisms with one nickname taking the blame, freeing the rest of the self from the burden of failure, guilt, or rebellion. Assigning blame to a variant nickname could be a wonderful coping mechanism for overly guilt-ridden women because it allows part of the personality to remain guilt free. Women with multiple names discuss the complexities of personality mirrored by their multiple names, a complexity they may even have attained thanks to their many names, as well as an acute awareness of how they relate to others and how others relate to them through their different names. Because of their multiple names, these women also seem to have more freedom to grow and change: they realize a single name represents a limited identity.

Chapter 5
NO NICKNAMES:
SOMETHING'S MISSING

What about women with no nicknames? How does having identity limited to one name affect the individual?

• • •

No Nicknames, Please
Elisabeth

I can still see and hear my dad as he explained to me that I was named "Elisabeth" for his mother. Even into his very old age, he could not speak about her in other than a whisper. The pain of her loss had not lessened with time, perhaps because she died prematurely. I remember he said that she was a wonderful woman, a farmer's wife, very gifted with needle and thread. She sewed all the clothes for their family of three—including the men's suits, shirts, coats, and, of course, her own clothes. I also remember that he told me never to let anyone call me by a nickname. I don't remember his exact words, but I sensed that a nickname would be a kind of desecration. Bearing her name was a sacred trust. Therefore, I never allowed myself to be addressed by a nickname. Names and people are too easily lost.

In writing this essay about my name, I realized for the first time that my father had managed to surround himself with three generations of mothers. His mother was Elizabeth; his Belgian wife was Betsy, a diminutive of Elizabeth. (My Belgian mother had an American name because it was fashionable to give European babies American names due to popular American films and American aid during WWI and WWII.) I was Elisabeth, like my paternal grandmother. My dad lived to be 91 with a disease that killed most people early in life. He survived thanks to good medical care and three moms. He was a very wise man. It was also only in writing this essay that I discovered "five," my favorite number, is the date for St. Elizabeth's feast day—an interesting coincidence.

Basically, I have always been Elisabeth, with an "s"—a long, formal name for a child. In elementary school, I remember wishing it were shorter. The "s" is for the French spelling, which made me different from all the other Elizabeths but also caused confusion. The "s" was a conversation starter because most people didn't know why it was spelled that way. It gave the shy child and adolescent I was the chance to talk about my parents rather than myself. The "s" was also a source of pride. I was descended from the Belgae, whom Caesar described as the bravest of the Gallic tribes. Belgium is also the birthplace of the medieval Emperor Charlemagne, father of modern Europe. My grandmother's village still spoke Walloon, an ancient French dialect, which explains why I became a medievalist. Belgian adults dropped

French and spoke Walloon when they didn't want me to understand. Many years later, my subconscious was still determined to win this communications battle, even after all the Walloon conversations ceased to exist except as faint memories. Medieval French took me back to those days and to ages even further past—a subconscious search for origins.

A search for ancestors laid bare a history of conflict. Because it is flat and located between Germany and France, Belgium has been the battleground of Europe—as real estate agents would say, "location, location, location." My Catholic uncle ended up in a concentration camp at the beginning of the WWII as a member of the quickly defeated Belgian army, which ignored King Leopold's promise of free passage to Hitler and tried to stop the German advance. By the end of the war, my uncle Camille had been in three different concentration camps. He was named for his mother Camille—a momma's boy who survived some of the worst history of the twentieth century. His war stories, his battered physical and psychic selves haunted me as a child.

Besides being the historic battleground of Europe, Belgium is a volatile mix of Flemings and Walloons. On my American father's side, the heritage was both Union and Confederate—another volatile mix. Because of my grandmother's premature death, my father's constant illness, and my cultural heritage on both sides of the family, I saw life as tenuous—a constant battle for survival. Even your own body could betray you. A new day was never a certainty.

I regret not having experienced the stability that would have allowed for evolving through a series of nicknames; but I had to be stable, unchanging, because life was too uncertain. "Elisabeth" is formal, weighty, with four syllables—a serious name. I think in some ways the formal name protected me and helped me grow up faster. I was a child with a grown-up name. I needed to grow up fast with a father whose life was always uncertain and a mother for whom I was a "translator," because people couldn't understand her accent in the small southern town where I grew up. I have always been proud of the family and cultural history my name carries with it. My name linked my two cultures. It gave me an anchor and endurance, which I needed to deal with doctors and hospitals, and the Ever-Lurking Shadow of Death.

Recently, in an old book, I discovered the name Lizzie written in the most beautiful script, full of fancy flourishes worthy of a Renaissance manuscript. It was my grandmother's nickname—the girl she was before she was my father's mom. Now, maybe, I'll have a chance to find the Lizzie in me....

・ ・ ・
A Very Plain Jane
Erin Towers

My name is Erin. (…) I have had it pronounced like urine and of course Aaron from the Bible. It was strange enough that I never had a nickname. Actually, now it is not that unusual a name. We think this change occurred when "The Waltons" T.V. show was popular.

———————

Women without a nickname express regret about not having one: they feel something is missing. Because they are diminutives, nicknames provide a playfulness and sense of affection not found in given names. Elisabeth and Erin are missing the time markers nicknames provide—the sense of evolution of the self that comes from going through one or more nicknames. One wonders if accessing memories from different periods in the past is harder for women without nicknames.

This feeling of being different because of a lack of a nickname leads one to wonder how women with unusual names feel about their unfamiliar names.

Chapter 6
UNUSUAL AND UNIQUE NAMES

Unusual names vary in degree. In the following essays, women describe the challenges of growing up with unusual and unique names.

– A –
SET APART

• • •

A Burden
Jaedene Levy

I was named after my grandfather. He died the year before I was born. They called him J.D. for Joseph David. But, really my father wanted me to be named after him. His name was Robert. I might have been Roberta. They worked it out somehow and named me Jaedene. They were adamant about the spelling, and they never allowed a nickname either. I hated my name when I was in grade school and high school. It felt like a burden that set me apart. I so wanted to be called Jane or Judy. But I changed my mind when I got to college. There was only one "Jaedene" out of 12,000 students and I was ready to be unique. The number of times I've spelled it or pronounced it is uncountable, but I think it's made me stronger. Of course it could have backfired. I'm grateful it didn't.

• • •

No Escape
Ellen "Taylor" Manson Watson

(…) Not being an easy child or teenager, the name got me in trouble. There was only one Taylor around in that generation, and I was IT! I had to learn to be wily like a fox and NOT get caught. Sure did have fun though! So the name made me strong and cagey! The Ellen made me more tender and softhearted, so I am blessed in both categories.

• • •

Who?
Ilanit S.

I was named after an Israeli singer. My name means little tree. I like not having an everyday name, but people can never remember Ilanit and completely mispronounce it. (I have been called everything from Internet to Iliana.)

...
The Good and the Bad
Dojelo

DOJELO comes from three female relatives: the most important is the "LO." My mother adored her aunt Loretta and wanted to name me after her but thought, thank goodness, that Loretta was not a very good name. So she took "DO" from my dad's mother, Dora, and the "JE" from her own mother, whom the family called Jennie. (This was a very creative step; Jennie's real name was Regina…let your mind wander over the possibilities in DORELO, and you will see I was lucky she didn't do that!)

I was born and grew up in a small southern town (Russellville, Arkansas) where ALL girl children had two names. You know that pattern: Mary Ellen, Sara Louise, Polly Anna, etc. Even the boys had two names: Van Andy, Bobby Deane, John Alden, etc. I had only one name, and it was odd. I can still recall quite vividly the day that I recognized that I (whatever my name was) was unique. I was in second grade, and I had a red leather coat that no one else had and a name no one else had—delightfully overpowering. I had to just sit down on a step and think about it!

The not-so-good: Having to spell it a lot and being taken for Male anytime there is no title. I get as much mail for Mr. Dojelo as I do for Ms. or Dr. I think that is not a good thing.

The good: On reflection, quite a lot. People don't seem to forget it. It can make a connection between two people who know me if my name is mentioned, and one or the other always seems to let me know that later. I am always asked where it "came from" so it has been a conversation icebreaker for as long as I can remember (though one does get tired of being asked sometimes). I never get mixed up with anyone else…no "which Betty," etc. It makes an easy nickname: "Doj" (sounded with a soft "j"). These were all three pretty wonderful ladies, and I like that my name honors them.

I have 13 step-great grandchildren, and none, of course, is named Dojelo. I understand that! I do have two namesakes, and I've lost track of both. One was the granddaughter of a long-time maid. The child lived in Chicago. The other was the child of a mentally retarded, legally blind client. I lost track of her when I moved to Virginia in the 1960s.

Once many years ago, I said something to my mother about some of the problems of an unusual name. Whereupon she drew herself up to her full height (not very high) and from her 70-something pedestal said, "If you don't like the damned thing, change it!" Just the kind of woman who'd name a kid such a name. I sometimes wish I had told her (she's been dead now for 13 years) that it ended up being more blessing than curse…and that's about the sum of it.

Jaedene and Taylor believe their unique names made them stronger. Taylor says her name required her to be "wily," i.e., more intelligent—a surprising plus one might not immediately contemplate in drawing up a list of the possible benefits of an unusual name. Jadene has to bear the burden of being unique, which made her "stronger," more self-reliant. Both women highlight the difficulties of growing up with an unusual name—of being set apart, with no namesakes for support or protection.

Dojelo is unique among the essayists with unusual names in that as a child, she discovers her distinctive name is "delightfully overpowering," rather than isolating. She creates her own story for her name: it is like her red coat, which makes her both different and special. Dojelo's red coat brings to mind associations with Little Red Riding Hood, which is about behavior and identity. Dojelo manages to escape being consumed by the wolf, i.e., the isolation of a unique name. She escapes by realizing that the name makes her unique—an indication she is not afraid of being different, even at a young age when most children are trying to fit in. Dojelo also has a name based on those of three female relatives, which may be another link to Little Red Riding Hood. If you "open up" her name with all its threatening possibilities for teasing and isolation, you find three living relatives and all their stories inside. The connections with all these living relatives and their stories may be another reason Dojelo easily adapts to her unique name as a child, as opposed to Jaedene (named for a male ancestor, who died before she was born) and Taylor (whose name is her middle name and a family surname, rather than her given name).

Jaedene's, Taylor's, and Dojelo's names create gender identity problems: on paper, they are easily mistaken for males because of their given names. Once grown, Jaedene and Taylor appreciate their unusual names. Dojelo highlights many positives of a unique name—people don't tend to forget it, and it's an "icebreaker." However, Ilanit finds people do not remember her unusual name. All the essayists with unusual names deal with being "set apart."

– B –
LONGING TO BELONG:
A PROCESS

. . .

A Process
Marlee Margulies

When I was in grade school I really hated my unusual moniker. It displeased me that I couldn't find anything with my name printed on it—like pencils, stickers or those little license plates for my bicycle. I vowed to give my children common names—I remember Amy and Michael topped my list.

I recall in 4th grade signing my school papers with different variations of the spelling: Marlie, Marley, and my favorite—Marleigh (which to me seemed very glamorous and sophisticated). The name was growing on me.... As I grew older I started to appreciate having a name that was unique and not shared by many others. After hearing it, people would often say, "That's a pretty name," or "I've never heard that before."

I have been a writer since high school. I have always enjoyed having "Marlee" as part of my byline. It's memorable and sets me apart from other writers.

After more than 30 years of becoming "Marlee" and truly loving it, it came time to name my own children. Amy and Michael didn't seem viable any more. And so came along: Grayson, Aria, Elisabeth and Asher. Although "Elisabeth" is a more common name than the others, I chose a less common variation on the spelling ("S" instead of "Z").

My children may have trouble finding pencils printed with their names on them, but my hope for them is that they will love growing into their own, special names.

• • •

Longing To Belong:
There's Nothing with My Name on It
Vanessa Allen

My parents named me Vanessa after an Austrian actress in the '50s, Vanessa Brown. I guess they used the family names up on my sisters. I've always loved my name, and gone by the whole name.... no nicknames. Even though all of my male cousins wanted to shorten it to Van, they thought Vanessa was too "girly." Now it is a little more popular. I think it does fit me, my personality/interests, etc....

Neither my sisters nor I ever found anything with our name on it, and neither can my children. You would have thought since I was so traumatized by that fact I would have named my children Bob and Ann...but, No!!! I picked Tilson and Alana, and they have always said, "Why did you give us unusual names, too?" It's just those darn family names. At my age now if I see something with my name on it I actually get excited. My sisters will buy funny stocking stuffers if they run across anything with Vanessa on it.

———————

Many women with unusual names mention the frustration of not being able to find anything with their name on it while they are growing up. When a name is unique, there are no others to refer to in comparison or in solidarity. A child looking at a rack of names without finding hers feels left out. Even

49

as adults, this isolation still haunts our essayists' childhood memories. Do you have memories like these?

Is there any way to overcome the feeling of isolation children feel with unusual names? Based on personal experience with our child's unusual name and her frustrations with it, I remember trying to console her by telling her that trinkets with names only make a profit if there are lots and lots and lots of children out there with the same name—so many kids with the same name that they are no longer special; they are just one of many, a drop of water in an ocean of names, a speck of sand on the beach. Despite this effort, her frustration continued. I will never forget the day we found a lovely little shop in Leesburg, VA with her name. The owner was very empathic: our little Adele left the store carrying a bag with her name printed on it. She was radiant; and her unusual name was never a problem after that. She had found one link—that was enough.

Today, it is very easy to personalize items, even storybooks, with your child's name. A child's sense of isolation that comes from not finding a namesake or something with her name on it is no longer the problem it was in the past. Finding as many namesakes as possible in as many different domains as possible—the family, mythology, history, art, music, science, religion, and nature—will inspire both you and your child.

– C –
ASSOCIATIONS:
LOOKING FOR CONNECTIONS

One of the surprising themes women discuss concerning their unique names is that of the associations either they or others make to their names.

• • •

Stories
Runa (Caquelard) Swofford

Growing up I always felt I had the weirdest name in the world. My name is RUNA MARY. My first name, RUNA, is my great-grandmother's nickname. Her given name was JERUSHA.

As the story goes, Mom was pregnant with me when she and Daddy went to the cemetery where my great-grandmother, JERUSHA, was buried. On the tombstone it read, JERUSHA PERMEILA JONES, in parenthesis under her name in it read, (Runa). Somehow out of Jerusha they came up with the nickname of RUNA! After seeing this, Daddy said to Mom, "If the baby is a girl, I want her name to be RUNA." And here I am!

50

Growing up I did not like my name at all, no one could ever pronounce it which embarrassed me and of course being called Runa-Tuna wasn't much fun either. Now, I love my name, and when asked, "Where did your parents get THAT name?!?" I am proud to tell my special cemetery story. My middle name MARY is not uncommon at all; the fun thing about my middle name is it is after my grandmother.

I always said if I had a daughter I would name her RUNA. I have been blessed with two sons. You never know, maybe some day one of my ancestors will see my name on my head stone fall in love with the name like my Father did and continue this little piece of family history. I am so very proud and thankful my father named me RUNA. Thank you Daddy!

• • •
An Abundance of Associations
Mima Suzanne Creed

My maiden name is Mima Suzanne Creed. While Mima is my full first name, it is my grandmother's nickname. Her name was Julia Jemima Creed, and some of her friends, and my grandfather, called her Mima. She always called me Mima Sue. I'm assuming Jemima is a southern name, which is usually associated with the Aunt Jemima pancake products, and therefore with Afro-Americans. (Julia Jemima was of Welsh origins.)

I was surprised to read in the Book of Job that after Job's tribulations, God restored everything that he lost, including a family. Job named his first "replacement" daughter Jemima (Jemima in the King James translation and Jemimah in the NIV).

Nicknames: In the upper grades of elementary school, everyone took to calling me Angela Mima (an expansion of Aunt Jemima). In high school someone called me Mima Bean (a take on Lima Bean), and the nickname Beanie took hold with my friends and family. My sisters call me Beanie to this day.

Interesting story: I recently went to my 40th high school reunion in Silver Spring, Maryland. I always submit a bio for the memory book, which is distributed to all who buy it. A short time after the reunion I received an e-mail from someone I didn't recognize referencing the reunion. The writer explained that she was a friend of someone I went to high school with, and they live in Chester, Maryland, (on the Eastern Shore). She happened to be reading her friend's memory book and my name "jumped" out at her. She contacted me and asked if by any chance I had lived in Turkey in the 1950s. I was jolted, realizing that I had, and wrote back, "How did you know me?" She had been in school with me in Istanbul, Turkey in 1958-1959. We were in the 3rd and 4th grades. She only remembered a few classmates, but she remembered my name. It was such a huge coincidence that after almost 50 years she happened to be reading a reunion book of a friend, in Maryland, halfway around the world from where we went to school together, and remembered my name. I venture to say she has not met another Mima, and neither have I.

Children love sound play; they remind us of the importance of sound in creativity. Growing up, we gradually lose this sensitivity as words (and names) are cemented in meaning and structure. For children, words are but another set of toys to play with. Rhyming and teasing are always a possibility with names, especially unusual names that attract attention because they are different. Nicknames created by children through wordplay become stories for unknown names: they reflect children's need to make the unknown, known—the unfamiliar, familiar. Children's fascination and discomfort with unusual names reveal a deep-seated human instinct concerning the unknown, which can be associated with malaise as well as curiosity.

Children find a host of associations for Mima's name—Aunt Jemima, Angela Mima, Mima Bean, and Beanie, which has an affectionate ring because of the *-ie* ending. Each new nickname creates another story for her unique name. Like Runa, Mima has a family story to go with her name. Family stories help both survive the inevitable childhood teasing. Mima acquires so many different stories for her unique name that she is no longer isolated by it. Name associations, made either by the individual or by others, are paramount because associations provide connections. Every new connection we find for our names gives new meaning and enriches our identity. If others do not create these connections, we can create them for ourselves.

• • •
New Associations
Arielle Bony

My first name is Arielle, a rare name in France (only 2,500 holders); and it is my only name. My mother chose it because she liked the name. She used to be an English teacher. Arielle could be Shakespeare's influence, but it also happens to be the name of my paternal great-grandmother. She was shot dead while pregnant at the very beginning of WWII in a part of Poland that is now the Ukraine.

A year after my birth, a new detergent named "Ariel" was launched and heavily promoted in France. During my childhood, until I was 10 or 11 years old, children often called me Persil, Skip or Omo, names of other brands of detergent. It bothered me a bit at first, but those comparisons were so silly, I ignored them and they quickly stopped.

When my parents broke up, my father returned to Israël. I'm Arielle in France and Ariela in Israël. When I was in junior high school, I discovered, amazed, that there were two other Arielle Sterns in my very small neighborhood in Paris. My maiden name, even if common, is not that widespread even in France. One of those Arielle Sterns was only one year younger than I. I met her because she played basketball against one of my school friends. The other Arielle Stern was about ten years older and practiced piano at our district council, but I never met her.

When I grew up, my uncommon name was sometimes twisted into "Muriel" or "Armelle" and more recently into "Amel" (probably because of the recent success of the French singer Amel Bent). The only period of time I didn't have to repeat my name twice was during my two-month student internship at Procter & Gamble's logistic service. They had launched "Ariel" twenty years ago and the brand was still a lead seller. People there got my name straight away, even the double "l" at the end. It was so pleasant! I suppose it would be like a left-handed person suddenly becoming right-handed. Life also started getting easier because I started to get a nickname—"Ariou"—invented by my young sister, who is 13 years younger than I am. She still uses "Ariou" now, twenty years later, and, sometimes, so does my mother or my husband.

Then my name took a new twist in people's minds about ten years ago when Walt Disney launched the movie "The Little Mermaid," whose name is Ariel. Today, I give gardening courses to children, and they have all heard of my name before. Now the only place I don't use my name Arielle is at Starbucks cafés. The bar is often noisy, and baristas, as they call waiters and waitresses, when asking my name, never get it right. So my Starbucks' name is "Adèle." They get it right although it is even more unusual than Arielle. Adèle is the name of the daughter of the French writer Victor Hugo. I find it so romantic before sipping an ice Moca!

Well, I like my name. It's the only one I've got anyway. It fits me. It is a rare name, widespread in people's minds, but seldom heard.

Children find associations for Arielle's name to make the unknown familiar just as they did with Runa and Mima.

• • •
No Associations:
The Only One
Ona

I have always been interested in the relationship of names to destinies. I was named after my maternal grandfather Oscar, who died before I was born. This follows a Jewish tradition of taking the first letter of a dead relative's name as a way of honoring them.

Ona means, I have been told, the first or only one. I was the first born of four and almost "the only." My mother had many problems conceiving and my parents were on the verge of adopting when I came along. My mother was 32 years old at the time and back then, it was considered "late in life" to have a child, let alone four.

I have never really related to my name. For a good part of my life nobody I met had heard of the name. For that reason, it often evoked one of several comments/ questions: "Oh what a beautiful name," "Where did you get that name?" and "What does Ona mean?" From the positive to the curious, these innocuous queries became over time, not only boring to me, but intrusive as well. I could never be just, "Ona." I was always "the only" Ona most people had ever met.

Being unheard of, as it were, my name constantly gets mispronounced, with the tendency to call me Oona and for the "mispronouncer" to remind me that was the name of Charlie Chaplin's wife.

Having a unique name carries a special burden, that of being different. True to form, and not in name only, I was always considered "different."

When you are young, that is a difficult thing. All you want to be is like everyone else. Now that I am older, I appreciate difference, but still don't relate to my name. Interestingly, I still have a hard time saying, "my name is Ona…, a name that has no reference, making it only self-reverential.

The people I am closest to call me O. I like that a lot. Maybe because it has many reference points—the alphabet, mathematics, a shape, nothing, empty, complete, etc.; it doesn't beckon intrusive questions (nobody asks me what O means) and it is, for better or worse, kind of sexy.

Research indicates that *Ona* means receiving grace, favored by God, and unity. These are all meanings that set Ona apart. Because all the associations highlight being set apart, they also reinforce the story of isolation. Ironically, *O* becomes a symbol and provides Ona with many associations for her name, including that of being "complete," which she never felt with *Ona*.

• • •

From Unique to Universal
Tana Sommer-Belin

Your birth certificate calls it your given name, your first name, and it's true you don't have a thing to say about it when you're just born and lying there in your bassinet. Your parents decide your name and the reasons for choosing certain names are as infinite as there are people to dream them up. Certain religions call for certain names. Beloved relatives live through their name given a newborn. Respect, honor, and cultural customs dictate certain naming around the globe. Some parents take inspiration from history, archetypes, astronomy, calendar days and months, movie and rock stars.

In my case my parents chose a name with a very short story. My name, Tana, was the name of a college girlfriend of my father's brother. They liked it. They used it. When I was small they pronounced it with a flat "a" as in the color "tan." By the time I got to high school and was studying foreign languages, I decided it was much prettier said with a long "a" as in the French or Italian way of saying "Anna." I also had a brief period in High School of using the name "Misty" that was derived from friends who started calling me "Miss T." and that morphed into "Misty." This name went along with my artistic inclinations and my tendency to gaze out of windows, seeming to be elsewhere. My parents more or less adapted to each new phase, but by college I was back to Tana with a long "A." Tana Naomi.

I don't remember a desire to change or modify my name until high school—at the age when we all tend to argue about and criticize anything we can find. I liked that my name was easy and quick to spell when doing schoolwork. Imagine having to write out Alexandra all day in each class at school or Theodore! The only trouble with it was that it was different. I have probably spent one percent of my life's conversation in spelling it for people to obtain the correct pronunciation. People in general have never heard the name and immediately go to the nearest name they do know such as Tanya or Tania. I was in college at UC Berkeley when Patty Hearst and her cohorts robbed a bank and she went into hiding. She unfortunately changed her name to Tanya and was in the news daily. This publicity had an impact on me because even those who had learned to call me Tana would slip into Tanya because that name was on their tongue and on the news.

I liked the esthetic quality of the name, with the "T" standing tall in front and the soft "a", the "n", and another soft "a". My height is above average and the "T" rather suits me.

The inevitable consequence of having an unusual name is that it sets you apart. It means that you are likely to be different or that your parents are out of the norm in some way to choose a rare name. Do they want to set themselves apart in naming their child with an original name, or do they want to imply that they wish this child to be different or more original in the way they live their lives?

With my unusual name I was set apart from day one at school with teachers stumbling over or changing my name with every roll call. I have always been shy anyway, and as a small child, I was unlikely to correct them. So, in fact, I probably was called by my real name only fifty-percent of the time. Maybe what looks like the handicap of having one's name bashed about phonetically on a daily basis, is actually an early life lesson in tolerance and diversity. It can make a shy person even more humble and it can be grounds for asserting oneself when the occasion warrants like on the receipt of a diploma. These are issues the Marys and Johns of the world don't have, at least when in their own country.

Now I have had my name for over sixty years. I know a lot more about it, in a global sense, now, than ever before. In the dictionary I learned there is a Lake

Tana in Ethiopia and that Tana is the name of a Sumatran shrew! In the '60s I met a sleek little female dachshund named Tana, with a long "a" too. I never met a person with the same name till a few years ago in the Von's supermarket—a pretty Eurasian girl became my husband's favorite cashier. Her lovely smile and her nametag with a boldly printed TANA made him feel right at home. Traveling in Mexico, I spied an optical shop named "Optica Tana," In Italy, a clothing store named Tana; in Paris, a chic boutique in St. Germain; and a jewelry maker in Santa Barbara, have all shown me I am not so alone with the name as I thought.

But the most spectacular surprise sighting of my name in public happened while I was driving from Amsterdam through Belgium on my way to France, just after sunset. The sky still glowed a soft pink and the autoroute was elevated so I was at the same level as the skyline of city buildings in dark silhouette. I drove around a big sweeping curve admiring the view and all of a sudden a huge pink neon script wrote across the sky "Tana." That's all. I had a short ego-filled moment of fantasy that the city of Maastricht was putting out the red carpet in a big way, and then I began wondering what the neon advertising was for. I inquired soon after and discovered that a famous company in Holland and Belgium supplies all of Europe with a shoe polish line called "Tana." I have been using this product ever since but I still don't know who the Tana is, who inspired the company name.

While Tana Naomi is on all my legal documents, driver's license, and social security, IRS, etc. I almost never say it or use it otherwise. Naomi is my mother's name. Her mother had done the same adding her own name as a middle name, making Naomi Johanna.

I suspect that most parents don't really think through all the repercussions of the name they choose for their child. Perhaps that is an impossible task because the child's personality is, as yet, unknown. Inevitably a name becomes a type of baggage that we carry all our lives, along with our genetic traits.

No sooner had I started to write this essay about my name, when I went to a reception where we wore nametags and the first person I am introduced to was named "Tana." I stared at her nametag in disbelief. A fellow Santa Barbarian with the same name, only she pronounced it "Tan–a" with the flat "a." I could not resist asking this stranger if she knew why her parents gave her this name. I must say her story was more interesting than mine. This Tana's mother was a nurse and took care of a sweet child with a fatal disease. The child's name was Tana. Caring for Tana touched the nurse's heart so much she declared to her family, "If I have daughter one day, I will name her Tana." Our mutual friend who introduced us said she has a devil of a time when she telephones one of us to remember the pronunciation of the Tana she is calling. I had no idea she'd been dealing with two Tanas for the last fifteen years.

If we have a common name, we are forced to add the middle name or first initial to be distinguished. If we have an unusual name, we risk being a source of *conversation at every meeting. For me, as a shy person, this meant blushing a lot in class. Now, I tend to just re-say it and spell it out right off the bat when I meet someone new, in an attempt to avoid a fuss, especially in foreign countries.*

A name is a brand and sticks with us just like on cattle. People we meet decide what our ethnic background is, whether we are noble or not, related to someone of importance or glean other clues or stereotypes when they hear our names.

When it came time to name my daughter, I felt like giving her the simplest, easiest name to spell (even backwards), a name that almost everyone in the world knows. I gave her the first female name, Eve.

Marlee describes a process of growing into her unusual name similar to that of women who grow out of their nicknames into their given names. This process may take a bit longer with unusual names, but once they have grown into their names, these women have the pleasure of being different and even unique. When her name becomes a common one after the release of a Disney film, Arielle picks another name for herself—a very unusual name, *Adele*, which suggests that Arielle has not only overcome the problems of an unusual name, but also that she may even yearn for the lost uniqueness of her name.

Finding associations for unusual names is not easy for these women or for the people they meet. Like children, adults are also uncomfortable with the unknown and will seek associations for an unknown name—either ethnic or social clues, or stereotypes as Tana observes.

For most of human history, our names have been badges or "brands" of ethnic and class distinctions that could hamper an individual's progress in life. Fortunately, this is less and less the case. As the world becomes more and more of a melting pot, the ability to decipher an individual's origins and class by their name is becoming more and more impossible and even misleading. Tana raises an important point: people bring multiple associations to a name based on their personal experience. Our personal associations to names can subconsciously color how we react when meeting an individual for the first time.

In naming her daughter, Tana chooses a name that is unusual but universal, Eve, one of the simplest and most recognizable of women's names. *Eve* has the additional magic of being a palindrome, which reinforces the message of universality: the name is the same forward or backward.

Chapter 7
COMMON GIVEN NAMES

Having considered unique names and their issues, what are the concerns women discuss relating to common names?

– A –
GIVEN NAME VERSUS NICKNAME

• • •

Susan, Please
Susan W. Hamilton

I don't remember why my parents named me Susan. I've always gone by that name except as a child when I was called Suzy (and as an Aunt, come to think of it!) and for a weeklong stint at a church camp with Peggy P. when we lied about our names and my name that week was Wendy. Several people, especially from NY, have tried to call me Sue over the years, which I absolutely hate.

———————

Various time frames, like adolescence, college years, and even summer camp, provide the opportunity for name changes.

• • •

Still Suzi
Suzi Caquelard

My name is Suzanne Marie. My maiden name is Caquelard. I have been married twice and don't really want those names anymore! Some day I will change back to my maiden name I am sure.

I was named after both grandmothers. My paternal grandmother was Susanne, the French way of spelling it. My parents spelled it with a Z. I don't really know why they did that. BUT my slightly goofy grandmother thought it was the Japanese spelling and would never write my name!? Almost immediately after my birth, my mom began calling me Suzi. A friend of hers sent me a card and wrote it that way and they liked it. I am Suzi still today. Sometimes it seems funny to be 58 years old and be called Suzi... oh, well. I really wish I had gone by Suzanne. It is a very pretty name, but people recognize Suzi easily. Usually I don't even have to write my last name and they know who I am! Marie came from my maternal grandmother. It was her middle name. I am so glad... her first name was Ethel!!

Judith, Please
Judith Sylvane King

My father named me Sylvane after one of his grandmothers. It was the only name I had until I was about one, when my mother added Judith. Since then I've been one of the Judy-Judiths.

I'm a Judith and have been since I saw the movie "A Date with Judy." (Not as soon as it came out around 1948, sometime in the television '50s.) Movie Judy was sooo cute. My mother just loved her and the nice-little-girls she represented. As a result, I tried hard not to be a stereotype.

I don't remember any other Judy-Judiths in high school or college.

I went to work at WTOP Radio in 1960. I replaced a "Judy" and a "Judy" followed me in the job. And, yes, I was still a "Judy" at WTOP. People don't listen.

I went to work at the National Zoo in 1970. I was the second Judith there, but the other Judith worked in a different department. No problem. In 1972, however, I transferred to the new Education dept., working for Judy White. It was easy when there were only two of us—she was "Judy" and I was "Judith." But then White went a little nuts and hired a third Judy and then a fourth! As a result, the five Judy-Judiths at the Zoo were known by their last names. It set us apart from other Judy-Judiths. Since then, many of my friends still call me King.

One Christmas a few years ago a friend gave me an art book, "Judith: Spiritual Warrior." It was unusual and enjoyable.

To this day most people automatically respond with "Judy" even though I say "Judith."

I could never retrain my mother.

• • •

Judy, Please
Judith Gottleib Herman

I have a relatively informal style so Judy suits me fine.... Judith is a bit too formal for me.

These essays illustrate why it may be more difficult to remember common names—which Susan is Suzi, not Susan, and vice versa. Americans love to use nicknames; however, women with common names carefully decide whether or not they want a nickname as a means of establishing their identity among their namesakes. Assuming the use of a nickname is preferable is not always the case as these essayists explain.

– B –
EASY TO REMEMBER?

• • •

An Easy Name
Judy Jones

I haven't thought about being a "Judy" for a long time. Believe it or not for such a popular name, I have only one other friend with the same name.

My parents had unusual names. My mother's name was Traba, an alteration of her father's name Traber, and my father's was Virgil. My guess is that growing up they had problems with their names and as a result were very quick to name their progeny, Bob, Bill and Judy. We fit right in to our generation.

I never really gave being named Judy much thought. I never counted the Judys in my high school or among my friends in college. I did however have some concern when I married and became Judy Jones. Everyone's first reaction is to say, "Oh you have an easy name to remember" and the next time they see me they promptly call me Barbara or Sue.

Contrary to what one might assume, a common name is not a key to freedom from name issues. Almost all of these women express something problematic about their common names. Ironically, the biggest problem for all these women is getting the name right—whether getting it right centers around the given name, nicknames, or spelling. Susan doesn't want any nicknames. Judith King wants to be Judith, not Judy; but Judith Herman prefers to be Judy. Things are never as simple as they seem.

– C –
SPELLING

Like nicknames, spelling is an important issue for women with common names.

• • •

Sarah with an "h"
Sarah Jones-Popiel

The name Sarah: a classic. Growing up, however, it irritated me. There were so many other Sarahs in my school! My mother insisted that Sarah was not a common name when I was born, but I never really appreciated that. The one bright point should've been that no one would ever misspell my name, but, of course, I always had to specify "Sarah with an 'h'"! When I named my own daughter, I chose a name I'd never even heard as a person's name, thinking she would have a unique one.

Now her name, Siena, is appearing on popular name lists... AND she'll have to specify "Siena with one 'n'." I suppose it's karma... hmm, Karma... that would've been a unique name!

• • •

To Distinguish Myself
Deborah Field Washburn

I didn't know any other Deborahs until about fifth grade, at which time I became "Debbie" to distinguish myself from the two "Debbys" in my class. People didn't use full names much in the early Fifties: Judiths were Judy, Sarahs were Sally, etc.

———————

If you have a common name, it makes sense that you want it spelled "right." Spelling is one of the few ways women can distinguish their common names. This explains, at least in part, why spelling is so important to so many of these women. Spelling provides either a means of bonding when girls decide to spell their names the same way or a means for asserting one's independence as Debbie does in order to distinguish herself from the Debbys in her class.

– D –
ONE OF MANY

• • •

Plain, Ordinary, Boring
Ann M.

My first name is Ann. My name at birth was Margaret Ann, after my mother. I was to have been called Peggy. Then at about the time I was born my father's younger brother's wife, Peggy, had a schizophrenic break and disappeared with her infant son. Obviously I was not going to be a Peggy. I also was not going to be Margaret because my mother had that name cornered. The fall back name was Ann.

I have always hated my name. I see it as being plain, ordinary and boring. I did not have the greatest relationship with my mother, so I have never been happy with the idea of having her name. At this point I feel rather neutral about my name. It has never encouraged me to be like some other Ann. It's just who I am. I have never had a nickname, nor been called anything but Ann.

I was precocious and entered kindergarten writing my name at four. My accomplishment was denigrated because there were only two different letters in my name. "Elaine" was the brilliant one.

Then there was the "Ann-Ann-Ants-in-Your-Pants" in about second grade. And Annie Fannie followed about a year later.

The younger sister of a friend of mine was also Anne, but she claimed to be special because she was "Ann with an E." She also got called Annie, a fate I was able to avoid. At about this time it was "Annie Get Your Gun," and I was no tomboy!

When I began college I almost changed my name to MegAnn, a name I would have loved. Counselors were going around the room calling out names. They got to mine and called out Margaret. I answered, "I am Margaret, but I go by Ann." I thought of the MegAnn about two minutes later, but by then it was too late.

My ex-husband wanted me to be MegAnn because he thought that sounded better with M_____, but at that point it would have been a major undertaking to make the change.

I converted to Judaism as an adult and the Rabbi who did the conversion gave me the Hebrew name Hannah. I kept that until I found out that I could come up with my own Hebrew name. I selected the name Alona Tzipporah, which means, "bird in an oak tree." I love the feeling of strength in an oak tree, but I don't want to stay in one place, hence the bird.

———————

Ann struggles with a variety of problems many women face with their names. She loses the first name picked for her, she is teased about her name, and her name lacks a nickname. She finds inspiration in a new, long name.

• • •
Easier
Amy Moore

Amy Rae Gaston was my given name. I grew up in Iowa. My father and mother wanted a short name for the first name as they said it would be easier to call my sister and me. My older sister is named Jill, which was a perfect one-syllable name. They stepped out of the box a bit and went for the two-syllable "Amy" when I was born.

• • •
Just Lisa
Lisa Baritone

My name is Lisa. It is not short for anything, I'm just Lisa. Sometimes I'm Lisa 1 or Lisa 2, depending on whom you are talking to and how they rank me, other times I am big Lisa ('cause the other Lisa is Little Lisa). In high school, I was in a chorus where there were 6 Lisas...I changed my name to Stan. That was a short-lived nickname. Lisa and I still refer to each other as Patsy and Eddie on occasion... homage to Absolutely Fabulous[8] and our alter egos, but we are the only ones who use those names.

I have no clue why my parents chose my name...one wanted me called Lisa Naomi and the other wanted Naomi Lisa...Lisa Naomi won. I don't really care for either but I guess I'd rather be a Lisa than a Naomi. Do I think I fit my name, I don't know, perhaps I do. I don't know what a Lisa is. I am just a Lisa, one of the many, often confused with one of the others. I honestly don't know what else I would like to be called, wish I had had a name which called me to greatness but after 50 years, it is too late and just a Lisa is fine.

• • •

Common Enough
Karen Lee Cole

(...My parents) also told me they believed "Karen" went well with our last name of "Cole," and was common enough to be spelled easily and remembered. It is a bit onomatopoeic, with the repetition of the hard "c/k" sound; however, I suppose they didn't consider how too much "in vogue" it was in 1957 when I was born. I recall five other "Karen Lees" in my high school graduating class of 656.

They told me they also considered "Laura Lee," but feared that name would make me the butt of teasing, singsong jokes, as in "Laura Lee, Laura Li." Of interest, my younger sister, four years later, was named Laura Ann. In junior high, I went through a brief period of hating my name because it seemed so ordinary and uninteresting. I wanted something more unusual and glamorous, and experimented with a variety of spellings.

Judy Jones notes that, "Everyone's first reaction is to say, 'Oh, you have an easy name to remember'; but the next time they see me they promptly call me Barbara or Sue." Lisa wonders what it would have been like to have a name that "called me to greatness," but is resigned to being "one of many, often confused with one of the others." When someone has a common name, it seems even more troubling when the name is misunderstood, forgotten, or spelled incorrectly since it is an "easy" name. From these essays, we make the surprising discovery that getting a common name right is not so easy. Whereas women with unusual names seek to find connections with others, women with common names seek to create a unique identity. Ironically, giving a child an unusual name can create a longing to belong and having a common name can create a longing to be different.

Chapter 8
AMBIVALENCE ABOUT THE GIVEN NAME

Although women usually transition into their given names over time, some are never totally at ease with their given names as we see in the chapters that address unusual names and common names. The following essayists describe other types of problematic relationships with names.

– A –
NO REAL FIT

. . .

Still Don't Really Like My Name
Maxine Penn

I've always hated my name, which is Maxine. I use it professionally. Actually, I decided it wasn't such a bad name after I was 50 because it is a grown-up name. My parents named me after my grandfather Max but really because my mother was a fan of the Andrews Sisters, a popular singing group of the time. I was called Max and Maxi the Taxi. Maxine, spoken with a Chicago accent, sounded flat and ugly and as I didn't feel exactly beautiful, I thought if I changed my name, it would change me. When I was a freshman in high school, I idolized a junior girl whose name was also Maxine. She called herself Micki and so, when I went off to camp that summer, I called myself Mickie, spelled differently from the other Micki, and came back with a new name. Eventually my parents even called me Mickie and mostly everyone does. When we took a slow boat to England for a year's stay when I was 25, I tried to choose an entirely new name but neither my husband nor I could think of anything that seemed to fit. I still don't really like my name and even feel uncomfortable recording the message on my answering machine. I remained Mickie (Maxine) and named my children the most ordinary, popular names of the late 60s. Steven, Michael and Jonathan. My husband's name is David and I took his last name easily because it is plain.

Maxine's ambivalence about her name may stem from teasing. An older namesake, summer camp, and a change in spelling help liberate her somewhat from her ambivalence about her given name.

• • •

Gotten Used to It
Rose O.

I have a fairly unusual name—Rose. I was named after my great grandmother. I have always disliked the name. As a child I thought it was too old-fashioned, too plain and all the flowers and smell jokes. As a teen the hokie quotes and a thorn and rose comments were annoying. I wanted a name that was not so feminine, more worldly, and something more appropriate for the career woman I wanted to be. Now as an adult I have just gotten used to it. I would even consider using it as a middle name.

Sometimes I think girls are not satisfied with what they have. My daughter was named for her great grandmother Laura. I thought Laura might be too plain so I chose to name her Lauren, which is a little more sophisticated. She tells me at least weekly that she does not like her name and wishes I had just named her Laura.

My son has never mentioned liking or disliking his name at all.

As the world changed and women entered the work place, certain names fell into disfavor—especially names linked to nature or names considered too feminine—because of stereotypes. Rose can now be proud of her name, which marks a dramatic change back to names drawn from Nature in the most recent census both in the U.S. and Britain.

Judging from her own children, Rose makes the interesting observation that girls seem to have more problems with respect to their names than boys do. If this is accurate, it suggests that girls are, perhaps, more sensitive to, or more expressive about, the complexities of identity than boys may be.

• • •

Never Liked It
Shirley

I never liked my name. My dad wanted to name me Shirley and my mom wanted to name me Louise. My dad won and I was named Shirley Louise. Because of Shirley Temple, I never felt like the name was mine. Everybody always said, "Oh, like Shirley Temple." Actually I was born before Shirley Temple: I wasn't named for her. In addition, I had four brothers who teased me mercilessly about my name.

I was born on Christmas. I would have preferred to be named Carol, but my sister got that as her middle name. Sometimes I feel like I've been "Shirlied to death" all my life.

Shirley points out one of the dangers of name associations. If people constantly point out your name is like somebody else's, eventually, you feel like the name doesn't really belong to you—especially in Shirley's case because, as she notes, she was born before the famous actress.

All these essayists suffer a common problem that affects their relationship with their given names throughout their lives—teasing. Maxine, Rose, and Shirley all have painful childhood memories of being teased because of their names. Negative associations and stereotypes can create a sense of rejection that is difficult to overcome.

– B –
NO NICKNAME AND NO STORY

• • •

Never Cared for It
Gloria

I've never cared for this name. I would have preferred Carolyn, my middle name. You can shorten it to "Carrie," which is less formal and more affectionate. I don't know why my parents named me Gloria. Carolyn is after my grandad Carl.

– C –
NEGATIVE MEANINGS

• • •

What Could Be Worse?
Sheila Seigal A.

I never liked my name. It was so difficult to say Sheila Seigal over the phone and always seemed to me to be a hard sounding name. My dad called me Susabellatish. When I went to college, during orientation week, we went around the room and gave our names. When I announced mine, someone called out, "We'll fix that after the meeting." So they did, and I went through college as Sue.

The meaning of my name is "gray-eyed and blind." What could be worse? Had I been a boy, my name would have been Shephard David. Not sure which is worse. Sheila is a name that has not been recycled, and most people I meet with the same name are about my age.

Sheila has many derivations depending on where in the world you come from. In Australia, it is a loose woman. It is not a soft name or one that can easily find a nickname.

Like Maxine, Sheila feels her name has a harsh sound. Like Gloria, Sheila doesn't like her name because it has no nickname. Women without

66

nicknames may feel that not having a nickname is like missing out on part of childhood.

Looking for stories about her name, Sheila discovers the negative associations of the name are even international. Rose, Gloria, and Sheila give no family stories about their given names. Maxine notes that her name is not a family name but that of one of the Andrews Sisters. Family stories are missing for many of these names or they are problematic.

• • •

Never Liked My Name
Dolores

Dolores. It means "sorrow" or "pain." That's a good send off to life! I come from an Irish very Catholic family who grew up in Georgia—four girls, each named after a variant of the "Blessed Virgin Mary" ("Our Lady of Sorrows"/Mater Dolorosa). And my sister, Regina ("Queen of Heaven") was certainly the crowned favored child. My middle name is Elizabeth, which I like much better, more personable, more "sexy;" but I never used it much. I wound up (?intentionally?) having the same initials as my father and struggled all my life (and even after his death) with my intense relationship with him. I have never liked my name, so "old-fashioned" (Dolores Del Rio?) and the only nickname was a friend who called me "dol" (pronounced "Dull") which needless to say was worse.

Yes, I wonder about names as family agendas!!!

• • •

A Family Name
Dolores Rice

Dolores is a family name, goes back for generations. Represents the Mother of God, the Lady of Sorrows. I was the only Dolores I knew until I was twelve and met another in seventh grade. Haven't met too many since then. I tried to be Dee for a few years in high school, but I was never cute enough, or silly enough to go by her forever—so Dolores has been my name since graduation. Except for my Dad, he, and only he, calls me Lola.

I've wrestled with pain throughout my adult life and attribute the addiction to my name. I don't seek to alleviate pain but seem to dwell in it, a strange perversion to being named for pain and sorrow.

Some call me empathetic, others say I'm very serious, spiritual, a wise woman, an elder and have been older than my years since the day I was born.

Dolores Toledo has a rolling sound and easily reveals my ethnicity. After I married and became Dolores Rice doors may have opened, however slightly, camouflaged in the anonymity of an American surname. Stripped of the language and culture that distinguished my ancestors I attempted to make a difference in American Education listening for the needs of the disenfranchised.

The woman who seems best able to cope with her problematic name is Dolores Rice, perhaps because of her name's story. Her given name is a testament not only to her family, but also to her lost heritage.

When creative writing was suggested as a means for exploring identity, Dolores provided a beautiful example—an elegiac poem, *Isleta Woman* (p.308).

• • •

If I'd Known....
Barbara Mattson

If I'd known "Barbara" was a derivative of Barbarian, or meant strange or foreign, when I was growing up, I might have wished harder to have my name changed to Patricia.

Sometimes ignorance is bliss; but ignorance about one's name is never an option because at some point, "the truth will out." As we have seen from many of the essays, there is sometimes confusion about the origins of a name or what a name means. Multiple sources should be considered in gathering information about a name: not all resources are accurate or complete. Sharing the multiple dimensions of her name with a child can provide a wonderful source of inspiration as she grows up. As we shall see later, the meaning of names can play an important role in a child's development; and as we saw with Molly, creating your own meaning for your name is an inspiring endeavor.

In addition to problems children may face with unusual or common names, name ambivalence may also result from teasing, from an old-fashioned name, from a name that belongs to someone else whose identity overshadows that of the child, from negative stories and associations to the name, or from a sense of isolation created when there are no nicknames or stories to go with the name. How can an individual overcome name ambivalence about her name no matter what the problem is?

Chapter 9
OVERCOMING TEASING

As we have seen, many women bear life-long scars from childhood teasing because of their names. The following essays offer tips on how to overcome this problem.

• • •

Prevailing
Clementine (from: France)

My name is Clementine. I can hear you sing the song "Oh my darling…." You know! Yes, Americans often sing this song when I introduce myself.

I am French. My parents first planned to call me Claire, which I really dislike! One day, at the end of her pregnancy, my mother came into a drugstore and heard a mother say to a very cute little girl—her daughter: "Clementine, come here!" My mother and father found this name really sweet and chose it eventually. I think, also, my father had an aunt by that name. She died a long time ago.

I was teased a lot in school because of my name, because of a very well-known animated TV series called "Clementine." Children my age would always sing the tune of the cartoon to annoy me. Not to mention the jokes: "Are you an orange?", "I am going to eat a clementine, Clementine!" etc. But as I grew up, people found that my name suited me a lot, because I am said to be sweet and calm.

I do have a Hebrew and an English name, additional names, but I never use them. Clementine is the only name I ever use.

My close family and friends do not call me Clementine usually. Most of them call me "Clem," a few call me "Clé" or even "Clems." As a joke, and because she knows I don't like it, one friend of mine calls me "Clémentin," (which does not sound the same as "Clementine" in French), to make it sound masculine.

Anyway, I quite like my name, because it is uncommon. When someone yells "Clementine" in the street, I always turn to see who it is, because I always think I'm being called.

• • •

Growing Up My Name Was the Bane of My Existence
Dorothy Escher Kerr

(…) Growing up my name was the bane of my existence. I wanted to be a Deb or a Susan or anything but Dorothy. Not only was it antiquated, but also no one else had it, and the association with the Wizard of Oz made for quite a bit of teasing. ("Where's the WIZ? Where's Toto? Auntie Em! Auntie Em!") Over the years I've really come to love being Dorothy. No one ever says, "Dorothy Who?" because it's so

unusual. In fact, both of our children have unusual names and I love that they do. Sometimes they're teased, but not too often.

• • •

Just Smile
Lula

My parents were both from the South, but met in the North. They named me Lula. Unfortunately, when I was little, there was a very popular song at the time about Lula, who's "back in town." Of course, the other children teased me mercilessly; and I was very unhappy. I was only five or six. I finally went to my mother to tell her about my problem. She smiled and said, "Why Lula, they wouldn't tease you if they didn't like you—they wouldn't bother. If they tease you, just smile and keep that little secret to yourself." So when they teased me after that, I'd just smile. The teasing didn't last long after that.

———————

Clementine is teased as a child because of associations with an animated TV series. She overcomes teasing for several reasons: her name has a family story, pleasant associations with a sweet fruit and a well-known historic American folksong, and it is unusual in France—a quality she appreciates when she grows up. In order to overcome childhood teasing, the individual needs to find more positive associations to the name than negative. For both Clementine and Dorothy, the characters with whom they are associated have more positives than negatives, so the teasing is more good-natured than malicious. Having her name associated with someone else is difficult for a child because she may feel her name does not belong to her: her identity feels threatened. Later in life, the fact their names are unusual helps Clementine and Dorothy overcome childhood teasing.

Like Arielle (p.52), Lula discovers that if she ignores the teasing, it stops. By ignoring the teasing, the victim takes away the power of her tormentors. Surviving teasing can make the victim stronger. Lula's mother provides a solution that offers her daughter several ironic advantages. Little Lula takes the teasing as a sign of being liked because her mother tells her that's what it means. By smiling, Lula appears to be happy, which is the exact opposite of what her tormentors want and expect. The smile raises the question of what she is smiling at. Could it be that she is happy despite the teasing (which is thus futile), that she is also teasing them, that she knows something they don't know? When I talked to Lula, the elderly woman smiled as she recalled her mother's words. When I questioned her about her mother's explanation, Lula just repeated the story and smiled: the strategy still works. Just smile: you can't beat the Mona Lisa. Ambiguity is a powerful psychological tool.

Were you teased about any of your names? If so, collecting more positive stories than negatives will help overcome painful memories and feelings of inadequacy, which is the message of the American film classic *It's a Beautiful Life*, starring Jimmy Stewart (1946).

Chapter 10
DOUBLE GIVEN NAMES

Women with double given names discuss some surprising issues.

– A –
DOUBLE NAMES ALTERED TO ONE

• • •

How Did I Get This Double Name?
Sue Martin

One question I wish I'd asked my mother before she died is, "Why did you name me Linda Sue?" "Linda Sue" has that two-name, three-syllable lilt that says I'm from the South, and, indeed I am. I was born in Birmingham, Alabama in 1946 to parents whose roots were also in the South. I was never called Linda Sue, thank God, but just Sue, or Susie (only by folks who knew me very well). The only time people called me Linda was on the first day of school when the teacher automatically focused on the first name of every student. Only in second grade, when I was too shy to correct her, did my teacher call me Linda all year.

I attempted to fix this problem in college when I signed all official documents "L. Sue." This strategy, I thought, would clearly point to "Sue" as the preferred name. But no. In my junior and senior years of college, all my friends called me "L. Sue." But I kind of liked that. It was certainly less common than plain Sue. And it went along with my then artsy persona (I was a theatre major). I would have preferred to just drop the "Linda" altogether and, to this day, if someone asks for my "first name," I'll say Sue. It just kills me that my driver's license says "Linda Sue." When they started checking ID more closely at the airport after 9/11, I would arrive at security with my boarding pass ("Sue Martin") and my driver's license ("Linda Sue Stevens Martin")—and the security folks weren't sure whether to let me through or not!

The only thing my mother ever told me about my name is that she wanted to call me Sue after her aunt Suella. I guess I should be grateful she didn't call me Suella, but that aunt was very dear to me, too, so I am honored to have a piece of her name. At one point during my work career, a good friend nicknamed me Suzella, the closest I've come to my mother's original inspiration....

Sue gives no particular reason for disliking her double given name except that it suggests a stereotype. She picks the part of her double name for which she has a story—a link to the family.

And So It Goes
Mary Rojcewicz

I was given the name Mary Alice. My father had a sister with that name, although she went by the name Mary. My mother had a sister named Mary Alice, but she was called Alice. I was always pleased with my name because both of my aunts were very kind and sweet, and I was happy to be named for them. I realized even as a child that I was continuing a name that was common to both sides of my family.

When I started middle school, I decided I wanted to be called Mary. I thought the double name sounded rather childish and that Mary sounded better. So all my friends in junior high, high school and college and now know me as Mary. However, my family and friends from my earlier days still call me Mary Alice. When I send out cards or letters I am conscious of my name change. My signature on some is Mary and on those to my brothers and sisters and cousins it is Mary Alice.

After the birth of my first daughter, my husband said that he would like to name her after me. Of course, I was very pleased that he wanted to. My daughter was known as Mary Alice until her entry into junior high when she changed her name to Mary. And so it goes.

A girl with a double name who wants to mark her growth out of childhood may drop one of her names if there is no nickname to drop. Stepping out of childhood often entails dropping the childhood name, be it a nickname or part of a double name.

. . .

Too Confusing
Mary Martin

I was named Mary Ida Martin after both of my grandmothers. In high school, the kids just dropped the Ida. I was happy to see "Ida" go because it just led to confusion. People would call me Mary Ann because they remembered it was a compound name, but couldn't remember Ida because it was a bit unusual and didn't fit as well as Ann.

Mary's essay points out that associations affect how people remember or misremember names. Remembering two names can be even more difficult than remembering just one. Mary's essay also highlights the role peers may play in shortening a name to one identity as opposed to two.

Confusion
Maryann F. Hunter

My given name is Mary Ann. My parents are Catholic and reportedly chose it to honor the Blessed Mother, Mary, and her mother, Ann. That said, my Mom also admits readily that the song with lyrics "All day all night Mary Ann, down by the seaside sifting sand...." was very popular in 1957 around the time I was born. The fact that there were several Mary Anns in my class at school may provide support for that notion.

I never minded my name, but I didn't particularly like it either, perhaps because it seemed a little old-fashioned. I spelled my name as two words until I went to college. The professors would get a computer printout list of students, and my name printed out as Mary A. A couple of times, a professor would trying to call on me by calling "Mary," and I never responded because I didn't recognize it as my name. I went to the records office and had the spelling changed to one word with a lowercase "a" and no e, and it has been that way ever since. To add to the confusion, because Ann was no longer my middle name, I added my maiden name (Friday) as my middle name when I got married. It was easier than hyphenating and let me keep a little piece of my former identity. The change in my name solved the problem in college, and I never thought about it again until we moved to Maryland and I tried to get a driver's license in the post 9/11 era. It took two trips to the DMV and several other forms of ID to convince them that the name on my license didn't have to match my birth certificate.

___

For Maryann, her two names are a single identity; so she fuses the two names to avoid losing half of who she is.

• • •

Legally Changed
MaryAnn

MaryAnn is intended to be one name, not two. It is my first name only. There is no middle name. I am the first-born and my mother prayed for a girl, making the commitment that "if God sent her a girl," she would name her Mary for the Blessed Mother and Anne for Mary's mother.

I went to Catholic schools where I was chronically called Mary, which I hated. Later in life, I legally changed my name—making one name with no space between the names—with the hope of being called MaryAnn, instead of the dreaded Mary.

___

Unlike Maryann Hunter, MaryAnn keeps *Ann* capitalized, which suggests that though fused into one, the names still retain something of a separate identity.

Living for Two?
Ann-Louise Schlesinger Silver

My parents chose my name, Ann-Louise, in memory of a Hannah on one side of the family and a Leah on the other, in keeping with Jewish tradition. They hyphenated the name in order not to "show favoritism," (an important principle for my mother, especially when my brother or I asked for something). I don't know anything about these two women, not even which one was on my father's and which on my mother's side of the family. I am sure I asked my parents about them when I was little, but can't remember what they said. I do remember feeling disappointed with their answers, and got the impression they might not even have known them, and now they are both gone, too. I imagined these women, and thought I liked Hannah better, mainly because I never liked "Louise." (Hannah, in my imagination was short, overweight, with graying black hair and was a great cook, and Leah had light brown hair, was thin, read a lot and was intimidating.) I have often signed my name accidentally omitting the "i" (louse). I usually do this when I am feeling guilty or grouchy. "Louise" sounds ugly to me in any case: Loo-EEZE. People say that names starting with "L" are especially beautiful, and that puzzles me.

I have worried that this double name means I have to live for both of them and do twice the "normal" one-name stuff. In middle school, (I had started in a new school) a classmate wanted to nickname me "Weezie," or "Weezle." I didn't like the sound, but thought a nickname would be nice, and I like weasels and otters, which fit my hyperactive personality. When I told my mother, she angrily said, "Tell her you cannot have a nickname. Your name is Ann-Louise. The hyphen is there for a reason. You cannot favor one side of the family over the other." So I dutifully told my classmate, who looked very puzzled, and that was the end of it.

I haven't ever met another Ann-Louise, but when I googled "Ann-Louise" today, I found quite a few, mostly in Europe: an athlete, a jeweler, a stripper, a tapestry-maker, a fashion designer, two directors in important posts, two Ph.D.s. I found myself a couple of times.

My cumbersome double name was with me until the first day of college when I introduced myself as Ann, and that's who I've been ever since, or sometimes Annie. I wanted to be "Granny Annie", but the kids just call me Grandma.

Anne is very sensitive to the double inheritance of her compound name and has, therefore, the intriguing awareness of living for two. One wonders how much other women with double names may share these emotions on a subconscious level. A compound name can be both a double gift and a double responsibility.

Why Do People Shorten Names?
Mary Giles
(by her mother Clicker Morgan)

We started w/Mary Giles. When she hit middle school, the kids just called her Mary. Giles is not a common name like Mary Ellen, Mary Catherine, etc. Those who knew her as a child still refer to her as Mary Giles. Maybe you can tell me why people seem to always trend towards shortening a name? A girl in our neighborhood was Mary Grace. Now they are starting to call her MG.

———————

Peers shorten names for a variety of reasons—to avoid confusion, to center identity on one name, and to make the name more informal.

All the essayists with double given names evolve into one given name: they pick one of their two given names, they fuse their double name into one name, or their peers drop the second name. Linda Sue becomes Sue, Mary Ida becomes Mary, Mary Alice becomes Mary, the two Mary Anns become either Maryann or MaryAnn, and Ann-Louise becomes Ann. They suggest different reasons for their name changes—Southern stereotypes, confusion, the double name sounds childish, old-fashioned, or it is too cumbersome, and finally problems with computer ID, which does not recognize double given names (but lists the second name as the middle name). In the cases of Maryann and MaryAnn, both women fuse their names. MaryAnn dreads being called *Mary*. Maryann does not recognize her name in college when professors call out *Mary* from the printouts, because part of her name is missing. For both MaryAnn and Maryann, their names are a single, not a dual, identity—even when the names were spelled separately as two names.

All these women pick one name for various reasons. Ann may actually give the psychological reason for picking one name—that of choosing a single identity. In addition, we see that if the individual does not shorten the double name, peers will shorten it as in the case of Mary Ida and Mary Giles. This suggests that a core identity is critical before we can think about other names and identities for ourselves—a need that echoes the Native American tradition of the spiritual name as the immutable center around which other names evolve.

Every essayist with a double name expressed some issues with it. How do you feel about double names?

While some women with double names drop one or consolidate the name, others do not.

• • •

A Puzzling Predicament
Mary Jo

I grew up Catholic. As a child I thought Mary referred to the Holy Mother and Jo was for Joseph. I thought that, somehow, I was supposed to be both of them. This was especially confusing since I thought one name was for a woman and the other was for a man. (Josephine is the feminized form Joseph.) I had four brothers and was dressed, like a boy, with my brothers' hand me downs. "Mary" represented a feminine, sweet identity that didn't fit in my childhood. In college, I was called "Mo Jo," which seemed robotic. "MJ" was sporty, but not feminine. It's taken me a long time to feel at ease with my double name and its double identity.

––––––––––

Mary Jo discusses the double identity that is subconsciously suggested by a double name. As a child, this was especially problematic for her because of the combined female-male identity. (One wonders if bisexual names, like *Mary Jo*, *Billy Jean*, *Jo Ann*, and *Peggy Lee,* are shortened less frequently because dropping one name would eliminate one sex.)

Chapter 11
THE NAME TRIBE:
A SISTERHOOD

Children have an intense desire to find something with their name on it—to belong to a group, a sisterhood, a name tribe. Finding a namesake is not always a positive experience, however.

· · ·
I Was Doomed
Beth

In grade school, I noticed that the other Beths I met were pudgy. I had a well-rounded face also, so I thought all Beths were fat and I was doomed to it. I fulfilled that prophecy pretty well. I still find that the pudgy Beths outnumber the skinny ones that I have met. Is there something to that?

· · ·
The "Amy" Curse
Amy Moore

Growing up in Iowa, I attended a small public school. There was one other Amy at my school and one Amy who attended my Sunday school class. They were both rather obese children and my sister, Jill, used to say to me "Amy, you're getting kind of heavy. You don't want to be like those other Amys!" It seemed every time I met an Amy I would check to see how they were built—and very rarely it seemed that I met a thin and beautiful "Amy." I ended up being a little pudgy in 4th and 5th grade and always had a complex that maybe it was the "Amy" curse.

· · ·
Why Was I Named After a Betsy-Wetsy Doll?
Betsy

My nickname is Betsy. I guess the choice was to prevent confusion with mom, who was called Betts. But as a child, I wondered, briefly, why I was named after a "Betsy Wetsy Doll."

———

Betsy's memories go back to a young age when children are still learning about names and identity and do not yet realize that one name can refer to different people or, in this case, even to something inanimate like a doll. This story, like those of Arielle and Clementine, reminds us that whenever a young child's name appears elsewhere, an explanation should be provided.

• • •
A Tyrant
Sheila Cahill

I didn't meet another Sheila until seventh grade. She turned out to be a ginger-haired tyrant whom I hated.

• • •
I & II
Vera Constance Chadwick Sky

(…) one of my very first friends who was actually named Connie joined us for a week on Lake Michigan one summer. My father christened us Connie I and Connie II. We both thought this great fun, including determining who was I or II, and remembering it.

Many women describe their childhood wish to belong, to find something with their name on it, to belong to a name tribe, which the child sees as recognition and social validation. Not finding a trinket with their name on it creates a sense of isolation and rejection which women remember even as adults.

Some girls manage to find an older namesake who serves as a role model and helps them grow into their given name (e.g., Martha, p.39, Maxine, p.64). Others find a namesake their age who becomes a good friend (Rebecca Snow, p.32). When girls with identical names become friends, they pick different nicknames, like Becca and Becky, the two Phyllises called Flies and Flees (p.213), and the two Lisas (p.62). Vera describes the delight the girls feel with trying to remember who is I and who is II—a playful game of both sharing and delineating identity. This game highlights the magical nature of a namesake, who is simultaneously a reflection—like a sister or a twin—and a different person, a double. These experiences with namesakes can be wonderful. However, girls can meet a namesake who is difficult, or even "a tyrant" as Sheila describes, which is a doubly disillusioning experience because not only is friendship not achieved, the "sisterhood" suggested by the name is not realized. In Betsy's case, the sisterhood takes on a strange dimension for the child who can't understand why she would have been named for a doll. When members of the name tribe share a common problem, essayists humorously describe the sense of a name "curse"—a projection that "frees" the individual from any guilt or responsibility for her problem.

The desire to be friends with a namesake goes back to our earliest understanding of our names as part of the self (Stephanie, p.27). Our desire to find a namesake, or at least something with our name on it reflects our desire to find a place in society as an extension of the family. The innate human desire to belong is one of the strongest indications of the social nature of our species: this desire manifests itself in childhood even with our names.

Chapter 12
THE MISSING MIDDLE NAME

Although women were only asked to discuss their given names, the subject of the missing middle name appeared so often, it needs to be addressed.

"Middle names (...) started to be used in the United States and England at the end of the eighteenth century. By the end of the nineteenth century most people in the United States were given middle names, and today only one to four percent of U.S. children do not have middle (...) names. Middle names, which served to convey status, first became popular among the upper classes and then were adopted by the general population. Middle names are useful in distinguishing one generation from the next when sons are named after their fathers, and sometimes they preserve a mother's maiden name."[9]

• • •

Why Didn't I Get One?
Beth

Why didn't I get a middle name? My older sister has one. Everyone else in the world has one. Why not me?

Maybe my parents figured that Elizabeth plus my 11 letter Italian last name was long enough. No need to try to squish "Ann" onto the birth certificate. Incidentally, I added the "Ann" myself at my confirmation, but it's never on any forms that I fill out. I leave that space blank as my folks intended. And just to make life even easier, I married a man with a 5 letter last name.

———————

Bonita (p.36) wonders why she does not have a biblical name like her siblings. Beth wonders why she does not have a middle name like her sister.

• • •

Why Didn't I Get One
Judy Moorman

Why didn't they give me a middle name like every other kid I knew?

• • •

I Was Horrified
Erin Towers

As my mother's mother never gave her a middle name, she never gave me one. When I graduated from a very formal high school, I was horrified that along with all the Lynden Garnett Ashby III's and Elenore Morehouse Fox Richmonds, there was I, Erin Thorpe, a very plain Jane. Mother always thought I'd get married anyway and drop my middle name; so it was no big deal. After watching Camelot, I remember signing all my school papers with Erin Guinevere Thorpe.

Erin's desire to have a middle name like her peers reflects her desire to fit into her social group, which becomes an extension of the family.

. . .

Why No Middle Names?
Maryanne Mundy

My grandmother's funeral was this weekend and everyone on my mom's side was there—7 children (and their spouses) ages 40-67, and 11 grandchildren ages 11-35, and 3 great-grandchildren. Well, I told them all about your book, and asked about the middle names and we dug though her records—my grandmother (who was Catholic and Lithuanian) did have a middle name, but since she was a confirmed Catholic, and an orphan, we do not know if it was given to her at birth or if it was her confirmation name (and there's no paperwork that goes that far back in her life).

As far as anyone can remember (he died 35 years ago), my grandfather (who was Dutch and didn't seem to come into the marriage with any religious affiliation) did not have a middle name. We couldn't find any paperwork on him like a birth certificate or marriage license, and there is no middle name on his gravestone. None of the seven children have a middle name, but no one knows why—some think it may have been their father's family tradition, some think it has to do with Catholic Confirmation names, some say "it was just the way it was back then" and some think that their parents just couldn't think of anything (the last two babies, who were twins, had to stay in the hospital for days because my grandparents couldn't come up with names for them).

A few of the grandchildren (my generation) were given middle names, and when I asked all the parents why they didn't given their children middle names, they didn't really have an answer beyond "its tradition, I thought" (our tradition if they didn't have a middle name, the spouses' tradition if they did), or "I just liked that name". All the great grandchildren (all born after 2000) have middle names regardless of whether or not their parents did.

Maryanne's essay illustrates how much confusion can result from the lack of a middle name. Originally Europeans only had first names. Gradually surnames and then additional given names were added as populations grew. Interestingly, the idea of a middle name seems to be a North American phenomenon. In many countries, women have multiple given names—as opposed to a given name and a middle name—which suggests an interesting difference in the concept of the self in North American versus the rest of the world. My Belgian mother, born at the end of WWI, had four given names—each to honor a family member. Although she never used all her names, it pleased relatives to know their names were part of her "official" name. *Wikipedia* discusses evolving Dutch naming traditions and notes that after 1945—by the end of WWII—about half of Dutch children received only one name despite a history of having as many as five names.[10] In France, multiple given names are now also considered old-fashioned. The decrease in the number of given names after WWII may represent a desire to simplify life and move away from the old ways of doing things, seen as a failure after two world wars. Because of computer databases, middle names are now a necessity. If there is no middle name, the box for the middle name has to be filled in with an X.

• • •

That Was Their Name to Choose
Judith Eisendtadt Horwich

Mother was both a wise and a silent woman. She taught things by example not verbiage. One was this. Her mother, a strong Russian woman who bore six children, did not give her children middle names. She told them that was their name to choose. The last name came from and was the family. The first was the parents who gave life to choose. But, the middle name was each child's own to pick. Mother picked Dorothy. I don't know why. She just liked it. She didn't use it very much. Sometimes only the initial D. But it was all hers. She repeated this practice by not giving me a middle name.

These essayists are concerned with missing middle names. Beth wonders why she doesn't have one like her sister does. Erin's story illustrates that the desire to fit in extends beyond the family to the social world of our peers. Maryanne's essay points out the confusion both within the family and society because of missing middle names.

After WWI, many European babies were given American names. My Belgian mother was named Betsy. After WWII, middle naming traditions changed in Europe. The most obvious answer is to break with the past; however, one of the primary ways the victors change history is by changing naming traditions as the vanquished seek to fit in with or to emulate the victorious. One of the earliest examples of this phenomenon is the popularity of French names in England after the Norman Conquest in 1066. This phenomenon can be traced across the world's maps as well as in individuals' names.[11]

Middle names can play an important role in the adolescent's development by providing the opportunity to pick her own name. Native Americans recognize the importance of acquiring a new name at adolescence. Catholicism also realizes this important transition with the confirmand's selection of a new name. If there is no formal tradition for changing the name at adolescence, many women modify their given name in some way. Judith's mother has the creative idea of not giving a middle name, so that the adolescent can choose a new name for herself when she wants. Ideally, choosing a new middle name offers the individual the opportunity to pick a name that provides a sense of purpose and inspiration. We should consider reviving this tradition where it has been lost; it offers a valuable opportunity for the adolescent to assess the traits and qualities she wants to develop.

During a conversation about names, psychotherapist Joanne Gold wondered if middle names, centered between the given and surname, represent the individual's hidden essence. This insight seems to be true for the German naming tradition, which traditionally placed more importance on the name immediately preceding the family name: e.g., Johan Sebastian Bach, whose name could be shortened to Sebastian Bach, but not Johan Bach. This centering would also be the case for confirmation names, which represent a spiritual essence; for family surnames names used as middle names, which represent the maternal line that would otherwise be lost; and for maiden names which traditionally became middle names after marriage in English speaking countries. In English speaking countries, maiden names traditionally became middle names. This marital name change literally requires "recentering" as the new bride loses her middle name, which is replaced by her maiden name: the emphasis is then on family names and family identity rather than on individual identity. In some cases, middle names are so significant they eventually replace the given name, as is the case for Taylor (p. 46). This centering of the individual in the middle name is also suggested by the expression: "My middle name is…(insert desired ability)." The fact that many women talked about missing middle names suggests that women see them as key to part of their identity. Society now requires middle names in order to assure identification.

Chapter 13
WOMEN'S LIBERATION AND NAME CONSCIOUSNESS

Cultural evolution has led to changes in women's names as we saw with Rose's essay (p.65). Vera, Judith, and Ginta discuss a wide range of cultural and social topics concerning women's names.

• • •

Vera Constance Chadwick Sky

My mother's parents died long before her marriage but she kept her heritage alive by always using her maiden name in her career and professional writing. I was forever conscious of my father's sorrow that his very old family name would not be passed on since I, a girl (!), was the only offspring from his generation. When I married I really liked my married name, Vera Sky, but I did hate to give up the old name and the identity that went with it. At first colleagues at work had a hard time switching, and despite my mother's example, it would have never occurred to me to fight convention and keep my maiden name or even hyphenate it. I am very glad that so many young women of today do so without hesitation!

• • •

Judith Eisenstadt Horwich

Language is our most basic form of communication. Our names are identity within that form. As a woman, I have struggled with the flow of identity shifts through life's cycles.

Mom and Dad named me Judith. I am told they liked a movie star who was named Judy. That speaks loudly for the power of visual communication. I was also given a Hebrew name of y'hoo diet' for Judith in the first testament. It says her beauty was so great she was able to stop warring armies. To me, it seems my parents, having just viewed a wrinkled red faced screaming babe, displayed quite a hopeful and positive attitude on their part.

Within the Jewish tradition, this business of naming babies is quite a precurser to attitudes toward males and females within the tribe. A male child has a formal "brit" or circumcision ceremony exactly eight days after birth. A party is made where all those in the community are welcome to attend. He is formally brought into the community at that time and is not considered a Jew till this is done. This act is supposed to be a reminder of the story of Abraham, when God asked him to slay his son to test his faith. Should this male child be a first-born, an even greater party is made called a "pit ni ha ben." A first-born male is of great significance. An even bigger celebration is made and monetary gifts are offered. A first-born male was slain by the Egyptians and this child, so to speak, belongs to God. Therefore money is exchanged to symbolically buy the boy back from God. I must say, I found the concept of buying anything from God a bit humorous. However, perhaps it is the one time it was fortunate to be born female since we did get to live! This little boy goes through a lot to get his name.

Now, this naming business is quite different for a girl. She has no guidelines of timing for the naming. Well maybe just a bit. She can be named any time at all during the first entire year. The honor belongs to her father who is called to the pulpit to read from the holy books. A blessing is said for her, wishing that she should grow to be like great Jewish women who have come before her. In the event she is a first born, no grand party is given for her. She does not have to be bought back from God. However, no "pit ni ha ben" for a brother born after her. She displaced him, now he cannot be called the family's first born. However, she has no special privileges as that first born. From the moment of birth as a woman, our human plumbing has a major importance starting with our naming ceremony.

Though I was named Judith during childhood, I was called Judy except for a week at summer camp when all the campers in my cabin got the stomach flu except me for some reason. I was in charge of bringing them—no forcing them—to down as much water as possible and have them stay put in the cabin. They were pretty angry with me and while they groaned and moaned with stomach aches, I pranced in and out of the cabin quite freely. I was a nine-year-old version of nurse Ratchet to them. For that lovely week I was called, not so affectionately "Stinky." I properly abhorred it. It was a powerful thing to do, and though being healthy, I would have rather joined my group, kept my name, and been as ill as they. Thank God, their recovery absolved me of the new name and I was returned to Judy.

The next shift in my name came in my self-absorbed teen years. I only changed the spelling. But, to me, it was a profound shift. I became Judi. That letter "i" was a small rebellion and a claim toward my self, separate from my parents. It was not a very brave move. I could not drift far. I even apologized to people for the change in spelling and would state, "All I did was take the "th" off of Judith that my folks gave me." I was declaring independence, but quite safely and not too loudly. The biggest teen announcement I could make with this shift was to dot the "i" with a circle or a heart. Independence is a hard thing to come by without the guilt of hurting those you care about, but need to become separate from.

The next powerful identity shift came with marriage. Talk about a name change!! In 1960 women in our circles were not yet hyphenating. Neither my husband nor myself could even think of my keeping my maiden name. This was a huge trauma to me. Mother was dying of cancer. I had no brothers to carry my maiden name. My father's last name ended with me and with my marriage. The endless declaration of that fact was painfully repeated with the enormous paperwork involved in driver licenses, library cards, charge cards, publications, and documents *galore. Judith Eisenstadt would no longer exist. She was changed, seemingly erased forever and reestablished as Judith Horwich. My personal identity was taken from me simultaneously as my mother lay dying. It was numbing, and part of me went with her. (…)*

After marriage, I took my maiden name as my middle name. It still is today, but it will die with me. It is a profound sadness.

The next name choice was another step toward independence. I was a suburban mom with two children. The women's movement was on its way. I have always been interested in language and words. The movement addressed their stance in part by looking at many words and how they affected attitudes toward females. Hence "history" became "herstory". In our prayer books not only were forefathers mentioned but also foremothers, though sounding foreign and awkward, were included. I had never bought a car for myself nor even had one. But here we were in the suburbs, and I needed one. My husband bought one for me through the years, always a lesser model and less expensive but still fine for me and the children. It was a time for vanity license plates. I got to pick what I would call this car of mine. His plate name spoke of his identity. I could speak of mine. What could I say? I was someone's wife, someone's daughter, someone's mother, but what was I separate from all these people? What was I just to me? It had to be more than Judy with an "I." If nothing else I was female—a separate identity from my powerful husband. I used the new spelling "W O M I N" for my license plate. And, so to speak, took the man out of woman. My son was furious! After all he just started to drive. How could he borrow the car and drive to school with that plate? It was an insult to his emerging manhood. My husband just laughed at it. How could he do anything but laugh since it was "just a word." I was totally dependent on him for most everything in our existence.

But that naming was significant though seemingly as weak as the teen change of Judy to Judi it began my independence from male monetary dominance. I went back to school, got a masters degree in design, followed by a job teaching on the college level and that brought me to my grown-up professional self. Hence the next name change. Professionally I am referred to as Judith. Never in my life did I get addressed orally as Judith. When I see someone from the past or someone asks me "Judy or Judith?" I reply that I am all grown up now and Judith sounds that way. I like it a lot… All my documents are signed Judith Eisenstadt Horwich. I did have one struggle with the signature on my artwork. If I signed the pieces Horwich, that was my husband's name. If I signed them Eisenstadt, that was my father's name. Finally, I decided that Vincent was a good enough signature for Van Gogh. Judith is a fine signature for my artwork.

It is almost humorous that after all these years I have returned to the name Pearl Dorothy Cohon Eisenstadt and George Eisenstadt chose for me. Now in my adult life I can hear it out loud for the first time—"Judith."

Like Native Americans, Judith talks about the "flow of life." As a woman she is particularly sensitive to life's cycles. Unlike men, for centuries many women have marked their transition from single to married life with a change in their names—losing *Miss*, their middle name, and maiden name to become *Mrs.* with a new surname. Both Judith and Vera miss their maiden names, which is a loss associated primarily with English speaking countries.[12] A friend commented that it is difficult to find old female friends if you don't know their married names—another name issue men don't face.

As our culture changes, there are more options for retaining maiden names. For centuries, fathers hoped for sons to carry on the family name. As times have changed, married women in English speaking countries no longer feel obliged to drop their maiden names.[13] There is no simple solution to the problem of naming children for both sides of the family, however, without a double surname or even a string of names reminiscent of royalty. Some families give their girls surnames (family names) as given names or as middle names. When marrying, some couples create a new surname by fusing their surnames into a new name. To get a better understanding of the complicated history of marriage and naming, delve into Julie Gilbert's *Committed*.

Judith discusses the Jewish historical favoritism shown to sons, especially to first-born sons. Jewish boys had a coming of age ceremony centuries before Jewish girls. The boys' ceremony, the Bar Mitzvah, began with Italian Jews around the sixteenth century during the late Renaissance.[14] A parallel ceremony for girls developed slowly—first in the mid-nineteenth century in Europe and finally in 1922 in the U.S., Rabbi Mordecai Kaplan, founder of Reconstructionist Judaism, performed the first Bat Mitzvah in the U.S. for his daughter Judith. The Bat Mitzvah, the coming of age ceremony for girls, is now firmly established.[15]

Following the circular naming pattern, when Judy attains independence with a master's degree and a teaching position, she becomes Judith, which is the only name she uses to sign her artwork. Her essay suggests that women identify first with their given name. Which one of your names do you primarily identify with?

• • •

Name Choices
Ginta Remeikis

I was late. My parents had chosen another name for me, Gražina. However, as it became clear that I would be born on February 16th, Lithuanian Independence Day, they named me Gintarė. This is the female version of "gintaras," meaning amber, the national gem. My parents had fled Soviet occupation of Lithuania as children and spent five years in displaced persons camps in Germany before arriving in the States as teens. It was the raison d'être of those who fled, and by extension their children, to keep Lithuanian culture alive and to work for Lithuanian independence. Amber carries the past within it. It should not be surprising that I became a psychoanalyst. Now every jewelry store offers a variety of amber. Until Baltic independence and "Jurassic Park," it seemed no one knew about amber but Balts and science teachers demonstrating magnetism.

My birth certificate, however, identifies me as Victoria Gintare. Everyone calls me Ginta, a common version of Gintar_, but my parents gave me an easy, acceptable, anglicized name, just in case. When my parents arrived in this country, they experienced strong pro-assimilation messages. The Catholic high school my mother attended would not allow the girls to use their ethnic, non-saint first names. So instead of Nijolė, my mother was known as Apollonia. Apollonia is an important woman's name in our family. My great grandmother chose it for my beloved grandmother because she was born on the feast of St. Apollonia, the patron saint of dentists. My mother, who was given the name as a middle name, in fact became a dentist in this country where that was not then seen as an appropriate possibility for women. I eventually chose Apollonia as my Confirmation name, out of love for my grandmother, and really, I think, in a type of feminist solidarity, as the daughter of an immigrant woman who pursued a career of her choosing. Since then, I have already passed it along to my oldest daughter as her middle name.

In Lithuanian, female last names have feminine endings and identify a woman as married or not. Thus, I was Remeikytė and my mother was Remeikienė. In the American realm, all family members used the masculine, Remeikis. This was not particularly confusing, as we basically took living in two cultures as a given. I did not change my name when I married. It represented both my professional identity and my ethnic identity. However, in Lithuanian, including when I write, I hyphenate my name, Remeikytė-Gedo. I no longer wanted to use the unmarried woman's ending. I think adding on my husband's last name also tells part of my own, and the Lithuanian diaspora's, story. Women's last names have become something of a controversy since independence. Some Lithuanian women have begun using the masculine ending. I ultimately prefer the solution arrived at by several poets to use a feminine ending, but not signify marital status. If I did not use the hyphenated form, I would be Remeik_ using that system.

A name carries one's past and one's identity within it.

Now this is interesting… As I am about to sign this essay, instead of the expected Ginta Remeikis, I am signing

Ginta Remeikyt-Gedo

Despite the difficulties of emigrating twice, Ginta's mother chooses dentistry, a profession not yet accepted for women. Perhaps she was inspired by her middle name, Apollonia, the patron saint of dentists. Dr. Randi Finger notes that Ginta's mother may have been inspired to become a dentist because she was an outsider; thereby reinforcing her identity as an outsider with her choice of dentistry as a career. As an emigrant, Apollonia's choice of a field not associated with women is doubly daunting.

Like her mother's name, Ginta's name links her to her profession. She also maintains the female family connection to the oral; for as a psychoanalyst, she listens to spoken words. Ginta further develops the ties between her name and her profession with a poem in the chapter on creative writing and identity (p.307).

The women's liberation movement Judith discusses took place during the Viet Nam War and the social upheaval of the '60s. The women's movement in the U.S. began just before the Civil War: the first suffragettes were also abolitionists. It was only after the social upheaval of two World Wars that the women's movement was able to regain momentum with Betty Friedan's *The Feminine Mystique* in 1965. The earliest feminists in Western culture were the Greek poetess Sappho, seventh century BCE, and Christine de Pisan in fourteenth century France. Sappho wrote as Greece struggled against conquest by the Persian Empire. Christine wrote during the Hundred Years' War, the Black Death, and the Papal Schism. Reconstructionist Judaism was founded at the end of WWI. Historically times of social turmoil have provided opportunities for more freedom for women. This gives us hope that Muslim women may gain more freedom during the current upheavals.

Chapter 14
WOMEN AND THEIR TITLES

Until recently in history, women could only add Miss or Mrs. or inherited titles, like Duchess or Countess to their names. In 1841, Mary Caroline Rudd, Mary Hosford, and Elizabeth Prall became the first women to graduate from an American college—Oberlin College in Ohio—with B.A. degrees.[16] (Oberlin was also the first college to admit African Americans.) Elizabeth Blackwell became the first American woman M.D. in 1849 with a degree from Geneva Medical College in New York. Lucy Hobbs was the first to graduate from dental school in 1866 with a degree from the Ohio College of Dentistry. Arabella Mansfield of Iowa was the first admitted to the bar in 1869. Helen Magill White was the first to get a Ph.D., graduating in 1877 from Boston University. Louise Bethune of Buffalo, NY, was the first woman architect, accredited in 1881.[17] America was slightly ahead of Europe in the admission of women to universities. Thanks to the organizing skills of Miss Alice Stokes Paul (a Swarthmore graduate and a Quaker), women won the right to vote with passage of the 19th amendment in 1920. The movie *Iron Jawed Angels* reminds us that American suffragettes were abused, and even tortured, while imprisoned for demonstrating peaceably for the right to vote. Miss Paul (who preferred this title despite her Ph.D.) was also the author of the original Equal Rights Amendment in 1923. Despite numerous attempts, the amendment has never been ratified although it simply states that men and women have equal rights under the law.

• • •

What a Role Model for a Girl...
Elizabeth Blackwell Hanes

I was born Elizabeth Blackwell Hanes. The "Elizabeth" part gained significance for me in combination with the "Blackwell" part, my father's middle name and the surname of my great grandparents, good Virginians all.

Already blessed with two daughters, my father was deeply disappointed that I was not born a boy, but accepting that there were to be no more children, he honored me with his name nonetheless. No reason to let it go to waste.

So I was Elizabeth Blackwell and came to feel quite special as my parents often reminded me that another Elizabeth Blackwell was famous as the first woman physician. What a model for a girl raised in the provincial South! The association was inspiring and, when asked as a child what I wanted to be when I grew up, I would respond with pride, "a doctor."

The patronizing laughter that followed, I took as encouragement and held fast to unrestrained ambition.

There is a family story related to this. My father was a pharmacist and ran the only drug store in the county. I loved to go to the store with him and examine all the wonders on the shelves: Coty face powder, boxes of Whitman's Sampler, Halo shampoo, packets of brown and black shoe laces, Epsom salts, Lifebuoy bar soap, Katy Keene comic books, and Timex watches.

One Sunday afternoon when I was about five, my father and I stopped by the drug store, even though it wasn't officially open on Sunday. He would often go by after church to fill a prescription for an indigent member of the community who was not able to get into town during the week. As I cruised the aisles (there were only two), my eyes fell on a white plastic box with a plus sign on it in red. I remember carefully sliding the box off the shelf, sitting down on the floor, and opening it. To my delight, the inside held a miniature drug store stocked with first aid supplies: a spool of white adhesive tape, in a tight tin wheel; a little glass bottle of mercurochrome; crackly paper squares of gauze; a small box of "Band-aids;" and other diminutive versions of curative aids the particulars of which escape my memory now. Seizing the opportunity, I asked if I could have the first aid kit. Ever parsimonious, my father said, "No." I persisted, and so did he. Finally, in exasperation, I declared in high volume, "Well, I don't see how you expect me to become a doctor if you won't even let me have a first aid kit!" I was incensed, while my father was unyielding, and I went home without the first aid kit.

I never pursued medicine but I did acquire the moniker, "Doctor," when I finally earned a Ph.D. in my fifties. I think my father would have been proud.

Growing up, I had two nicknames: "Lilibet" when I was very young, and "Buff" awarded by my younger cousin, Houston, as his best effort to pronounce my cumbersome Christian name. In my thirties, I came to realize that I hated the name "Buff" and so reverted to "Elizabeth," which is a name I love. When she was born, I blessed my first daughter with the middle name "Blackwell."

• • •

The First Female Ph.D. from My Hometown
Dr. Lovely Ulmer-Sottong

(...) As an aside, I was the first female Ph.D. from my hometown—that I got a 4.0 was less important than that the folks who knew me all my life could call me Doctor. Although I haven't been back to my hometown since my mother died in 2001, I smile every time at the memory.

A Never-Ending Process
Anonymous

Once you've earned a Ph.D., you've arrived—at the beginning, not the end. You defend your dissertation before a panel of Ph.D.'s, whose job it is to make sure you don't graduate thinking you know it all; but rather, that you have just started on a long journey. The same is true of every profession, including motherhood—everything keeps changing. There are no laurels to rest on. Maybe that's why the Greeks awarded laurel wreaths, which would eventually dry and crumble, a symbol of both glory and transience – a reminder that the record would not stand forever.

. . .

Different Options
Barbara Mattson

(...) I consider my amateur radio call sign (KA4UIV) as part of my name. However, I've known many amateur radio operators who changed their call—some to reflect the class of license they earned. Likewise, I've known people who've changed their name. I can't help but wonder if some do that to try to start a new life or personality.

———————

Barbara reminds us that numbers can have positive associations for identity. Numbers and identity often have negative associations, e.g., government ID, prisoners, and concentration camps. In the computer age, numbers are becoming increasingly important for thought and identity, as we shall see.

———————

When Elizabeth meets with laughter upon announcing she wants to become a doctor, she interprets it as encouragement and "holds fast to ambition"—just as Lula (p.70) interpreted teasing as a sign of affection. Both girls make the laughter positive, reminding us that we underestimate the potential of our mindset to turn negatives into positives. The main theme in Elizabeth's essay is the inspiration provided by her ancestor. Whatever your field, researching the history of your ancestors and discovering spiritual archetypes, inside and outside of the family, will provide life-long inspiration and guidance.

Following the circular naming pattern, when Judy obtains her degree, she becomes Judith and finally feels that she has become her "grown-up professional self." It is only recently in history that women have been allowed into schools to study and obtain titles, which entail an identity outside the family.

Reading the essays, I wondered why more women did not comment on their titles, which leads to speculation that in some respects, a woman's acquisition of a title may not bear the same psychological weight it does for a man. For centuries, Western women have been accustomed to changing their names upon marriage. Unlike men, whose identity has been centered on their occupation or title, women are used to acquiring different names and playing different roles in life. A title simply provides one more role to play. Now many women put off having children until they are older so they can establish their careers before they have children. One of the inevitable problems with having children later in life after careers are established and titles acquired is that women face increased difficulty in conceiving as they grow older. Women's sensitive biological time clocks pose a challenge to women trying to balance work and family, titles and motherhood.

Chapter 15
CHOOSING A NEW GIVEN NAME

Women adjust their names in many different ways. Some women change the spelling of their names, mainly during adolescence. A few women pick their own nicknames. Some women with double names center their identity on one name by either dropping one or by fusing the two into one. A few women pick completely different names. The desire for a new name may first manifest itself in childhood and may be part of the process of searching for one's identity.

– A –
TRYING OUT A NEW NAME

• • •

A Period of Wishing for a Different Name
Leslie Kent

When I was 11 or 12, I went through a period of wishing for a different name, specifically Tanya. At that time, Leslie seemed kind of boring and ordinary, while Tanya was exotic, sophisticated and adventurous. I think I kept my wish to myself. After maybe a year, Tanya didn't seem so great anymore, and I came to terms with Leslie. To me that development goes along with a growing sense that I could define myself by what I did, thought and felt, and what kind of person I was, rather than trying to seem exotic, glamorous, grown-up or impressive based on some external attribute like my name.

I do like my name. It seems calm, orderly, feminine. I don't wish for any other name.

• • •

The Oh, So Short-Lived Nancy
Kerry

My attitude towards my name, Kerry, went through as many changes as my budding identity. As far as I can recall my initial feelings were initially all positive ones. I was pleased with the story my mother would tell of her being 9 months pregnant and panicked that she still didn't have a name for me. She related how she was dining in a restaurant and overheard someone talking about County Kerry, Ireland and how in an instant she knew that Kerry would be my name. I felt proud of my Irish roots and this connection to the home country. My pleasure was further enhanced when I learned that the much-admired Kennedy family also had a daughter named Kerry, Robert and Ethyl's seventh child.

95

Yet at the same time I also recall hating my name. This was strongest on the days I watched Romper Room on TV. Each day I would sit and anxiously wait for Miss Sally to hold up her magic mirror and say goodbye to all the little children she saw at home—Mary, Bobby, Joanne, Michael, Kathy, Ellen, name after name, show after show, but never a Kerry in the group. Each day I eagerly waited for my name to be called, only to once again be crushed she couldn't see me. I would wave my hands at the TV trying to get her attention. How could she not see me, I thought, when I worked so hard to be a good "do-bee" just like Miss Sally said I should.

Despite these disappointments my name generally remained a good-enough name. That is until the September I turned 8 years old. At that time I was in Miss McCarthy's 3rd grade. I was busy collecting whatever was the latest fad, jumping rope and playing jacks. I loved grilled cheese sandwiches, Campbell's tomato soup, and Twister. But what I truly loved most was listening to music. My repertoire of music choices came mostly from my older sister's collection and included The Beatles, The Monkeys and Herman's Hermits. But my secret personal favorite was Nancy Sinatra's "These Boots are Made for Walking." This black 45, with the faithful yellow spider in the center, was permanently fixed to my pink Dansette record player.

It was for that 8th birthday that I told my mother I desperately wanted white leather Go-Go boots, just like the one's Nancy Sinatra wore on the Ed Sullivan show. My mother, certain Go-Go boots were not an appropriate gift for an 8-year-old, offered up an array of enticing items instead, a dollhouse, an Easy Bake oven, even a much sought-after purple bicycle with a banana seat. No, I was firm. I couldn't be bought off with some silly little kid stuff. It was Go-Go boots or nothing. Finally she succumbed to my barrage of pleading and on that September morning I awoke to find a large box at the end of my bed.

Breathless, I threw open the box, grabbed my boot, slipped my foot in, slowly zipped up the side and stood tall in my new boots. I imagined I looked just like Nancy Sinatra. With shoulder length hair in a flip, baby blue miniskirt, I grabbed my microphone, a well-used egg beater, strutted up to the mirror, and in a sultry voice said, "Are you ready boots, start walking," and proceeded to belt out an off-key full rendition of "These Boots are Made for Walking." I was in heaven, of course never noticing the boots were not even leather, just a cheap vinyl. They were perfect. The only problem now was that Kerry was clearly no longer a suitable name for someone with white Go-Go boots and a future singing career. At that moment, I was no longer Kerry. I was Nancy. I reasoned that it was my name and I certainly could decide to change it to another name if I wanted to.

The next day, shod in my new boots, I proudly paraded into Miss McCarthy's 3rd grade classroom, marched up to the front of the room and handed in my homework. A yellow-lined paper with the name Nancy Leddy carefully printed on the top right corner. Later that day, I was shocked and bewildered when Miss

McCarthy pulled me aside and told me I could absolutely could not write Nancy on my papers any longer. So quickly my hopes of a new name dashed.

• • •

I Decided to Take Care of the Problem Myself
Sheila M. Cahill

I hated my name during all my childhood and most of my youth. When I hit first grade, I asked to be renamed "Jane." No dice. When I was around 10, I decided to take care of the problem myself: "I'm not going to be called Sheila anymore," I announced. "From now on I'm 'Debbie'." This held up for about three days, until I caved because I couldn't withstand the venomous sarcasm in my mother's voice as she would call out for "Sheila, ohhhhh, I forgot—I mean DEBBIE!" Obviously, I longed to fit in, to sound like everyone else.

I didn't meet another Sheila until seventh grade. She turned out to be a ginger-haired tyrant whom I hated. But by my mid-teens, I no longer considered my name a problem, and had settled into it with relative comfort. Still, I thought it an ill fit with my last name, which was Delsol. Talk about a name no one had ever heard of! And definitely one no one could spell.

Playing "pretend" allows children to assume different roles—different ways of relating to the world. Children may attempt to extend these new identities into their everyday lives with a new name, which inevitably causes a clash between reality and fantasy. Do you remember your favorite pretend roles? Did you ever dream about, or actually try to change your given name as a child? What aspects of your personality were you trying to explore in your world of pretend? What do your childhood fantasies reveal and how have those desires been fulfilled or forgotten? How did adults react to your new name?

In preadolescence, Leslie, Kerry, and Sheila dream, not simply of a new nickname, but of a new given name. After trying out a new given name, Leslie finally "comes to terms" with her name: she grows into her identity. Who she is depends on what she does, not her name, which she sees simply as an "external attribute." Both Kerry and Sheila try changing their names. Kerry's elementary school teacher quickly puts an end to her fantasies. Sheila struggles with hurting family feelings, getting people to change their habits, and teasing. She finally "settles" into her given name as a teen despite "an ill fit." Sheila never gets to grow into her name: it is imposed.

Kerry, Leslie, and Sheila do not have nicknames: there are no name variations to grow into or out of without picking a new name. Are children without nicknames more likely to want to change their given names? Kerry seems the most able to grow into her name because she has stories for it.

Leslie and Sheila do not give any stories about their names. None of the essayists relate any helpful adult suggestions about fantasy, names, or identity. Surprisingly, the adults seem threatened by the children's name play. Adults should be able to nurture a child's imagination while also upholding reality. Fantasy is, after all, the key to the imagination and creativity. Talking with a child or adolescent about why she wants to change her name and what her fantasy name represents for her is a wonderful opportunity to communicate about identity—needs, hopes, desires, and dreams.

– B –
A NEW NAME AS A GOAL

• • •

Then I Can Change My Name...
Beth

(...) I'm on a diet. I've lost 15 pounds so far. Another 40 pounds, and I can change my name to "Liz."

A new name inspires Beth to shed both her old image and her weight: the new name personifies her goal, a new self.

– C –
PICKING A NEW NAME

• • •

My Name Incarnations:
Judy Spector, Judy Moorman, Judith Moorman
Judith Felix Moorman

I didn't wind up in the therapist's chair over this issue but I always resented the name my parents chose for me. Why didn't they give me a middle name like every other kid I knew? I now tell people that we were so poor they couldn't afford to give me one. And why did they name me, in the Jewish tradition of choosing a name in memory of the deceased, after a third cousin? It wasn't fair that my brother, Gus, was named after our maternal grandmother, Bubbeh Gussie, someone you could hear stories about, while I received the name of an anonymous relative with the unromantic appellation Jake.

Although Judith Spector is on my birth certificate, I was always called Judy. However, at age 40, I decided Judy was a name for a cute little girl always smiling and trying to please everyone. A woman who'd just gone through breast cancer surgery was no longer a Judy so why not choose a new name? I obsessed upon possibilities until I realized that my given name, Judith, was very beautiful and fit the woman I'd become. And so, I announced to family, coworkers and friends that I wanted them to call me by this name.

People tried but many couldn't make the change. "I've known you as Judy all these years and can't stop calling you that," they'd tell me. I finally allowed a retroactive naming clause to those used to Judy when it got old constantly correcting them.

At age 42, after some more stressful life events, I decided to take a writing class. This was something I'd always wanted to do but had put off. Now that I'd adopted the naming habit, I decided to select a pen name for this new phase of my life. I again obsessed upon names. This time, I would choose someone I admired. They could be dead or alive since there was no need to follow the tradition of my parents. It also had to be a name that I liked. I couldn't think of anyone who met these criteria until my cat sat beside me one day and began licking my face. "Here's someone who knows how to live life right," I thought. "He's very loving and even the smallest thing like basking in a spot of sunlight makes him happy." So, in my writing class, I introduced myself as Felix.

The last time I changed my name, and for no particular reason except that I could, happened about ten years after I became Felix. I decided it was finally time to bestow upon myself a middle name. I was using Judith Spector Moorman for legal documents but that had little zest. The majority of people in my life recognized me as Judith and I still liked the whimsicality of the name Felix. I began writing my name as Judith Felix Moorman.

I have to admit that at age 61, I still think about renaming myself. I like to tell people when these obsessions occur that they're due to a childhood trauma known as name deprivation. The only way to relieve its symptoms is to grant oneself a new name.

According to the Apocryphal *Book of Judith,* Judith saved the Jews from Nebuchadnezzar's invading army by killing Holfernes, the leader of the invading Assyrian army—an apt story for a woman who has struggled to stop and prevail over an invasive cancer. With all the resources available on the Internet, readers can research their names to find out the stories behind them, the meaning of the name in other languages, and any other information that can lead them to think creatively about their names.

In her writing class, Judith introduces herself with a new name *Felix,* which means "happiness": the new name sheds the sorrows of the past. Felix is delighted by sunshine: the sun is an ancient symbol for life and the spirit. *Felix* is also a male name: men are not associated with breast cancer. Judith's willingness to continue considering new names reflects her desire to embrace personal growth and change.

A New Name
Tara Arlene Innmon

My maiden name was Arlene Katherine Bangsund. I was born in 1950 of a Norwegian father and a Swedish mother. My father named me Arlene for the movie star or TV celebrity, Arlene Francis, or Arlene Dahl. I don't remember which. One of them was on a game show, "What's My Line." She had dark hair and a small chin. I wasn't named after her; I was named after the pretty one with lighter hair. I didn't like the name Arlene because it seemed sort of old-fashioned and nobody else in school had that name. It didn't mean anything either.

At home I was called Deany because my baby brother couldn't pronounce Arlene. I like that name better than Arlene.

When I was forty-four I became totally blind and changed my first name to Tara. I didn't change my name legally because I didn't want to completely lose Arlene. I felt Arlene had been a shy girl, who had to hide that she couldn't see well, and who had become an adult who would rather read a book and not be noticed. While I was going blind I became bolder and tried doing things I wasn't sure I could do, because I realized my life, like my sight, would end. A Sufi teacher gave me the name Tara when I was involved with the Sufis. It comes from the Tibetan Goddess of healing. I think of myself as the green Tara.

I liked my middle name, Katherine, because it was the name of my Swedish grandmother, whom I loved deeply. I didn't want to use it because it was so common in the 1950s.

As a child I hated my last name, Bangsund. It was given to my Norwegian grandfather when he came to this country. It is the name of the town he came from. It means ice sound, and is a fjord in northern Norway. I didn't like spelling it out all the time and people miss-spelling it. When I got married I took my husband's name, thinking it would be better. It is Innmon. I didn't realize it was an unusual spelling too.

I think of Tara as someone who is bolder, wiser, and more confident than Arlene. It might have helped me accept total blindness. Tara doesn't have to try to do things the ways sighted people do, as Arlene tried and sometimes failed.

Tara is the Tibetan Buddhist goddess of healing. Tara identifies specifically with Green Tara, who embodies the highest enlightenment.[18] The goddess Tara represents compassion and mercy: she is considered to be the protector of all living things. She helps humans deal with the eight traditional Buddhist dangers—pride, delusion, anger, envy, avarice, wrong views, attachment, and doubt.[19] (The seven capital sins are pride, anger, envy, avarice, lust, gluttony, and sloth. Pride, anger, envy, and avarice are on both the Christian and Buddhist lists.)

The Green Tara is also the goddess for the feminist movement in Buddhism: she refuses to give up her sex and become a man. She saves millions of souls from suffering by centuries of meditation, thus attaining the highest level of enlightenment.[20]

By adopting this divinity's name, Tara is able to tap into the healing nature of the goddess, her divine mercy and compassion, as well as the help the goddess offers with the eight Buddhist dangers. The goddess is a female savior figure, associated with Buddhist feminism and female empowerment. Tara, the goddess, teaches Arlene to see in new ways. As Tara, she is a new being in a new world, who will develop new talents Arlene never dreamed of.

• • •
A Legal Change
Elizabeth

At age 50, I legally dropped my first name, which I had never liked and had never used. Even as a little child in school, I would not respond unless I was called by the "acceptable" nickname.

I changed my name for two reasons. (1) I was experiencing a transitional time marked by severe chronic illnesses among close family members. I seriously needed a change. (2) I recognized myself (finally) to be an adult, and an accomplished one. The nickname made me feel emotionally vulnerable and seemed silly professionally. I suppose I simply outgrew it.

My parents had no objection to my dropping the given first name. They explained that my maternal grandmother had chosen the alien name simply because she had liked it. My parents and sister had called me by a nickname from the start. My given middle name, however, had been my mother's choice reflecting the names of generations of predecessors in her family.

I hired an attorney to officially renounce the other name and claim my middle name—Elizabeth—as my only and correct name. I love the history and the sound and the meaning of my name. It IS who I am.

Elizabeth's grandmother imposes a name which is not a family name just like Heather's grandmother did (p.34). With her new name, Elizabeth reasserts her family ties and personifies her personal change.

• • •
New Names and the Evolution of Identity
Francesca Ruth

I grew up in the '50s. My given names are Frances Ruth. My mother's name was Frances, so I went by Ruthie as a child. At work I used Ruth, a strong name meaning "beautiful friend" from the Old Testament. I wanted to be taken seriously, not an easy situation in those days.

I was married twice. I preferred my own identity: I did not use Mrs. or his last name—that sounds like property. Many assume it appropriate to call one "Mrs." about the age of 25, thinking it is respectful—teachers, clerks, neighbors, etc. I do not use a surname.

After retirement I prefer Francesca, a Latin name meaning "free spirit." Now I am responsible only for myself. I enjoy life by doing as I choose without negative stress. I enjoy my grandchildren, paint watercolors, do yoga & meditation, and dance ballet tap, & jazz for exercise, read and attend lectures. Life is precious.

When I questioned further about her lack of a surname and how she handled her name change, Francesca sent the following reply.

I am surprised that this name situation is unusual.

What happened to the consciousness-raising sessions of the '70s? I talked about this then. Many women may not think they can change their names or reinvent themselves.

My legal and professional name is Ruth Frances (as I was known as Ruth at work). I had it legalized in the '70s at the divorce from my first husband. It is easy to change one's name at marriage or divorce; otherwise it is quite difficult and expensive. At that time I also dropped my long unusual family name (always having to spell it.)

After retirement I prefer Francesca, using just one name, it simplifies and it suits my lifestyle of dance, painting and just enjoying life with no one to be responsible for but myself. If asked for my last name I say Ruth.

I did have someone ask me if I disliked my family to not use a surname. I replied that is not the issue, self-identity is. I'm not the same person I was as a child, a young wife, mother, or even the same person as last year. Guilt was not a factor. As a political scientist, I understand people rarely change their religion (born into), their family's political party, or, so it seems, their names either—except for women when they marry, which is tradition and not a legal matter.

My children laugh when a sibling calls me Ruthie or when someone calls me Mrs. ("married to") Baker, it is out of character for them also. Thank you again for this wake up call to women who want to be known for themselves. I am the creative type and a born reformer and comfortable in my own skin.

———————

Francesca is very unusual in that she uses neither her husband's surname nor Mrs.: she uses only given names. She also picks a new name to mirror her newfound freedom in retirement. Francesca's essay calls to mind that of

Judith Horwich (p.83) who signs her artwork with her given name because she realizes, as Francesca does, that it is only women's first names that belong uniquely to them, with the exception of given names that are surnames.

Francesca's concept of the evolving self is strikingly like that of the Native Americans. She is a great example of how women can change and reinvent themselves: change is essential for growth. One way to keep our minds evolving is to keep our sense of identity evolving.

• • •

A Spiritual Name
Shyama

On a cold day in late January, I was born with the name "Nina", suggested to my parents by my older sister. Considered one of the "lucky ones" for being one of the few Indian kids with an easy to pronounce name, around my preteen years I began to feel a lack of spiritual depth and meaning with this name. Many would appreciate "Nina" as a fairly uncommon yet not too strange multiracial name with several intriguing meanings such as "pretty eyes" in Hindi or "strong" among certain Native American tribes, yet none of these lovely meanings were quite satisfying enough. The summer after my 9th grade year in high school, the name "Shyama" was given to me by my guru, or a Hindu saint and spiritual leader. In Hinduism, we believe in one loving God who appears in many different forms and is called several different names that describe His virtues. "Shyama" is a name referring to the dark bluish-gray "rain cloud" colored glow of Lord Krishna. The receiving of a spiritual name is a gift that signifies a new birth, meant to strengthen understanding of an eternal relationship with and a sense of belonging to God. I've whole-heartedly embraced this beautiful new name and have encouraged and reminded all friends and family to begin to address me only as "Shyama".

———————

Judith and Tara pick new names after facing traumatic physical challenges. Elizabeth picks her new name because she says she needs a psychological change. Francesca changes her name because she wants to acknowledge a change in her life. Shyama picks her name for spiritual reasons: she wants a name with greater spiritual depth. For Judith, Tara, Liz, Elizabeth, Francesca, and Shyama, the meaning of the new names they pick is important for inspiration and regeneration.

Changing names is seen as a spiritual turning point in the most ancient naming traditions as we saw with Native Americans in Chapter I. We find the same tradition in the Bible. Abram's name is changed to Abraham and Sarai's name is changed to Sarah when they are told they will be the parents of many nations. Jacob's name is changed to Israel when he is told he will be the father

103

of a nation. Jesus changes *Simon* to *Cephas* (Aramaic for *rock*), translated as *Petros* in Greek, which is then translated to *Peter*.[21] Hadassah becomes Esther, Queen of the Persians. Changing the name to represent a new self is an ancient naming tradition.

"The Old Testament has nearly one thousand and four hundred different names. Most biblical names have two parts: one name is a designation of the deity (the spiritual name) and the other is the 'real' (given) name.[22] The New Testament also refers to a new name with words that echo the Native American tradition. "To him who overcomes, I will (...) give him a white stone and a new name written on the stone which no one knows but him who receives it" (Revelation 2:17). Ancient traditions recognized that different names helped address different aspects of the personality: a spiritual name was crucial for addressing the spiritual essence of the self. As we saw in Chapter IV, having several names seems to spark creativity. As we see in this chapter, adopting a new name is a liberating decision that can stimulate creativity, healing, and spiritual renewal.

God has at least eight names in the Old Testament; and the name Jehovah has many qualifiers, which describe His different attributes. The Christian God is referred to as Three in One—God the Father, God the Son, and God the Holy Ghost. Muslims have ninety-nine names for God. Understanding the self requires the vocabulary to do so. Plato speaks of the soul, reason, and appetite. Freud uses the terms the ego, the superego, and the id. We cannot understand who we are through the use of one name: we can only limit our understanding of who we are and what we are capable of imagining and creating.

Western culture readily changes packaging and product names to increase sales. Advertising understands the importance of chameleon changes for surviving in a fickle public that is always searching for something better— "the new and improved." Therefore, we are suspicious of change, which is often simply a superficial marketing gimmick. Obviously in our modern world, names are necessarily fixed and unchanging out of necessity for purposes of identification. By fixing our names, however, we no longer readily think of ourselves as constantly evolving. A static name creates a fixed sense of who we are. Our names risk becoming a kind of box in which we think of ourselves. If we think about the Native American naming tradition in which a name is fluid and evolves as the individual evolves, we can think of ourselves out of the box our names risk becoming—we can think of ourselves in more flexible and creative ways.

A few essayists describe innovative ways of thinking about identity using their names. These essays can inspire all of us to think more imaginatively about ourselves. If we are to succeed, this evaluation becomes not simply an exercise in creativity, but also an exercise in spirituality.

In thinking about our identity, we can choose new names to make different parts of our personality more accessible. These names don't necessarily have to be public. They can be names we keep private, which help us access parts of our identity that get lost in the pressures of everyday life. I have come to a new self-understanding with the discovery of my grandmother's nickname *Lizzie*. It has come to represent the artistic side of my personality, which is rarely given the time it needs for self-expression. Even though Lizzie still doesn't get the time she needs, just acknowledging those needs with her name has helped me attain a new self-awareness and peace with that part of myself—an ability I did not have before *Lizzie* appeared to help me deal with these frustrations. I've discovered that the power of the name *Lizzie* to summon the artistic side of my personality is remarkable. When I pick up a paintbrush and say to myself, "Okay, Lizzie, here's your chance," I literally feel a surge of creative energy. I've also been amused to find that I can censure myself by using the name *Liz*: "Liz would do that, but not Elisabeth." When I need to get to work and be more efficient, I call on Liz to organize things and keep them on track. This strategy has also been very helpful. I have to put some serious thought into choosing a spiritual name, which will require research that will lead me in new spiritual directions.

- OVERVIEW -
PART ONE
THE NAME FROM THE INSIDE OUT

Native Americans represent our richest and most ancient naming tradition. Because their tradition is very different from ours, they offer us the possibility of thinking more creatively about our names. Life, identity, and names flow linearly like a river. Ever-evolving names encourage constant growth. A new name is bestowed by society to recognize a changed individual: a new name has to be earned. Because their culture does not hesitate to name shortcomings, names provide a powerful incentive for positive change. Their secret, sacred names protect and center the individual. Native American names have psychological, social, natural, and spiritual links that constantly reinforce the multiple dimensions of identity. The Native American naming tradition invites us to renew our exploration of our names and our identity and to continue that quest throughout our lives.

Women describe their awakening to the complexities of identity through the use of names. One essayist observes her child beginning to understand the multifaceted nature of identity when she questions her mother's different names—*Mommy* versus her given name—that represent two different identities, familial and social. Another essayist recalls her young child's efforts to determine when to use her social given name or her family nickname. Essayists also describe our childhood feeling of owning our names and the surprise we feel when we first hear someone else has our name. Different names for the same person, as well as the same name for different people, play a key role in the child's gradual awareness of the complexities of identity.

The Foundling Fantasy appears in the midst of all this naming turmoil and allows the child to expand identity through fantasy. The child begins to realize identity is not as simple as a name suggests; therefore, reality may not be as simple as it appears. The role-play of the Foundling Fantasy allows the child to imagine the unknown as full of possibilities, which make it less frightening. The child can take control by creating her own, new identities, which allow her to explore different aspects of herself.

The transition between *Mommy* and *Mom* and between the child's nickname and given name mirrors the development of a social sense of identity. Society urges the child to step into a more grown-up role by exercising pressure to relinquish *Mommy* for *Mom* and to relinquish her nickname for her given name. Besides revealing the complexities of identity, nicknames can help, even enjoin, a child to grow up. Some women retain their nicknames, which can be a regenerating oasis that allows them to constantly tap into their earliest memories of being loved and cared for. Nicknames may also elicit these emotions in others. The direct link to the informal, innermost self may be one of the reasons Americans gravitate to nicknames: nicknames bypass the defensive barriers of formal names.

Nicknames are the closest we come to the Native American tradition of evolving names. Women with various nicknames use them as time markers in their lives—a linear progression similar to that of Native Americans. One wonders if it is easier for women with nicknames to access past memories and emotions because their different names provide keys to different time periods by linking specific names to specific memories. Women with nicknames describe name changes primarily at adolescence, in college, upon marriage, and when entering the work force. As opposed to the linear Native American naming tradition, essayists describe growing into their given names—a circular evolution returning to one's roots. Women consider growing into their given names to be a rite of passage, of finally attaining adulthood. Since antiquity, closing the circle has been a symbol of completion, which may lead us to feel our development is complete, however, rather than ongoing.

Women with many different nicknames describe a questioning and a multifaceted understanding of reality that includes not only nicknames they pick for themselves but also nicknames picked by others—an awareness not only of their own point of view but also that of others and how these different perspectives interact. The more names women have, the more creative they seem to be because each name provides a different perspective—i.e., new insight, a slightly different way of seeing and relating to the world. The various nicknames described by so many women suggest that evolving names are extremely helpful in the development and understanding of the self.

Women without nicknames regret that absence. They have no name time-markers to help access memories from different stages of life. Women with unusual names usually adjust happily to them because they provide a distinctive identity. However, as children, they may feel isolated when they have no namesakes or other associations for their name. Women with very common names, which they describe as surprisingly difficult for others to remember, constantly strive to find ways to maintain a distinctive identity. For them the primary issues concerning name identity are not belonging, but asserting a personal identity, different from that of their many namesakes. For these women nicknames, pronunciation, and spelling are important issues for their name identity. Ironically, giving a child an unusual name can create the desire to belong and giving a common name can create the desire to be different.

Women also discuss the negative aspects of names. Nicknames can be seen as too childish, they may lead to teasing and negative associations, they may be "indomitable," refusing to enter the Netherworld of Nicknames. Teasing causes life-long scars for many women. Names may feel dated as culture changes, the namesake may be problematic, or there may not be any stories to go with the name. Names that are "imposed" on the nuclear family by an outside figure cause problems, even if "the outsider" is a grandmother. Negative meanings of names are also problematic. Women discuss the associations others have to their names, which may be inaccurate. Women with no stories for their names do not relate to their names. Any of these issues may cause a woman to feel ambivalent about her name. However, women who collect more positive than negative stories for their names can overcome the negativity associated with the name and the accompanying feelings of inadequacy or rejection. The more stories we can find for our names, the more we can enrich our identity.

Women with double names address issues of double identity. They may decide to fuse the double name into one or they may drop one of the names. Peers may shorten the double name to one, even if the individual does not. If the double name represents two sexes, like *Mary Jo*, dropping one name may not be feasible. These essayists and their peers suggest a preference for a single given name.

After adjusting to the surprising reality that other children share the same name, children seek out namesakes—their name tribe. Children also look for their names on trinkets—a subconscious desire for social recognition. When a child cannot find her name, she feels left out. Essayists describe special friendships with namesakes or disappointment when a namesake turns out to be unpleasant. The subconscious desire is to see the namesake as an extension of the self, as a "sister" or soul mate. Essayists describe the inspiration an older namesake can provide in helping them grow into their names. They also describe with a great deal of humor, "the name curse," which is a subconscious desire to place the blame for a personal problem on the name by finding other namesakes with the same problem—a self-mocking wish that the fault might be "not in ourselves, but in our...(names)."

Besides seeking names on trinkets or with a namesake, the desire to belong to a name tribe is manifested by a desire to conform with spelling changes to the name so that it is the same as the predominant spelling among peers and, even, in the desire to have exactly the same number of names as peers. These anecdotes are drawn from adolescence when girls are trying to establish their social identity. An extension of the concept of "a name tribe" is also found in the surprising number of essays about missing middle names. Women with no middle name wonder why they don't have one, and families wonder why some members have middle names while others do not. Middle names were discussed so often that they may represent an inner core identity as psychotherapist Joanne Gold suggests.

A few women discuss titles they have earned. Women do not discuss their titles as much as one might expect, perhaps because women play so many different roles in life; and perhaps because until recently, most American women had no permanent attachment to names or titles. *Miss* became *Mrs.* and maiden names were dropped for married names. Two of the essayists observe their identity is to be found more in their given name than in their family names, married names, or titles because their given names are the only names that belong just to them. Essayists admitted feeling nostalgia, if not sadness, at the loss of their maiden name, unless the maiden name was problematic. One wonders about the psychological impact of losing the family name after marriage, which involves many losses as well as gains. In European culture, marriage does not entail the same loss of the maiden name. Because most American women are used to name changes, a name change with the addition of a new title may not have as much of an impact as it would for men, who, traditionally, have not changed their family names.

Although name changes are not unusual in childhood, when children readily assume different names in role-play and when different names or nicknames are picked at adolescence or in college, most American women do not change their names once they are established as adults. The essayists who show the greatest strength in determining their own identity are those who actually change their names. They describe name changes when facing major transitional points—illness, a psychological re-evaluation, or a spiritual awakening. They think about what they want their new name to represent, and what they want it to inspire. In addition to mirroring change, new names spark creative changes in the way women think about themselves—especially different aspects of identity which they may want to develop, as Judith does when she picks *Felix* as her pen name to represent the healthy, happy writer within herself, or as Beth does when she picks *Liz* to represent the thinner self she aspires to. Their new names facilitate a revitalization of the self and provide a sense of empowerment. Ancient cultures, like the Native American and the biblical, recognize the importance of a new name to acknowledge a changed individual. Although changing names may not be as easy as it used to be in smaller societies that accepted this tradition, women can privately identify parts of their personality with which they readily want to connect. Naming Lizzie, the artistic part of myself, and Liz, the assertive part of myself, has definitely helped me function better. A spiritual name would also help reach that innermost part of myself. I look forward to that spiritual quest. A new name is a powerful and energizing source of creativity and self-renewal.

Ancient naming traditions, like the Native American and the biblical, recognize this need for more than one name in order for the individual to change and grow. If I use the word "spirituality," it is an abstraction with no easy definition. If I think about the spiritual part of myself, it is an undefined, uncertain essence. But if I have a name for the spiritual, artistic, or creative part of my personality, I have access to a human being with all the complexities that the name evokes rather than an abstraction. Names allow us to access complex thoughts and feelings immediately. If we strive to constantly grow and evolve, we need new ways of thinking about ourselves. The Native American essayists teach us that names can mirror and inspire change. Eastern traditions, like Hinduism and Buddhism, also believe change is key to spiritual evolution. Our identity should never be "fixed" because at that point, we stop developing. Growth requires change.

Ironically, it is only through others that we can see ourselves by how they react to what we say and do. In this sense, our identity is always outside of us, not within us, just as we can only see ourselves by reflection, whether it is in a mirror, a pool of water, or another's eyes. To paraphrase Matthew 16:24-28, to find the self, you must lose it: you can only find your self outside yourself. In a strange paradox, our self does not belong to us: in the external world, we only exist and only have meaning through others. Basically, our existence is only of value as it affects others. Some of the essayists address this theme when they maintain it is not their name but their deeds that define them—a metaphysical definition by negation, which seeks to reach beyond the name.

Dr. Randi Finger, a psychoanalyst, raises the critical question of the chicken and the egg vis-à-vis names and identity. Are the issues women describe being played out through their names rather than the names being the sources of their conflict? I think the answer to Dr. Finger's question is that both concepts are accurate and are not mutually exclusive. I think women discuss their identity issues through their names, and I think names are the source of certain issues. In other words, I think that naming is more complex than an either/or question. However, I want to make it clear that a name is not one's destiny. A name is what you make of it. Dojelo is a good illustration of this point because although she has a unique name, she is not isolated by it as a child like other essayists were by their unusual names. As a child, Dojelo realizes that her unique name makes her feel "special," rather than isolated. This positive reaction to being different requires a self-assurance not all children have. The purpose of examining the essays thematically is to discover the identity issues women face, no matter what their names are, and to re-energize how we think about ourselves, which leads us to the second part of our name quest—the given name from the outside in. What are the external influences that determine our names and how we relate to them, as opposed to the internal, psychological dimensions of names?

Part Two

**The Name from the Outside In:
How We Get Our Names and
What They Mean to Us**

The first part of the book considers the internal, psychological, dimension of names—how women feel about their names, how they adjust, adapt to, and grow into their names, and why they may change their names. The second half of the book addresses the many external dimensions of names—familial, social, cultural, and religious, which determine how women get their names.

Chapter 16
FAMILY NAMES

Let us begin our quest once again with our oldest naming traditions, this time beginning with Africa, which anthropologists believe to be the birthplace of mankind.

– A –
ANCIENT AFRICAN NAMING TRADITIONS:
ANCESTORS AND TIME

*Reading this essay requires very careful attention to generations, their continuity, and even their fluidity, because Elvira Kituyi's sense of time and identity is very different from ours in the West.

• • •

The Eternal Present
Elvira Kituyi Moschetta Ransom

I was born on November 21, 1945 at Ruaka, in Colonial Kenya on a plantation of coffee, fruits and flowers. My father, Ferruccio Marco Moschetta, was a Catholic Italian from Pordenone, Italy. He came to Kenya as a prisoner of World War II, and settled here as an employee in the nursery section of the plantation. Fruit, flowers, and roses were his specialties. He was also a mechanic for all the vehicles.

My mother, Helena Nambuya, was a Kenya born Protestant. Her parents were from the Kenya-Uganda border area. Her father Jowash Mungoma was from Kenya and her mother Turkasi Wekosasa was from Uganda. They were among the first Christians from their area. They liked Christianity because it forbade polygamy; otherwise, for them, there was very little other change. My grandmother Wekosasa minded the home. Most of her children went to school in Nairobi, and the rest of the family was employed on the plantation. My mother, Helena Nambuya, was a nanny for one of the landlords' families. She could read, write, and speak a little English. She kept the children busy, singing, learning their alphabets, and playing. She fed them, saw to their naps, study time, play indoors and outdoors, she ironed their clothes, and kept the place clean. They called her Yaya or Aya.

To get to work, my mother, Helena Nambuya, had to pass through the nursery of the plantation where my father worked. On their way to and from work, they greeted each other as they crossed paths by the clear brook that was hidden by the yellow bamboo bush. Everyday he gave her little gifts of fresh fruits and berries from the nursery, and that's how they fell in love—a secret love, because by law black Africans and white people were not allowed to be seen together.

The plantation was very international. Temporary workers came from the near by Kikuyu villages; but those who lived on the plantation were from various far parts of Kenya, Uganda, Tanganyika, India, and Europe.

My grandmother Wekosasa and her two friends Mama Leah, from Tanganyika, and Mumbi, from the village of Chief Koinange, were the only lay midwives on the plantation. Like most African children at the time, I spent my first seven years on Wekosasa's back, by her side, and or within hearing range. Sometimes I was with Mama Leah or with Mumbi. From them I learned how to garden, to draw water from the pond, wash clothes, how to safely wander through the plains and bushes on the plantation in search of wild vegetables, mushrooms and fruits, how to gather fire wood, light the hearth, cook simple meals, heal the sick, listen to people and their problems, receive guests, and about life in general.

Most of all I learned about my names. Mama Leah was a devout Christian. She called me "Elvira," which she pronounced "Labpila," soft and sweet, even though it did not sound the same as the way my father or the other white folks said it. She always reminded me that Elvira was a Catholic name from Italy, where my father came from, and that someday when I would go to Italy, I would learn more about it. I felt unique, beautiful, happy and mysterious like the name Elvira. To me it was always the sound of love when uttered by my parents

My grandmother Wekosasa named me Kituyi after her Matanda great-grandmother, who had passed away only a few months before I was born. I was reminded that Kituyi had been waiting for my arrival so as to pass her name on to me and the other female relatives who were born during this period. Kituyi was a jovial, social, generous, hard working and adventurous little lady whom everybody loved. Everything about her was good.

There is method for naming children amongst the Matanda people. Often families have to consult with the elders who have up to date knowledge of the births and deaths regarding a couple who wants to get married and also regarding newborn children. After a woman passes away, that name will be passed down to her newborn female relatives until another female relative passes away. Sometimes a family will get two or more girls within a short period of time, their names will roll backwards from the latest to pass away. Sometimes two girls (or boys) will have the same name in the same family – what keeps them apart is the second name from the second parent. There are cases where the spirit is unable or refuses to take responsibility for the newborn child in which case, the child is ill and has to be renamed, thus given a new guiding spirit. The purpose of this method of naming is to keep couples from intermarrying with close relatives. It also answers the everlasting questions of our origin and the afterlife.

When my grandmother Wekosasa fell ill with tuberculosis. There was no cure. She often told me that she would soon be leaving for Matanda, as soon as a suitable bride was found for Uncle Grishon Wandiba. They would take care of me. I often cried and wanted to go with her, but she told me that it was a long journey and that she was going to die. I asked her what dying meant, and she explained that it is when the body ceases to have a shadow. It is buried underground where it continues to live the same life as we live now, and the shadow is what is given to a new born child. Thus my shadow is that of Kituyi. She is my guide. Kituyi goes a long way back. My grandmother Wekosasa's great-grandmother was not the first one. It goes way back to creation, created by a greater power named Were, or God in English, whose name is too sacred to be uttered. When I need help I ask Kituyi to speak to the Creator on my behalf. Kituyi is an ancient name. Some say that it means the seeker, the wanderer; and it may be the sound of a bird. People will keep my name alive only if I live a good life – if I am good to my family, to people in general and to nature.

One early morning at dawn, I was still in bed, not asleep, but pretending to be. My eyes were slightly open. I knew this was the last day that I'd ever see my grandmother. Wekosasa stood tall and slender outside our hut, her small load of belongings balanced on her head, her kanga neatly wrapped around her up to the arm pits, covering her chest from the cold, leaving her hands free to carry only a walking stick. She looked toward where I was sleeping and said "Alinde, Kukhu," may HE care for you, my grandmother."

My heart replied, "Tsia bpulai, Mayii, Safe journey, mother." I remained there frozen with sadness. My heart was empty, without joy and meaning. Only the spirit and shadow of Kituyi remained by my side with fond memories of Wekosasa, my great-great-grand-daughter, grandmother, whom I always called Mayii—mother. She must have passed away a few months after she left. Everyone was sad. My uncle Grishon often held me on his lap and wept for her. We were inseparable. His wife Mary was a jewel, and she is still precious and loving. She gave birth to a Wekosasa, and so did all my other four uncles' wives. Mary, now "mayii umutini" (younger mother), calls me Kituyi, sometimes Elvira, and when she is most affectionate she calls me Kituyi Kukhu.

Until 1960, just before Kenya's independence, schools for children from mixed marriages were scarce. As much as I felt loved, accepted and appreciated, I was not accepted in African, European or Asian schools. I was wait listed at the Thika, White Sisters' Boarding School. In early 1956 my parents and I were *invited for an interview and enrollment. One of the sisters asked me my name, and I happily replied "Kituyi Elvira," only to see her horrified. She looked at me and sternly said, "Only Elvira, for the time being. You will have to find yourself a proper Christian name for your baptism by the time you join us." I was shocked and confused, but my father came to my rescue. He assured the sister that Elvira was a good Catholic name and that it was, indeed, my name.*

One year after I entered the boarding school at the age of eleven, I was baptized, Elvira. My father and everybody, especially Sister St. Aristide, my religious teacher, were very happy. Sister St. Aristide taught me about Adam and Eve, Mary, Joseph, Jesus, the catechism, the New Testament and the Saints, I was fascinated. For seven years she was my teacher in religion and geography. Until she died in the '90s, she was the replacement of Mayii, Wekosasa. It is to her that I owe my gratitude for the opportunities I had to study in the Netherlands. My husband Bob took our children and me to visit her in her retirement home in Canada. I was already in my forties. My name Kituyi was only being used in my mother's family in Kenya. In America and the rest of the world, people knew me only as Elvira.

There came a time when I suffered from depression. I explained to my husband Bob that there was no reason for me to be feeling unwell for such a long period of time. Kituyi must be feeling upset that I had not used her name in a long time. I needed her in my daily life, side by side with Elvira – the way it is supposed to be. I wanted to be called Elvira Kituyi or Kituyi Elvira because that is who I am. Bob is gentle and understanding. I expected him to just start calling me Kituyi Elvira, but instead he surprised me by mentioning it in our Christmas cards, that henceforth my name was also Kituyi. It created a little stir and discomfort in some people, and I still find myself having to explain to people that both are my names: they are of equal importance to me. That was ten years ago, I am Elvira Ransom on paper; but many people now call me Kituyi or Elvira. I feel wonderful, alive, and I'd like the world to know that I love both my names. They are special to me – they are my parents, my history, and my anchor. …

According to African tradition, I am simply Elvira Kituyi, wife of Robert (Bob) Ransom, mother of Myles and Andrew Ransom, daughter of Marco Ferruccio Moschetta and Helena Nambuya—a whole family tree for one to memorize. It is often needed when talking to old people from the countryside, or just family members. Amongst friends and relatives, people call me Mama Myles, after my elder son. Others who know Andrew better call me Mama Andrew. If I had only daughters, I'd be called mama (girl's name), and if I had no children, I'd be called Mama Bob or Robert. In Pordenone, Italy, where my father comes from my family calls me Elvira Moschetta Ransom. If more explanation is needed, again one has to go through the family tree, which inevitably boils down to: Elvira Kituyi. …

Modern parents name their children the way they please, but underneath it all the older relatives breathe in the names of the Ancestors. ... This naming system is coming to an end. It is closed in, old-fashioned, complicated, and too tedious for modern families.

Elvira Kituyi

_____

The most striking theme in Elvira Kituyi's essay is that of the ancestors. Her grandmother Wekosasa names her Kituyi for her great-great-great grandmother, the most recent female to die, a span of five living generations rarely seen in the West today. Wekosasa explains death symbolically to her granddaughter: someone is dead when she no longer casts a shadow. The shadow, which is given to the newborn child, is a symbol for the spirit. Death is not frightening: it is a gift, not a loss. Kituyi prays to her namesake great-great-great-grandmother when she needs help in the same way Catholics pray to the saints for whom they are named. Kituyi's namesake, her great-great-great-grandmother, is her spiritual guide. For Africans, family members are spiritual links to the afterlife as well as well physical links to the past.

Elvira Kituyi makes the continuity of generations very clear by joining the different generations when she calls her grandmother Wekosasa, "my great-great-granddaughter, grandmother, whom I always called Mayii—mother." The generations are joined again when Wekosasa addresses Kituyi not only as her granddaughter but also as her grandmother, a role reversal, to remind the child that she is a link to the past, which reaches all the way back to creation. Kituyi is both Wekosasa's granddaughter and the shadow of Wekosasa's great-grandmother, for whom she is named. Kituyi carries with her the spirit of all past Kituyis, and her spirit will reach into the future as new Kituyis are born. This sense of universal time within the individual is called "the Eternal Present."

The generations are linked: past, present, and future are artificial, man-made divisions that allow us to clarify physical relationships and the passage of time. Although we can remember the past and imagine the future, we only experience the present—a truth we easily forget. We are often so busy thinking about the past or the future that we forget to enjoy the present.

Elvira Kituyi points out that "people will keep my name alive only if I live a good life—if I am good to my family, to people in general, and to nature." In the African naming tradition, like the Native American, the name provides an acute sense of the individual's link to society and to nature. The individual must "be good" in all three dimensions—social, environmental, and spiritual.

Elvira Kituyi sent me an addendum that highlights even more family relationships. She is known as Elvira Kituyi, Bob's wife, or as the mother of either of her two children—Mama Myles or Mama Andrew. The last two names are tekonyms (mother+child's name). Even if she had no children, the name Mother would not be taken away from her: she could be called Mama Bob (or Mama Robert) for her husband, which is a kind way to deal with childlessness. For centuries in European cultures, childlessness was often considered a curse: the wife was blamed and could be repudiated. Elvira Kituyi notes that in her family in Italy, her maiden name is kept after marriage; so she becomes Elvira Kituyi Moschetta Ransom. There is no trauma for the loss of the maiden name as seen in previous essays.

Elvira Kituyi rightly considers herself most fortunate to carry both her cultures in her double given name. With these names, she has "her parents, her history, and her anchor" with her at all times. As we saw in Native American culture, and as we will see again in other cultures, women who are deprived of their ethnic first names are often unable to identify with the first names they are given. It is crucial that given names reflect ethnicity, and even ethnicities, as we see with Elvira Kituyi. In a new culture, the ethnic given name serves as a means of retaining and honoring the original culture, the original life source.

Elvira Kituyi reminds us that our names transcend time and link us simultaneously to the past, the present, and the future. To delve more into African culture try *African Culture* by K. Asante, *Faces of Africa* by Beckwith and Fisher, or *Once Upon a Time in Africa* by J.G. Healey. *African Traditional Religion* (http://www.afrikaworld.net/afrel/) is a wonderful website with links to bibliographies and many other websites. Another very good site is *The Africa Guide: People & Culture* (http://www.africaguide.com/culture/tribes/index.htm), which also includes bibliographies.

Elvira Kituyi's essay prompts us to ask if we in the West still have a spiritual and physical sense of connection through our names.

– B –
NAMED FOR A FAMILY MEMBER

America has been called a "melting pot" or "a salad bowl," as Eleanor Roosevelt quipped; therefore, traditions for naming children after relatives vary greatly. Some are purely family decisions while others are based on faith traditions. African and Native American naming traditions maintain that the name carries the spirit. Ashkenazi Jews (Jews of Eastern European and German descent) traditionally name children after deceased relatives: superstition did not allow a child to be named for a living relative for fear the Angel of Death might get confused and take the wrong person. Sephardic Jews (Jews descended from the Iberian Peninsula and northern Africa) traditionally name children after their grandparents or other relatives, whether they are living or dead.[23]

Families of Scots-Irish descent followed traditional naming patterns, more or less, until the 19th century. (As early as the 14th century, the English tried to eliminate Irish culture by suppressing Irish names, laws, and customs. Scots-Irish refers to Protestant Scottish and English families who settled in Ireland on land confiscated from the Irish in an effort to officially "colonize" Ireland with British subjects. These immigration programs were formally called "plantations"; they started in the 16th century and continued into the 18th.[24]) Many of the Irish forced off their lands by the British immigrated to America. Because of these settlements, the Scots-Irish and English naming traditions are linked. The first daughter was named after the mother's mother, the second daughter after the father's mother, the third daughter after the mother, and the fourth daughter after the mother's eldest sister, and the fifth after the father's eldest sister.[25] "Sometimes after the third daughter, subsequent daughters were named after great-grandparents, aunts, cousins, neighbors, minister's wife, doctor's wife, schoolmaster's wife, laird's wife etc."[26] These naming patterns played an important part in maintaining family connections; but as families became smaller, these traditions were gradually lost. We will see remnants of them in some of the essays that follow.

More than half of all North American children get one name from a relative, although it is more likely to be a middle rather than a first name: this very old custom of naming a child for a relative does not appear to be weakening in the U.S.[27]

– 1 –
Named for a Living Relative

– a –
A Direct Link:
First and Second Generation

• • •

Named for Mother:
A Name with a Diminutive
Lyn Oakes Miller

My given name is Evelyn, which is the same as my mother's. This is not a huge surprise since my brother, who is one year older, was named after my father (and he got stuck with the winner "Herbert"). I was called "Lyn" and my mother was called "Evelyn." While I am not crazy about the name Lyn, I have never used the name Evelyn because I thought it was "old-fashioned," I was just happy they did not name me after a grandmother. I would be either "Ora" or "Bertha." Don't know which is worse.

Lyn's family follows the American tradition, which does not skip a generation, but names daughters for mothers and sons for fathers. Lyn uses the diminutive of her mother's name, which eliminates the confusion caused by two people in the family having the same name. Although Lyn expresses no problems with her name, when mother and daughter have the same name, the daughter may have a profound sense of stepping into her mother's shoes or of becoming like her mother when she grows into her mother's full name. This may be one reason why Lyn considers Evelyn to be an "old-fashioned" name: it belongs to an older generation—her mother's.

Lyn also highlights name cycles that doom some names to the Netherworld of Names, from which they may or may not return, according to ever evolving name cycles. *Bertha* and *Ora* are both names that have dropped off the naming charts.

Mother-Daughter Nicknames
Elizabeth M. Brunner

My mother was Elizabeth M. Morrell. She went by Betts. (...) I was nicknamed Betsy as an infant. I guess the choice was made to prevent confusion with Mom.

———————

Like Lyn, Betsy has a diminutive of her mother's name, which helps avoid confusion and gives the child an independent name identity.

If a mother can retain her nickname as one different from that of her daughter, the mother can symbolically retain her younger self—represented by her nickname—without having to forfeit it, and the younger self the nickname carries with it, to her daughter.

. . .

"Big" and "Little"
Judy McGowan

I bet you don't know too many Judys under the age of 60. The name went out of fashion in about 1945, but that didn't stop my parents from giving it to me! I am the fifth child, born six years after my next oldest sibling. In other words, there were four kids with strong opinions about what to name me. Every name my parents came up with (all from the Bible in a good Catholic family like ours) was shot down by one or another of my brothers and sisters. Finally my mom, Judy, suggested JUDY. "Anybody have a problem with that?" Well the story goes that no one did so here I am.

It was very tricky having the exact name as my mother (we both share the middle name Mary, too). When she had me, she became Big Judy and I became Baby Judy (and eventually Little Judy or Judy Junior). I preferred my name to hers, she was never crazy about being "Big" Judy, though I remained "baby" Judy for a lot longer than I thought was necessary. I became Little Judy. (She became Big.) When I got a bit older (high school age) we both had bank accounts at the same bank... same name, same address, very different balances. A bit confusing for the bank!

Somewhere along the line the bank started depositing her checks from her job into my account! I had no problem with this, but it didn't sit as well with my mom. It was probably about this time that she changed her middle name from Mary to her maiden name, Kuhn.

———————

All of Judy's nicknames are based on her relationship with her mother—"Baby," "Little," and "Junior." "Junior" could perhaps provide Judy with a bit of male perspective on hierarchy. Because of the confusion, her mother starts using her maiden name as her middle name, which allows her to recover part of her younger identity.

"Big" and "Little"
Marty

Martha was a family name. My grandmother, my mother, and I were all Marthas. I remember at one point my mother was Big Martha and I was Little Martha. My mother wasn't too fond of this. But then, my brother was John; and so was our dad, so we also had a Big John and a Little John. At some point, my brothers started calling me Matt, which then cleared up the confusion inside the family. But I was still Martha outside the family—which did not clear up the confusion there.

Apparently, mothers do not consider "Big" to be an appealing epithet.

• • •

"Little"
Madeleine Mayen

My mother's first name is also Madeleine, her maternal aunt. The name is a family tradition. My second name is Camille, like my grandfather and a maternal aunt.

My first name is an old-fashioned name. When I was younger I didn't like it. And it was difficult to recognize who was being called: my mother or me. "Madeleine, please come on"… which one? Often people said: "little Madeleine come on." It was difficult to bear this inferiority.

About mail, it was confusion. When I was teenager, my mother opened my mail. I hated that. That's why I preferred that people called me Mado.

But now my first name is up to date. I can meet baby girls called Madeleine. I am always surprised to hear my name and to see a little girl answers.

Madeleine, who is French, is as frustrated with the use of "little" as the U.S. essayists are. She explains why: the term makes her feel inferior. Madeleine's French mother escapes the designation of "Big," because the French equivalent *grand* (tall, important, grand) is used uniquely for grandmothers, which leaves no other French word meaning *big* except for *grosse*, which means fat or pregnant, both of which are unacceptable: so, French mothers escape being described as "Big."

The pleasure Madeleine describes on hearing her name repeated in a new generation is one of the comforts of belonging to a name tribe, a universal family.

• • •
Named for an Aunt
Marcia L.

My first name is that of one of my mother's sisters; my middle name is for an older relative whom I never knew. Growing up with the same name as my aunt, who always lived nearby and whose personality is best described as difficult, posed an interesting situation. I don't have a special relationship with her, nor an especially close one, and I've often said to family members, "That's not me—that's Aunt Marcia!"

But I would never wish to have a different name. Somehow, this one fits me very well. It's just unusual enough to help me stand out a bit from the crowd, but it's not strange or unpronounceable.

Because I like my name so much, I took special care with naming my children, none of whom has a family name. I chose names that weren't trendy or traditional, but I did choose slightly different spellings for two names. While I've never had this conversation with them, my impression is that all three are happy with their names, too.

When the namesake is problematic, the need to distinguish one's identity is essential. Perhaps as a result of her own experience, Marcia does not give any of her children family names.

• • •
Named for a Friend (Aunt?)
Helen Jo

I was named Helen Jo Burget when I was born. My mother said she met someone in California with the name and liked it very well, but my aunt who reared me was Helen Josephine, so who knows? When I was a year old, my sister was born with a heart condition. As a result, I went to live with my grandparents and my aunt Helen. Although my mom and dad had seven kids, my aunt had none except for me. Because I was so young when I went to live with her, I remember once asking her if she were my mother. When my parents moved to another city close by, Aunt Helen begged my parents to leave me with her. My mother and Aunt Helen were very close, so my mother agreed.

My aunt Helen was a very special person. I had a wonderful childhood and adolescence with her. She made sure I stayed connected with my siblings. She always saw to it that I was with my family for all holidays. My parents came over on the weekends I didn't go to their place. I lived with my aunt and uncle until I graduated from high school, and then I moved in with my parents to go to college in the town where they lived.

All of my family called me Helen Jo and my aunt was Helen. I guess my mother liked to call us by both our given names, but when I became an adult, I dropped the middle name and only went by my first name. I can't say this holds true for my family members. I can tell when in my life people knew me by what they call me.

When I was younger, there were three Helens in the high school, but I was the only girl in our class of seventeen.

I was privileged to care for my aunt Helen the last nine months she lived by going to the nursing home every night after school and weekends. My husband knew how important this was to me, so he made sure he was home to take care of our sons, two and four. We never know what will be required of us; and at the time, I didn't think of anything but taking care of her.

After that time, I figured my name sounded like an old woman's name. I guess I finally aged into my name. Now nearly all the baby girls are being christened "Old Women's Names."

A generational gap in naming provides more space for the child to discover her own identity without the intensified sense of competing with, displacing, or being confused with her mother. Nicknames and middle names can provide solutions for the confusion. "The North American practice of naming children after their parents, and especially naming sons after their fathers, is rare in other societies. Of all relatives, grandparents are typically the preferred name sources."[28]

There is also the issue of becoming an adult as the namesake is growing old which Lyn and Helen Jo discuss. Namesakes directly linked by generations may be more sensitive to aging and the passage of time especially as daughters see their mothers aging and feel themselves "turning into" their mothers as they age. Time takes on a generational aspect, the shortest time span in a family.

– b –
An Intermediate Link:
Named for a Living Grandparent

• • •

Closing the Circle:
The Same Name I Called My Grandmother
Marie Gaarder

In the Greek Orthodox religion, children are named for the saints the grandparents are named after. My name Marie was given to me in honor of my grandmother, whose name was Mary after the Virgin Mary. Since my cousin's name was Mary

and she lived across the street, her mother (my aunt Georgia) did not want another
Mary in the family. Therefore I was named Marie, but I wanted to be called Maria,
which is my name in Greek. My grandmother gave me a nickname. Since I was
the baby in the family, she started calling me "Bebeka," which means little baby in
Greek. My brothers loved calling me "Babeka," and teased me by taking my doll
away or hiding her some place and making me cry, and then singing, "Babeka,"
"Babeka," and making fun if me.

When my friends thought my name was Rebecca, I was relieved. I associated
the name with the book, "Rebecca of Sunnybrook Farm." I was Babeka or Rebecca
until I went to elementary school. But even after I became Marie, my grandmother
called me her "Bebeka," the name she gave me and loved to call me by until the day
she died. Being named after my grandmother and having her give me a nickname I
got teased about it in the family and by a few neighborhood kids; but it was worth
it because she favored me, and gave me of her knowledge, wisdom, and love. She
wanted me to go to college and become educated, because she never learned English.

I am grateful that she inspired me and wanted me to do more in life as a
woman. She taught me to celebrate life and we had a lot of fun together. I am
more like my grandmother in personality than in name. Now my granddaughter
Annemarie, who is six years old, is learning about things my grandmother taught
me. Now I have a new name because she calls me "Yayia," in Greek, which means
grandmother; and all her friends and her mother call me by the same name I called
my grandmother.

Marie points out that Greek Orthodox children are traditionally
named for their grandparents. Grandparents are the preferred namesakes
because they represent the longest generational span within which family
members can usually significantly interact. The grandmother looks back
in time to a world unknown by either the parents or the grandchildren.
She can give her grandchild valuable life lessons based on her life and the
changes she has seen, which other family members have not experienced.
She can help the grandchild avoid her mistakes and take advantage of
opportunities she did not have. A generational gap between namesakes
provides a more relaxed time cycle, in which one generation does not
threaten to topple the next, but rather, carries on the heritage of the
grandparents, who are ready to see future generations continue their legacy
after they are gone.

By adopting *Yayia*, the same name once used for her own grandmother,
Marie becomes part of the complete cycle of life as it links past, present, and
future. Here we see the name circle not simply through one individual, but
through three generations, as the child becomes the grandmother. Maria's

essay recalls Elvira Kituyi's essay: the interlocking circles take on a linear aspect with multiple generations.

Grand comes from Old French and was a term used to describe famous and important people, places or things. Grand was used for "grandparents" by the 15th century (OED). Because of war and disease, life spans in this era were only 35 to 40 years: living to see grandchildren was a "grand" (great) accomplishment. Today, with increased life spans, we often take grandparents for granted in a child's life.

For all of these reasons, it is understandable that of all relatives, grandparents are typically the preferred name sources.

– c –
Three Coexisting Generations

What are the possible consequences of three living namesakes within three generations?

• • •
There Wasn't Going to Be a IV
Marty

My grandmother, my mother, and I were all named Martha. Sometimes the conversation was confusing.... I was Martha III, but I was determined that there wasn't going to be a Martha IV; so I gave my daughters different names. I broke the mold to free my girls from the confusion and to give them more of a sense of their own unique individuality.

Marty has a name shared by three living generations. Nicknames, "Big" and "Little," and numbers help differentiate the generations. The numbers call to mind royalty, an association Marty clearly takes a stance against with her decision that there will not be a *Martha IV.* Marty makes no reference to a fourth generation in the past, or to any deceased relative, who would give the name a greater sense of history.

The confusion resulting from names repeated directly from one generation to the next, as well as the increased difficulty this creates for a sense of individual identity, may explain why many cultures avoid direct generational repetition of first names. We also need to ask why having a dead namesake should make any difference. Perhaps the deceased namesake allows for sublimation, relating to a different time dimension in which the namesakes are no longer in competition with one another, but are, instead, part of an ongoing chain of being as Elvira Kituyi describes.

– d –
Named for Two or More Living Relatives

(1) Double Names

Double names are common in the South because of the Scots-Irish-English, French, and German double naming traditions. With a compound name both living and deceased family members can be remembered, and both sides of the family can be honored.

• • •
Ella Frances

I was named for my mother, Ella Frances Baird Brown, who was in turn named after her maternal grandparents, Ella Cannon McCullough and Francis Marion McCullough.

• • •
Frances Mary Giles Morgan

My great grandmother, grandmother, mother, and now I was a Mary Giles (and my youngest daughter is the 5th Mary Giles).

———————

Clicker avoids the pitfalls of repeated family names by using the family name Mary Giles as a middle name: this allows her both to continue the family naming tradition and to have her own personal given name.

(2) Composite Names

Two essayists describe composite names—new names made by combining two or more relatives' names.

• • •
Three in Me
Dojelo

"Dojelo" comes from three female relatives…

• • •
Too Similar
Pinkie Byrd

When I was born, a month after Pearl Harbor, I was the first granddaughter on both sides of the family. Consequently my parents named me for both grandmothers,

Helen and May. Not wanting to give preferential treatment to either woman, they dropped the "Y" from May and the "H" from Helen and named me Maelen, pronounced May Ellen. On my birth certificate, the name has a dieresis over the first e to denote starting a new syllable here, but that didn't get on school records and other legal stuff. At age 66 I still have to correct those who see this name and call me Marlene, Mayleen, Mary Ellen, and other M-names too numerous to write. Therefore I go by my nickname, Pinkie.

Dojelo's unique name provides a topic of conversation that may help others remember it. However, Maelen discovers that her composite name is confused with lots of other *M* names; so she uses her nickname Pinkie. Composite names must be different enough that they are not confused with established, similar sounding names.

– 2 –
Named for a Deceased Relative

– a –
The Broken Link: Missing Grandparents

Parents who want their daughters named for a deceased relative can use the deceased's given name, nickname, a composite name based on the deceased relative's names, or they may simply repeat the first letter of the given name.

• • •

Before I Was Born
Ona

I was named after my maternal grandfather Oscar, who died before I was born. This follows a Jewish tradition of taking the first letter of a dead relative's name as a way of honoring them.

• • •

The Year Before I Was Born
Jaedene Levy

I was named after my grandfather. He died the year before I was born. They called him J.D. for Joseph David. (...) They worked it out somehow and named me Jaedene.

I Never Met Her
Deborah Silverton Rosenfelt

I was named after my father's mother, D'vorah, whom I never met. She died in the great influenza epidemic of 1919, when my father was six years old.

• • •

Before I Was Born
Anne

I was named after my grandmother Agnes who died before I was born.

• • •

She Died Prematurely
Elisabeth

I can still hear my dad's subdued voice when he told me that I was named Elisabeth for his mother.

These essayists are named for deceased grandparents. Unlike in ages past, not having a grandparent today is considered a premature loss. When a child is named for a deceased grandparent, each time the name is used, it will remind the parent of her own lost parent. Through her name, the child is a recipient for both the parent's love of the child and the parent's love of the missing grandparent. The child helps replace the missing link for the parents by keeping the parental love for the grandparents alive in the present with the name. This is the spiritual link that Elvira Kituyi describes in her essay. Once we feel this emotion, we begin to understand how the spirit of the deceased is not lost, but is transmitted throughout the generations as Elvira Kituyi explains.

Depending on how parents handle the loss, a child named for a deceased relative may grow up with a heightened sense of heritage, duty, and the fragility of life. Because deceased namesakes cannot tell their stories, the parents have to become the storytellers. Stories are extremely important for the woman's relationship with her name (e.g., Marie, p.124 and Nina, p.19). Basically, we are a collection of memories. If the stories are not told, if they are not told often enough, or if they are not written down, the memories are lost.

– b –
Four or More Generations:
Names Keep The Past Alive

• • •

Family Names Should Be Carried
Through Generations
Beth

My Italian grandmother was Julia. Her great-granddaughter is Julia. I think that was very nice of my cousin to name her daughter after her grandmother. I think it's a sign of love, and of a desire for the memory of the grandmother to live on. Family names should be carried through generations. It gives pride to the original owner, and a sense of belonging to the recipient. Sometimes pressure to "live up to" something. I think the pros outweigh the cons there.

• • •

She Was Shot Dead
Arielle Bony

"(Arielle) ... happens to be the name of my paternal great-grandmother. She was shot dead while pregnant at the very beginning of WWII in a part of Poland, which is now in the Ukraine."

• • •

Family Names
Elizabeth Catherine Tauke

My name is Elizabeth Catherine Tauke. My parents named me Elizabeth Catherine for several reasons. Elizabeth was my great-grandmother's name. Catherine was my other great-grandmother's name.

• • •

Family Names and Stories
Julia Gertrude Hawks Perlman

I am named for my father's sisters. They were named after my great grandmother and my grandmother's sister. My father's sister, Julia, died at 22 in 1935. She began work as a nurse at Bellevue Hospital in NYC, immediately contracted something, and was dead in three days. She was much loved in the family. I have her scrapbooks. I was called "Doodie" for a while because no one could bear to say her name. She was named after my grandfather's mother, Julia Babcock Hawks. Both she and my grandfather are buried in Sleepy Hollow cemetery in William Rockefeller's family plot. My grandfather was the manager of his estate on the

Hudson River. My aunt Gertrude was named after my grandmother's sister,
Gertrude. I have all of their pictures on my nightstand.

———————

Once a given name represents a deceased relative, name repetition directly from mother to daughter seems to be less of a challenge to personal identity: history beyond living memory makes repeated names less problematic.

Photographs, as well as stories, help keep the memory of multiple generations alive. Julia's essay leads us to consider the importance of family photographs. Keeping generations of family photographs is not easy because of calamities like war and fire, and problems of space and preservation. With the advent of the computer, retaining a family's pictorial history will be much easier but less visible.

Photography was invented in France in 1839 and spread quickly to the U.S. If a family had the resources, the first family photographs were often large and framed—a bourgeois imitation of traditional portrait paintings. These photographs were complicated affairs requiring a professional photographer, usually a trip to the shop (where a backdrop could be chosen as if for a painting), and sitting for a long timed exposure, which made smiling impossible. Like a painted portrait, the first photographs were made for posterity, which led to formal poses and attire. In our world of instant, informal photographs, it is difficult for us to relate to the stilted photogravures (beautiful and stark like etchings), daguerreotypes, ambrotypes (on glass), and tintypes of the past. Googling the different types of photographs takes you to bygone days and provides a glimpse into how much things have changed since the 1800s. The Daguerrian Society and the American Antiquarian Society have nice collections you can view online. Looking at these faces is a moving experience.

Many old photographs were never labeled so relatives' and friends' names were lost, which may explain why so many of these old photographs of unidentified relatives are found in antique shops or the Cracker Barrel. In the digital age, the need to identify those photographed for future generations remains, lest these digital images also present unknown strangers for future generations. CDs are subject to deterioration with time and need to be replaced periodically to prevent loss of stored data. Check your CDs to see how often they need to be renewed.

131

• • •

Named for Mother, a Great-aunt, and a Great-great aunt
Taylor Manson

My full name is Ellen Taylor Manson Watson. I am named for my mother Ellen Alvira Taylor (thanks be they didn't call me Alvira although a song was written about her!) and my great aunt Ellen Gregg Ingalls and her mom Ellen Ely Gregg.

• • •

Family Names and History
Elizabeth Bonner

My formal, legal name is Elizabeth Morrill Brunner. Two Morrell brothers came to the "Bay Colony" in the 1600s. They were English yeomen (a person who owns and cultivates a small farm; specifically: one belonging to a class of English freeholders below the gentry from London: http://www.merriam-webster.com/dictionary/ yeoman). I suspect because people's spelling was so poor that Morrills, Merrills, etc. may be variations of a common root.

My mother was Elizabeth Middleton Morrill. She went by Betts. Middleton is also a very old English/American name. Lots of Middletons settled in the South. Some were even dastardly absent landlords in Ireland. John and Elizabeth Middleton were two witches in Bermuda. John got the noose. She was dunked.

• • •

Only Three Choices
Dorothy Schuyler Escher Kerr

My parents chose my name out of three choices: Margaret, Caroline, and Dorothy. Those are the only names that have been used on my mother's side for as long as we have documentation. Two aunts and my maternal grandmother were also Dorothy so I was next.

I was VERY much aware of these names on the family tree because in our family there was more emphasis put on the past in our family than on the future. Every generation of women updated the next generation on who everyone was and family history was discussed with great frequency. There are published family trees on my maternal (Livingstons and Armstrongs of NY...very well documented) and paternal (Escher vom Glas family celebrated their 600th anniversary in Zurich in 1985) sides so there wasn't need for a lot of research as it was pretty much done for us, although my great grandmother had to redocument to get into the National Society of Colonial Dames in the State of NY and it had to be reviewed by their genealogist. I thought most families knew their history the way we did and it wasn't until much later as an adult that I realized that our family was more preoccupied by history than most!

• • •
The Feminized Male Name:
Women Carrying on Male Given Names
Edie

I was named after my mother—her name was Edythe Chapman. Family lore was that her parents selected it because it was the female version of the English name Edward—the name of their first-born—Edythe was the second child. The name Edward goes back five generations and is repeated generationally for four generations.

Out of curiosity I've done some research on the name and learned that the popularity of the name Edythe, a variant of Edith, peaked in 1915—my mother was born in 1913. Much to my surprise I learned there was an American stage and silent film actress named Edythe Chapman, 1863-1948.

————————————

Edie's sense of time is similar to that described by Elvira Kituyi. The origins of *Edith* predate the Norman invasion of 1066, reaching all the way back to the Anglo-Saxons (fifth century ACE).[29] Feminizing a male name is an ancient tradition. For much of Roman history, women's names were primarily a feminized form of the family name followed by a number, to distinguish one daughter from another.

Visually, *Edie* reinforces the ties with *Ed* and *Eddy* even more so than *Edythe*. Donna (p.138), Leona (p.172), and Jacqueline (p.218) also have feminized male names. There are many names in this subcategory, such as *Georgia, Roberta, Michelle, Denise, Harriet,* and *Josephine.* Many cultures have feminized male names; they allow the family to continue a male given name even if there is no male progeny.

Until recently, travel and communication were slow and expensive. In the early days of the U.S., mailing a letter from the frontier to foreign relatives was almost impossible. In addition, American culture has been driven by the desire to innovate and to create, which has centered us in the present and the future. Essayists rarely discuss family history beyond three generations. Few mention a country of origin.

If we knew more about our family histories, it would help us feel more connected to world history. What are the forces of history or nature that caused your family to immigrate to the U.S.? From what countries did they emigrate? Where did they originally settle in the U.S.? Do you have relatives not only in the U.S., but also in foreign countries?

In the past, ancestry was associated with the upper classes because only the wealthy had surviving family records. Now there are many genealogical research sources available online. *Ancestry.com* is an excellent site. Families can trace their ancestry from government and religious records even if their ancestors could not write. Affordable genetic testing is available which can awaken women to an identity that reaches beyond national boundaries.

According to genetic specialists, Black Americans will discover that they have both European and African ancestry. All American families are a genetic mix of many different ethnic groups. New genetic discoveries have redefined the meaning of race. "Race is a social concept, not a scientific one," according to Dr. Craig Venter, former head of the Celera Genomics Corporation: scientists at NIH have unanimously declared, "There is only one race—the human race."[30] Dr. Harold Freemen of the North General Hospital in Manhattan told the *New York Times* that only about .01% of our genes are responsible for our external appearance, on which we base our racial categorizations.[31] Many scientists and academics believe that this new information challenges the legitimacy of racial categorizations and shows that race is a meaningless notion."[32]

Discussion with geneticists reveals that it is impossible to trace Black American ancestry back to specific tribes because of the massive Bantu migration across much of Africa beginning around 3000 BCE: genetics does not recognize tribal distinctions. We may look at an Ethiopian or a Zulu and claim a distinction, but our genes tell us another story—namely, that we are much more alike than we are different from one another. In fact, Alan Templeton, Professor of Biology, proved in 1998 that…"Race is a real cultural, political and economic concept in society; but it is not a biological concept, and that unfortunately is what many people wrongfully consider to be the essence of race in humans—genetic differences (...). There's nothing even like a really distinct subdivision of humanity."[33] The biblical story of Adam and Eve, the Baha'i faith, and the concept of a universal soul found in many Eastern religions teach us the same lesson: mankind is united within its diversity. We often fail to recognize this important fact, taught first by the world's religions and now proven by science.

If you know what country your ancestors emigrated from, you have only the first step in the history of your family. The story of the human race is one of perpetual migration. If traced to its origins, all our family histories would eventually take us back to the beginning of the human race; and an understanding that we are all related. We divide ourselves based on visual distinctions that are as meaningless as the color of a dress.

– C –
SURNAMES AS GIVEN NAMES:
NAMED FOR A FAMILY

Women are sometimes given family names as first names, which links them not to just one individual, but to an entire family. The use of surnames in human history has a surprising, inconstant history. The ancient Greeks, Hebrews, and Romans had surnames, which were those of different tribes or families. After the fall of the Roman Empire, however, surnames disappeared in Europe until the tenth century. The earliest surname in Europe, found in Irish historical records, is that of *O'Clery* (Ó Cleirigh, son of Cleirigh), dating back to 916.[34] Although these patronymic Celtic names of Scotland and Ireland were not originally hereditary because they changed with each generation according to the father's given name, they did allow for tracing genealogy, which was important for clan identification. In 1465, in an effort to dismantle and weaken the Irish clans, King Edward VI decreed the Irish had to take surnames based on the towns they were from, colors, occupations, or trades.[35] This is one of the earliest examples of an attempt to suppress ethnicity by forcing name changes.

Surname derives from Old French and was introduced to England as a result of the Norman Conquest in 1066. Hereditary surnames existed among Norman nobility in England by the early 12th century and among common people by the 13th century. English surnames did not become common, however, until after the Crusades. (The last crusade was the Ninth, 1271-1272.) Surnames were nearly universal by end of 14th century. The process took longer in the north of England, which was less settled, than the south.[36]

Surnames became necessary to distinguish one individual from another as populations grew. Family names were created based on occupations (e.g., *Smith, Cooper, Miller,* etc.), description (*Strong, Brown, White, Short,* etc.), relationships (*Cousins, Brothers, Haraldsson* [son of Harrald: -son names are primarily associated with Nordic—Viking—heritage]), and even place names (*Banks, Easton* [east of town], *Waterford, London,* etc.).

"Giving a child a surname for a first name was originally a practice of the aristocrats, the people most concerned with family ties and legacies. For generations, surnames were only used as first names when the families were related: e.g., Percy Shelley was a cousin of the Percy family. In 17th century Scotland, a new custom arose: the practice of giving surnames for first names, usually only among Protestants. The pressure to name one's children only after saints was gone; parents were free to experiment with 'new names.' Protestants used 'new names' because they wanted to avoid traditional Catholic names."[37]

In Scotland, boys (often first-born) were given their mother's maiden name as a first name in order to honor her family. Nineteenth century American upper classes took to using surnames so frequently that the usage filtered down through all classes. Although the South continues the use of surnames to maintain the maternal lineage, surnames are now commonly used as given names without any family relationships.

As late as the 19th century, Napoleon issued several decrees (in 1806 and 1811) to firmly establish surnames throughout Europe. With the exception of clan names, the history of surnames is surprisingly recent in western history. Few girls were given surnames for given names until the early 20th century. By the end of the 20th century, however, they had become quite common. Most of them end in the long *e* sound—e.g., *Kelly, Chelsea, and Casey*—which softens them.[38] The trend to use surnames as given names for women is a relatively recent naming phenomenon.

$$\bullet \; \bullet \; \bullet$$

Windy for Winslow
Frances Margaret Winslow

When we were in school, I used my nickname Windy, but my full first names are Margaret Winslow. I continue to use Windy and Winslow but have never used Margaret (…). I am the namesake of my father's maternal grandmother, Frances Margaret Winslow. My father was from south Alabama. I have never tried to do any genealogical research on the Winslow family, but I have often thought it would be fun to do so, particularly since there were two Winslow brothers on the Mayflower and they had a sister Margaret. Alabama is a long way from Plymouth, and my great grandmother was born on a farm in Alabama 230+ years after the Mayflower's landing. But on to my name in particular. My parents nicknamed me Windy from the beginning, but they must have called me Winslow sometimes.

I prefer to use M. Winslow professionally (…). An additional twist is that Winslow as a first name is often thought to be a man's name and I have over the years received mail addressed to Mr.

This may be more than you really wanted to know, but I have always found names to be fascinating—perhaps because mine is unusual. Nowadays, many people give their children first names that are family surnames, but in 1947 I don't think it was a terribly common practice.

• • •

Mabry, Not Margaret
Mabry Debuys

My first name is Margaret. I was named for my paternal grandmother. Because I am one of 18 first cousins on my father's side of the family, there were many of us (females) named Margaret. Because of this, I was never called Margaret. My middle name is Mabry. It is my mother's maiden name. (My maternal grandmother was named Mabry Turner. She married Nathan Mabry. Thus, her married name was Mabry Mabry.) I was the first grandchild for my maternal grandmother, so I was given her name.

• • •

Taylor, Not Ellen
Ellen "Taylor" Manson Watson

(…) I am named for my mother Ellen Alvira Taylor (…) and my great aunt Ellen Gregg Ingalls and her mom Ellen Ely Gregg. Mom's dad was the first Republican Federal judge appointed in TN since Reconstruction, and the University of TN law school is named after him. Mom and Dad tried for seven years to have me; and regardless of sex, the baby would be called Taylor – hence, me.

• • •

An English Name
Tarpley Long

Tarpley Blair Mann is my birth name. (…) Tarpley is an English name (…) My parents named me after my paternal grandmother (…).

Windy observes that although using surnames as given names was rare when they were young, this is no longer the case. Surnames are becoming more and more popular as given names for girls. Given names that are surnames can cause gender confusion, which is not necessarily a negative, as we shall see (p.212). Surnames used as given names honor female lineage. Because they have a surname for a given name, Windy, Mabry, Taylor, and Tarpley all have a deep sense of history about their given-surnames. In previous essays, women discussed their childhood desire to belong to a name tribe, which represents an extension of the family into society. For women with given names that are surnames, their name tribe is in their given name, which is a family name representing males as well as females. One wonders if these androgynous given-surnames, which identify the individual with an entire lineage, make these women feel stronger.

Women named for lost grandparents discuss these losses with equanimity because they never knew their grandparents. They are one generation removed from the sorrow. Usually, the degree of loss felt depends on how recent it is—although there are exceptions such as premature or traumatic bereavement, which take much longer to heal. The following essays provide very different examples of how to handle premature loss.

– 1 –
The Power of a Name

• • •

Multiple Losses:
My Name Was Proof Positive
Donna Shaft

Married nine years, my parents neared forty saddened by the reality that they might not be able to have a child. Both had lost their mothers as children and a family of their own was central to the happy life they wanted together. My dad, Don, was raised by his father's sister, Ada. My mother, Ena Mary Emma, lived with maternal relatives and was particularly influenced by a cousin named Helen who was ten years older than she. Helen was to be a formidable force in Mother's life for the next eighty years, and commanded a large presence in my life as well.

When Mother's pregnancy was confirmed, everyone was overjoyed. There was some strong pressure to name this unexpected blessing-child for Helen, but Mother also felt a sentimental wish to name the baby for her beloved half-sister Frances, who died in childbirth at the age of twenty-two.

It must have required enormous personal conviction for my parents to name me Donna after my father, in the face of Helen's wishes. She had been very involved in raising Mother and continued to direct much of her adult life. It is also relevant, I think, that Helen lost her only child to cancer not long before my birth. I often wondered whether she regarded me as her child too in some fashion.

Mom and Dad always declared that they particularly wanted to have a daughter to name Donna. I grew up secure in the belief that I was the child they really wanted—and my name was proof positive, to my thinking. It didn't occur to me that I was obligated by my name to be like him; they loved me just because I was me, a girl, their girl. I was loved unconditionally, just for showing up.

They were exceptional and consistently loving parents and, while I am absolutely sure they would have been equally excellent parents to a son, I always knew that if the only child they could have had been born a boy, they would have named him Steven.

In my professional life I use my full-married name and add the first initial of my maiden name as a second middle initial—as a loving gesture to Don and Mary Green.

In picking a name, Donna's parents have five possible female namesakes. They wisely choose to name her for a living male relative—her father—thereby avoiding the problem of choosing one deceased relative over another, or one female relative over another. Being named for her father removes Donna from the overwhelming female losses, which reminds us of Judy's name change to the masculine Felix. Donna sees her name as proof of her unique identity because her parents create her name just for her, not as a memorial. When family losses are overwhelming, a new family name can provide liberation from the cycle of loss and sorrow.

– 2 –
Physical Links: Inherited Traits

• • •

My Name Was Very Special
Rachel L. Spencer

My name is Rachel Lynda Spencer and I am not married as of yet. My mother always told me that my name was very special and would not let friends and family create a nickname for me. She was adamant that she named my sister and me names that had no accepted shortened version. My sister's name is Ashley. I began to ask about the spelling of my middle name when it was often miswritten as "Lynn." My mother corrected the misinterpretation and I finally asked her what the big deal was. It was then that she told me about my Aunt Linda, her older sister, who had died a year before I was born. My Aunt was her best friend and losing a sister at such an important time in my mother's life was very hard for her.

We do not have any pictures of my aunt in our family home, save one. It is a picture of Linda a few years before her death, sitting in front of the Christmas tree in her nightgown. So, I found that I did not know much of the woman for whom my middle name was chosen. Middle names seem to grow increasingly important during high school when filling out graduation documents and college applications. But, it wasn't until I graduated from college (the first in my family to do so), and I heard my name read at commencement, that I felt like I wanted to know more of my aunt. I began asking questions about her. I talked with my grandfather and grandmother. I talked with her husband and my cousins. I asked what they remembered about her. The more that I asked, the more I found out how much we resembled each other. We laugh the same, have the same habit of chewing the inside of our lips when nervous, we both have a sarcastic sense of humor and our body shape is almost exact. I wore my hair very long until I graduated from high school and I believe my mother chose that style to remind her of Linda's hair.

When my grandfather died in 2003, it was at the end of a long illness. I was living several states away from him and we talked on the phone every few weeks. Toward the end, he began to confuse me for Linda who had died some 25 years earlier. He would ask me about my travels and when I was coming home. I kept telling him that I would see him in the summer and he would talk about how we would go sailing. My aunt Linda drowned in a boating accident with my grandfather. The last time that I spoke to him, he told me he was very tired, but that he would wait for me. He called me Linda in this conversation, which I found creepy at the time. I didn't get home to see him in person before he died, but my mother had an interesting story to share with me. My grandfather had molded mine and Linda's lives in such a way that he truly thought we were one person. During his last day, he talked about how he was going to get the boat ready for our sailing trip and how he missed Linda very much.

I suppose there have been other instances where family members have remarked how much I look like Linda and how similar we are. Even her children, my cousins, do not look as much like her as I do. I am older now than she was when she died, but somehow I am still envious of the life that she led and the way that she touched people's lives. When my grandmother mistakenly calls me Linda at a family BBQ, I don't correct her much anymore. I consider it a compliment and keep my middle initial securely in each representation of my name.

Most of the essayists named for deceased relatives simply mention for whom they are named. Sometimes, if the loss is traumatic, it is carried through multiple generations, as we saw in Julia's and Elisabeth's essays. Both women observe that relatives have difficulty saying the name of the lost namesake. In Julia's case, the family uses a nickname to avoid the given name. Both Elisabeth's and Rachel's families suffer premature losses, and neither girl is allowed to have a nickname: perhaps because the nickname represents a diminishment of the given name, a loss, which is a subconscious link to the premature loss of the beloved namesake.

Rachel's essay describes one way of handling traumatic loss in a family. Her mother only tells Rachel of the loss when Rachel asks about her name. By letting Rachel ask the questions, the family allows her to absorb the loss when she is ready. The only displayed photograph of her aunt is one taken at Christmas time, which has joyful associations with birth and the promise

140

of resurrection. Sometimes women do not think to ask, or are unable to ask, these questions when they can still be answered; and the stories are lost.

Although it bothers her at first when her aging grandfather confuses her with her deceased aunt, Rachel accepts that he molded them into one person. In doing so, her grandfather can overcome the unavoidable sense of guilt he must have felt for Linda's death. He sees Linda in Rachel: Linda is not completely lost. Because the boat is tied to Linda's death, the grandfather's reference to it on the day he dies suggests he sensed his imminent demise. The sailing boat is an ancient symbol used by the Sumerians, Egyptians, Greeks, Romans, and Vikings for the passage of the soul into the next life.

Now that Rachel's grandmother is confusing her with Linda, Rachel is not only able to accept the confusion but also to appreciate her aunt's life and to accept that, for her family, part of her aunt lives within her. Rachel gives a double gift to her family—her own unique life and reflections of her deceased aunt. Rachel's story highlights dramatically the theme of the physical link between generations described in Elvira Kituyi's essay. We keep people's memory alive not only with photos, stories, and emotions, but also with our DNA. Our ancestors are never completely lost, as Elvira explains so beautifully and as Rachel comes to realize. In Rachel's case, the resemblance is especially striking since she and her aunt are only a generation apart.

Rachel's essay invites us to ponder our physical links with the past. As you go through your daily life, you carry with you a physical history of an amazing past—the genetic code of ancestors who survived unparalleled disasters like ice ages, war, and disease—a survival that is a testament to both the pertinacity and the fragility of life. We are physical mirrors of ancestors whom we will never know, but they have made us who we are, as Elvira Kituyi explains. Stories like Rachel's remind us that, ultimately, we are all physically linked to one another in "the Eternal Present"—a realization that can be a source of gratitude, strength, and inspiration.

———————

In the African tradition Elvira Kituyi describes, ancestors play a critical role in the individual's sense of time and identity. Her great-great-great-grandmother, her namesake, is her spiritual guide. Praying through her ancestors gives Elvira Kituyi a physical as well as a spiritual connectedness to time. In Catholicism, the spiritual guides are not family members, but saints, designated by the church. By replacing family members with saints, our family ties, our physical links, to the spiritual realm are lost. In the Protestant church, the idea of intermediate spiritual communion is dropped altogether for a direct and personal relationship with the divine, leaving the individual with more freedom, but more isolated. By losing the understanding of the ancients that the past, present, and future co-exist within us both physically and spiritually, the present risks becoming disproportionately important.

Jews observe the Yizkor (Remembrance) service four times a year with a commemoration for deceased relatives, a donation to charity, and a remembrance of Jewish communities destroyed through the ages.[39] They also observe Yahrzeit to remember specific individuals. Jewish memorial services influenced the Christian Church. Catholics commemorate the saints with All Saints' Day. All Souls' Day is for all the other deceased; and special masses can be said for a deceased family member. Eastern Orthodox Churches are closer to the Jewish tradition in that they celebrate several All Souls' Days during the year. Episcopalians and Protestants remember the deceased on All Souls' Day. The Mexicans observe *el Dia de los Muertos*,[40] the Hindus celebrate Shraddham,[41] the Chinese have the Ghost Festival,[42] and the Japanese observe Obon Week.[43] Diverse cultures remember the dead with traditions that vary greatly in length from a day to a month. These commemorative traditions help provide the individual with a heightened sense of being part of a chain of being along with the accompanying sense of gratitude for the past and responsibility for the future. The more these ties are celebrated, the greater this sense of belonging will be. More frequent thanks to our forbearers and hope for our descendants in our Protestant religious services could help strengthen our sense of spiritual communion with the past and the future. Although we may not consider our distant ancestors very important to us personally, the "butterfly effect" proves otherwise.[44]

The Western world tends to separate the physical and the spiritual. Through our DNA, we have physical ties to the ancient past and the distant future. With $E = mc^2$, Einstein proved that energy is never destroyed but only transformed. Spiritual evolution and physical evolution are linked in ways we do not yet understand. Perhaps there are lessons that the spirit can only learn through the body and the body can only learn through the spirit—a concept inherent in Hinduism.

Due to the influence of the Enlightenment and the deification of Reason, the West has come to think of the world strictly as we can perceive it scientifically in three dimensions. Scientists no longer agree, however, on the actual number of dimensions. There may be as many as twenty-six. The concept that time has a direction doesn't even exist in physics: time is a much broader, multidimensional concept. Black holes, wormholes, countless galaxies, countless universes, and string theory, all open up unlimited possibilities in both the physical and spiritual planes. In *Unbelievable: Investigations into Ghosts, Poltergeists, Telepathy, Clairvoyance*, (2009), Stacy Horn notes that after years of research, scientists at Duke University concluded there is a field of human communication that simply cannot be explained or understood. As scientists discover ever-expanding dimensions and complexities in the universe, physical and spiritual realities reveal more and more potential, not less. Transpersonal psychology, a relatively new field, endeavors to study the spiritual with scientific methods.[45] Gradually, we are regaining a more complex understanding of the interconnectedness of the spiritual and physical worlds espoused by ancient knowledge and religions.

Time is an artificial construct that helps us organize our lives but divides us from the past and the future linked within us. Elvira Kituyi's essay inspired me to say a prayer of thanks to my grandmother, whom I never met and for whom I am named. I had never done anything like this before and found it to be a moving spiritual experience, which the reader may also wish to undertake. Our deceased relatives are not gone: we carry them within us both spiritually and physically. Remembering our ties to those who have gone before us and to those who will come after us can be a great source of inspiration, consolation, and hope.

Chapter 17
NAMES OTHER THAN FAMILY NAMES

Besides family names, names are picked from a wide array of sources including friends, godmothers, the performing arts, the fine arts, mythology, and places.

– A –
A FRIEND

There were only two essays in which the given name was inspired by a friend's name rather than a family name: Rondi (p.192) and Helen Jo (p.123), whose name is the same as her mother's friend and her mother's sister. Naming a child after a friend, rather than a relative, supposedly occurs more frequently with girls than boys.

– B –
A GODMOTHER

• • •

Yvonne Rollins

My name Yvonne comes from my godmother, Yvonne Courtil. My mother chose her as my godmother because it's thanks to her that my parents met. It's a very romantic story, and I think that my mother was right to give me that name. My godmother played an important role in my youth. It's thanks to her that I entered the Conservatoire de Musique, and that I undertook advanced piano study. I was never ashamed of my name even thought I discovered as an adolescent that the name was out of fashion. I thought it was beautiful. It's a typical Breton name; and my mother was Bretonne. My best friend (whom I have known since we were two years old) is Maryvonne, because her mother was also Bretonne. My middle name is Marie; and it's not clear if there was a dash between the two names. (A dash would make a single name out of the two.) I think my mother would have liked to call me Yvonne-Marie. But that name was too long, so it wasn't hyphenated. The name Mary comes from French Catholicism, especially from Brittany. My grandmother was very religious; and it was to make her happy, I think, that my parents chose that middle name.

I continued the tradition with my daughter, Sophia, whose middle name is also Marie, although I wasn't still Catholic when she was born. Her paternal great-grandmother, much loved in the family, was named Marie. Marie was born in Utah, but the family was originally from France.

In the past, godparents were always present at the christening of the child. They were responsible not only for overseeing the child's religious education, but also for taking care of the child until grown should anything happen to the parents. Today, if the godparents are to be the foster parents, this must be arranged legally.[46]

– C –
THE PERFORMING ARTS

– 1 –
Starlets

• • •

A Media Idol
Deborah Knight

My name is Deborah. My parents said that was one of the most popular names at that time, and stars like Deborah Kerr and Debbie Reynolds were media idols. It's funny now that whenever I meet someone named Debbie I can almost always tell her age...

• • •

An Austrian Actress
Vanessa Allen

My parents named me Vanessa after an Austrian actress in the 50s, Vanessa Brown. I guess they used the family names up on my sisters. I've always loved my name, and gone by the whole name.... no nicknames.

• • •

An Actress and A Meaning
Vivienne Lassmann

I grew up in Edinburgh Scotland and my mother chose the name Vivien because she loved Gone with the Wind and Vivien Leigh. But Vivien is not a known name in Scotland. I decided when I was about 11 or 12 based on a short stay in France that I didn't like the way it looked with my last name which I despised and was teased at school and by friends—Hogg. There were all kinds of variations that only children can devise for Hogg. So I added the NE to make it Vivienne and more French. In terms of origin it means alive which is a wonderful name to have and I have always enjoyed it. (Viviane is another variation and goes back to Arthurian legend of the lady of the lake.) I gave my daughter the name

Justine and hers means fair or just and she truly embodies that for disenfranchised people. Vivien is the English female version (as opposed to my French one), and Vivian is the male French spelling.

As an adolescent, when girls are usually trying to fit in, Vivienne is brave enough to differentiate herself by giving her name the French spelling. As she explains, the meaning of a name can be an inspiration throughout life. Vivienne has researched the cultural and literary dimensions of her name.

• • •
A TV Soap Star
Marguerite Gwendolyn Mathews Isley

My name is Marguerite Gwendolyn Mathews Isley. Marguerite is a family name. Gwendolyn was a TV soap star. The star was young, blonde and beautiful and my mom loved the name. Gwen is my nickname. Love the name Gwen. Not happy with Marguerite when I was younger, so I named my daughter Charlotte Marie and stopped the line with me. I am very sorry that I did not give my daughter our family name.

• • •
A Movie Star
Pamela Kirby

My understanding is that my mother heard the name Pamela in a movie and liked it. I have rarely used it socially, and go by Pam instead. I do use Pamela in my business signature block and for legal documents. Either way, I guess I've always felt satisfied with my name ... no objections, that is.

– 2 –
Music

• • •
A Song
Linda Rieger

My parents named me Linda because of a song that was popular at the time. Linda was a very popular name for early boomer women. I didn't like my first name used with my middle name. Linda Jane sounded Appalachian to me.

The Beach Boys
Barbara Ann

When I was in jr. high I wanted people to call me "Barbara Ann." There was one boy who was eager to win my heart, so he complied. Now I can't listen to the Beach Boys' song with the lyrics, "Ba ba ba, ba Barbara Ann" without thinking about this.

———————

Barbara reminds us that sound is an important sense, with powerful subconscious associations of which we are rarely fully cognizant—fortunately, sometimes.

– 3 –
BALLET

• • •

A Ballet
Giselle L. Pole

I really didn't think much about my name until I was about 10 years old. I was looking through a photo album my mom created, and saw my name in the newspaper type. I asked her if I was in the paper, and she told me about the ballet, Giselle. Apparently, it was playing in Miami when she was pregnant with me, and she really liked the name. I've always loved the name because it's so unique. I have never given much thought to an alternate name. Perhaps if I'd been named Mary or Sue....

———————

Giselle's name is inspired by a work of art that demands a mastery of different disciplines: music, dance, and story telling. It is a story of love, forgiveness, and fidelity. The name means "a pledge"—thus inspiring dedication and determination. In addition, Giselle has a family story to go with her name—her mother's desire to name her for a beautiful work of art. She expresses no problems with her unusual name most probably because of the positive associations with art, spirituality, and family.

• • •

Dancing on Ice
Sonja Cowie

It took me many years to grow into my name Sonja and to get over having no middle name to choose instead; however, I eventually grew to accept that my choice of name had perhaps not been the most pressing concern in the lives of my parents at the time of my birth – and may also be why they did not get around to choosing a middle name. My younger brother – "the Victory baby" – did get a middle name.

My parents were young, and I was born in Wales in the same week that Winston Churchill made his famous "We are Now a Country at War" speech. My father had already enlisted in the army and was being trained to be sent overseas. I have no memory of him until after the war. He was fighting in North Africa. Not surprisingly then, I don't think my parents agonized for long over my name choice. I was called after Sonja Heine—a then famous ice skater—and I have no middle name. I was not christened as a child, but eventually got the job done as an adult in Baltimore Cathedral by the Bishop of Maryland.

As a child, I was an avid reader (no one had television yet!)—and I loved to read the books about British Boarding Schools. The head girls, who were also heroines, were usually called Rosalind or Mary or Margaret; the villains were often Monica. Then, of course, in Enid Blyton's "Famous Five books, the tomboy heroine Georgina was always called George; and Anne, as in so many books, was gentle; and Elizabeth was dependable. The names of these fictional characters often "set the stage" for their stories.

Sonja reminds us that WWII affected everything—even the naming of children. She also points out that in popular literature, many characters' names are associated with female stereotypes, such as the tomboy, the gentle, the dependable, and even the villainous, which brings us to the topic of names and the fine arts.

– D –
THE FINE ARTS

– 1 –
A Novel

• • •

Lynette Ann Osborne

My name is Lynette Ann Osborne. My first name, as far as I know, was derived from an Agatha Christie novel that my mother was reading when she was pregnant with me. For most of my life I have gone by "Lynette," although in high school, I did shorten it to Lyne for about a year. It didn't stick, so I went back to Lynette. Now I have friends who call me "L"; but in general, I am known personally and professionally as Lynette. I like that I have a distinct name, and I think it fits me well. I think the only other name I would easily embody would be Nicole. I've been told this by other people too, "You look like a Nicole."

Lynette feels the only other name she could assume would be Nicole—another French name, a mirror image that would preserve French associations.

• • •

Janice Poland

While growing up, I never met many Janices. My mother named me for a character in a book, Janice Meredith. Now I hear my name much more frequently in the younger generation.

Janice Meredith is a novel by Paul Leicester Ford, an eminent historian and the grandson of Noah Webster. The book, also known as *The Beautiful Rebel*, concerns an intelligent and courageous heroine who helps George Washington and Paul Revere during the American Revolution. The book was so popular it was made into a movie. The website *Baby Names Pedia* indicates *Janice* is Hebrew in origin and means "God is gracious," that it evolved as a variant of *Jane* in English, and that Paul L. Ford is the first to use the name in the title of a book.

When I asked Janice about the origins of her name, she explained that she associates the name with Janus, the two-headed Roman god, who sees both the past and the future simultaneously, a reminder not to center the self uniquely in the present. A little research about Janus leads to the Far East, Jewish, Etruscan, Roman, and medieval European history. Janice has a deep well of meaning and inspiration to draw from with these associations.

– 2 –
French Literature and Philosophy

• • •

Je Ne Sais Quoi
Renée Cochrane Edson

I did not feel very proud, attached to, or fond of my given name "Renée," which is spelled in the traditional French way. All I wanted was to have a name that seemed familiar—and girlish and sweet or innocent like many of my friends of that era—Jenny, Amy, Sandy, Karen, Mary, or Stephanie. Somehow my name seemed too mature or rather haughty to me. (…) I wanted to belong to the "ee" club as in "Jen-nee;" not exactly the club that would have my name as a member despite all those "e's." It didn't have that softer sound.

Teachers butchered the pronunciation and almost everyone misspelled my name. Nobody knew to highlight the second "e" with an accent aigu. It wasn't until my high school French class that I began to appreciate having a name that actually sounded beautiful when spoken by a native speaker from which it originated. I can't remember, however, if my name inspired my choice in language study—it wasn't as if my family was ethnically unusual for our rural town. Why was I given a "French" name anyway—when I wasn't of French origin? My parents loved beautiful, unique names. They were Midwestern born hippies, Bohemian, lazy intellectuals (that is possible if you smoke too much...) who struggled to make ends meet, but were well read and named all of us children names from great literature and philosophy.

Into adulthood, I have traveled with my name in comfort. I believe that it does fit me, or I have come to fit my name in that unique way that our names define us. For me, it's that "je ne sais quoi" quality.

• • •

A Provençal Heroine
Mireille

"Mireille" is Mary in Provençal, and there is a book by Frederic Mistral about a young girl named Mireille. The story is that Mireille is the daughter of a rich landowner. She falls in love with a foreigner and wants to marry him against her father's wish. An opera named Mireille by Gounod was inspired by the story. Also, there is a statue in Provence (I do not know which village) of Mireille as the "patronne" of lovers. There are always flowers there placed by young lovers.

Mireille's name is associated not only with lovers but also with the rebirth of Provençal, the medieval *langue d'oc* dialect of southern France. The earliest vernacular love poems in European literature were written in Provençal—love poems written by the troubadour poets in the 12th century. These poems introduced romantic love to the literature of the Western world.

Mireille is the heroine of a story about star-crossed lovers, written in Provençal by Frederic Mistral, who worked to restore the ancient dialect in the 19th century. *Mirèio* was published in 1859 and marked the beginning of the resurrection of Provençal from oblivion. Mireille's name is associated with love, literature, history, and rebirth.

– 3 –
Shakespeare

• • •

Cymbeline
Imogen Wade

I was born in Brighton, England. I was named after the heroine of Shakespeare's play Cymbeline. As my mum told me in explaining why she named me Imogen, it was a combination of unusualness and the personality of Imogen in Cymbeline that clinched it:

"First of all, I wanted it to have a nice but not too girly sound and to be attractive in French. Also, I wanted something unusual but not too weird so that it would be distinctive but not peculiar. That was sort of in reaction to my own name Susan." (My mother told me she chose my name because she thought it was "so pretty and unusual"—the only problem was that she had her head in the sand at the time and didn't notice that it had quickly become the most common choice of all among her peers. My sister's name, "Araminta"—shortened to Minty—was indeed unusual, but a little too far out, and had been something of a liability for her.) "Next, I knew of 2 or 3 people with that name, musicians and artists which seemed a nice flavor (Imogen Holst, Gustav's daughter, Imogen Cooper the pianist, Imogen Stubbs the actress). Last and most important I knew that Imogen was the heroine of Cymbeline so I reread the play before you were born and was quite bowled over by the character—such a marvelous, lively, fresh, energetic, intelligent, enthusiastic, right-thinking, strong-principled, unselfconscious, kind and enterprising person; and I must admit that I really liked her getting out of a fix by pretending to be a man for a while. That clinched it. And guess what—that is exactly how you have turned out! Long live Shakespeare!"

Although the play has never been one of Shakespeare's most popular, Imogen is admired for her courage and steadfastness. (She is wrongly accused of adultery by her husband, and has to flee to save her life.)

Whenever I tell people my name, people always ask where the name comes from and what it means. It is a good conversation starter for someone who is shy by nature. Some people think that Shakespeare (or the printers) made a mistake transcribing a much-earlier girl's name—Innogen—when writing (publishing) Cymbeline. Innogen (inghean) meant "girl or maiden"/innocence in Gaelic.

I feel that my unusual first name has helped me form my own personal identity and that it has helped me feel unique and special, which in turn has contributed to alleviating my shyness.

Middle English & Shakespeare
Cate Mueller

My parents named me Catherine (no middle name) Tinkler in order to call me "Cate." My father was an English professor specializing in Old and Middle English. My mother was ABD (all but dissertation) and did [for] most of her course work Elizabethan era things. Anyway, they always told me that "cate" was a Middle English word for "a sweet tidbit…something sweet to eat." I believe it's used in a Shakespeare play…maybe Taming of the Shrew since it would make a nice pun with the shrew "Kate." I think the line is that they are picnicking on "cates and meats."

Other than an interesting naming story…at least to me… I think I qualify in the unusual spelling. I never met another Cate with a "c" before adulthood… and frankly still haven't met one in person. I'm older than Cate Blanchett, but maybe they use the nickname for Catherine spelled as Cate more frequently in Australia or England. It may be her popularity that has led recently to more children named "Cate." I was also struck with how much the name has grown in popularity when I recently saw a children's apron monogrammed "Cate" in a Lands End, or similar catalogue.

I remember as a child searching fruitlessly through the named key rings and doorplates and other things one would buy at a Stuckey's and never finding a "Cate." Well, I guess there still aren't any "Cate" items, but it's now among names that people would monogram on something!

I have always enjoyed having a distinctive name. My maiden name is "Tinkler" and despite being humorous to some, I still liked having that as well. I have actually in the last month received an email from another "Cate Mueller" in Arizona and have, when googling myself, found a "Cate Mueller" who lives in the next county over in Northern Virginia from me! So I guess the name isn't all that distinctive or unusual anymore, but I still get people asking me about the spelling and how I got it.

Imogen and Cate both know the stories behind their names, which link them to family and to literature.

By way of a slight digression, it is worth pondering one of the greatest puzzles of literary history—that having created heroines like Imogen, Katherine, Cordelia, Lady Macbeth, and a host of others, William Shakespeare's two daughters were illiterate, his six signatures (the only handwriting of his that we have) are those of someone who had a great deal of difficulty writing, and his estate had no books—*non sequiturs sans pareil;* and a hint that, indeed, "Something is rotten in the state of Denmark" (*Hamlet*, I, iv, 90). Who was the Shakespeare who wrote the divine plays and the sublime poetry? "What's in a name? That which we call a rose/ By any other name would smell as sweet" (*Romeo and Juliet*, 2, ii, 43-44). Anyone interested in the latest on the Shakespeare wars should check out Mark Anderson's *Shakespeare by Another Name* (2005), or *Der Mann, der Shakespeare erfand: Edward de Vere, Earl of Oxford* by Kurt Kreiler (2009), which has also received excellent reviews and will soon be available in English. James Shapiro tries to put out the fires with *Contested Will: Who Wrote Shakespeare?*

As Imogen points out, literary names provide a variety of topics for conversation, which is especially valuable for those who are shy. Renée observes that she believes her name "… does fit me, or I have come to fit my name in that unique way that our names define us": our names can influence us and help shape our identity. Besides family stories, literary names invite an exploration of the literature, culture, and history from which the names are drawn. All of us can undergo a quest to find our literary namesakes, which will take us through different eras and cultures, leading us to discoveries we would never make otherwise.

– E –
PLACES

• • •

A County
Devon Hannan
(Generation Y)

My name is Devon Hannan. Though I am not sure what the name Devon means, I know it is Irish and is the name of a large county in England. Hannan, however, has a deeper origin and was chosen by my father. It was his aunt's name. And he liked the way it sounded with Devon.

Devon feels a deeper attachment to her middle name, Hannan, because she has a story and a person to link it with. She does not yet have a specific story for her given name. If she googles *Devon*, she will discover a trove of stories. Devon is an ancient land settled by the Celts, who created a rich mythology and intricate artwork. Devon has beautiful moorland, thatched villages, ports, and a magnificent cathedral. It is known for mariners like Sir Frances Drake and Sir Walter Raleigh, authors like Samuel Coleridge and Agatha Christie; and the members of the rock band, Muse. If Devon has ancestors from this area, her ties to the name will be even greater.

A Place and a Tree
Orna

My brother who is seven years older than me chose the name Orna (feminine for a pine tree) since I was born on Mt. Carmel in Israel, which is rich in pine trees like California. My family calls me Ornik.

Orna suits me; and at the time, it suited the four other Orna who were in my class in high school on Mount Carmel. By the way, we named our elder daughter Carmel.

Orna links herself and her daughter with names associated with Mt. Carmel, an extremely ancient site. One of the most important Neanderthal skeletons ever discovered was found in one of Mt. Carmel's caves. In addition to ancient pagan religious sites, four of the world's great religions are now represented there—Judaism, Christianity, Islam, and the Bahá'í faith. Bahais believe in mankind's spiritual unity and the evolution of religion through prophets who will continue to enlighten mankind as our ability to understand evolves. Mt. Carmel is a testament to mankind's enduring spirituality, united within its diversity.

• • •

A Mountain
Carmelo

I was named after a mountain located in Israel. Easier said than done. That's how mountains are.

In an Internet conversation about names, when asked if she felt being named after a mountain made her strong, Carmelo answered...

I don't think I'm "the" strong one; but, yes, my friends know that they can lean on me when they need to. I do the same with them at times.

For Jewish women, bearing a name associated with a place in Israel may assume particular significance since the recreation of the country after the Holocaust. Jewish names invite studies in history, religions, and languages because Israel has been a crossroad for different civilizations since ancient times. All names offer these possibilities because all names are ethnic names. English names have ties to many languages and cultures because so many different ethnic groups settled in England from the dawn of civilization— Picts, Anglo-Saxons, Danes, Celts, Gauls, Romans, Vikings, and French-

Normans in the ancient past, plus a multitude of cultures since then, all of which made contributions to English names both in England and abroad.

Many names drawn from the Bible have Semitic origins, which include Hebrew and Arab names. Arabs and Jews are of the same Semitic family: Abraham is the patriarch of both, which makes their current strife even more tragic. Tracing Jewish history even further back to Genesis 10, Noah is the patriarch of all of mankind through his three sons Ham, Shem, and Japheth. Once again, the Bible teaches that we are all related.

Researching the origins of your name will take you through many different cultures. Seeking its equivalent in other languages will take you around the world, through history and different religions and cultures.

• • •

A French Tower
Eiffelene

I am named after the Eiffel Tower in Paris. (-:

Eiffelene's name could lead to the study of engineering and architecture as well as that of history, culture, and art.

• • •

Thai Jade
Veronica Li

My Chinese name is Tai Ying, which means Thai Jade. Tai also means peace. My grandfather was the one who christened me. He had a tradition of naming his grandchildren according to their birthplace. Because of the Chinese diaspora, he had plenty of cities to be creative with. Three days before I was born, the military staged a coup in Thailand. Violence broke out and the government imposed a curfew. My parents were worried sick that I would arrive in the midst of the chaos. Fortunately, I appeared the day after a truce was reached. My grandfather sent a telegram from Taiwan, naming me Tai Ding for Thai Calm. My mom tweaked it a little and came up with Tai Ying. I'm so thankful she did that.

• • •

An American Icon
Quincy Martel

My parents met in Boston and named me after Quincy Market.

Quincy Market goes back to 1742 and played an important role in early American history as a meeting place for American revolutionaries, who voiced their anti-royalist rhetoric and fanned the flames of insurrection there. As a shopping center that has existed for 267 years, it is a symbol of enduring vitality as well as a link to the past.[47] (*Martel* also echoes *market*.)

In ancient times, a place name was a way of locating someone: gradually they became family names. Place names are still a source for names today. When they provide a link to origins, a former home, or special memories, place names are very nostalgic, highly emotive names. They invite learning about history, different cultures, languages, and religions.

– F –
MYTHOLOGY

• • •

A Beautiful Queen
Helen Marie Margaret F.
(Generation Y)

My parents thought I was so beautiful when I was born, they named me Helen after Helen of Troy. Marie is my aunt's middle name.

• • •

The Goddess of the Hunt
Diana Ziemniak

I have always loved my name, Diana, and feel like it's a perfect fit for me. Diana is the mythical Roman goddess of the hunt, protecting all that is wild and free. She is projected as being strong with the ability to survive. I am known by my friends as being the strongest, most resourceful person they know.

I was born in 1950 and the name Diane was fairly popular at the time. My Italian grandmother's name (I never knew her) was Damiana, and I am told I was named after her. I have never cared for the name Diane—it is not the same or a nickname, as many believe. It also sounds nasally to me. For me, Diana has not only another syllable, but also a smoother rhythmic flow to it. When people call me Diane, I rarely correct them anymore unless I believe I will have further contact with them. However, it still grates on me like "nails on a chalkboard." I feel like someone was not paying attention or caring enough to know who I really am.

Diana Lynn (my name) was a fairly popular star at the time so perhaps that entered into my parents thinking at the time also. The goddess Diana is also considered a witch and a healer. I also teach women's studies as an adjunct, and as a feminist, I feel like I am helping to empower other women (and men) and give them the "tools" (knowledge) for a more enriching life journey. I would never want another name and as you can see, I strongly connect with it.

Diana's name has links to popular culture, family history, and mythology. As a teacher of women's studies, she identifies with the image of the goddess as protectress, survivor, witch (meaning "wise woman") and healer. Diana reminds us of the Native American naming tradition with the multiple meanings she has created for her name. In ancient traditions, witches were primarily associated with good. It was only after the advent of Christianity that witches were considered to be forces of evil. Many people only know about the negative history of witches.

Witch derives from *wicce*, the Anglo-Saxon of these invading Germanic tribes who settled in the south and west of England and eventually gave us Old English. Our *w* words are very old words derived from Germanic and Nordic languages. Neither Latin nor the romance languages have words beginning with *w*, except for Walloon (an Old French dialect). *W* words still echo the wonder of the wilder ancient culture that helped shape the sound of English. The difference is readily felt in comparing *w* words to romance based synonyms: *witch* versus *sorcerer* or *magician*, *woman* versus *female*, *wild* versus *uncivilized*, *wise* versus *sensible* or *sage*, *word* versus *mot* or *parlance*. To mirror her strong character, Diana is not afraid to use "witch" in its ancient meaning, which is connected to the very beginning of English history.

• • •

The Ulster Cycle: An Irish Queen
Deirdre Grace Callanan

I open the small, blue book, a 1930 edition of A Golden Treasury of Irish Verse, to page 94. James Stephens' Deirdre is nine tercets of melancholy, longing, and regret. That "poor queen" dead for "more than a thousand years" is still mourned. I whisper the lines, remembering...

Even before I could read, my mother recited Deirdre, often by the fire at bedtime, or so it now seems. I grieved for this lost and lonely woman whom no man could befriend or love. The grass she trod and the clouds she saw remained, yet she was now "but a story that is told/Beside the fire!"

As I listened beside our glittering hearth, it was as if my soul were already vanished, drawn through the chimney on the coals' sparks, blotted to nothingness in the sky.

Thus I have lived these 60 years preferring to traipse trails and beaches which, too, will remain long after I am gone.

I've read many versions of this Ulster Cycle legend about Deirdre's love for Naoise, one of the three Sons of Uisneach, and of King Conachur's love of her and the "great tain" it caused. The poet Cathfa called her the "Troubler."

Though I've no interest in inciting a civil war, I'm nonetheless proud to bear a name so central to Irish mythology. It's a birthmark that grounds me in a specific history. I may claim it in silence and privacy, but it is mine to the bone.

I allowed my naming to make me reckless but rarely careless, sad but seldom sorry. What might I have become as a Maureen or a Susan? Hopefully someone kind and curious. Definitely someone else.

The ancient queen continues to weave her magic spell through Deirdre as she enraptures us with her own poetic story. Deidre personifies her name and makes it a source of poetic inspiration.

To discover the ethereal story of Deirdre check out *Celtic Fairy Tales: The Story of Deirdre,* which tells the fable in contemporary prose: http://www.luminarium.org/mythology/ireland/deirdre.htm.

• • •
The Greek Moon Goddess
Cynthia Campbell

Cynthia...a lot to be said about Cynthia. It is Greek and means "Goddess of the Moon." (Cynthia is of Greek origin. Kynthia was one of the names of Artemis, the goddess of the moon, referring to her birthplace on Mount Kynthos.) Everyone knows how old I am. No one uses that name any more. I had seven people in my German class in high school. Two of us were Cindy's. There is a Cindy right across the street from me; but neither of my two sons, who are in a very large middle school, has a female classmate named Cindy.

Then there is the nickname Cindy, which can be spelled Cyndi, Cindi, Cindie, or Cindy. You would really think the proper way would be Cyndi, since the full name is Cynthia.

Cynthia sounds snotty. But Cindy's so cutesy. I can't imagine being a wrinkled 80-year-old and having the name Cindy. On the bright side, I could always find one of those little license plates with my name in it when I was little.

My mother still loves the name, but regrets calling me by my nickname, Cindy. My in-laws told me if they were to have had a girl, her name would have been Cynthia. They got their Cynthia after all.

In answer to the question of how being named after a goddess might have affected her, Cindy humorously turned the tables.

I don't think the meaning of my name was considered at all when given. Of course it is wonderful to think you are some sort of goddess? I wonder what the moon thinks of me?

158

Mt. Kynthos, on the island of Delos, is one of most sacred Greek sites, birthplace of the twins Apollo and Artemis (the Roman goddess Diana) and home of the Delian League, the confederation of the ancient Greek city-states. The tiny island has temples to all the gods, including the "Unknown God," because polytheists accept all gods: there were never any religious wars between polytheists. Today you can still see the crowded, eerie remnants of the temples, market places, and patrician mansions standing in stately ruins, a testament to the transience of all earthly glories. Like Delos, *Cynthia* was largely forgotten. *Cynthia* was revived by Renaissance historians, but not commonly used in English before the 19th century[48] when French archaeologists revived the story of Delos. The rediscovery of Delos and *Cynthia* are, therefore, linked. As she says, "… there is a lot to be said about 'Cynthia.'"

• • •

Names, Myths, and Symbols
Peggy Heller

When my parents were dating (for six years while they saved money to get married), my father's hobby was racing motorcycles on cinder paths. It was a very dangerous activity that required great skill and also probably great foolhardiness. Although several of my father's buddies were severely injured and one died, he loved the sport. One of his motorcycle buddies was a "girl" named Peggy. My father thought she was super and somehow even got my mother to agree. Also around the time that my parents were expecting me, they were enchanted by a child movie star named "Baby Peggy." That settled it for both of them. My father called me Peg or Pegasus; my mother called me Pegala, a Yiddish diminutive. I liked my name and my nicknames. I loved my dad's attitude that a girl can do anything. That's what my name symbolized for him.

The only problem came in school where teachers invariably argued that my name was a nickname for Margaret, which they insisted, was my real name. I always had to tell them that my sister's name was Marjorie, and they'd desist.

One of my father's brothers was married to a woman from Ireland, Annie Flynn, whom I loved dearly. She was the nurse who took care of me in the hospital when I had my tonsils out. She called me Peggy O'Neill and would sing that song to me. I called her Aunt Nurse.

Because of her and because I didn't like my middle name, Osna, I called myself Peggy O' and my family name that was not at all Irish. It wasn't until I was a late teen that I learned the story of my middle name. It was the name of my mother's favorite sister who died in childbirth before I was born. My mother was the eleventh and last child born in her family. Only seven survived past early childhood. Her father, a biblical scholar, an apostate, and the last of many generations of rabbis, had chosen that name for his daughter. It was a name from the Old Testament story of Joseph of the many colored cloak fame. The English spelling was Osna, Asena, or Asenat. She was Joseph's Egyptian wife, given to him by the pharaoh in appreciation for Joseph's dream interpretations. I did some research and learned that Asena was the name of the Egyptian mythological Minerva or Athena. I claimed it mine and have used it ever since. I like to remind myself that my middle name identifies me as one who has a good head and good hands.

What's in a name? Significant clues to how a person makes meaning and choices in her life.

Although a child movie star inspired her name, Peggy's father takes the name into new realms by associating it with Pegasus, thus introducing the world of mythology, symbolism, and multifaceted reality. Peggy creates her own mythology for the name Pegasus, as a symbol that "a girl can do anything." Following her example, we can make our names into empowering symbols by creating our own stories for our names, which will make our names uniquely ours and serve to inspire and energize us.

Family members introduce more dimensions with Yiddish and Irish associations to her name. As a child, Peggy grows up with a rich, multicultural history—a wonderful gift a parent can give a child through her name by simply googling the name to discover as many connections as possible. The more connections we have, the more possibilities we have.

By linking the Roman Minerva and the Greek Athena to refer to the Egyptian Osna, Peggy adds yet more cultural layers to her name. She explores different cultures and religions as she engages in a constant quest for knowledge. One can only wonder at the inspiration provided by Peggy's name, since she is active in the field of poetry therapy: Pegasus has been considered the steed of the Muses in the modern era and a symbol for poetry. Peggy's name has inspired her to take flight in her own life, and she has given wings to others.

She also contributed poetry for the chapter on literary writing and names (pp.308–310).

• • •

The Goddess
Meredith Heller

Meredith is Poseidon's sister. She rises up from the waves on the back of a shimmering seahorse. Raising her jeweled trident to the sky, she calls down the summer storms. Lightning inspires her.

With her long turquoise hair and prism eyes, she is regal and mystical and a bit wild. Like the Ocean, she has many moods, and she allows herself full, embodied expression. One of her favorite things to do on a Sunday afternoon is to take the hands of the Wind and the Sun and dance across the water.

If you're walking along the shore at dusk, you may hear her singing. Sometimes she weaves her songs with sorrow, sometimes with joy, and always with the soulful melody of truth.

When you find yourself alone at night in a small blue boat, drifting too far out to sea, Meredith will whisper your name until you are no longer afraid, and then she will gently guide you back home with one long breath. When your feet feel the Earth again, you will put your left hand in your pocket and pull out a round iridescent shell, like a small cup of light—a token from Meredith and the Sea—should you ever choose to return.

———————————

Like Molly (p.23), Meredith provides a wonderful example of how to create powerful associations for a name. Molly's name means happiness to her, the exact opposite of what the name meant traditionally. *Meredith* is of Celtic origin; but contemporary culture has recreated the name, associating it to *mer* (French for "sea") and *Edith* (interpreted as meaning *guardian*).[49] Although this meaning may not be linguistically or historically correct, names endure, like words, by taking on new meanings and associations with the passage of time and cultures. Seeing names change meanings is an affirmation of the creativity of the human spirit. Meredith makes her name into what it means for her—a link to inspiration and the supernatural. To hear Meredith sing with the dolphins, go to her website: http://www.myspace.com/meredithheller.

– G –
HISTORY

• • •

Roman Origins
Sabine Bourgey

My given name is Sabine, of Latin origin—Roman empress. I was the first in my family to have it. I had a half-sister whose name was Nadine. My mother liked this type of tone.

I never had any nicknames.

I really like my name because it's classic and original. You don't find too many women named Sabine.

I always had a fascination with Roman civilization. I am a coin dealer. My specialty is Roman coins. My thesis was about Roman archaeology. My names are Sabine, Pauline (my grandma's) and Jane (my aunt's, but curiously written in English: her name was Jeanne. Maybe the anglicized spelling was a mistake made by the "etat-civil.") "Jane" was a sort of premonition, because I've always been fascinated by Anglo-Saxon culture (GB and U.S.).

Sabine believes that names have a powerful influence on people's lives and that her name has greatly influenced her interests.

Only a small percentage of women's names are not family names.[50] Names from the performing arts and fine arts can inspire an interest not only in the arts but also in history, literature, and culture. Place names have historical, cultural, and religious dimensions. Learning about the past can lead to new paths in the present. Mythological names provide multiple layers of meaning and links to diverse cultures. The essays by Deirdre, Peggy, and Meredith tempt us not only to look into the meaning of our names and the stories behind them, but also to create our own name stories. We can add multiple layers of meaning to our identity through our names with a bit of research and imagination.

Chapter 18
NAMING PATTERNS

In Chapter XVI, women discuss family names and relationships. In this chapter, women discuss naming patterns. Naming patterns are both visual and oral.

– A –
REPEATING GIVEN NAMES

– 1 –
The Power of the Given Name
Linking Generations and Families

Judy McGowan gives us a fascinating glimpse into what naming patterns were like in mostly by-gone generations when families had many children and relatives were close by. Her essay depicts an intense awareness of naming patterns in ways we do not often see today and helps to explain why Americans, unlike most other cultures, may have chosen to link generations by repeating the same given name directly from one generation to the next.

• • •
Only a Few Names to Pick From
Judy McGowan

Our family has only a few names that we choose from. My mom is Judy. I'm Judy and I have a niece Judy. I have a sister Katie, named after my grandmother, and I named my daughter Katie as well. I have an aunt Susie, a sister Susie, and a niece Susie. Most of the girls in the family, starting with my mom and her sisters, have the middle name Mary.

My grandfather was a Michael, as is an uncle, a brother, and a nephew. My dad is Robert, as is a brother and a nephew. See the pattern here? It keeps remembering names simple, though one time my dad was leaving a gathering, taking a few of us with him. Someone asked him whom he was taking and he said, "Judy, Judy, Judy, Katie and Katie!" It was a bit strange! That was my mom, my niece, my sister, my daughter, and I. My sister Katie has a daughter Judy and I have a daughter Katie.

My mom and her 3 sisters and me and my 2 sisters all have Mary as one of our given names. None of us go by Mary, however. I think we repeated a lot of the names because my mom loves her brothers and sisters so much that the names bring good things to mind. Popular names the extended family uses: Aggie (2), Maggie/

Margaret (4), Susie (3), Katie/Catherine (3), Judy (4), Mike/Mikey/Michael (4). This includes names from my grandparents down to my kids' generation. It does get confusing in family conversations! Of course, my dad has been calling my siblings and me by the wrong names all our lives (down to the dog's name sometimes!). We usually just tell newcomers to guess Judy or Katie and they'll have a pretty good chance of being right!

When asked how names are kept straight in a conversation, Judy answered with the following.

To specifically answer your question the best I can, I guess we refer to someone with a repeated name by their parent. For example, my daughter Katie would be "Judy's Katie." My sister's daughter Judy is "Katie's Judy." Mostly, though, we've learned to associate by context! The many Michaels usually start as Mikeys and gradually grow older into a Mike.

Another story: when my mom's father was near death, we went to visit him one last time. He had developed dementia and didn't recognize too many people. When he saw me he said, "Hi Judy." We were never quite sure if he recognized me or thought I was my mom when she was younger (we share a strong resemblance).

———————————

Judy's family repeats given names directly from one generation to the next, which makes for a lot of name repetition—four Michaels, three Roberts, three Susies, two Judys, and three Katies. As Judy notes, it keeps things simple but also offers multiple opportunities for confusion. These naming patterns create the sense of a chain of being like Elvira Kituyi describes. The repetition of the given names to include not just mother/daughter, father/son relationships but also uncles, aunts, cousins, nieces, and nephews broadens the sense of family beyond a linear concept to that of a group—a family tree.

Judy alludes to the fact that the repeated names call to mind several relatives simultaneously: "I think we repeated a lot of the names because my mom loves her brothers and sisters so much that the names bring good things to mind." Namesakes have a special bond: by creating more given namesakes, family bonds are magnified by both first and last names. When Judy's extended family gets together, the intergenerational, interfamilial links are constantly reinforced by first names, which subconsciously erase the generational gaps and create an ongoing sense of time, a continuum, within the family—"the Eternal Present." As we saw with Elvira Kituyi, Judy's family uses tekonyms to help avoid confusion. These are all the positive aspects of repeated first names.

164

Judy highlights the sense of belonging, the history, and the links between individuals that a family naming pattern provides—all of which help overcome her personal identity issues.

She closes with a story reminiscent of Rachel's (pp.139–140). Close to death, Judy's father is able to name her; but "We were never quite sure if he recognized me or thought I was my mom when she was younger." For the dying grandfather, the generations are linked as they are in Elvira Kituy's essay and in Rachel's essay. Judy's dying father sees the physical link between the generations—the cycle of life. Stories like Judy's and Rachel's remind us of how emotionally powerful, how sustaining, our physical links can be.

– 2 –
The Special Bond:
Given Names Linking Grandchildren and Grandparents

Beth verbalizes the transcendental feeling of touching the future with names repeated throughout multiple generations.

• • •

Awfully Comforting
Beth Boswell Jacks

Beth Boswell Dowdy is a precious 5-year-old now. She crawls in my lap, gives me a kiss, and says, "Bebe . . . two Beths. You. Me." And I melt.

All of Beth's life, you see, when I'm long gone and forgotten by almost everybody else, she'll tell folks, "I was named for my maternal grandmother." And there will probably be many more Beths in our family in the generations to come. There's something awfully comforting about that.[51]

Beth's use of *awfully* is especially meaningful because it is a biblical term, based on the Middle English *aweful* meaning "awe-inspiring."[52] Her usage is an example of how some Southernisms have maintained a much older meaning, now largely forgotten, which dates back to our first European immigrants. "Awfully" conveys the sense of wonder that is found in Elvira Kituyi's essay. With her name, Beth feels part of a chain that stretches from the present into a future beyond that of her granddaughter—a future she will touch through her descendants even though she will never see it herself.

Historic Given Names:
A Living Link to the Past

Names repeated for generations can provide women with the sense of fitting into a pattern—with a sense of destiny—the continuation of the family lineage.

• • •

Dorothy Kerr

My name is Dorothy Schuyler Escher Kerr. My parents chose my name out of three choices: Margaret, Caroline, and Dorothy. Those are the only names that have been used on my mother's side for as long as we have documentation. Two aunts and my maternal grandmother were also Dorothy, so I was next.

• • •

Back to the 18th Century
Caroline Claire Willis

I was named for my Grandmother Caroline Bryan Tillman Hamilton. She was named for her mother Rachel Caroline Bryan Tillman. The Caroline in my mother's generation died in infancy. The Carolines in earlier generations go back to the 18th century. Growing up I was called Caroline Claire, and then again in adulthood, to distinguish me from my niece, Caroline Elizabeth Nichol Campbell.

For Judy, Dorothy, and Caroline, the name tribe is found within the family. Because the names go so far back in time, they provide a sense of history that helps overcome issues centered on individuality. Their names are like a musical leitmotif. These individuals have a strong sense of being part of an ongoing tradition, a chain of being that stretches from the past and the present into the future, the chain of being that Elvira describes.

– B –
SIBLING-NAMING PATTERNS

– 1 –
The Importance of Maintaining the Pattern

Although parents may not always think about sibling-naming patterns, especially when choosing the name for the first child, siblings relate to one another via their names. Sibling-naming patterns play a much more important role than parents may realize.

• • •

It Wasn't Fair
Judith Moorman

And why did they name me, in the Jewish tradition of choosing a name in memory of the deceased, after a third cousin? It wasn't fair that my brother Gus was named after our maternal grandmother, Bubble Guise, someone you could hear stories about, while I received the name of a "storyless" relative with the unromantic appellation Jake.

• • •

The Whole Naming Thing
Bonita Winner

My favorite psychoanalyst has another theory that the unconscious does funny things to avoid hurt. If, for instance, all your siblings have biblical names like Joseph, Sarah, Rebecca, John and your name was something decidedly exotic like Bonita, your unconscious might try to ignore the whole naming thing.

By failing to include a child in the naming pattern, the parents figuratively place her outside the family unit: subconsciously she risks feeling like an outsider.

• • •

Inextricably Tied to Hostility
Lynne Marie

My parents were divorced when I was in fifth grade. Prior to that, I don't remember them ever showing any signs of physical affection or emotional support for one another. The history of my name is inextricably tied to the hostility between my mother and father. The story goes that my parents, who could never agree on anything, made a deal with each other that she would name the first child, and he would name the second. My brother, who was born four years before me, is named Edward Matthew for my maternal and paternal grandfathers respectively. When my family gets together, people from both sides always discuss and debate with pride which attributes he shares with each of the two great men.

However, Lynne Marie is not a name that appears on any branch of my family tree. Lynne is an uncommon spelling of an uncommon name and was always a major source of anxiety during my childhood; I could never buy a license plate with my name on it for my bike without adding an E in magic marker, and I never had a namesake song like my friends Maggie, Beth, and Sue. For my 13th birthday I received a decorative plaque explaining that my name is derived from an Old English word meaning "beautiful waterfall." When I asked my mother why my father chose to name me Lynne Marie, I was picturing a waterfall nestled in the English countryside, with a peasant woman reading a book beside it, every few minutes she would lift her eyes from the pages to admire the calm and beauty of the clean cascading water. My mother interrupted my daydream when she turned to me and with ample bitterness told me that my father wouldn't tell her where he got the name from, and that I was probably named after one of his ex-girlfriends or mistresses.

By linking Lynne to one of her father's girlfriends, her mother puts *Lynne* outside the family and, inadvertently, gives Lynne the feeling she does not belong. This feeling of being an outsider is exacerbated by the fact her brother has a family given name and she does not.

Research on the name *Lynne* reveals that it is an ancient Celtic/Welsh name meaning "lake." It can be considered a nickname for *Linda*, which is an old Germanic name meaning "tender," the emotion Lynne is seeking but missing in her name story. A study of water and its symbolism of life and the spirit could inspire a healing journey through mythology, world religions, and literature.

• • •

No Explanation
Sheila C.

And so, in haste, I was named "Sheila". No explanation for WHY that name in particular. The name has no history in my family—whereas the three subsequent kids got named after Grandma, Dad and Aunt Elaine, respectively.

I hated my name during all my childhood and most of my youth.

• • •

Grandmother Was Furious
Clicker Morgan

When I was 18 months of age, my parents legally changed my name to Frances Mary Giles Hamilton. Why? My mom said that my Dad adored me so much that she wanted to name me after him. He was Francis (called Frank) so I became Frances. "Cynthia" was a whim, not a "family" name. And the Mary was added because my grandmother was furious that my mom didn't keep with the tradition. My great grandmother, grandmother, mother, and now I was a Mary Giles (and my youngest daughter is the 5th Mary Giles).

Sometimes the sibling-naming pattern needs to be maintained not for the sake of the child or the parent, but for the grandparent, as Clicker's and Heather's (p.34) essays illustrate.

Chinese Sibling-Naming Patterns

Chinese naming traditions are very sensitive to sibling relationships. One wonders if they avoid some of the problems Westerners face when they do not follow sibling-naming patterns.

• • •

Siblings Share a Name
Katherine Mei Hwei Lee Rieger

Naming became a big issue when I was pregnant and thinking about names for my son. It was important to me that he had a Chinese middle name since he was going to have a Western first and last name. My vague understanding of Chinese naming traditions came from knowing that my grandmother visited a Chinese fortuneteller to choose Chinese names for at least her granddaughters. My cousin, sisters and I have middle names that start with Mei, which means beautiful in Mandarin. Our second names are all different and to my knowledge unrelated. My name is Mei Hwei, my sister's name is Mei Hsien, etc. Chinese names generally suggest good fortune or other desirable qualities; my name means beautiful and intelligent.

My cousin and I had had conversations about wanting our children to have Chinese names so she contacted her Chinese friends in China to help us. This is what I learned. Within the same generation, families choose a common name—one for boys and one for girls. Then each child has a second name from an idiom. So, in my son's generation all the boys will have the common name Dao (meaning way or path) and a word from an idiom that says zhen xin shi yi (meaning true heart). So my son's name is Daozhen and the next boy in his generation will be Daoxin.

Katherine explains that Chinese families choose a shared name that will be the thread linking all the siblings just as Western families link siblings not only with repeated family names but also with the repetition of the initial sound (e.g., *Julia* and *Julius*), rhyming names, shared initials, shared middle names, and various names for the Virgin Mary, as we shall see.

• • •

Birth Order is Very Important
Veronica Tai Ying

My nickname is Ah Mui, Cantonese for Little Sister. Hierarchy is paramount in a Chinese family. The order of birth is key to shaping a person's character. As this is something one has no control over, it's pure luck that I got the plum position-number four out of five. Believing that "a bad older child will set a bad example," my mom was very strict with my eldest sister and brother. I'm also lucky not to be Baby Sister, because that's what she'll always be. Even at fifty, we treat her like a baby.

Having gotten the best bargain, I feel it's only fair that I do my best for the family. When my parents could no longer live independently, I invited them to move from California to stay with me in Virginia. My siblings chip in, but I chose the lion's share and am most grateful for it. I taped my mother's stories and wove them into a memoir.

Women whose names do not fit the family naming pattern express varying degrees of discomfort with their names. The only exceptions were Vanessa, who knows "...they used the family names up on my sisters" (p.49), so she does not feel left out, and Clicker, who also knows why she does not have the generational family name as her given name. Thanks to her grandmother, Clicker continues the family tradition with her middle name; and she continues the tradition with her daughter. The sibling naming-pattern is set with the first child's name: it is important not to break the pattern for subsequent children without an adequate explanation.

Chinese siblings are linked not only by a shared name, but also by another name that is part of a proverb. The siblings only fulfill the meaning of the proverb when they are united, a wonderful way to strengthen the sense of family unity with the siblings' names. Birth order also plays an important role in maintaining Chinese sibling relationships.

– C –
MIDDLE NAMING PATTERNS

Once again, the middle name insisted on being part of the discussion. Women describe a surprising variety of middle naming patterns.

– 1 –
Generation to Generation:
Mother's Given Name as Daughter's Middle Name

• • •
I Had My Mother's Full Name
Tana Sommer-Belin

While Tana Naomi is on all my legal documents, driver's license and social security, IRS, etc., I almost never say it or use it otherwise. Naomi is my mother's name. Her mother had done the same thing adding her own name as a middle name, making it Naomi Johanna.

Middle naming traditions vary greatly, including the use of surnames, double names, or no name at all. In Tana's family, the tradition is to give the mother's first name as the middle name, which allows Tana to have her own separate identity while keeping her mother's entire name, first and last. This is a powerful visual image of the link between mother and child. The loss of the mother's given name upon marriage reflects the transition from daughter to wife when Tana loses her mother's full name to start her own family. She observes the name link is never totally lost because her full name is preserved in all her legal documents.

– 2 –
Linking Siblings with the Middle Initial

• • •

I Changed My Name, but Followed the Pattern
Carolyn Vivian Walker

My mother Clara Virginia named her first two daughters Evelyn Virginia and Madelyn Violet. Following the system, she named me, her third daughter, Carolyn Veda. The fourth child might have been named Marilyn but he turned out to be Carl Vernon. I didn't like the name Veda, so I asked my mother if she might change it. "All right," said my mother, "but don't tell Aunt Veda." So I became Carolyn Vivian Walker.

Linking the siblings with initials is a faint echo of the Chinese naming pattern: it reinforces the siblings name ties by giving them an additional name bond—the middle initial.

– 3 –
Skipping a Generation:
Linking Grandchildren and Grandparents with the Middle Name

• • •

I Did Feel Special
Karen Lee

My given name is Karen Lee, my middle name having come from my paternal grandmother. She was "Nellie Lee," and I was told that she always hated the "Nellie" part of her name, because it sounded diminutive, like a nickname or only a child's name.

171

(...) Even though I only used "Lee" as a middle name, I was told that Nellie was honored to have a namesake. I was not her first female grandchild (I was her third), but neither of the others was named for her. Nellie gave me a beautiful and delicate bird's eye maple desk, dresser and chair set, a wonderful, loving and feminine gift. My female cousins did not receive any such present following their births, so I did feel special. Nellie also seemed to love my pale blonde hair and asked my mother for a lock of it. Many years later, years after Nellie died, I found a tiny envelope still holding that lock of hair amongst her possessions. I was one of the few towheaded members of our largely brunette clan.

In Karen Lee's essay, we see that bestowing even part of the grandparent's name is enough for the grandparent to feel a special bond with the grandchild.

• • •
Unsettling
Anonymous

Since I was named for my paternal grandmother, my middle name was given to me to honor my mother's side of the family—my maternal grandfather. My mother was extremely fond of her dad, so she gave me his name Leon and added an "a" to feminize it—Leona. He died before I was born. It is a name that has always been unsettling to me. At best, it sounded awkwardly feminine. At worst, it brought to mind images of a wild beast.

As a teenager, I discovered from my dad that Leon was, alas, a cad. Later, my mother told me stories about him that curled my hair. I could never understand why she continued to worship the ground he walked on despite all the suffering he had caused in the family. For her, he was like Zeus, a divinity, albeit, flawed.

The name could be very empowering for a woman, if only I could conjure up associations with C.S. Lewis or Boudica, but the name always seemed to bring up images more à propos of Dickens' Marley or Don Juan. Then there was the Leona Helmsley scandal....

Middle names can honor male relatives while allowing the woman to receive a more feminine given name. Naming a child for a family member with a difficult family history is problematic.

– 4 –
Linking Multiple Generations
with the Middle Name

• • •

Three Generations
Carol Armstrong

Our daughter Stacy Anne was named after no one in particular. We just liked the name; however, her middle name (like mine) is Anne, and this was after my grandmother.

• • •

Multiple Generations
Mary Giles

My great grandmother, grandmother, mother, and now I was a Mary Giles. My youngest daughter is the 5th Mary Giles.

• • •

Bridging Cultures
Deborah Field Washburn

I was born a few months before Pearl Harbor, to a mother and father from Tennessee and Maine, respectively. They named me Deborah Farwell Field. The name Farwell is from my mother's side, an eighteenth-century New England connection that perhaps helped bridge the gap between her Southern roots and my father's profoundly Yankee heritage.

Despite the request to discuss their given names, essayists frequently discussed middle names, which suggests middle names carry more meaning for women than one might assume. Women's middle names serve several functions. They provide the opportunity to honor both sides of the family, to link generations, to maintain the matriarchal line, to distinguish family members with the same given names, and traditionally to preserve the maiden name after marriage, when the other middle names are usually dropped. Society's ideas concerning marriage and surname usage are currently changing, offering women the opportunity to keep both their middle names and their maiden name. Once again, it appears that the middle name is central to women's identity as Joanne Gold suggests (p.84).

– 5 –
Maiden Name Becomes Middle Name

. . .

An Altered Identity
Elisabeth Pearson Waugaman

I remember after I first got married, it felt a little odd when I signed my new married name. I was proud of my new last name and happy to be married to such a great guy; but I also felt a bit strange—like I was no longer who I had been, a kind of Alice in Wonderland feeling. Miss had become Mrs.: I had lost the singular i of Miss, but gained an r (are), a reinforcement of the plurality of marriage. That was lovely to think about, but my maiden name had shrunk, like Alice—in this case, to a single letter "P.;" or sometimes, like the White Rabbit, it disappeared altogether. It was a bit disconcerting. I remember saying something to my dad about not being a "Pearson" anymore. He looked me in the eye and said, "You'll always be a "Pearson." It was a reassuring paradox.

Established marital naming patterns are changing. Some American wives now choose to keep their maiden names. In most cultures the maiden name is kept: losing the maiden name is a loss associated primarily with English speaking nations. In continental Europe, the wife traditionally adds her husband's name socially; but her maiden name remains her legal name. For European women, the husband's name is an addition without the loss of the maiden name. Some European women are now choosing not to use their husband's name socially. Spanish speaking countries have complicated surnames, probably due to the Arab influence. The Arabs ruled Spain for almost 800 years—from 711 to 1492. Muslim wives use only the maiden name. Spain had a matrilineal naming system until the 18th century, when it became patrilinear. Hispanics have two surnames—the first is the father's and the second is the mother's. The child takes the father's first surname and the mother's first surname, which means it is only the paternal family names that are maintained. People are addressed by the paternal surname only. In the U.S., Hispanics either drop one name or use a hyphenated last name to avoid confusing Americans, who mistake the first surname for a middle name.

As we have seen, losing the maiden name can be traumatic for women. "The Council of Europe officially enacted legislation requiring member governments to take measures to adopt equality of rights in the transmission of family names in 1978, a measure that was reinforced by the United Nations in 1979. Similar measures were adopted by Germany (1976), Sweden (1982), Denmark (1983) and Spain (1999)."[53] Now the European

Union allows some flexibility in choosing family names and even combining family names for children. Because of the problems with spaces on forms and the formatting of software, the U.S. is still a long way from accepting even hyphenated last names.[54]

– D –
DOUBLE NAMING PATTERNS

The Southern double naming tradition has many sources. "In the mid-to-late 18th century, large groups of Scots and Ulster Scots (later called the Scots-Irish) immigrated and settled in the back country of Appalachia and the Piedmont. They were the largest group of immigrants from the British Isles before the American Revolution."[55] They were predominately Protestant. In Ireland and Scotland, there was a tradition of double names because there were so many common surnames: e.g., Patrick Murphy, whose dad was Joseph could be Patrick Joseph Murphy (or Paddy Joe). As the name in brackets indicates, a double name could include one or more nicknames referring to different generations: nicknames could be inherited.[56] A double naming pattern was also used for girls to distinguish one namesake from another, a tradition Mary Giles describes (p.176).

The Catholic tradition of a given name and a saint's name, chosen at confirmation, also leads to double names like *Mary Anne*. Europe has a tradition of double hyphenated names: the hyphen indicates that the name is to be considered as one name. We now see this usage in the U.S., but it may cause problems for computer databases. Like the Scots-Irish and English, French and German Catholic immigrants had double names.

A double given name allows parents to honor both sides of the family. In another widely used Southern convention, women's names are created from a combination of male and female names with names like *Annie Earl, Bobbie Sue, Jeri Lynn,* and any woman's name followed by *Jo, like Betty Jo or Mary Jo.*[57] One theory is that masculine names like *Bobbie Lynn* were given because "in the not so distant past it was rare for all babies to live to adulthood. If the first born was a daughter, the father's name was often given as well as a popular Southern female name of the day just in case there were no surviving sons to carry the name in future generations."[58] This usage mirrors the French tradition of mixing male and female given names for both boys and girls with names like *Jean-Marie* for a boy and *Marie-Josephine* for a girl. This bi-sexual naming pattern allows children to be named for favorite relatives or saints, despite gender—the gender of the names is simply altered as necessary.

175

African slaves also had a double naming tradition. Slaves listed on registers with both a European and an African name were Christian. Slaves with one African name were animist, and slaves with two African names were of African nobility.[59] Islam appeared as early as the 7th century in the Horn (Ethiopia and Somalia: the north-east) of Africa and the 11th century in western Africa. Christian missionaries reached central Africa by the 15th century: Congo converted to Catholicism in 1491. Portuguese slave traders brought Christianity to western Africa in 1483. Experts can only give educated guesses for the percentages of slaves who were animist, Muslim, or Christian. Most are believed to have been animist, with ten to thirty percent being Muslim, and a smaller number (three to five percent) being Christian. Prof. Donald Wright provides an excellent discussion of slavery and the role of Africans, European Christians, and Muslims in this sad history with his web article, "Slavery in Africa."[60]

Double names present special problems for databases: "in common use, it is quite difficult to make a 'double-barreled' name stick. As we saw in Maryann's essay (p.74), they're a database nightmare. In fact, common double names like *Mary Anne, Mary Beth* and *Mary Jane* don't appear in the Social Security's Top 1000 names list, doubtless because they're all counted under *Mary.*"[61]

· · ·

The Importance of the Middle Name for Identity
Mary Giles
(by her mother Clicker M.)

Mary Giles doesn't really care for the Giles part because it's not highly familiar and people often say it wrong so...she was probably happy to just let her friends and teachers call her Mary. On the other hand, she definitely becomes Mary Giles when she's around her godmother Mary, great aunt Mary, aunt Mary, or 2nd cousin Mary Claire! It helps to distinguish her....

Mary Giles' name provides double bonding with a given name and a surname. Because there are so many Marys in the family, *Giles* establishes her individual identity within the family.

· · ·

Multiple Double Naming Patterns
Ella Frances

I was named for my mother, Ella Frances Baird Brown, who was in turn named after her maternal grandparents, Ella Cannon McCullough and Francis Marion

McCullough. (He was apparently named after the Revolutionary War guerilla, the South Carolina "Swamp Fox.") My mother was always called "Ella Frances," except by her in-laws, who unintentionally annoyed her by calling her "Ella."

An aside about my nickname Tister/Sister: calling a sibling thus is another Southern tradition, and I often address my brother Charles as "Brother." My sons call him "Uncle Brother," and now that he is an Anglican priest, occasionally "Father Brother."

Factoid: Billy Burke, the actress who most famously played the Good Witch of the West in The Wizard of Oz, was christened Mary William, but called Billy Burke after her father, a circus performer.

P.S. Texas must be the center of odd double names. My mother-in-law has female friends named Johnny Marie, Betty Sue, and Lida Lee. (...) My husband's aunt was named "Reube Gene." Friends in her hometown mispronounced it as "Ruby Gene" to feminize it, and she received a draft notice in World War II because of the masculine name. She was named for her father, Dr. Reube Franklin Shaw, who was in turn named for the doctor who delivered him. His brother-in-law was named for the same man. The parents probably did not realize the name was most likely short for Reuben.

Aunt Gene knows no other Reubes besides herself, her father, and her uncle. She has always hated her name and now calls herself just Gene. She feels her parents used the masculine form of Gene out of unfamiliarity with other spellings. All of Aunt Gene's friends in the small East Texas town where she grew up had double names, but none so unusual as hers.

An unusual name, although not a double name, in my family is my father's grandfather, who was named Marquis de LaFayette Brown after the famous Frenchman.

Ella Frances discusses her double name, the same as her mother's, which is based on those of her maternal grandmother and grandfather. At times, she addresses her brother Charles as "Brother." This use of a kinship name has many possible sources. In the past when families were large, kinship names helped to designate "Brother Charles" from "Father Charles" or "Cousin Charles." Numerous religious traditions, past and present, (e.g., the Puritans, the Shakers, and the Mormons) used "Brother" and "Sister" plus the given name to emphasize their spiritual relationship.[62] (One wonders what the psychological implications might be if all of us addressed one another as "Brother" and "Sister" to remind ourselves that we are all one family.) None of these religious traditions has the playfulness that Ella Frances describes, however, with the variety of double names used to describe one person depending on which relatives are in the room and which relationship they

177

want to emphasize: e.g., "Uncle-Brother" and "Father-Brother." The Scots-Irish tee-names, which were often based on family relationships, come closest to the playfulness she describes. These double names are not only amusing but also affectionate: the emphasis on family relationships is in keeping with the strong family ties associated with the South.

She also notes the tradition of masculine names given to women. Besides her name, Ella Frances provides other examples like her husband's aunt, Reube Gene, named for a physician; and Billy Burke, a famous actress, named for her father. We also saw essays in which women had surnames as given names, like Winslow, Mabry, and Tarpley. Both Tarpley and Reube received draft notices.

Her aunt's name "Reube" is very unusual. It's not surprising that people call her "Ruby," a more familiar and, seemingly, more feminine name, although *Ruby* can also be a nickname for *Reuben*.[63] However, if as Ella Frances suggests, the pronunciation was "Reube" (with a silent final syllable) as opposed to "Ruby" (with a voiced final syllable), the doctor's given name is the unusual, but documented surname, Reube. Reube Gene's first name is a surname, and *Gene* is androgynous.

Because of the tradition of the Southern Belle, it seems contradictory that Southern women would receive surnames and male names as part of their given names. As we have seen, when a male heir was not available to carry on a family name, the female could carry it on with a male name or a surname. Surnames were also part of the Protestant Scots-Irish naming tradition. One wonders, however, if the common usage of surnames or male names for given names was not another result of the Civil War, which led to a 25% decline in the white male population.[64] Many of the men who returned were severely injured both physically and psychologically. Women were left alone to take care of homes, farms, and businesses, which led to the formation of very strong women, a phenomenon which James McPherson notes as needing further study in *Battle Cry of Freedom*.

In addition to giving surnames as first names, the Southern tradition of unusual names deserves scrutiny. Strong Southern women are sometimes described as "Steel Magnolias." These strong personalities can be found in Southern women's nicknames: "(...) all Old South. There's Pokey, Beezie, Honey, Lib, Tayloe, Saysee, Lo, Flo, Hope, Georgia, Happy, JinJan, Fair, Muffet, and so many more" as listed by Erin Towers. One can theorize that during and after the Civil War, Southern women joined together to help one another like an extended family while Northern women bonded to start the beginnings of the women's liberation movement. Female bonding for

Southern women was on a family-like basis whereas female bonding in the North took on a more formal aspect out of necessity to deal with a male business world. These radically different worlds help us to understand both the differences in naming traditions for women in the North and South and the differences in ideas concerning femininity. As the U.S. is becoming more homogeneous, these differences are disappearing.

For good reason, the agrarian society of the Old South has often been compared to that of an aristocracy. We tend to forget that Northern society also had an aristocracy, which was based on industry. Social registers were first published in the North in 1886,[65] rather than the South, probably because they weren't as necessary in the much smaller Southern population, which allowed people to know one another's social status without the aid of a directory. The North also has the Boston Brahmins.[66] (Brahmin refers to one of the highest Indian castes—the scholars. Boston has long been a center for education with almost 40 institutions for advanced learning located in the city; so the term "Brahmin" is quite *à propos*.) The U.S. is not totally free from class distinctions, although they remain less important than in most countries.

In comparing the North and the South, the South often serves as the evil twin. We fail to remember that the industrialized age began with horrific exploitation of workers, including children. Many industrial workers were never able to pay their debts to the company store and were, therefore, like indentured servants, who could never earn their freedom. Slowly democratic principles prevailed: the slaves were freed, and workers gradually got better working conditions and pay. However, today the disparity between the rich and the poor is greater than at any time in human history. When the G20 met in Toronto in July 2010, Maude Barlow, internationally known for her work on global water issues, warned that, "The richest 2% own more than half the household wealth in the world. The richest 10% hold 85% of total global assets and the bottom half of humanity owns less than 1% of the wealth in the world. The three richest men in the world have more money than the poorest 48 countries"—to read the rest of her speech, go to http://www.democracynow.org/2010/7/2/maude. Plato warns that anything taken to excess will eventually collapse. The world's great religious teachers also warn repeatedly against excess, which leads us to our next topic.

179

Chapter 19
SOUND

Because we are literally drowning in sound, we have lost our sensitivity to its importance. A silent walk through a forest or along an empty stretch of road immediately restores an appreciation for sound: how empty the world seems without it. Religions understand the importance of sound in ways we have forgotten and, perhaps, never completely understood. Science is now proving what the ancients knew long ago. Genesis describes creation as the result of the sound of God's voice. Science tells us creation started with a big bang. Hindus believe sound is at the center of creation. Many Eastern religions (Hinduism, Buddhism, Sikhism, and Jainism) emphasize the importance of sound. *In Sacred Sound, Sacred Space*, Susan Hale explores the relationship of sound, space, and worship beginning with cave men in Lescaux. For the world's religions and for science, sound is at the heart of creation.

Greek mathematician and philosopher Pythagoras believed all things in the universe are interrelated, including sound; and he believed these relationships could be proven mathematically. Science has now shown Pythagoras' theories to be accurate with the discovery of chemistry's octaves and with the very structure of nature according to the Fibonacci number pattern.[67] Because Pythagoras understood the interrelationship of all things, he realized the importance of sound in astonishing ways. He believed every building has a sympathetic note that will make the building vibrate—a principle validated by acoustics and the study of earthquakes, which is a study of resonance, i.e. sound vibrations.[68] Thinking on a much smaller scale, since sound is vibration, it is also touch. On a personal level, when you speak of being "touched" by someone's words, that is literally true. Emily Dickenson understood the power of the sound of words intuitively when she wrote, "A word is dead/ When it is said/ Some say. / I say it just/Begins to live/That day."

Because Pythagoras believed that everything is interconnected, he believed that every individual has his own tonality[69] and that sound is an important tool in healing. The human voice and music can be powerful healing instruments.[70] Ancient peoples understood this implicitly as we see in the biblical story of David and his harp. Contemporary poetry therapy is another example of the power of sound and healing, which engages the mind to heal the spirit. There are many new books dealing with sound and healing, such as *The Seven Secrets of Sound Healing* (ancient, modern, and futuristic) and *The Healing Power of Sound*. Medicine has recently discovered the use of sound waves to break up kidney stones. Taking this mathematical and acoustic relationship to its ultimate expression, Pythagoras believed in the harmony of the spheres—that the universe created a kind of music as it moved through space. A computer music group at Princeton University has now made a recording of the harmony of the spheres.[71] Sound is a means for connecting to and mirroring the divine essence of creation.

You can use your name as a mantra, a spiritual tool. Chant or repeat your name until you reach sonic disassociation—that is, until your name turns into unintelligible sound. With training, it is then possible to attain a mystic liberation from the self.[72] Paradoxically, the name becomes a means for transcending the self. You can teach yourself the art of the mantra with books like *The Yoga of Sound* and *Following Sound into Silence*, or you can buy CDs like *Chakra Chants* and mantras sung by artists like Devra Premal. In the West, Gregorian chants offer some of the West's most beautiful chanted music. The most popular is *Chant* by the Benedictine monks of Santo Domingo. Chanting is a universal religious tradition, which recenters and re-energizes the soul.

The relationship of chanting and singing to worship reminds us that music has been key to mankind's spiritual and literary quests since our origins. Our first written literature—the epics—are poetry that was sung. The ancient Greek tragedies were also sung. (*Chant* derives from Latin, whereas *song* comes from Germanic and Nordic languages.) Musicality is even key to our speech. Babies learn words better from the singsong speech of their parents (using *real* words) rather than from normal adult speech patterns. Our speech patterns are even musical, with some individuals being more musical than others. Prosody is the study of the musicality of speech.

Neuroscientists at Duke University have now proven Pythagoras' theory of our physical tonality: they "(...) discovered that the tones of the chromatic scale are dominated by the harmonic ratios found in the sound of the human voice."[73] Music is, therefore, a mirror of our own vocalization. When someone hears an idea expressed that they like, they may respond by saying, "That's music to my ears": now we know the idiomatic expression is literally true. This neurobiological discovery also gives new meaning to the idea that music is language without words. Music is a reflection of our most basic human nature—our voice. Although English is not, most of the world's languages are tonal, which further strengthens the bonds between music and language. Drs. Ross, Choi, and Purves also discovered that "(...) 75% of the intervals of female utterances were chromatic compared with 60% in male utterances,"[74] which suggests that female speech is more musical than male speech if judged by tonal variations. Anyone who has overheard female conversation versus male conversation in any public space can attest to this phenomenon: female conversations go up and down in tone more than male conversations.

181

All of this leads us to wonder if male and female names have similar sound variations and mirroring.

We can usually gain insights into ourselves by considering discoveries made in the natural world. To give us some idea of the importance of sound and courtship, a recent study of mosquitoes provides some interesting insights. When mosquitoes are courting, the male will coordinate his sound vibrations to those of the female, creating "Harmonic Convergence."[75] This correlation between sound and courtship is also found in birds and may help explain why some human voices and why some names are more appealing to us than others.

According to the U.S. census,[76] male names are overwhelmingly dominated by names beginning with consonants. There are no male names beginning with a vowel in the top ten names from the 1880s to the 1980s with the exception of *Edward*, which appears as number nine in the 1900s and 1910s, number eight in the 1920s, and number ten in the 1930s. For fifty years, 1940s through the 80s, there are no male names in the top ten beginning with a vowel. One male name beginning with a vowel appears in the 1990s in seventh place—*Andrew*. In the 2000s there is a rapid increase in male names beginning with vowels until there are three in the top ten in 2003, 2005, 2006, and 2007—*Ethan, Anthony, and Andrew*. This increase in male names beginning with a vowel represents a dramatic change from the 1880s through the 1980s. Is there a parallel evolution in women's names?

Five out of the ten most popular women's names start with a vowel in the 1880s, four in the 1890s, three in the 1900s, two in the 1910s, and 1920s. No women's names in the top ten begin with a vowel again for forty years, 1930-1960, until the 1970s. One wonders why the top ten most popular women's names should be missing names beginning with vowels for such a long time—the sexual revolution of the twenties, the war years, the feminist desire to project a stronger image? In the 1970s we find two women's names beginning with vowels in the top ten, then three with vowels in the 1980s and 1990s, increasing to a surprising seven in 2003–2005, holding at six from 2006–2009. This is a dramatic increase in female names beginning with a vowel—more than at any time since the census was first taken in the 1880s. In addition, from 2002 to 2009, there is simultaneously a dramatic increase in the number of women's names ending in -*a*. Women's names ending in -*a* have been steadily increasing in number in the U.S. since the beginning of the 21st century with half or more of the top ten names ending with –*a* since 2007. The only decade with more was that of the 1960s, which had seven. Not surprisingly, the names are taking on more of a Hispanic flavor with names like *Mia, Ava, Sophia, Olivia*, and *Isabella* as opposed to *Samantha, Hannah, Sarah*, or *Emma*. It appears that the Hispanic influence may be feminizing women's names after the repercussions of the feminist movement on women's names, which led to a desire to avoid names considered to be dated or stereotypical.

In 2009, *Elizabeth* and a variant, *Isabella*, appear twice in the top ten names. For forty years (1880s–1910) *Mary* was so popular, two of the top ten names were either Mary or a variation of Mary—*Minnie* or *Marie*. This phenomenon occurs one more time in the 1960s with the names *Debra* and *Deborah*. In comparing this doubling, it is interesting to note that Marie has French origins whereas Isabella is undoubtedly due to Hispanic influence. Isabella suggests the Hispanic population will be playing an increasing role in influencing American names since it is estimated that 30% of the U.S. population will be Hispanic by 2050 according to the U.S. census bureau. Isabella represents the first time since the U.S. census started in the 1880s that the number one name is not either of English or Germanic origins, but a result of the Hispanic influence. The ongoing bilingual development in America could help Americans overcome their language limitations: exposure to Spanish will make it easier to learn not only the other romance languages, but languages in general.

The reappearance of female names beginning with a vowel in the 1970s coincides with the appearance of androgynous names. The first androgynous names, *Kimberly* and *Tracy*, softened a bit by their *y* endings, appear in the top ten in the 70s. Three out of the top ten names are androgynous from 2000 to 2004—*Madison, Ashley,* and *Alexis*—dropping to one, *Madison,* by 2006. The increase in female names beginning with vowels serves as a counterweight to the increasing use of androgynous names. Two of the most popular androgynous names begin with a vowel, and one ends with a *y,* which helps to temper them. If androgynous names disappear from the top ten, it may suggest parents feel a social balancing of the sexes has taken place and androgynous names are no longer felt to be advantageous for job applications.

The rapid increase in names beginning with vowel sounds is mirrored in both male and female names in the 2000s, which is an intriguing "harmonic convergence"—considering names beginning with vowels are almost totally absent from the top ten men's names for a century (1880s–1980s). There are none in the top ten for men for fifty years straight (1940s–1980s), just as there are none for women in the top ten for forty years straight (1930s–1960s). These sound patterns suggest that men's names adjust to women's names with a bit of a lag.

There is also a dramatic increase in the popularity of names beginning with a vowel for both men and women. Why? Their resurgence is long overdue and may indicate a new subconscious sensitivity to the sound of names—the lack of a need for strong sounding names: a gentler sense of self and the projection of that self with an initial vowel as opposed to consonants. Although *Ethan*, *Andrew*, and *Anthony* begin with vowels, they have powerful meanings. Ethan and Andrew are associated with the Bible and Anthony with Roman history. Despite three androgynous names for women in the 2000s, the other top ten names—*Emily, Emma, Hannah, Sarah, Samantha, Abigail, Elizabeth,* and *Isabella* could be considered standard, even old-fashioned names.

Women's names beginning with *M* are subliminally associated with mother.[77] They also undergo an interesting evolution. From the 1880s through the 1910s, *M* names increase in popularity until there are four in the top ten—*Mary, Margaret, Mildred,* and *Marie.* Even in the 1930s, when all female names beginning with vowels are dropped, there are still two women's names beginning with *M—Mary* and *Margaret.* By the 1940s there is only one—*Mary. Mary* is the most popular woman's name from 1880s through the 1960s (with a drop to second place in the 1950s.) The name is unavoidably associated with the Virgin Mary, who is universally associated with the image of a beautiful young woman. By the 1970s, *Mary* drops to ninth place and is then no longer found in the top ten names. In 2007, *Mary* is ranked at #93, still in the top one hundred, but by 2009, *Mary* is #102, a constant and dramatic decline, which reflects both a decline in religiosity and a desire to abandon female stereotypes. With the Hispanic influence, *Mary* will probably reappear and regain status as *Maria.*

Although women's names beginning with vowels were completely dropped from the top ten for forty years (1930s–1960s), there has always been a woman's name beginning with an *M* in the top ten since the U.S. census has kept records beginning in 1880 except for the 1990s. After that gap with no *M* names, there is a surprising change in that the *M* name in the top ten in the 2000s is *Madison*, an androgynous name, which ranks first, second, third, and fifth in the 2000s through 2009 (the last available census before publication). This shift to a single androgynous *M* name represents a dramatic cultural change for women's *M* names, although *Madison* retains a subliminal feminine link with its initial syllable, *Ma.* A male name beginning with an *M* does not appear in the top ten from 1880 until the 1950s when *Michael* appears. *Michael* stays in the top ten from the 1950s through 2007. *Matthew* joins *Michael* in the 1970s and the pair remains in the top ten through 2007. It is interesting to observe that as *M* names in the top ten were disappearing for women, they were appearing for men.

Overall, there is a historical movement in the U.S. towards longer names in both sexes in the top ten names. There are more one-syllable male names in the top ten in the 1880s than two- or three-syllable names. Male names are evenly split between one- and two-syllable names from the 1890s through 1920s. From the 1930s through 2008 (78 years), two-syllable male names dominate in the top ten, but beginning in 1970, one three-syllable male name appears, then two (1980s–1990s), and finally three in the top ten from 2001- 2007 (with a momentary drop to two in 2003 and 2004). In 2008, there are again three names with three syllables; and for the first time there is a four-syllable male name—Alexander—in the top ten. In 2009, two-syllable names make a slight gain, which serves to balance the trend towards longer names and suggests the trend towards longer names maybe slowing. We may nostalgically return to the shorter names found in the early days of the census when life was simpler with a slower pace; internet communication shortens names faster than nostalgia, however.

From the 1880s–1970s, two-syllable female names dominate (with the exception of the 1930s). Beginning in the 1900s, three-syllable female names become more and more common (with the exception of the 1940s—the war years). From the 1980s through 2007, three- and four-syllable female names dominate. Historically, women tend to have longer names than men. Women's names lead men's names by one syllable in the trend towards longer names. As women's names have gotten longer, men's names have slowly followed suit: there is a tendency towards "harmonic convergence" in men and women's names. The changes in the sound of our names provide subtle indications of social change. They also indicate that sound still plays a more important role in our identity than we consciously realize.

– A –
NAMES PICKED JUST FOR SOUND

• • •

We Liked the Sound of It
Carol Armstrong

In discussing the choice of her daughter's name, Carol wrote, *"It's not a family name, but we liked the sound of it."*

If notes are the language of music, then letters are the music of names. Carol picks a name based purely on the sound, rather than on family tradition. Literary references at the end of the book describe the evocative importance of the sound of a name.

. . .

It Sounded Beautiful to Us
Renée Cochrane Edson

By the way, my daughter's name is "Kyra" which actually morphed from "Kayla," "Kendra," and "Kara," while I was in labor and discussing names with my husband that sounded beautiful to us—and it stuck.

In picking her name, Renée's parents gave her not only a French name, but also a given name that visually mirrors her maiden name with the *r, n,* and the *e*.

In considering their daughter's name, Renée and her husband exhibit great sensitivity to aural nuances. *Kyra* and *Edson* are both iambs: the names are perfectly balanced aurally.

The visual pattern of names reminds us that we distinguish names by sight and by sound, by the written and spoken word, which leads us to consider the signature as a reflection of the self. Penmanship in Europe is considered more of an art than it is here in the U.S. At a certain point in history, the signature was, indeed, "a measure of the man" as evidenced by the ornate signatures of European aristocracy. This aristocratic influence may be one of the reasons autography was and continues to be so much more important in Europe than it is in the U.S. With computers, the art of developing beautiful handwriting as an artistic expression of the self is disappearing: people are writing less and less.

Graphology is the analysis of character based on handwriting. You can read an analysis of the handwriting of the famous and see what traits you may share with them at *Digg—Handwriting Analysis of Famous People* (http://digg.com/celebrity/Handwriting_Analysis_of_Famous_People) and learn a bit about the basics of graphology at the same site under "Career Test Lessons"—which will allow you to analyze your own handwriting and see if you agree, disagree, or make some discoveries about yourself.

The *New York Times* provides a quick lesson to help deteriorating American orthography with *Op-Art: The Write Stuff* by Inga DuBay and Barbara Getty (9/8/2009) at http://www.nytimes.com/interactive/2009/09/04/opinion/20090908_opart.html. If you want something a bit more challenging, try *Learn Calligraphy* at http://cmcgavren.home.sprynet.com/chiselpt.html. If you have some old family letters or signatures in old books, they can be a wonderful way to learn beautiful lettering from ancestors who were writing when school children learned an elegant script. Tracing over an ancestor's writing will allow you to experience how they moved as they wrote and may even provide a glimpse into their personality.

– B –
SOUND PATTERNS

– 1 –
Names Linked by the First Syllable

• • •

Paula Worth

My first name is Paula. It is a family name. I am named after my maternal grandmother, Pauline. My aunt is Paulette. I named my daughter Molly Pauline to continue the family name, but she goes by Molly.

• • •

Karen Lee

My mother's name was Kathryn. I was told my mom longed for a female child after the birth of my two older brothers. Her mother, in turn, was Kate; Kathryn and Karen are both forms of Kate. My mother felt she wanted to continue this family tradition and was thrilled to name me, her first daughter, Karen.

My mother and I have been connected all our lives by the similarity of our names. She has always gone by "Katie," which is even closer to the name "Karen" than "Kathryn" is. She often told me that she wanted to have a granddaughter named Kathleen; and I, no stranger to fantasies myself, dreamed of someday having a daughter of my own, a Katelyn, Caitlyn or Kaitlin to carry on the related names. (I chose the name many years before it too became so commonplace.) Now, unfortunately, it is too late. I am 50, my husband died this past April, and I have no children. Sometimes, I dream of adoption.

– 2 –
Names Linked by the Last Syllable

• • •

Roman Names
Lydia Esquerdo Varaona

Lydia means beauty and beloved. Julia means soft haired, youthful, gentle; Emilia means eager, friendly, and soft. Yes, my parents are obviously fond of Roman names.

The sounds of names provide clues to ethnic origins, which do not necessarily reflect that of the namesake. Some examples: Latin names ending with *-a* (e.g., *Julia*), Italian names with *-ella* or *-etta* (*Antoinetta, Giulietta*), French names with *-ette* and *-ine* (*Juliette, Christine*), Spanish names in *-ita (Julieta, Anita)*, Greek in *-andra (Alexandra)*, Indian names in *-enda (Narenda)*.[78] *Julia* was originally a Roman name, the feminine form of *Julius*. It was adapted and modified by different cultures. Tracing the history of your name will lead across continents, through diverse cultures and different religions.

– 3 –
Linking Twins' Names with Sound

• • •

Charlie Toledo

My first name is Charlene. I'm a second to a twin brother Charles. My mother was going to name us Jess & Jessica after my father's anglicized forename Jess, from the Hispanic Jesus. I don't know why she chose Charles & Charlene.

• • •

Julia Elaine

My name is Julia Elaine. I go by Julie and I was named from my paternal grandfather Julius. My twin brother's name is William Julius. He was named for the maternal and paternal grandfathers.

When linking twins' names by sound, if the twins are a boy and a girl, the girl has a feminized male name as illustrated by Charlene and Julia. Do feminized male names help make girls more assertive?

– 4 –
One-Syllable Names

• • •

Like Dogs?
Amy Rae Gaston

My father and mother wanted a short name for the first name as they said it would be easier to call my sister and me. (…) Looking back, it was as if we were dogs… typical dog names are quick –"Jack", "Bud", etc.

⋯

An Explosion About to Happen
Fay Sunshine

I have an old-fashioned name, Fay, and I've always disliked it. My parents were going to name me Julia or Elizabeth (which is my middle name), but my father feared there were too many derivatives for these names that he didn't like or didn't intend (Betsy, Liza, Lizzie, etc. for Elizabeth and Julie for Julia, I guess). I didn't mind so much that it was unusual, and I kind of liked that they left off the "e" at the end since they felt it was extraneous, but I objected, and still object, to the hard sound of "F" at the beginning. It has always sounded masculine and awkward to me, like an explosion is about to happen. And the name ends so quickly, there's nothing but the hard "F" and long "a" sound. It didn't help when they told me Fay means "fairy" in French, "so it must be feminine." (I never identified with Tinkerbelle.) I knew that if I were a boy, they would have named me Charles, and called me Chip, which sounded like a fine butch name for a boy. Couldn't they have applied the same logic to naming a girl?

In junior high and high school, people nicknamed me "Faye Wray," after the actress in the original King Kong movie because I screamed a lot. That was okay, but I hated the other nickname, "Fay-Baby," since it was conferred on me by the fast crowd I sometimes ran with as an indication of my reluctance to engage in their more risky behaviors. I think it began when my mom packed some leftovers in my lunch bag using a baby food jar (duh!).

One time I was taking a ski lesson in frigid weather on the slopes of Vermont and the instructor asked us to introduce ourselves. In the cold and wind, he thought I said "Fang!" and I think that sums up my feelings about the lack of beauty and grace the sound of my name evokes. Of course, my dislike for my name has mellowed with age and I would never consider changing it. I loved my parents and I know they named me with love in their hearts, I just wish they'd gone with their first instinct.

My husband's last name is Sunshine, and though I often use Fay Sunshine in social or school situations, I have never officially changed it. Since everyone comments on our last name, I was careful to name my boys very established, obviously male names--Benjamin Wheeler Sunshine and Daniel Wheeler Sunshine. Before we named them, I practiced saying their names as if they were television anchors, "This is Ben Sunshine, signing off from New York," for example. Actually, I've found that Fay Sunshine rolls off the tongue a little better than Fay Wheeler, so I ended up using it more than I originally intended, and I think the novelty of Sunshine takes the focus off Fay.

My father was from old-time Protestant Midwestern stock and my mother was second generation Italian-American (Italian was her first language) from Kennett Square, PA. Though proud of her heritage, I think naming her daughters Laura and Fay was part of her desire to assimilate.

My husband asked me how my name has affected my life and I thought, well, I DO consider my name to be one of my faults, like stringy hair and flat feet, so I guess it's made me the tiniest bit more insecure. And yes, if my name were Julia, I'd feel a little bit better about myself, which is strange to admit since I am a pretty secure person.

—————

Fay's feelings about the sound of her married name remind us that many women may recall writing their name and their sweetheart's name on a sheet of paper, saying the names, and even writing their future married name to see how it looks. This exercise is part of adapting to the new name the bride will acquire. As we saw earlier, because sound is vibration, it is also touch. Shakespeare captures young lovers' fascination with the beloved's name in *Romeo and Juliet* with their incessant repetition of each other's names: e.g., "Oh Romeo, Romeo! Wherefore art thou Romeo?"

Ann (p.61), Amy, and Fay all express some dissatisfaction with their short names. One-syllable names do not have true diminutives. Ann makes this clear when she maintains *Annie* is a nickname for *Anne* but not *Ann*. Amy and Fay do not have nicknames. Ann, Amy, and Fay all find the brevity of their names demeaning in some way. Fay's description of the masculine, explosive sound of her name and Amy's assertion that one-syllable names are "short" and "quick" like dogs' names highlight the subliminal power of the sound of names.

– 5 –
Three-Syllable Double Names

• • •

That Three-Syllable Lilt
Sue Martin

"Linda Sue" has that two-name, three-syllable lilt that says I'm from the South (...).

—————

Many popular Southern double names have three syllables, like *Linda Sue, Betty Jean,* or *Rita Mae.*[79] Sue Martin describes this three-syllable beat as a "lilt." A list of Southern girls' double names reveals that many have three beats, which can be scanned either as an *amphimacer* (long/short/long) or as an *anapest,* if spoken quickly (short/short/long). Sue's description of these double names as "a three-syllable lilt" is perfect because a "lilt" is defined as a rhythmic swing or cadence,[80] a light, happy tune or song.[81] The amphimacer is common in folk poetry, proverbs, tags, slogans, and adages because of its lively beat.[82] The anapest is described as a "rolling" beat. It is used frequently in limericks and light verse like Clement Moore's *The Night Before Christmas* and T.S. Elliot's *Book of Practical Cats*.[83]

Considering their association with light verse, limericks, and songs,[84] these three-syllable beats are inherently light-hearted and affect us subconsciously in a very different way than names with longer or weightier beats. Both the amphimacer and the anapest are spirited poetic meters that were used for songs by the Greeks. The anapest was extremely popular in 19th century European lyric poetry[85] when many European immigrants were coming into the U.S. Because of cultural changes, negative stereotypes, and even subconscious associations with advertising jingles, the three-meter beat of Southern names is no longer as appealing to some as it once was.

The three-syllable beat of Southern names leads to a consideration of the Southern accent. The Southern accent is the result of a fusion of West Country English (found in the south of England), Irish, Scottish, and French.[86] Black Americans also contributed to the Southern accent just as they contributed to Southern cooking, music, and worship. Is there another explanation for our Southern accent besides the ethnic mixing of accents? Many nations have southern accents. The French in the south of France, the Italian in the south of Italy, and even the German in the south of Germany are all slower, softer, more melodic, than the accents found in the north. Why? Are southern regions universally more agrarian? Is there a universal sensitivity to the warmth of the sun, the seasons and nature in "the South," in whatever country it may be? Will southern accents survive in the future?

International stereotypes associated with Southern accents continue despite changing demographics and serve, like color, as another example of how we evaluate people quickly and superficially. Lost accents, like lost languages, reflect the loss of a different perception of life. As the world continues to unify around fewer languages and fewer accents, we will find fewer ways of discriminating against one another and fewer ways of contemplating and hearing the world.

– C –
THE MULTICULTURAL DIMENSION OF SOUND

• • •

International Links
Violette Yacoubian

My name is Violette. I was named after my mother's youngest sister: she was number six. Lebanon was under French mandate, so it was very common to have a French name specifically among the Christian community. My grandfather who did not speak French could not pronounce my name for in Arabic there is no "V", it could be "B" instead. That did not bother me. I did not like it when kids teased me by singing mockingly a tune from the Opera "La Traviata". I survived that too. Finally my name for friends and family shrunk to "Viol" or "Viul." When I moved to the United States my name was pronounced Violet. I insisted that it really is Violette I prefer not to change the spelling, thus the pronunciation. Now I am happy because that is my name, and new acquaintances find it a pretty name.

• • •

Norwegian Ties
Rondi Levin

When I was born, my mom wanted her best friend, Rondi O'Gara, to be my godmother. Back then, a godparent needed to be Catholic; and while I am not sure what religion Rondi was, I know she wasn't Catholic. So Mom gave me Rondi's name instead which I think was a much better choice!

Rondi's mother was Norwegian; and the spelling was originally "Randi" with an umlaut over the "a"—turning the vowel into an "o" sound. When she came to the States, everyone started calling her daughter "Randi" which she hated, so she changed the spelling of the name to "Rondi."

I would say that at least 50% of the time, people ask me about my name; and about 25% of the time, they ask what it is short for, or if my "real" name is Rhonda, Rhoda, or Randy. On the few occasions I have met a person of Norwegian descent, they smile and tell me they are pleased that someone here in the States has my name. It is a fairly common name in Norway. And caused quite a stir with the teenagers of our friends from the UK when they first met me. They thought it a riot that people in the U.S. named their kids "Randi/Randy"—no wonder Rondi's mom wanted to change the spelling and I'm grateful that she did....

• • •

Wonder Bread World
Renée Cochrane Wilson

(My name)… was too "worldly" sounding in a "Wonder Bread" world.

• • •

Longing
Evelyn Torton Beck

But what I have really missed all these years, is the sound of Evi in German, where the E is neither clipped nor drawn out, but softly iterated in a sound that does not exist in English. The sound of my name before we were cast out.

– D –
SOUND AND SENSITIVITY

Essayists describe both their own sensitivity and that of others to the sound of their names.

• • •

Evocations
Vera Constance Chadwick Sky

Recently I telephoned a new acquaintance named Constance and hearing myself saying, "Connie, this is Vera" evoked a vision of my father. Occasionally I will overhear a stranger on the street speaking in his soft baritone, and viscerally, I'm Connie again!

Vera describes the power of the sound of her nickname to reconnect her with her childhood just as Evelyn, Vera, and Sophy (pp.33–34) do.

• • •

A Rose by Any Other Name Is Not a Rose
Deborah Field Washburn

At around age 45, when beginning a new job, I reclaimed my full name, Deborah. I am just as fussy about the spelling as when I was Debbie. It's extremely annoying when people spell my name D-e- B –r-a. To me, that's another name altogether, but apparently most people can't hear the difference in pronunciation.

Lately I've been called Barbara (or possibly Barbra): often, even by those who should know better. I have nothing against people named Barbara, but I am not a Barbara. A rose by any other name is not a rose. Call me Deborah, and spell it right.

According to audiologists, initial consonants become more and more difficult to distinguish as people age.[87] Confusing *Deborah* with *Barbara* could be a problem with older individuals. Since Deborah does not indicate the confusion is limited to older folks, we have to assume people are not listening or they assume it is all right to use a nickname. As we have seen, nicknames are not always acceptable.

One should assume the individual introduces herself with the name she wants used. If we say the name of the person we have just met, it helps us remember it, assures that we have heard the name correctly, and establishes a bond, which is not created if the name is not acknowledged by being spoken because sound is touch.

People Mispronounce My Name
Laura
(Gen. Y)

My name is Laura N___. I am of mostly Irish and German heritage. I grew up and live in Tennessee. My mother named me Laura because she has loved the name ever since she was young and could not wait to name her child Laura if she ever had a little girl. Laura is derived from the flower Laurel. The name is Latin although the pronunciation has altered from the original, being "lou" – as in loud and – "ra" as in the Egyptian sun god, with the "r" being trilled. My name is pronounced the modern way. It drives me crazy when people mispronounce my name. They will say "Lora" instead of "Laura" which gives it a somewhat unflattering sound. I go and have always gone by Laura and not any another name. I have had a few nicknames such as Laura Belle or a combination of my first and middle name: Laura Lizzi. I don't know an excruciating number of people named Laura although this name is not rare. Laura is a name that I think sounds classic, calm, ladylike, and sweet. All the other Lauras I have met could be described by these words. My name suits me perfectly. I feel like a Laura. I look like a Laura. I honestly could not imagine a name that fits me better.

One of our youngest essayists, Laura has discovered her name tribe. Because of her youth, she is more sensitive to sound than adults, who gradually learn to block out sound—i.e., not to hear—because of our noisy world; whereas young people are still carefully listening. Pronunciation is key to her sensibility of who she is.

– E –
SOUND AND ADAPTABILITY

. . .

A Tool
Karen Betaque

I don't have a middle name, which is just as well. The two names I got were trouble enough. My parents chose my first name when I turned out not to be the Roger they expected. They found it in a tiny leather bound book of names that my grandparents brought with them when they emigrated from Sweden. I became Karen with the Swedish pronunciation, a soft "a" (as in alms, art, calm). This sound is made obvious in Swedish with an umlaut over the "a." However, umlauts failed to emigrate along with my Swedish kin so my first name stands naked and vulnerable to dominant American assumptions that I am a Karen with a hard "a" (like air and dare).

Every September of my California childhood, a teacher called the roll on the first day of school in crisp, staccato tones designed to establish authority over the class and every situation in it. Before she got far she came across my last name, Betaque. The "que" in Betaque stopped most people and annoyed teachers in particular as it distracted from an otherwise efficient commencement of class. "Karen, how do you pronounce your last name?" She tossed the hard "a" in Karen across the room with an impatient tone.

Unfailingly, I had to correct the mistaken assumption that I was the usual sort of Karen by gathering courage to tell the newest authority figure in my life that she had made a mistake. My face reddened, my hands got sweaty and my stomach fluttered as I corrected her pronunciation of my first name. I felt apologetic for causing a distraction from the more important business at hand. But I had to plunge ahead into the additional explanation about how she should attack the queer spelling of my last name. The phonetic of Betaque is close to "bettack" based on its French-Huguenot source. Generally failed attempts say beta-queue or bet-teek. I was just too shy a young girl in kindergarten for a name with so much responsibility. Still, even as a five-year-old, I knew that my station in the playground pecking order would be at risk if I failed to summon the pluck to stand up for my own name; so I spoke out. Being the first student to correct a new teacher was uncomfortable; but each year, I got better at covering my embarrassment. Then at some point in my young adulthood, it became useful to interrupt the flow of adult business for the purpose of putting pronunciation of my name to rights. The uniqueness of my name allowed me to measure the character of the people I met.

Now I introduce myself, pronouncing my name slowly and distinctly; then I listen. Some people ignore what I say or proceed to correct me with the more common pronunciation of Karen. I find these are the people who stick with their preconceived views on just about everything. Others, however, make an immediate note of the unique pronunciation and proceed to use it carefully. They express curiosity about the origin of my names. These people are open to discovering who I am, what I think, what I know. These are people I want in my life. The burden of my childhood has become a tool.

Karen has discovered that people who make an effort to adapt to new pronunciation of a name are more likely to be open to new ideas. She can judge the adaptability of people, and even their creativity, by how they react or fail to react to the sound of her name.

Because America was primarily monolingual until recently, Americans do not seem to have the ability to hear and articulate different sounds like Europeans and other cultures with multiple languages. The ability to learn new languages is greatest during childhood. Generally, American schools start

195

teaching foreign languages too late: language specialists agree that foreign languages need to be taught as early as possible, beginning from birth within the family and with day care or nursery school, then kindergarten, continuing through elementary school, with a second (or third) language started in middle school. Experts now suggest that each adult at home speak only one language to the child to avoid confusion. If languages and speakers are constantly mixed, children may be slower to speak. They will overcome this momentary glitch, however; and learning a second language is a benefit in many different ways.

– F –
SUBLIMINAL HEARING:
SUBCONSCIOUS ASSOCIATIONS

A name is never simply a sound. The following essayists discuss subtle associations with family, friends, literature, history, music, and culture. These associations float in and out of our consciousness. The sound of a name evokes hidden emotions, which color how names affect us. Often, we may not even realize how these associations affect us.

• • •

Subconsciously
Rosalie Lepeltier

I love my name "Rosalie." I know it means "little Rose," and it is a French name. My mother gave me her first name—Hazel—as a real first name, but I've always been "Rosalie"—my middle name. No nicknames have ever supplanted it although I have variously been called "Rosa," "Rosie," "Mamma Rose." Perhaps it subconsciously lured me to France, connected me with a Frenchman, and subsequently added "Lepeletier" as a last name. Now, even though I am divorced, I would never give up the sweet sound of Rosalie Lepeletier—also because I have been the mother of seven children who ported the name "Lepeletier." "Rosalie" is my identity. To me it is musical and beautiful—two attributes I highly value—and I am thankful that my mother saw me as "a little rose."

• • •

Eve and Evelyne
Yvonne Rollins

I always heard her name as three distinct syllables, "E-ve-lyne." As a child, it was music to my ears. Of course, the name invoked Eve, the mother of all of us. I thought the name was almost too beautiful for my little cousin, who was more tomboy than gracious Eve. As far as I was concerned, "Evelyne" should be some sort of angel, very romantic—just the opposite of my cousin.

It was a name I liked.

———

Yvonne describes the powerful associations even part of a name can carry with it. As a child, *Evelyne* and *Eve* are united in her mind by their sound. (The French pronunciation emphasizes the connection more than the English.) She describes her childhood shock upon discovering that her cousin does not match her expectations for the name, which is yet another example of how children come to understand the complex aspects of names and identity discussed earlier. Yvonne observes how we are primed by sound. Most people might hear the *Eve-lyne* without being conscious of associations to *Eve*; but upon seeing the written name, the subconscious associations are unavoidable.

• • •

Maggy Was Different
Yvonne Rollins

The name seemed mysterious to me growing up. It was derived from "Marguerite" but nobody ever mentioned that to us. I think my uncle chose the name because he was romantic, a big fan of Lamartine and all the Anglomania prevalent at that time. Maggy was a truly exotic name in Auvergne where I grew up. And Maggy was not like all the other children: she was a dreamer, sometimes withdrawn. She lived in her own world. I think she liked her name.

———

As an adult, Yvonne discovers that *Maggy* becomes a key to understanding her uncle. Names are tools that can help us understand both others and ourselves in surprising ways.

• • •

Not Another Josette!
Yvonne Rollins

My uncle's first wife was so disliked in the family that when I meet any Josettes, even to this day, I momentarily flinch.

———

Fortunately, Yvonne is aware of her negative associations to the name *Josette*. We may not always be aware of our negative stereotypes, or we may not be able to overcome them. Yvonne's essay is a humorous reminder of the subconscious power of prejudice—associations that are deeply embedded in our psyche.

Sound is at the very essence of the creation of the universe and our own personal sense of identity. Women discuss pure sound, sound patterns, and the cultural, ethnic, and psychological dimensions of the sound of names. Of all the name issues women discuss, sound is one of the most intuitive because it is one of our five senses.

Throughout the essays, women describe the varied emotions the sound of a name can elicit with words like *pleasure, music, ugly, hard, explosion, girly, cutsie, snotty, silly, childish, trendy, cool, diminutive, awkwardly feminine,* or *masculine.* The sound of a name evokes specific emotions. Elvira hears "the sound of love" in her name (pp.113–116). After her aunt's death, Helen Jo feels her name sounds "like an old woman's name" (pp.123–124). Renée realizes that when she was growing up her name was too "worldly" for a "Wonder Bread world" (p.192). Her use of *w* words to describe her sense of isolation is intriguing because French does not have native words beginning with *w.* Sheila remembers wanting "to sound like everyone else" (p.89).

Elvira Kituyi, Sophy (pp.32–34), and Evelyn (p.192) are nostalgic for the way their names were pronounced when they were children. Elizabeth identifies with the sound of her new name as who she is (p.101). Sound touches the heartstrings, the innermost core of who we feel we are. Sound rekindles memories. Sensitivity to sound can even be a measure of an individual's adaptability, creativity, and age.

Rosalie feels the sound of her name helped shape her destiny, and Fay believes the sound of her name increased her sense of insecurity. Names are never simply sound. When we meet someone, our subconscious associations to the name may affect how we feel about her. If you don't understand your reaction to someone upon first meeting them, consider other people you have known with that name and your associations to it.

Chapter 20
SPELLING

– A –
CULTURAL TIES

• • •

Emilie Kimball

Currently there are four Emilys living in my hall at Wesleyan so it is a great relief that my name is spelled differently from the other three girls. Although when you type my name in a Word document it underlines my name in red indicating it is spelled wrong, having my name spelled differently has always been nice. If anyone ever needs to write my name for anything I will mention the fact that it's spelled differently and that always serves as an exciting conversation—it's the French way of spelling and I was named after my grandmother who also spells her name this way.

Growing up I always loved having a cool name. I love spending time with my Grandmother who I'm named after, and I love telling people I am named after her. Every time the uniqueness of my name is brought up, I am reminded of the wonderful memories I have and of the memories to come while sharing time with my Grandmother. We remain very close—I spend my entire summers with my grandparents and we get together for New Years as well. The spelling isn't too out of the ordinary from Emily so most people when they see it during roll call, etc. won't pronounce my name wrong.

• • •

A Spelling Change
Patti G.

I was born and raised in Italy and given the birth name "Patrizia." After moving to America, I changed the "z" to a "c," but go by the nickname "Patti."

My parents chose the name simply because they liked it as it was a fairly common Italian name. I never thought about whether my name suits me. I do not like to be called "Pat" nor do I like my nickname spelled with a "y."

Spelling may reflect ethnicity and culture. If the spelling is not Americanized, it probably represents the individual's desire to maintain family ties. One can understand why Patti would prefer the spelling ending with an *-i* as opposed to a *-y*: the *-i* is more Italian.

– B –
UNIQUE SPELLING:
CREATING A PERSONAL IDENTITY

• • •

I Like the Unique Spelling
Cathy Trauernicht

My first name is Catharine (spelled with two "a's" as you can see). I was named after my great aunt Catharine Wallace Parrish on my mother's side. I have many friends my age who are named Catherine/ Katherine/ Kathryn: perhaps the name was popular in the '50s. Although I've always liked Catharine and the unique spelling, I go by Cathy.

Spelling variations establish subgroups within the name. Originally variations in spelling would have provided some clues as to heritage, but this is now less and less true.

• • •

Distinctively Mine
Cristy West

My first name is Cristy. That is spelled C-R– I –S-T-Y. Okay, so I know you probably put in an "h" after the C, right? Everyone does that. I am resigned to people correcting me on the spelling of my own name. It is not short for anything, like Christine. It was in fact a family name of my paternal grandmother, whom I never knew. Her name was Mary Cristy and I understand there are Cristy relatives out in the Midwest somewhere but I have never met them.

I have to admit I have longed for an "ordinary" name like Jane or Mary. I have also relished the distinctiveness of my name. A tomboy when young, I loved to be mistaken as a boy and called "Cris." My brother was given the similarly androgynous name of Robin--short for Robinson--in this case a family name on my mother's side.

My last name is West. My parents didn't give me a middle name since they figured I'd be marrying anyway and therefore taking on a different family name. Marriage was held up as the ultimate goal of my life. In fact I had two short stints at marriage and in both cases took on the names of my husbands, only to revert to West. West is a fairly ordinary, straightforward name and I like it for that. I associate it with wide-open spaces of the American West, which I'm drawn to, and the spirit of exploration. I guess for me the West has always been a bit "wild" and my eastern origins by contrast relatively subdued. Yet I'm also aware that in some systems the West can call up a sense of rootedness in the past just as the east calls up new beginnings. If I ever were to remarry, I would never change my name again. It is also perhaps worth mentioning that my parents – may their souls rest in peace – were avid Anglophiles, looking to England and especially the English upper classes for inspiration. But for me, in claiming myself as a West, I feel decidedly American – and post-women's lib at that. I think this is all to do with where the sun rises and sets. An interesting paradox! In writing the essay, I suddenly saw how, in the choice of first names, my parents had subtly tied in both my brother and myself to a sense of family and past generations.

In the course of my lifetime I have evolved into the artist I am still becoming. As a young girl, I used to sign my paintings just "Cristy" since my last name seemed so tentative and, like me, unsure of itself. But I have settled on "C West" for a signature. The simplicity of the signature is in contrast to the freedom and spontaneity I strive for in my working process.

I was born way before my name – or, at least other spellings of it – Christie, Kristi, Krista etc. – came into fashion. One of the advantages of the peculiar spelling of my name is that no one else tries to lay claim to it as their Internet domain name. You can visit my website at http://www.cristywest.com. That's c–r– I –s–t–y–w– E –s–t – just ten letters. It's a name I've learned to live with, for better or worse, distinctively mine.

– C –
FASHION TRENDS

• • •
i for *y*
Judith Gottlieb Herman

I always spelled my "Judy" with a "y" until one day at Thomas Williams Junior High, I was in a class with three other Judis, and I was the only one that spelled it with a "y." So wanting to be part of the crowd, I became Judi with an "i" for a short period of time. I am back to "y."

• • •
ie for *y*
Deborah Field Washburn

I didn't know any other Deborahs until about fifth grade, at which time I became "Debbie" to distinguish myself from the two "Debbys" in my class. People didn't use full names much in the early Fifties....

y not *i?*
Marcy Markowitz

I'm the third daughter in the family. I am 12 and 14 years younger than my sisters Caryn and Linda. My mother wanted to name me Martha, but my sisters thought it was old-fashioned and they picked Marci instead.

When I was two years old, I was often in the hospital with high fevers and people thought I was a boy (I never quite understood this) so they changed the spelling on my birth certificate to Marcy. My sister Linda named her fourth child Martha—Marcy Joseph Markowitz.

• • •

i not *y?*
Randi Finger

Randy Finger was the way my name had been spelled, but I changed it informally for my business cards so that I would be identifiable as a woman.

Spelling can help retain cultural ties. Spelling changes allow the individual to either fit in or stand apart. Marcy and Randi note the confusion about gender associated with the spelling of their names. Ironically, they find opposite solutions. The *-ie, -i,* and *-y* endings for women's names undergo constant fashion shifts. Originally *-ie* endings were French and *-y* endings were English. Using *-ie* at the end of the name actually started in England after the Norman Conquest in 1066. Harold Glendon wrote in a *New York Times* article on January 10, 1869 that women were playing with their names too much: "(…) changing the spelling from 'Molly' to 'Mollie,' 'Fannie,' 'Jennie,' and 'Sallie' (…) the incongruity (of) Frenchifying it with an '*-ie*' instead of using a good plain English '*-y,*'" as Mr. Glendon put it. He was quite annoyed by all this frivolity and concluded, "Ladies, don't you think you'd better drop the name mania before you talk any more about your rights."[88] Currently, one finds names ending in *-i* instead of *-ie* or *-y*. Dropping the *e* seems to make the name gender neutral according to Marcy's personal experience.

• • •

Dated by Spelling
Sabine Bourgey

Names ending in "ine" (Francine, Catherine, Pauline, Nadine...) came after those ending in "ette"(women now in their eighties and more: Odette, Arlette, Huguette, Annette...).

Sabine is French. Her observation indicates that spelling cycles are a cross-cultural phenomenon.

– D –
BUREAUCRACY: THE SPELLING NIGHTMARE
WELCOME TO THE WONDERFUL WORLD OF SOFTWARE

• • •

Maryanne Mundy

(...) I don't mind when a person spells my name wrong, but when it is a large organization, that is a different matter. When I was only four months from graduating NYU, I was suddenly un-enrolled. When I returned my diploma request forms to the appropriate office, they informed me that I was not enrolled as a student there since October of that year. This made no sense, so I got a friend in the office of my department to look me up in the computer. He could not find me, but when he ran my social security number, up came my name, minus an "N". So according to their records, no one with my name was enrolled in the school. I went to the registrar's office (NYU is a big bureaucracy) with my social security card and driver's license to try and get them to correct it. However, their rule was they were not allowed to change a name in the record without an official name change order signed by a judge. I tried to explain that this was my real name, and had been correct in the computer for 3 and a half years, and someone must've accidentally deleted a letter... the social security number was the same... but, they would not budge on the policy. So, in order to become re-enrolled and graduate on time, I had to go to court and get my name changed to my name. The clerk of court was very confused at first, but everyone can understand the ridiculousness of large organizations. So, I had my name legally changed to the same exact name that was on all my documents. Then, I had the signed Order I needed, brought it back to the registrar's office, they changed it in like two seconds, and I was able to graduate.

This was a long time before Homeland Security; I bet it would be a lot harder now since I am once again having a spelling problem and it seems impossible to correct.

On my first passport, everything was fine. They copied my name exactly from my social security card. Everything correct. Then, my passport expired, so I sent it in for renewal. When my new passport arrived, my middle name was now missing an "E". No big deal, again, this was before 9/11, so nobody really cared when I used it. My SS card and NY driver's license were correct, so it wasn't a big deal. Until now. I have been able to get correct licenses in Florida, and then South Carolina, but when I moved to Virginia in 2006, I gave them my SC driver's license, and they gave me a Virginia one. But, instead of copying my information from the old license, they must've gotten my name off some federal database, where it is spelled as it is on my passport, missing an "E." (They also did not transfer my motorcycle endorsement, which they are supposed to, but that is a different story.) So now, my passport and driver's license match each other but not my social security card, employment records, or medical records. I have had problems getting checks cashed and gotten hassled at the airport, but only traveled domestically so they eventually let me through. I have contacted the DMV several times, and the passport office and there seems to be no way to get it changed without- you guessed it- an official name change order signed by a judge! (I checked but cannot use the one from last time) Hopefully, I will not have to go through that again, because I am getting married in June, and may be able to change my name to the correct name when I get all new documents then. Unless another letter disappears...

Mary Anne Mundy describes the same problems as Maryann Hunter (p.74). Double names cause problems for databases.

Spelling is important for retaining cultural heritage, highlighting correct punctuation, providing a topic of conversation, allowing for individuality, mirroring fashion changes (which may be associated with cultural changes), bonding with peers by adopting a common spelling, and, unfortunately, for causing bureaucratic problems.

Chapter 21
WHO NAMES THE CHILD

The answer to the question of who names the child is an amazing variety of "namers," i.e. nomenclators. Wealthy Romans had nomenclators, highly prized slaves whose job it was to know everybody's name. When someone approached, the nomenclator would whisper the name into the master's ear, thus avoiding the embarrassment of not knowing a name.[89]

– A –
THE FATHER

• • •

The Honor Belongs to Her Father
Judith Eisenstadt Horwich

The honor belongs to her father who is called to the pulpit to read from the holy books. A blessing is said for her, wishing that she should grow to be like great Jewish women who have come before her.

———————————

This concept is similar to Elvira Kituyi's essay and her awareness of her ancestors, except the Jewish tradition expands from one direct line of ancestors to the history of an entire group, the Jewish people. The more you can broaden the connections to your name, the richer your sense of belonging will be.

• • •

Don't Forget
Sandra Delgado

My name is Sandra. My father, an Italian descendant, chose this name while he and my mother were still dating. My mother approved. However, after my parents got married, their first baby was a boy, and they decided to call my brother after our grandfather, Julio. So, when I was born, my mom was thinking about calling me Juliana. However, my father reminded her that they have agreed before, and I got my name.

• • •

So Fond of Her
Clicker Morgan

I was christened Cynthia Giles Hamilton. Around 18 months of age, my parents legally changed my name to Frances Mary Giles Hamilton. Why? My mom said that my Dad adored me so much that she wanted to name me after him. He was Francis (called Frank) so I became Frances.

– B –
THE MOTHER

• • •

Anybody Have a Problem with That?
Judy McGowan

I am the fifth child, born six years after my next oldest sibling. In other words, there were four kids with strong opinions about what to name me. Every name my parents came up with (all from the Bible in a good Catholic family like ours) was shot down by one or another of my brothers and sisters. Finally my mom, Judy, suggested JUDY. "Anybody have a problem with that?" Well the story goes that no one did so here I am.

The irony of including more and more family members in the naming of the newest addition to the family is that picking the baby's name becomes more, rather than less, difficult.

– C –
BOTH PARENTS DECIDE

• • •

A Timid Proposal
Sheila M. Cahill

While she was expecting me, her first child, my mother was 24. Dad was 29. They agreed that a boy would be named after him, and a girl would be called "Kathleen." In due time, I arrived. Mom came out of the anesthesia, learned she had a daughter, and fell back asleep. When next she woke, my Dad was at her side. "Oh honey," she said, "Have you seen our darling Kathleen?"

Dad looks down sheepishly. "Uhmmmm…" he says. (Dad was never a great one for speaking up.)

"Joe?" Mom says, "You haven't been to look at her yet?"

He had. "Yes, indeed, that baby is quite a beauty."

"So what are you telling me?" says Mom. "What's 'uhmmmm' all about?"

"Well," Dad says. "The thing is, I never liked the name Kathleen." He looks sheepish.

"Well for heaven's sake," says my exasperated Mom. "Why did you not say so before?"

Dad grins his characteristically impish irresistible young Navy seaman's grin: "Well, you know, I figured there was a 50/50 chance it wouldn't become an issue."

This much she told me. And so, in haste, I was named "Sheila". No explanation for WHY that name in particular. The name has no history in my family—whereas the three subsequent kids got named after Grandma, Dad and Aunt Elaine, respectively.

• • •

Serendipity or Destiny?
Paul Tucker

We named our daughter Dulcimer Hope which we translate as Sweet Song of Hope; my youngest son got Isaac Steward because we wanted him to take care of the things we've been given but with a sense of humor; my middle child got Seth Moran because we liked the name Seth and Moran is my mothers maiden name. My daughter interestingly then named her daughter Sylvie Irene. Sylvie for the trees and Irene for peace. One of my favorite authors was George Macdonald. In his At the Back of the North Wind there is a little girl name Dulcimer. When I read that in college I put it in the back of my mind that if I ever got married and was going to have a daughter I'd like that for a name. My wife Kimberly grew up watching a western TV show called Cimarron Strip. On the show there was a saloon girl name Dulcy. She tucked that name away for the future. When we sat down to discuss names when we got pregnant I told her that I had a name that I liked but I was afraid that she wouldn't like it. She said the same thing so when I said the name that I liked was Dulcimer she screamed. I didn't think anyone would hate a name so much but then she told me her choice was Dulcy. So that was that! When she was born it was good she was a girl because we hadn't decided on a boys name yet.

———————

When both parents decide, some compromise is necessary, unless both parents happen to have chosen the same name. The essays describe both fathers who are timid about naming and fathers who are more assertive. In the Jewish and Muslim religious traditions, the father traditionally plays an important role in the child's naming.

– D –
GRANDMOTHERS

• • •

Furious
Clicker Morgan

And the Mary was added because my grandmother was furious that my mom didn't keep with the tradition. My great-grandmother, grandmother, mother, I , and my youngest daughter are all Mary Giles. My daughter is the 5th.

Bossy
Heather Frances Perram Frank

*My grandmother, Elva (I was always told she was named for England's queens
Elizabeth and Victoria), told my mother that Jane was a "boring" name and
suggested giving me a Scottish name, Heather. My parents liked the name (and my
grandmother was bossy), so they changed the birth certificate. Since we were still in
the hospital, apparently it was easy to do.*

• • •

Outraged
Deborah Field Washburn

*Deborah was chosen simply because my parents liked the name. My Memphis
grandmother was outraged. "People from good families do not make up names!" she
fumed. In fact, genealogical research has revealed that there were Deborahs on both
sides of the family. My grandmother just did not like the name.*

Grandmothers are often the keepers of the family legacy—therefore,
maintaining family names is very important to them, as we also see in
Heather's (pp.34–35) and Peggy Kay's (p.243–245) essays.

Besides considering the role grandmothers play in the naming of their
grandchildren, we should also consider the names they choose for themselves
as grandmothers. It quickly became apparent in conversation that many
did not want to be called "grandmother" or "grandma." There is a vast array
of names for grandmother derived from different cultures: *Nani* (Hindi),
Nana (English), *Nonna* (Italian), *Nini* (Chinese), *Mima* (Spanish), and *Oma*
(German). French offers: *Mémé, Mamie* (the probable source for both the
16th century English and the Southern American Mammy), *Mimi,* and
Bonne Maman, which literally means "Good Mother," as opposed to *Maman*
"Mother." Other possibilities include *YaYa* (Greek), *Bubbe* (Yiddish), *Babushka*
or *Baba* (Russian).[90] Using a nickname instead of *grandmother* or *grandma*
cuts the associations with *mother,* making the name less hierarchical, more
affectionate, and provides the grandmother with her own personal nickname,
not shared with the mother. One wonders if these nicknames that drop
mother all together may not simultaneously serve to help eliminate feelings
of competition with the mother and free the grandmother to enjoy the child
more—with less need to discipline.

• • •

A Family Affair
Tricia Larkin

When the baby was born, we still hadn't decided. We asked a few people what they thought of the names. My sister liked them both. My husband's brother liked Lucie because he thought it was cuter and Camille was too serious. My husband's parents liked both but preferred Lucie because my mother-in-law had a grandmother in Brazil named Lucie (or Lucy).

• • •

Untold Stories
Erin Towers

My name is Erin. My mother knew of a woman named Erin and she liked the name. (…) And the strangest thing is that my mother never even researched my name or knew that it was Irish. My paternal grandparents were second-generation German immigrants who hated the poor Irish peasants whom they had to compete against for employment. So the story goes that when Nana heard I was born and named Erin, she was chopping vegetables and with each chop she would say, "Erin. Erin. Why name her Erin?" Nana was a wonderful woman and a great cook. We loved each other very much, so she overcame the prejudice she felt towards my name.

Discussing baby names with the family is not only inclusive but is also an honor and a sign of respect. The naming process can provide for family bonding that might not occur otherwise and may reveal stories that might otherwise never be discovered, as Katherine Lee found by consulting her family (p.235); and it can save a child from unnecessary family dilemmas like Erin's.

– F –
YOUNGER SIBLINGS

A few essays tell us about younger siblings who provide beloved nicknames, sometimes because of difficulties with pronunciation. These nicknames may or may not be used outside the family. Ella Francis gives the example of *Tis* from Tister, used by her little brother (p.177). Ruth Stenstrom tells of Memo, the grandmother so named by a young cousin (pp.221–222). Nina V. loves the name *Wia*, given to her by her young nephew (p.19). Rorie says that her name was the result of a child's failed attempt to say *Rosemarie,* which became *Rorie.* *Rorie* has the powerful sound of the roar of a lion followed by the diminutive *-ie,* which makes her name simultaneously strong but sweet.

These naming essays indicate that the nomenclator—who names the child—varies with each family. Fathers, mothers, siblings, grandmothers, relatives, and even friends are described as possible nomenclators. The older generations, especially grandmothers, are the most culturally and historically sensitive to the role of names in the family and may therefore play an important role in naming a new baby. At the other age extreme, siblings may not only choose a name but also create a new name based on their personal mispronunciation. Often the nicknames created by a sibling are especially emotive because they vividly recall childhood memories.

Chapter 22
NAMES BASED ON APPEARANCE:
"WHO DOES SHE OR DOESN'T SHE LOOK LIKE?"

• • •

Norwegian-looking
Karen Lee

My parents chose my first name, Karen, because I was blonde and blue-eyed. They had originally thought to name me "Laura," but decided "Karen" fit better with a Norwegian-looking child.

• • •

This Teeny Baby
Tarpley Long

"We can't call this teeny baby, Tarpley!" declared my 6'5" father, as he cradled me in his arms shortly after birth. "How about Miss T?"

• • •

So Beautiful
Helen Marie Margaret F.
(Generation Y)

My parents thought I was so beautiful when I was born, they named me Helen after Helen of Troy.

• • •

She Doesn't Look Like....
Katie Fontana

Up until the day I was born, I was to be named Elizabeth Mary. However, when I came into the world, my mother looked at me and said, "She doesn't look like an Elizabeth, she looks like a Kathleen." I was then named Kathleen Mary, but I have always gone by Katie and I'm happy with my name.

When a name is based on the child's appearance, the name is especially personal—picked specifically for her and her attributes, just as Native Americans pick names for children based on characteristics they note in them.

Chapter 23
ANDROGYNOUS NAMES

As you remember, French and German Catholic immigrants brought a double naming tradition in which one of the two names could be a masculine name that was feminized—e.g., *Marie Josephine*; and Scots-Irish Protestants brought the tradition of giving girls surnames as given names beginning in the 17th century. The use of androgynous names only began to spread in the mid-twentieth century. At the beginning of the women's liberation movement when women first started applying for jobs that had previously belonged only to men, having an androgynous name could be, and may still be, a benefit.

• • •

I Always Hated My Name
Reube Gene
(by Ella Frances)

My husband's aunt was named "Reube Gene." Friends in her hometown mispronounced it as "Ruby Gene" to feminize it, and she received a draft notice in World War II because of the masculine name. (…) She has always hated her name and now calls herself just Gene. (…)

———————

Reube Gene has not one, but two androgynous names. Because of the gender confusion associated with *Reube,* she drops it and keeps the second name *Gene,* a more common androgynous name. Like Tarpley Long (p.217), she had to appear before the draft board.

• • •

I Was Unique
Dojelo

(…) One negative…being taken for MALE anytime there is no title. I get as much mail for Mr. Dojelo as I do for Ms. or Dr. I think that is not a good thing.

• • •

Confusion
Ellen "Taylor" Manson Watson

I was always told that Ellen was from Sir Walter Scott's Lady of the Lake, a beautiful diminutive brunette. I got the brunette, but certainly not the diminutive at 5 ft. 10. So the Taylor is who I am, often mistaken for a boy! WRONG!!! Although my size and being the only girl in an extended family of all boys, I did learn to throw a ball and play football with the boys, sometimes to my benefit, other times to my detriment.

. . .

Phyl, Not Phil
Phyllis Claire Steinman Caplan Nest

– I was named after my grandmother Paula, my father's mother. She lived and died in Vilnius, Russia. Being Jewish, I was named after her in her memory and honor.

– Nicknames: several—my brother called me Flees—my first husband called me phylips. Phyl is generally used.

– Had a friend in high school—also a Phyllis—she was Flies and I was Flees

– My middle name "Claire" was self-chosen. I needed a passport when I was 17 and we could not locate my birth certificate; so in the process of applying for a new one, I gave myself the middle name of "Claire" in memory of my French cousin Cecile—we were born a week apart. She was killed in Auschwitz.

– I like my name; but when I was very little, I had much trouble with saying my name, Phyllis Steinman. You see, I had an awful lisp (thank goodness for speech therapists).

– I like the roots of my name (pun intended). In Greek, "Phyllis" means a "green bough." I do love trees and unashamedly am a tree hugger.

– Also, my mother loved a movie actress working at the time of my birth –Phyllis Love, hence, Phyllis, rather than any other name starting with P.

– I do get pretty annoyed when people spell my name Phil.

– I do like it when people call me Phyl.

– Have taught for many years. My favorite name (one of my students) is "Velvet Satin"—parents had an interesting sense of humor....

Women who rename themselves are not afraid to break with tradition to assert their creativity and independence. They are willing to break the mold in order to see themselves in new ways.

. . .

She Misspelled My Name
Jaime
(Generation Y)

I was always mad at my mom because I say she misspelled my name. I was also angry because there are a lot of guys named Jamie.

213

• • •
I Am Unique
Quincy Martel

My name is Quincy Maris Martel. There is no E in Quincy.

Often times, I receive mail addressed as a male, Mr. Quincy Martel. Common mistake, and no offense taken.

My Christian name definitely has a ring to it. I should be a movie star, or famous with a name like Quincy Maris Martel...but I am not. I am ok with who I am and where I came from.

My parents met in Boston and named me after Quincy Market. I recently ran the Boston Marathon this past year, and it was nice to see the Ole Quincy Market.

The decision-making process of my name was a toss up between Quincy or Phoebe, and thank goodness the later choice was not applied. I think I would be a totally different personality if I were a Phoebe or anything else for that matter. I like my name. I am unique.

Not many people are named Quincy, not to mention white women. I get a little annoyed when people ask me if my last name is Jones. So limited.

I have been called many names, but most of the times go by Quince, Q or plain Quincy.

———————

Although Quincy has a unique name, she is happy with it and appreciates its uniqueness. She has a story and a place to associate with her name—Quincy Market, an enduring American icon, which has survived and adapted to centuries of change. *Quincy* is an empowering symbol for a name.

• • •
Advantages
Pat Long

My full name growing up was Patricia Ann Long. I was called Patty. While I was in elementary school, kids quoted a rhyme: Patty, fatty, two by four, couldn't get through the bathroom door, so she did it on the floor!—Licked it up and did some more!! (P.S. At that time in my life, I was neither fat nor particularly gross, but have disliked the name "Patty" ever since. To this day, I hate to be called Patty and it always brings that rhyme to mind.

When I went to college (one of the few times in life when you can meet a whole new group of people and change your name), I changed my name to Pat. I chose this rather than Patricia because whenever I heard "Patricia Ann!!" I assumed I was in TROUBLE!; and the name "Patricia" connoted dainty and ladylike to me. I'm not sure why it had that connotation—but I certainly did not fit the "ladylike" or "dainty" picture.

Well...Pat turned out to be a good choice for me and I believe it gave me strength. Although not popular now as a name, the name "Patty" was associated with a vivacious girl-next-door type person thanks to Patty Duke. All through high school I adopted the friendly, slightly ditsy, Patty Duke persona. I found it much more appealing than the "Patty" of the rhyme....

To continue with this saga, I never met a female "Pat" before college, so it gave me a chance to be a bit more myself. I was more daring, outspoken, less afraid to be an individual, etc. It is possible that this was all part of growing up or it could have been thanks to adopting a plain (could be considered masculine) name which had no preconceived person for me. To some extent, it may also have helped in business at times (particularly in the late seventies/early eighties) when it certainly did not hurt to leave business correspondents wondering whether I was male or female.

Persona is defined as "an individual's social facade or front" that reflects the role the individual plays in life—the outer as opposed to the inner self according to the analytic psychology of C.G. Jung. Like Rebecca Snow (p.32), Pat finds her voice with her new name: she is more "outspoken." She thinks her growth may be thanks to adopting a "plain," "masculine," and therefore, more assertive name. Like Tarpley, Pat feels her androgynous name is an asset in the business world.

For those interested, Jung's *Red Book* has finally been translated and published (Oct., 2009). *The Portable Jung* or *Man and His Symbols* are good for beginning a Jungian exploration of the self.

• • •

The Quest for My Name Tribe
Frances A. Zwenig

I was named after my two grandmothers—Frances for my maternal grandmother and Anne for my paternal grandmother. "Frances" is a very southern and old-fashioned name, and that is why I love it. It also amuses me that the name is consistently misspelled as "Francis" and I receive lots of Mr. Francis messages. Then I explain to people—it is "e" before "i" in the alphabet, and ladies before gentlemen—to help them remember how to spell my name correctly.

When I was young I loved to see who else was named "Frances" or "Francis"— Francis of Assisi, Francis Bacon, Frances Farmer, but was not so happy with "Francis the Talking Mule."

My family and friends always called me "Francie," but when I got to GPS a classmate was also named "Francie," so I let her have that name and "Frances" became my moniker. Close friends and relatives still call me "Francie," which I really prefer. My other nickname is FAZ—for my initials. Now that you ask, I have to admit that I like all my names.

Frances is the feminine of *Francis*. At an early age, Frances searches for namesakes, both male and female, in a fascinating quest for her name tribe. She discovers the holy, the learned, and even the ridiculous, which provides both humor and humility. Making such discoveries at a young age enriches her concept of identity and the possibilities life offers. Searching for our namesakes is an activity we can all engage in to spark our creativity. [91]

She assumes *Frances* as her "moniker." *Moniker* has a variety of meanings—"slang for a name, a nickname, and a pseudonym or stage name."[92] The word *moniker* implies an awareness of the name as something coined or added and appears rarely in the essays. *Moniker* suggests that Frances does not feel as close to *Frances* as she did to *Francie*.

She brings up the increasing use of initials to replace names. In this age of ever increasingly rapid communication, many women sign off with their initials or a single letter, which offers the possibility of creating a new identity in the real world as well as the virtual world.

• • •

The Spirit of a Name
Tracy Spencer

My name is Tracy—"cy," no "e"! That is the worst part about my name—Spelling IT! But I have loved it more since I have been married, because I am Spencer Tracy backwards! If you are 45 or older, you know who that is! And doctors always make the remark (due to their filing systems). My parents heard the name and liked it. It fits my personality too! I am 45 and have only met a handful of Tracys, usually Tracey.

I think the name Tracy suits me. It is ageless! It is still given to girls even to this day. (Sometimes even to boys, but I have never met one in my 40 something years.) Ageless remember! Never getting old! That's me!

I believe the spelling is a last name spelling (i.e. Spencer Tracy), and for boys first names. I think the girly way is with an "e"—Tracey! I have even seen it spelled "Tracie" but that is a bit too cute!

I have always wondered if your name made a difference in who you become in life—if so then I will be young forever!

Tracy's enthusiasm for her name and its youthful spirit is reminiscent of Molly's essay. For both women their names embody an inspiring spirit: for Molly, it is happiness; and for Tracy, it is youthfulness.

. . .

Social History
Tarpley Long

(...) Tarpley Blair Mann is my birth name. My parents also considered naming me Matilda Blair, with the nickname, "Til," which sounds worse than being named Tarpley. When I entered elementary school, the "Miss" was dropped, and the "T" became "Tee" because "T Mann" looked incomplete. Where I grew up in Mississippi, plenty of my classmates had initials for first names but they customarily came in pairs, as in "PJ" Reeves or "JR" Walker. Until I was 30 and began my career, I was known as Tee Mann. To this day my family and close friends call me Tee; professionally I am known as Tarpley. Upon hearing my name for the first time, most people ask me how Tarpley is spelled, and then they ask the origin of the name. Tarpley is an English name. The last time I visited colonial Williamsburg, there was a business called Tarpley's Coffee Shop. I have never met another person with the given name Tarpley.

The worst part of being named Tarpley is how it is mispronounced and/or misspelled, sometimes to comical effect, other times I feel insulted. About ten years ago I received a Saks card with my name spelled Turdley. I was not amused. The most frequent misspelling is Trapley, followed by Tardley, Tripley, Parpley, and Partley. Once when I worked on a substance abuse ward, a patient persisted in addressing me as Titley. And mail invariably comes addressed to Mr. Tarpley Long. In 1955, I received a notice to register for the draft and had to appear in person with my social security card to prove that I was not a male. There has been an advantage professionally in being named Tarpley. Early in my career in the substance abuse field, dominated by men in their 70s, having the perceived male name of Tarpley opened many doors that otherwise might have been closed to me. For example, if I called an agency to schedule a meeting with the director, the female scheduling the appointment assumed that I was making the appointment for my male boss who had the name Tarpley.

Why did my parents name me Tarpley after my paternal grandmother whom everyone hated? When I asked them they said, "We thought it was such a pretty name." Grandmother Tarpley was never called Tarpley; she was referred to by my grandfather as "Tarp," which is about as ugly sounding a name as you can get. Once a colleague called me Tarp and I told him in no uncertain terms to never say Tarp to me again. The last time I saw my grandfather was in 1972. He had escaped from his nursing home in Florida and hitchhiked up to DC. Sitting in my living room, he stared at me for a minute and said, "You look like my wife, uh, uh what was her name?" Grandfather is not the only one in the family who has forgotten the name Tarpley. My daughters never considered passing it along to any of my six grandchildren. Maybe 100 years from now Tarpley will be rediscovered by one of my great-great-great grandchildren, who like my parents, will think it is a pretty name.

• • •
Just Like the Boys
Marty Vaughn

My name is Martha. My mother named me that because she liked it! There are no other Marthas in our family. The diminutive of my name is Marty, and it's a name my family always called me. My mother still calls me Marty Party. Cute Huh? When I went to GPS (Girls Preparatory School), I remember that they wanted to know what I wanted to be called—Martha, Mart, or Marty; and I chose Marty. Up until that time I was always known as Martha outside my family. Later I learned that boys named Martin shorten their names to Marty, so I always tell people that I spell my name just like the boys – with a "y."

• • •
Profound Repercussions
Jackie
by Jacqueline Pirson

I got my given name somewhat by chance. My father had always wanted to have a son. A girl's name was not even considered. So when I was born, he was caught by surprise. "Well, since she was supposed to be Jacques, we'll call her Jacqueline."

My father's desire for a son had many, profound, repercussions in my life.

For a long time, I wanted to be a boy and I had people call me Jaky; but I changed it to Jackie because Jackie is a bit more feminine. I also like the name Michèle as a first name. As for believing that a given name influences the person, I don't know about that. I think the family melieu is the most important influence.

Michèle, the other name Jackie would give herself, also has an interesting history. The traditional spelling would be *Michelle*, but *Michèle* appears in the Roaring Twenties and suggests a tilt towards more masculine names just as we saw in the U.S. in that era. (The masculine form of *Michael* in French is *Michel*.)

• • •
Not Very Common
Kylie
(Generation Y)

My name is Kylie _____. I am 12 & 3/4 years old. I have a nickname, "Buggie" because of a play that I was in, but only a few of my friends call me that. I like my name, but I mostly like my middle name.

Kylie is not a very common name. Nothing has the name Kylie on it (you know like the pencils, key chains, etc....) even though quite a few have the name

Kyle. It gets pretty annoying, especially since a lot of people spell my name wrong. Examples: 1. Kaylee 2. Kiley 3. Kylee 4. Kiyle 5. Kyile 6. Kilee etc..... Also, people say my name wrong. Once, someone called me Kaylee, also, someone once called me Kyle, and thought I was a boy because of a stupid haircut I had. I hate it. I mean, what if your name was Laura, but I called you Larry? How would you feel? This is how I feel a lot. P.S. I doubt anyone who is in this book is named Kylie.

Kylie is one of the youngest essayists. Her essay confirms adults' memories of having an unusual name with little name tribe identity—no trinkets, no social validation of the name. Because her name is both unusual and androgynous, Kylie thinks about the nuances of identity in ways other girls may not.

One of the surprises in these essays is the number of women with androgynous names. Most of the essayists seem happy with these names with the exception of Reube Gene, who is part of an older generation. Reube, Dojelo, Taylor, and Tarpley all have to deal with confusion about their gender, which they find annoying. Tarpley notes, however, that her androgynous given name was helpful in her career. Frances notes that she found both male and female namesakes, an empowering discovery. Pat thinks the masculine ring to her name may have helped free her from her timidity. Phyl chooses her androgynous nickname, as does Marty. The women with androgynous given names that are family surnames have a strong sense of family history. Jackie feels her name, which reflected her father's unfulfilled desire for a son, had profound repercussions in her life. Most of these women exhibit a sense of power and liberation in describing their given names—the only exception is the youngest essayist, who has not yet grown into her name at the age of "12 & 3/4." (We all remember how important the 3/4 is at an age when a year seems like a decade.)

Many of the Native American women who contacted me had androgynous names—Brooke, Charlie, and Sammye. Is this a coincidence or does it suggest that these women are stronger, more achievement oriented? Do their epicene (androgynous) names also suggest that as displaced Native Americans, they have to be assertive in order to maintain their ethnic identity? Charlie notes that she now sees more women with men's names. Judging from the essays received, this seems to be a cross-cultural phenomenon.

The subject of androgynous names brings up the topic of women's roles in history. Specialists are now calling for new studies of women in the past: their history has not been told. Spartan women competed in sports and were educated, unlike other Greek women. Archaeologists have discovered the tombs of Roman gladiatrix and female warriors buried in Roman military camps in Britain: they are believed to be Amazons, well-known female warriors of the ancient world. Celtic women fought alongside their men. Many different cultures, and even the Bible, tell stories of women who take up arms. The most famous female soldier is Joan of Arc, who saved France from the English. Women now serve in the American armed forces. Following the enduring and sacred Albanian tradition of Knun, women, who pledge virginity, have the right to become men. They dress, speak, act as men, and take on men's jobs. Society recognizes them as men in this ancient tradition.

In the 1970s the study of women's contributions to history began in earnest thanks to the feminist movement. Since women's activities were historically very restricted, almost any field they contributed to could be considered a crossing of the gender line until fairly recently. You could begin your own discovery of the role women played in the past with *Women Writers of Ancient Greece and Rome* by Ian M. Plant. *The Encyclopedia of Women in the Middle Ages,* the multi-volume *History of Women in the West,* and the *Encyclopedia of Women in the Renaissance: Italy, France and England* provide comprehensive sources for women who played important roles in history. Reading about European queens also makes it abundantly clear that many medieval women were forces to be reckoned with. *Eleanor: Crown Jewel of Aquitaine* by Kristiana Gregory is a good introduction to one of the Middle Ages' most assertive queens. In American history, you might consider *Early American Women: A Documentary History 1600–1900.* To read about women soldiers try *They Fought Like Demons: Women Soldiers in the Civil War* or *Band of Sisters: American Women at War in Iraq.* On the Internet you can discover women authors who used male pseudonyms or androgynous names by googling "list women pseudonyms." Google "female wartime spies" to discover the stories of famous female spies, many of whom were disguised at times as men. Google "200 famous women" for an interesting list of famous women in many different fields—e.g., sculptors, photographers, economists, composers, conductors, playwrights, physicians, writers, diplomats, astronauts. "4000 years of women in science" (http://www.astr.ua.edu/4000WS/) is a wonderful website to learn about women in science. *Wikipedia* has extensive lists of women in different fields as well as a list of websites (web-based projects) and journals that specialize in women's studies.

Chapter 24
NAMES AND ADOPTION

Individuals who are adopted may have naming traditions from different families and different cultures.

• • •

I Had the Greatest Interest in Family History
Ruth Stenstrom

I was adopted and I had never given thought that my given name was any different from my first name. It turns out that when I finally searched for my birth parents, the first document that I received was a document that stated that my name was "Baby Girl O...." Since I was adopted at six weeks of age, I never imagined that I might have had another first name. On the other hand, I spent a great deal of time thinking about all of the possible last names that I could have had—my birth father's, my adoptive family's, my adoptive mother's maiden name, my birth mother's birth family (yes she was adopted at birth too!), and my birth mother's maiden and married names....

When I was trying to first digest the news that my name for the first six weeks of my life was Baby Girl O, I unhappily realized that in some ways as I grew up I managed to look like my name as I was blessed with being short and looking eternally (or infernally) young. I was talking about this with a young couple who lived next door at the time and was blessed with hearing the story that the young man (whose name I now forget!) told which let me know that I was not alone. His parents could not think of a name for him for the first six months of his life. So he was known officially as Baby Boy for that whole time!

I was named after my adoptive father's mother. His parents had named their son and daughter after themselves, so each of them went by their middle names instead. But I didn't think of myself being named after my grandmother as a special link to her (or my aunt) because I knew her by a different, more affectionate name, Memo.

In my school year there were three other Ruth Anns. I come from a generation of many girls given Ann for a middle name. My mother insisted that Ruth Ann was my first name, so I had an interminable time deciding how to fill out forms that made me choose to put Ann in the first name blank or the one for middle names. Everyone who knows me from my childhood calls me Ruth Ann. I used to think that it made me seem too young; perhaps from the intonation used by my brothers. So when I went to college, I introduced myself as Ruth and gradually outgrew the nickname "Ruthie" by the time I was about 25.

Sometimes I miss being called Ruth Ann. A lovely artist, who gave me her studio to house sit, said the name of her friend Ruth Ann so respectfully that I felt a little bit jealous. Perhaps I would have kept the name Ann if it had had an "e" on the end.

Another friend of mine whose name was Pam, surprised me by changing her name one day to her middle name "Ann." At the time I thought that this was a silly idea. Who would want to be called by their middle, kind of bland, name as by that time I had callously dropped the Ann from my own name? But Pam stubbornly insisted and we gradually adjusted to her new name. We of course had problems learning her new name and referred to her as Ann Pam. Perhaps if she had chosen a longer or a more unusual new name we would have understood.

About that time I traveled in Europe and went to Sweden to look up my father's family tree. (Ironically as the only adopted child in my family, I had the greatest interest in family history.) I found the Swedish records office in the town that my great grandfather was from, and received a list of Stenstrom antecedents. When I gave the list to my mother, she became enchanted with a relative named Carlotta. She told me that if she had known it at the time, she would have named me after her. Visions of the potential nicknames of "Lottie" and the propinquity of the exotic name to "car lot," make me think that my name was a better choice. Now that I have grown into my identity as an artist, I am happy to keep my professional name: Ruth Stenstrom

––––––––––––––

Like Sophy (pp.32-34), Evelyn (p.192), and Heather (pp.34–35), Ruth is nostalgic for her childhood name. She even finds a resemblance to her very first name, *Baby Girl O*, in which she sees her "short," "young" self mirrored in the *O*.

Making the discovery about *Baby Boy*, Ruth discovers that children who are not adopted may also have to wait before getting a name. Native Americans accept waiting before naming a child in order to pick an appropriate name and may even change a child's name if it does not seem right. Society today does not allow for this because papers have to be filled out before the child leaves the hospital. In addition, many Christian parents are eager to baptize their babies as soon as possible due to a lingering fear that the souls of unbaptized babies cannot go to heaven. Until recently, the Catholic Church taught that the souls of unbaptized babies remained in limbo.[93]

Although Ruth is named for her adoptive grandmother, she does not feel linked to her grandmother by her given name because she knows her grandmother by the affectionate nickname, *Memo*. Although Ruth may not have known it growing up, she is linked to her grandmother by her "first" name—by the *O* of *Baby Girl O* and the *o* of *Grandmother Memo*—an endearing, serendipitous sound link.

Ruth is the family member with the most interest in names because she seeks answers not only about her natural parents, but also about her adopted family. She discovers missing history for her adopted family—thus providing them with identity, just as they did for her. Ruth's story echoes that of the biblical Ruth in many ways—she loses her family, becomes part of another family, and provides missing genealogy for her adopted family. Seeking out stories about namesakes inspires and empowers.

Chapter 25
ASSIMILATION

Names and assimilation have an ancient history. When the biblical Joseph goes to Egypt, he is honored with the new Egyptian name *Ramses*. Mordecai changes Hadassah's name to *Esther* to protect her from discrimination in Babylonia. When families move from one country to another or when one culture suppresses another, names may be changed voluntarily or involuntarily. The history of the United States is one of immigration and name assimilation. The following essayists explain what works and what does not with respect to names and assimilation.

– A –
NATIVE AMERICAN

• • •
Roots
Shiakoda Qkalokqua Saunders

I was born with a Native American name and then adopted by my "white" family who gave me an American English name. My birth name was Shiakoda Qkalokqua Saunders. My American name was Sandra Lynn Mansfield. My second stepfather adopted me when my adopted mother remarried and my name was then Sandra Lynn Gallentine.

I knew I was Native (through eavesdropping as a child), but knew nothing about my family. As I got older I did some research and found out that my dad died when I was in my early twenties. My adopted family didn't tell me anything about him. I really resented that since they knew him and knew that he was my dad. I could have spent lots more time learning from him! I found my dad had a sister and I looked her up and went to talk to her. She filled me in about my roots. That's how I found out about my Native name. When I was little I was told my dad called me "Little Girl Who Dances on Fire" because he said I would dance so fast, it was like I was on the hot flames of the fire.

When I reached my thirties, I traced back and found out that I was Mohegan. I legally discarded my American name and took on my Native name as my legal name. I tracked down my tribe and started getting involved. I am now tribal secretary, organizer of ceremonies and tribal council member. I had my naming ceremony where my Chief named me "Autumn Wolf Moon" which I wear proudly! Autumn is my season, Wolf is for my people, and Moon is for the mother. I have now reached grandmother status and I am very proud of this. I have been teaching young ones what I have learned—this is what it is all about. I also help people trace their roots by giving them information on where to look and what to do next. So I also have the name of "grandmother."

I guess going to school when I was young, the name Sandra Mansfield made my life a little easier. I didn't have to explain my Native name. Back then names like... "Ann, Betty, Joan," etc. were normal. Shiakoda was not a "normal" name!!

Now I wear my names with pride. Some call me "Shi," others call me "Wolf Moon." I answer to these plus any combination of names, but Native only! There are only a handful of people that knew me by my English name and still call me by that. I don't use it very often so sometimes it takes a while to realize they are talking to me! :>)

I think all the searching and looking I had to do made me more determined to use only my Native American name. It took a while to get here and there is no looking back. I am very proud to be: Shiakoda Autumn Wolf Moon Qkalokqua, aka, Grandmother.

I also have some English blood in my veins but I do not feel a connection there.

———————

Because Shiakoda's native name, culture, and father were all denied to her, she rejects as she was taught by renouncing her English name. "As you sow, so shall you reap" (Job 4:8). If she had been allowed to keep her native identity, she could have grown up with both cultures.

The elimination of ethnic names is one of the first steps in forced assimilation, which has been used against indigenous ethnic groups all over the world. As we see from Shiakoda's essay, this technique does not work. Having been denied her own culture, Shiakoda understands the magnitude of this loss and helps others trace their roots. This search can be very difficult for Native Americans because the U.S. government systematically broke up the tribes with constant relocations, splitting them into smaller and smaller groups. This constant fracturing made it increasingly difficult for them to maintain their ethnic identity.

– B –
JEWISH

• • •
What's in a Name?
Evelyn Torton Beck

"Synchronicity strikes again," was my response to this invitation to contemplate what my name means to me, since I had just asked that very question of a group of women at a conference (focusing on the Power of Language) from which I had just returned. With these women I freely shared the fact that I had never liked my given

name "Evelyn" and that my parents had never called me anything but "Evi" and that is the name by which my family, friends and even professional colleagues know me today. The only person who calls me Evelyn is my brother when he is teasing me because he knows I don't like it, and my ex-husband who gave up the more intimate Evi when we were divorced. He no doubt also remembers that I don't like it. I also told a story of how I had embarrassed myself in junior high school, when I decided to shed my name and introduce myself as "Lynn" to a new teacher, but did not answer to that name when she called the roll--friends had to prod me to respond and my ruse was up. I became Evelyn once again.

What I did not share with these women whom I had only recently met, was that my name was given to me under a dark cloud and is no doubt associated with the shame of being slated for annihilation, for I am a Jew, born in Vienna in 1933 under the shadow of Hitler's coming to power. My mother often told me that because of the threat Hitler posed to all Jews, she had given me a British sounding name so that I would fit in better if we had to immigrate to England. For the same reason she had named my brother Edgar. Within a few years, the worst did happen, and after my father was deported to a camp and miraculously returned a year later, we had to flee Vienna—lucky to escape to Italy whose borders were not yet closed, but leaving many loved ones behind whom we never saw again.

I had no real idea of why I did not like my name, but the Nazis were not satisfied with my name either, and like all other Jewish females, I was renamed "Sarah" on my passport that was also stamped with a large black J. I was never really a Sarah, but like most Jews, I had been given a Hebrew name, Nachama, meaning "comfort." My mother said she gave me this name because she had had a difficult pregnancy resulting in a caesarian birth and needed comfort. I did use this name years later, when I was enrolled in Hebrew school and again when I was active in the Zionist movement prior to the existence of the state of Israel. I liked my Hebrew name, still do, and I especially liked the idea of being a comfort to others, even when I could not comfort myself.

But in Italy there had been another name change. When I was enrolled in school I became "Evelina," and a star pupil. I do remember Italy, but cannot remember answering to that name; after we arrived in the United States my mother sometimes used it playfully. She had loved Italy, though the sorrow of leaving her mother (who was killed in Auschwitz) never left her.

In my professional life I usually write under the name of Evelyn Torton Beck. I created this name, for when I married right out of college and entered graduate school, I took my "maiden" name and made it my middle name; Americans all seemed to have middle names, and I had none, and it was a way of not giving up my former identity entirely. Strangely, and I am not sure how it happened, my essays (not my books) appear under many different names, Evelyn Torton Beck,

Evelyn T. Beck, Evelyn Beck, E. T. Beck and in Germany and Austria (where I have published in German) they list me under Evelyn Torton-Beck, although I have repeatedly told them my last name is Beck. This will make it hard to find my work if anyone ever decides to look up my oeuvre.

One last observation may be of interest. When I retired from university teaching and decided not to practice as a psychotherapist, a profession for which I had trained, I shifted from the academy to the arts, one of my earliest passions. Now, when I teach my dance/poetry workshops, unless I need my credentials, I simply call myself "Evi Beck." It is a relief to shed my old formal name with all its histories— Evi represents a fresh start, and it is also a return. But what I have really missed all these years, is the sound of Evi in German, where the E is neither clipped nor drawn out, but softly iterated in a sound that does not exist in English. The sound of my name before we were cast out.

Taking away the individual's identity by giving all Jewish women the name of *Sarah* was one of the first steps in the process of dehumanizing them. The same is true for the "big black J" stamped on the passport, which reduces an ethnic group to a letter—something without a name, another obliteration of their humanity. By choosing the name *Sarah* for all Jewish women, the Nazi's chose a powerful symbol for annihilation—the mother of the Jewish nation (Genesis 17:15). The Nazi name change was a dual obliteration—of their given name, which may have been German, and their Hebrew name, which was not necessarily *Sarah*.

Evelyn is unable to remember being called *Evelina*. Forgetting about *Evelina* may help erase painful memories. *Evelina* was a name given in exile, and Evelyn has exiled those memories.

Evelyn notes that although her books appear under a fixed name with no variations, "Strangely, and I am not sure how it happened, my essays (not my books) appear under many different names...." The variations may express subtly some of the different Evelyns she has been and, perhaps, an unconscious desire to escape obliteration with multiple names.

Evelyn's story is circular. Her return to *Evi* represents both a fresh start and a return. With *Evi*, the name given to her before they were "cast out," she recaptures the best of the past. With her first name, she returns to art—one of her first loves. Just like Judy F. Moorman (pp.98–99), Tara (p.100), and Francesca (pp.101–102), Evi chooses a new name, which revitalizes *Evelyn*, i.e., *"life"* (in Hebrew).

• • •

For Many Reasons
Carol

My maiden name is Cole. My parents named me Carol Sue Cole. My father's name was Cohn in Germany. They fled the Holocaust in 1939, the day after Kristalnacht. After a few years, he was drafted into the U.S. Army and worked as a German translator in a prisoner of war camp in Greeley, Colorado, where I was born in 1945. He said that he was asked to change his name so that the prisoners would not know that he was Jewish. He said that he decided to do that because his parents in Germany had been already forced by Hitler to change their name to "Kohn" so that it sounded more German. He said that he was not concerned about carrying on the family name because Cohn was a very common name in the U.S. So he and my mother chose "Cole."

All of my grandparents died in concentration camps. I was the first child, and was named Carol (after my maternal grandmother Clara) and Sue (after my paternal grandmother Selma). I always used the name Carol. I never had a nickname. After I married at age 21, I substituted my maiden name for my middle name and have kind of dropped my given middle name.

My paternal grandmother helped my paternal grandfather in their large shoe business in Koblentz, Germany. When I decided that I wanted to have a profession, and not be a full time homemaker, I used to fantasize that some of my internal drive came from her. My maternal grandmother was a full-time homemaker, and my mother used to tell me that I should not be too caught up in making everything perfect in my home—saying that was a waste of time—e.g., making sure that all of the linen was perfectly folded in the linen closets. Those anecdotes somehow stuck with me. But my parents never told me that much about their mothers' personalities with one exception. My father used to talk about how close he was to his mother (he also was a first born child). He said that his mother was very unhappy in her marriage because my paternal grandfather either worked or played cards all the time, and spent very little time at home. Consequently, my father went into his own business in Kansas City as soon as he could, and if he was not traveling on business (he was in the wholesale floor covering business), he was always home for dinner by 5 pm, and was very involved with his family.

I have been comfortable with the name Carol, but after Kennedy was elected president, I remember thinking that I thought that Caroline was a prettier, more feminine name, and wished that my parents had named me Caroline. But I never changed my name, or anything like that.

I grew up in Kansas City, and I was glad growing up that my name was not an ethnic one. My parents gave all of their three children American—generic names- and were happy that we could not easily be identified as being Jewish.

When I was growing up in Kansas City, there were certain neighborhoods where Jews could not buy homes, etc. All of that has changed long ago—thank goodness.

I don't think that Carol is used much now. People seem to go for more old-fashioned, complicated names at this particular time.

Names given in order to facilitate assimilation may have an element of fear hidden within them—the fear of renewed discrimination, which Carol describes. It may come as a surprise to many readers that problems with anti-Semitism were as acute as those Carol describes in the Midwest in the 1950s—a reminder that the U.S., home of the free and the brave, has struggled and continues to struggle with racism.

· · ·

A Double Name Anyway
Karen

Having grown up in the south in a Jewish family with all these people with double names...Eastern European Jews who wanted their kids to assimilate into southern culture. Thank god I only ended up with one name; but then my father gave me a name that was not my legal name that somehow everyone assumed was my real one. Go figure....

Ironically, Karen managed to fit into the double naming pattern without actually being a part of it. Perhaps all this was due to a subconscious desire to fit in, to be assimilated.

· · ·

What It Means to Others
Joan Goldhammer Hart

In preadolescence I became irritated about my name, realizing at that time that not only was Joan out of date, but I wasn't sure I liked the sound of it. My mother explained that the alternate possibility had been Nancy. When I heard that, I was much relieved and never gave it much thought after that. (I still breathe a sigh of relief when I consider the alternative.) It could have been so much worse. I guess actress Joan Crawford was on my parents' collective minds. When studying foreign languages, I always preferred their alternatives for "Joan": Juanita, Johanna, and Joanna, among others. It has been a very long time since I have given any thought to my name; it is simply the moniker that I respond to, nothing more or less. It is relatively rare as a first name, which is a plus, and the J sound, is not unpleasant. It has no great meaning to me, but hope it might have positive resonance to those who know me.

All of the Jews in Portland, Oregon of my parents' generation gave their children Brit/Scot/even Irish names. Assimilating meant blending in. Our last names were clearly not any of the above, but we could have "American" first names. My thoughts on my last name are much more interesting, I would have to say. Where did that come from? Austria-Hungary I was told by my grandmother, not knowing what a vast place it was. My uncle claimed that Goldhammer was some kind of transliteration of Maccabee. And why did we have an Anglo name in the middle of Central Europe, now Slovakia??? All mysteries yet to be solved.

Joan doesn't seem to have any stories to go with her name; it's just a moniker. Her real interest is in her family name because it has stories waiting to be discovered.

– C –
PERSIAN

In 1935, the Shah requested that Persia be called Iran. Iran is derived from Aryāna, the country of the Aryans, which predates Persia. The Iranians are not Arabs; they are Indo-Europeans. Indo-Europeans, inhabitants primarily of Europe, Iran, and India, are all members of the same language family. Although we may have forgotten our common origins from thousands of years ago, our languages have not.

The Iranians became known as Persians in the 6th century BCE, when Cyrus the Great, a member of the Pars tribe, conquered a vast area—stretching from Central Asia to the Mediterranean and the Black Sea, including Tajikistan, Uzbekistan, Northern Pakistan, Azerbaijan, Armenia, Turkey, Georgia, and the Caucasus region of Russia—which became known as the Persian Empire, based on the name of his tribe.

The Persian language has different names in different countries: Dari in Afghanistan, Tajiki in Tajikistan, Parsi, and Farsi (which is the name the invading Arabs gave Parsi because Arabic has no f $(/p/)$ sound. Arabs are descendants of the tribes of Arabia and speak Arabic. Arabs and Jews are related: both speak Semitic languages. Semitic languages are spoken primarily in the Middle East, Saudi Arabia, and Northern Africa. Turkish is neither Indo-European nor Semitic but has ties to Asian languages, like Mongolian, Korean, and Japanese.[94] As its languages indicate, the Near East has been a cultural mix for thousands of years.

Farsi is what Iranians call their language; but linguists prefer the name Persian, which is associated with the large ancient empire rather than specific countries. Because the Arabs conquered Persia in the 7th century, Persian is written in Arabic script and has assimilated many Arabic words. Like all history, Persian history is a complex story of assimilation.[95] Iranians are predominately Shia Muslim (a minority sect in Islam), followed by Sunni (the majority sect in Islam), and then by members of the Bahá'í faith, which originated in 19th century Persia and teaches the underlying unity of all religions—the spiritual unity of all mankind. Persian and Arab countries have Christian and Jewish minorities as well as followers of ancient religions such as Zoroasterism and Manichaeism.

(*Aryan* is a word that was completely distorted by Nazi Germany to refer to Nordic blond types and has no correlation to the historical meaning of the word. *Aryan* originally described any of the Indo-European speakers, who live in a geographic area that stretches from India to Iceland and includes, therefore, both dark- and light-skinned peoples.)

• • •

The Perfect Mix
Kathleen T. M.

There is a scene in the movie Forrest Gump, where the title character introduces himself in the following way: "My name is Forrest, Forrest Gump. People call me Forrest Gump." In many ways, I can relate to this comical scene. My nickname is Katie. However, every class or group I have been in has had a handful of Katies, so people call me Katie M. I am certain that the only reason people have learned how to pronounce my last name is because my first name is so common.

My full name, Kathleen T. M., is the brainchild of my mother, an American who found herself married to an Iranian after a great blind date in the 1970s. My mother originally wanted to give me a melodious, non–belly-dancer Persian name (her words, not mine); however after a turn through the Persian baby name book, she found very few names that she could pronounce and even fewer that she liked. Realizing that her half-breed children would already have a mouthful with the last name "M.," she and my father opted to pick Persian middle names and American first names. My initials, K. T., turned into my nickname, Katie, which I have been called since the week after my birth. (I was born prematurely before my parents had picked a name, so I was first called "it.")

With a short, cute nickname like Katie, I have always been thankful to have longer, classier and more professional sounding names for my alter egos. My resumé has always said Kathleen, and when interviewing as Kathleen, I wear pearls, speak eloquently and act qualified. My extended, Iranian side of the family calls me T., and when interacting as T., I wear gold, speak Farsi and act graciously. "K.T." is the combination of my upbringing, cultures, education, and experiences, but with my own personality thrown in the mix. When I was a little

231

kid, everyone told me that I would grow out of the name Katie. On the contrary, I think I grew into it.

With a wry sense of humor, Katie describes her experience of assimilating her American and Persian cultures socially, linguistically, and even stylistically. Even her name is a perfect balance between her two cultures. Katie is so at ease with her cultural identity because she "grew into it": it was not imposed.

– D –
ARAB

Although many of us are familiar with *How the Irish Saved Western Civilization* by Thomas Cahill, *How The Arabs Saved Western Civilization* has yet to be written. When Europe was brought into the Dark Ages by wave upon wave of barbarian invasions after the fall of the Roman Empire in 476 ACE, the Arab world was undergoing a Golden Age, maintaining Greek and Roman knowledge, creating new inventions in many different fields, and linking East and West. European Crusaders (1095–1291) started bringing back both new and lost knowledge as well as a desire to emulate the luxuries of Arabic civilization, which helped launch what scholars call the Medieval Renaissance in twelfth century Europe.

• • •

On Being an Arab American Today
Mariam

My name is Mariam. People call me Miriam, Marion, and even Merriam. Over the years, I've learned the best way to clear up the confusion is to say, "It's Maria with an 'm' at the end: M-a-r-i-a-m. It's Arabic for 'Mary.'" Then depending on their curiosity, I might have mentioned that one of the books in the Koran is named for Mariam, the mother of Jesus. Often people were intrigued: my name was a great icebreaker. But that was before 9/11. I don't do that anymore. In this post 9/11 world, that conversation has to wait; and maybe, it will never take place. Now Islam is associated with terrorists. What's happened to Islam makes me sad. It's such a distortion. I remember the horror of 9/11; and then the horror of discovering all the hijackers were Arab Muslims. For Muslims like me, we lived through 9/11 twice. First we went through the sickening anguish of watching human beings and towers fall, then we watched as our religion was transformed in the eyes of the world from one of peace and tolerance to one of hate and violence. At first I was in shock. Then, for a long time, I was filled with rage and tears. My world had been turned upside down. The madness seemed contagious, like a plague.

I am a second generation American Arab. My parents came to the U.S. during very bad times in their country. Getting into the U.S. was a dream come true. In thinking about my identity, the first thing that comes to mind is that I'm an American: an American Arab Muslim, to be precise. I wonder why it is that traditionally, we say Black American, Irish American, Native American, etc. Seems like it should be the reverse: American Black, American Irish, American Native. I guess people always want to be able to distinguish themselves. I have always answered questions about ethnicity saying, "I am an American Arab Muslim." A lot of my friends feel the same way. We want to be like everybody else. America is my home. I could never go back to my parents' country of origin.

It took a long time for the anguish surrounding 9/11 and the ensuing catastrophes to subside. It's not easy. People are afraid: they see every Arab as a potential terrorist. You can see it in their eyes—a momentary flinch when they discover I'm an Arab Muslim. One of the things that helped me heal was my name. Muslims believe your name should have meaning and should inspire. Mary, the Mother of Jesus, is such an inspiring figure. Why? Because she is allmerciful. What makes someone merciful? You have to understand why people behave the way the do: you have to have compassion. Compassion. That is what helped to heal my own spiritual wounds. People don't lash out for no reason. If you can understand why they act as they do, you're on your way to helping resolve the problem. Because you can feel their anguish, you know what they need to cure it. But to understand, you have to have compassion. If we could only realize that an angry person is a person in pain, we wouldn't react with anger. If your reaction to anger is anger, then both of you are in pain and nothing has been resolved. The situation has only been made worse. That's why Jesus said, "If someone strikes you, turn the other cheek." Will mankind ever learn to react like that? We can't lose hope. Gandhi and Martin Luther King showed us it is possible.

My father wanted my name spelled with an "i" rather than a "y": Mariam. He says it makes the name more international. The "i" suggests a visual triplicate: Mari/y, Maria, and Mariam. Each name represents a different culture, which inspired discussions about the international dimensions of religion and identity. I grew up looking at all kinds of paintings and sculptures of Mary—everything from medieval to contemporary art, which led to a fascination with art, history, religion, and ethnic studies.

Traditional Arab naming traditions are complicated because they include names that are religious, descriptive, patriarchal, and even place names. Arab middle names often include the father and grandfather's first names, which tracks paternal lineage. This complexity reflects the tribal origins of the Arabs. Many Arabs simplify their names in order to fit into contemporary culture. And finally, did you know that Muslim women keep their family names when they marry?

I've finally accepted that the world has changed radically. Many of my friends are now having kids. Naming them is a challenge. There's a tendency to give them American given names, because parents want to protect their kids from discrimination. Who knows what's going to happen. We think about the Japanese internment camps. We think about airports. We think about difficult economic times and scarce jobs. We think about Hindus murdered because the killer mistakenly thought they were Arabs. We worry. Because I am an American Arab Muslim, I weep for both sides and I pray for peace.

– E –
GREEK

• • •

Tradition and Assimilation
Roula S. Manton

I am a Greek American lady 69 years old, and I often wondered how people get their names. I was born and raised in Thessaloniki, Greece and I was the first born of my parents. It is a Greek tradition to name your first-born child after the father's parent—I should say it was a tradition when I was born to name the child after a grandparent. My name is Roula a nickname for Rodi, my paternal grandmother's name. When I was a child I didn't like to be called Rodi, actually Rothee, so the nickname Roula stuck. I married and came to the USA in September of 1962. The following September our daughter was born and we named her Eriphylli, my husband's mother's name. Eriphylli is an ancient Greek name.

The name sounded too old to us so we called our daughter Phyllis and felt it was a good name for her. Our second child a boy was named after my dad and his name is Stephanos. He is called Stephen most of the time. Children in Greece take their father's name as a middle name. The "S" of my middle name is for Stephanos, my dad's name.

In the Greek Church we use our baptismal name when we receive Holy Communion. Our priest and few friends now call me Rodi, and I am used to it. In fact I kind of like it.

People are always curious about my name Roula. They ask me what it means and how I got it. I have been a Realtor for the last 31 years and my name didn't bring me more business because it's different and didn't stop me from achieving my goals in Real Estate. Most of my friends at the office call me Bula, Bula. Sometimes it aggravates me, other times I don't pay attention to them: it depends on my state of mind.

Roula feels her Greek name has neither helped nor hurt her—an indication she feels integrated. This sense of assimilation also appears with her children's names. Eriphylli becomes Phyllis, and Stephanos becomes Stephen. The only problem Roula has concerns her office nickname, *Bula-Bula*, which means *"hello"* in Figi—a nickname that sounds like *Roula*, but is a bit easier to say and perhaps more familiar, since sporting equipment and resorts bear the name.

– F –
CHINESE

• • •

Name and Appearance
Katherine Mei Hwei Lee Rieger
(3rd/4th Generation Chinese Americans)

I didn't know how important my family name was to me until I got married and legally took my husband's family name. I am Chinese American and my husband is Irish/English/German American. I was proud to use my husband's name, but also felt a loss of my family and cultural connections. I had not realized how interconnected being a Lee was with my self-identity. Both my mother and father's families have been in America for many generations. Neither of my parents speaks Chinese, nor do I. My family has preserved some Chinese cultural traditions, but we are also very American. After I changed my name, it occurred to me that my Chinese-ness was based in name and appearance; otherwise I was completely American. I never dealt with this discomfort until I got pregnant.

(...)

As I raise my bi-cultural, bi-racial son, I realize how many of the choices I make on his behalf have to do with being raised a Lee, in a Chinese and American family. I realize that human beings are complex animals whose personal identities are shaped by countless factors. I realize that while names connote meaning, they are not the only ties I have to my Chinese-ness. But at school, I ask children to call me Mrs. Lee.

• • •

A Fortunate Mismatch
Veronica Tai Ying

Veronica is my baptismal name. When I was a week old, my mother brought me to a church in Bangkok, my birthplace, to be baptized. My mom is a devout Catholic who attended a convent school in Hong Kong. Because all her classmates had

Christian names, she had a rich roster to pick from. However, for her fourth child, she had run out of ideas. She asked the Italian priest to pick a name. He opened the Bible to a page and read the first female name he saw: Veronica, the woman who wiped Jesus' face.

When I immigrated to the U.S. in the 1960s, the immigration officer in Honolulu asked me where I got that name. Fifteen years old and wary of trick questions that could be used to deport me, I mumbled something about the priest who baptized me. The officer stamped my passport, and since then many Americans have asked me the same question. They feel it's most unusual for a Chinese to be called Veronica.

For a long time, the mismatch made me uncomfortable, but I recently discovered the advantage of being a Chinese with an unusual English name. After publishing a book about my mother's life, I put up a Web site to promote my title, Journey across the Four Seas. The domain name Veronicali.com had no other contender. It was all mine.

Veronica feels like her name is a mismatch, perhaps because so many Americans tell her how "unusual" her name is for her ethnicity. Two names or a name that unites different cultures seems to be the best choice for successfully integrating the old culture and the new as we saw in Katie's essay and in those submitted by Jewish essayists. Veronica's "mismatched" name redeems itself by providing her with a unique identity.

– G –
LITHUANIAN

• • •

Layers of Meaning
Ginta Remeikis

My parents had fled Soviet occupation of Lithuania as children and spent five years in displaced persons camps in Germany before arriving in the States as teens. It was the raison d'être of those who fled, and by extension their children, to keep Lithuanian culture alive and to work for Lithuanian independence.

Ginta reminds us that today with rapid, affordable communication, immigrants stay in touch with their homeland. Many get an education, send money, and work for freedom in their native country. Lithuania deserves special recognition as part of the world's biggest political demonstration, staged on August 23 of 1989, exactly fifty years after the Soviet Union took over the Baltic nations, when two million people in

Latvia, Estonia, and Lithuania held hands to form a 600 km (373 mile) human chain between their capital cities to draw attention to their calls for independence. This peaceful demonstration is called the *Baltic Way*. It was part of a wave of passive resistance—including the *Singing Revolution* in Estonia (1987–90), the *Solidarity* movement in Poland (1980s), and in 1989 the *Velvet Revolution* in Czechoslovakia, the fall of the Berlin Wall, and the Tiananmen Square protests in China. This history reminds us that contemporary passive resistance, inspired by Gandhi and Martin Luther King, Jr., is a formidable tool for bringing about change peacefully. The *Rose Revolution* in Georgia in 2003 the *Orange Revolution* in Ukraine in 2005 are among the most recent passive revolutions, with another now underway in Iran, which has yet to be named. The recent spread of passive revolutions is a sign of hope in mankind's evolution towards handling disputes without killing and warfare.

The planet seems to be undergoing the same kind of identity crisis that the individual also now faces. After centuries of creating a unified vision of mankind and a singular mind ruled by reason, the world seems to be moving back to the concept of mini-states just as we are relearning that an individual's singular identity is made up of multiple facets. Smaller states, which mirror our ancient history, may actually be more ecologically and socially viable. Economists are now advocating that nations become more self sufficient in order to boost local economies and to help the environment by reducing pollution caused by shipping goods for thousands of miles across continents and oceans. We see time revealed in amber—in the past—in the current thinking about both the world and the individual.

• • •

<h2 style="text-align:center">Diversity
Gabrielle Lina Gedo
(Generation Y)</h2>

I was born in 1998. Before I was born, my grandparents sent my parents a card congratulating them. On the front was a picture of the Annunciation. My parents had three name options for me: Lina, a Lithuanian name which means flax or linen; Gabrielle, because of Archangel Gabriel on the card; and Matthew, after my great-grandfather Mathias and my father's mother's maiden name, Mathews. My parents discussed which name they would give me if I were a girl; the other name would be my middle name. My mother wanted me to be Lina Gabrielle. My father wanted it the other way around: Gabrielle Lina. He pointed out that my older sister had a Lithuanian first name. My mother claimed Gabrielle was not a Lithuanian name. But my non-Lithuanian father held on, saying that Gabrielle can be translated into Lithuanian as Gabriel_. Finally, my mother consented. And so I became Gabrielle Lina.

Of course, most people who are named Gabrielle have a nickname. Most Gabrielle's nicknames are Gabby, but my parents did not want to call me Gabby, as it also means you talk too much. They decided Gabi would be better. This turned out to be a little ironic, however, as I have become a very gabby person.

My last name was Anglicized. When my grandfather and his parents came to America from Morocco (although they were originally Hungarians from Czechoslovakia) their last name was Gedö. The American authorities changed their last name to Gedo and it's been so ever since.

For story contests at my Lithuanian school, I have to use a pen name. In the past I have Lithuanianized the names of people I admire: first: Clara Clemens (Mark Twain's daughter) to Klara Klementait_, second: Martina von Trapp (one of the Trapp Family Singers) to Martina Trapyt_, and finally: Crown Princess Victoria of Sweden (and her father, too) to Viktorija Gustauftait_. What will my future names be?

Gabrielle's name is universally recognized because of its associations with the archangel Gabriel, the messenger of God, a powerful symbol of the link between the human and the divine. Gabriel is the communicator, who puts God's will into words. Gabrielle explains that she is both *Gabi* and *gabby:* she is already beginning to fulfill her name as a communicator. She also fulfills Gabriel's role in another way: for as Gabriel communicates between two worlds, the spiritual and the physical, Gabrielle is at home in either American or Lithuanian culture.

Different languages enrich our perceptions. Gabrielle's Lithuanian pen name adds yet another dimension to her identity. When she asks, "What will my future names be?" she reveals that even as a preadolescent she sees identity as multifaceted and evolving.

– H –
BLACK AMERICAN

• • •

Something Conventional
Kimberly Walker, Ph.D.

I was named by a family committee. In the '60s Kimberly was a really popular name…and my parents were determined to name me something "conventional" (I am African American) so as to make it harder to discriminate outright. My middle name is Elaine, which was chosen by my godfather and uncle. My uncles called me

238

"the Fugitive" for years because that show was popular at the time and apparently I was born or my mother went into labor during an episode. I call myself Kimberly, although my colleagues call me Kim. I think my name suits me very well.

Kimberly's parents choose her name with the hope of avoiding "outright" discrimination. Names offer protection. (The star of *The Fugitive* was a doctor, and so is Kimberly.)

• • •
A Changing History
Joycelyn LaBranch

My name is Joycelyn. It is of English origin and it means cheerful, merry. I was born in the south—New Orleans, LA. The ethnic group I claim was at that time identified as Negro. Interestingly enough, and as time and events transpired, the names used to identify me and my ancestry have changed. I am uncertain of why or who may be responsible for the confounded identity, or if the current racial identification is due for its millennial revelation. Rather than assigning all people to the human race each identity or title assigns a graphic description (Negro, Black, African American) that references color or hue. I associate the above names with historical reflections that communicate the struggles, challenges, travailing, colors of the flag (red, green and black), the sweat, tears, and the victories of generations of people.

As a teenager I wanted my name to reflect who I thought I was or whom I was attempting to portray. To me Joycelyn was a mouthful and was not attractive or cute. I asked my mother how or why she chose this moniker; and although a real reason escapes me, I do remember her saying during the signing of the birth certificate there was an error. My mother said that the nurse should have written "Joyce Lynn," which would have given me a first name and a middle name; but in the nurse's erroneous transcription, I got "Joycelyn."

I use my name in my profession, on résumés, and when I introduce myself. I had no other choice. I have come to realize that the meaning "cheerful," "merry" actually describes me. In the 7th grade a very cute young man, whom I was quite smitten with nicknamed me "Smiley"—that name caught on and I would be Smiley until I graduated from high school. Subsequently, eight years ago in church, a gentleman, whom I only acknowledged in polite greetings of the day, stopped me and told me that he was going to call me "Smiley" because I had a cheerful demeanor.

My mother's name choice was not indicative of tradition, ancestry, or religious meaning; but it was predicated on love. What now is a funny memory is how I could immediately distinguish, by tone, volume and the elongated extending of the syllables, as my name rolled off her tongue, if trouble loomed or if she simply needed my attention. How I wish to hear that voice again. My mother is gone now, and I cherish those memories. I love my name just because it was her choice.

Presented in 1884, a gift from France, created by Frederic Auguste Bartholdi, the Statue of Liberty bears a tablet with these words, "Give me your tired, your poor, your huddled masses yearning to breathe free." Unfortunately, we also had immigrants brought to these shores as slaves. The election of President Obama is proof that the prejudices of the past are giving way.

Jocelyn's discussion of the changing terminology used over the years to describe Black Americans highlights their slow assimilation and the problems with racial categorization. They have been called *Negro, Colored, Black,* and *African American.* Now because many African Arabs have immigrated to the U.S., the name has changed yet again to *Black African Americans* or *Black Americans,* the latter distinguishing them from newly arrived Black Africans. Terminology is facing a constantly evolving, and eventually, losing battle.

Negro derives from the Spanish, Portuguese, and Italian, which are all mutations of the Latin *niger* (black). The origins of the Latin are unknown. The Roman author Ptolemy (first century BCE), mentions the Niger River in Africa, a name derived from the Berber (Tuareg) name for the river.[97] Niger could originally have been a geographic description like Caucasian, which refers to the Caucasus Mountains. While understanding the etymology is helpful, it does not resolve the fact that color labels are dehumanizing distortions just like numbers or a letter. All the colors used to describe human beings are inaccurate: Blacks are not black, Whites are not white, Native Americans are not red, Asians are not yellow.

Finding a label for Black Americans is difficult because they defy categorization. All Americans do, but we fail to realize this. Americans are, by definition, a mix of different cultures. Jocelyn believes that there is only one human race, which is a belief geneticists have now proven to be true, as you remember (p.134).

The black, green, and red flag Joycelyn describes is the flag initially designed in 1920 to be "the official banner of the African race."[98] The flag was created in direct response to a very popular, racist song of the day, "Every Race Has a Flag Except the Coon."[99] Marcus Garvey designed a Pan-African flag and founded the UNIA-ACL (Universal Negro Improvement Association and African Communities League), which worked to promote the liberation of Blacks all over the world. The red symbolizes the noble blood of the African people, black represents the African race, and green is for the fertile land of Africa. Many newly formed African countries picked red, black, and green colors for their flags based on his flag. In the 1960s the flag became a "symbol for the worldwide liberation of people of African origin" and "an emblem of Black pride" for Blacks all over the world.[100] Joycelyn gives a very moving description of the pride the flag confers amid all the toils and tribulations Black Americans have undergone.

Like other essayists, she undergoes a modification of her name due to an intrusive functionary; and following a common pattern, she grows into her name. *Joy-ce-lyn* reinforces joy every time it is spoken or read—an uplifting association that may subconsciously affect her and others. She closes the circular narrative of her name with a description of the sound of her mother's voice saying her name, reminding us of the tactile sensations that accompany hearing. Her memories remind us of Sophy's and Evelyn's recollections of the sound of their childhood names.

Tradition and family ties were impossible to maintain during slavery ("officially": 1619–1850)[101] because families were separated. The Civil Rights Act of 1965 finally made discrimination illegal. Black families have survived years of discrimination with faith and love. For Joycelyn, love represents the essence of her name.

In less than 50 years after the passage of the Civil Rights Act, America elected a Black president. Obama's historical election proves that the country has come a long way in overcoming the prejudices of the past although much remains to be done.

More than 55 million people, one out of every five Americans, is a first or second-generation immigrant.[102] These essays indicate that the attempt to suppress any cultural aspect of an individual's identity creates rejection of the imposed culture. The essayists do not identify completely with their names if they were simply given to facilitate assimilation and they have no stories to go with them. Names given out of fear foster an inherent anxiety. The essayists who are the happiest with their names have multicultural names or they feel that their names have helped them assimilate successfully: they do no relate to their cultures as "either… or" but as "both…and." Although we often fail to realize it, being American automatically means your heritage is from elsewhere, unless you are a Native American. This diversity is key to America's strength and creativity.

Forming a sense of identity is like putting together a puzzle: the individual parts have to be recognized before they can fit together as a whole. The same is true on a global level: the paradox is that in order for different cultures to coexist, they must first recognize and honor their diversity. Ironically, it is only by acknowledging differences that unity can be achieved.

To delve further into assimilation in America, consider *Assimilation in American Life* by M. Gordon, *Legacies: The Stories of the Immigrant Second Generation* by A. Portes, or *Remaking the American Mainstream* by Alba and Nee. To ponder further color symbolism in the Black American community, read Alice Walker's Pulitzer Prize winning novel *The Color Purple*.

Chapter 26
THE SHRINKING PLANET:
INTERNATIONAL AND MULTICULTURAL NAMES

With ever increasing travel and global awareness, we are exposed to different cultures and different ways of thinking, which can enrich our understanding of identity.

· · ·

Spiritual and Cultural Dimensions
Peggy Kay

The story I am told about my naming at birth comes from the German tradition of my mother's side of my family. Both my mother and grandmother are very strong and assertive women, and I am told that my grandmother thought that I should be named Gretchen, a good stalwart German name for an evidently strong, strapping baby girl. My mother says at the last minute in filling out the birth certificate, she put her foot down and said that my name would be Peggy. I think Peggy is gentler, more artistic, and feels like me, whereas Gretchen does not. Peggy also has a more contemporary feel, whereas Gretchen is more old-fashioned. Since my family is Protestant by tradition, Peggy has no connection with the traditional Catholic name Margaret from which Peggy comes. So, even though I am often asked if my name is really Margaret, I say it is Peggy, which I like very much because it is fairly uncommon.

The middle name given to me was my mother's nickname. Her maiden name was Koenig, a fairly common German name meaning "king", so many people who knew her well called her "Kay." My last name was Demaree. I got very weary of having to spell it, and explain it, and it never meant anything, so I ended up just changing it. In 1986, I dropped Demaree, and my legal name became Peggy Kay. My mother's nickname was now my last name.

In grade school in Minneapolis, I was constantly teased by school kids who used to call me "Piggy" because I was so fat. When I went to a different high school, thankfully the nickname did not make the transition, so I became Peggy again to my classmates. In French class, we had to choose French names so I chose the name of Colette. Why, I do not know. I guess because it has the same feminine, intellectual quality as Peggy does—at least that is my sense of the two names. I had the same comfort level in both. Even today when I text-message someone in French, I sign off with the name "Colette", and they know it is me texting in French.

In the mid 1990s I made a friend—more like a sister—from Ghana. I have two older brothers, and always wanted a sister. When I met Ami she seemed familiar, just like a sister, and included me from the start in her family of five sisters.

Over the next few years as we became closer, one of the sisters, Mansa, was visiting from Accra with her children, who immediately became my children. They said if I was to be a proper African I must have a proper African name, asked me what day of the week I was born, and named me Adjowa, meaning "girl born on a Monday." It can be spelled any number of ways. It is a simple, traditional name, kind of a nickname or common name, given to all Ghanaians, boys and girls. ("Kofi", the first name used by Kofi Annan, means "boy born on a Friday", and it is very interesting that he uses it as his public, international name, rather than his birth first name.) So, having been named Adjowa and thinking that millions of women born on a Monday could be called the same thing, I said, "That's kind of dull, isn't it?", at which they howled with laughter. Okay, they said, we'll call you Ewuradjowa, which indicates a woman of social stature, a more proper ladylike term meaning known and respected in the community. So my name became Ewuradjowa Peggy, which means "Lady Peggy, born on a Monday." "That's more like it," I said, and they howled again.

At the same time I had a good friend with whom I would meditate and pray, a fellow devotee of Paramahansa Yogananda, a Hindu-Christian saint, swami, and yogi. We would discuss eastern traditions and spiritual principles and try to define Sanskrit and Hindi words with profound spiritual meanings in ways that could be spiritually adapted by American culture. In conversation one day, as we struggled to get to essence of concepts, we thought about the spiritual features we would highlight in each other. She said she would name me Samyama, which she translated as "angel of self-mastery." To this day I accept this as an enormous spiritual complement in the sense of a desirable spirituality, which I hope to live up to.

In 1997 in the middle of my Masters degree I received a grant and went on a research trip to South Africa, to the eastern province of KwaZulu/Natal. Apartheid had legally ended in 1994. I went to visit some Christian pastors from Ghana and Zambia, who had gone to the mostly Zulu province in 1982, twelve years before the end of apartheid, as fellow black Africans to teach the Bible to the Zulu people in the hope of quelling intra-tribal violence. I went deep into the province with them where whites do not often go. As it becomes increasingly rural, people live closer and closer to traditional tribal ways. We were headed for Nongoma, which is the town in which the Zulu King Goodwill Zwelithini lives and around which most of the churches were located. "Church" in this context is not a lovely building or even a building at all, but simply a place where people gather to worship—sing, dance, and bring offerings such as fruit or grain or beer (locally made with corn, a traditional drink with little alcohol). When we were almost to Nongoma, we were in a terrible motor vehicle wreck. The Ghanaian pastor and his Ghanaian colleague died. I had major injuries, the Zambian pastor lost much of his face, and our Zulu driver had minor injuries. While in the hospital as Zulu folk

came to visit me and heard my life story, they named me "Nomathemba." "Themba"
is the Zulu word for hope, and is also sometimes a man's name. "No" is a prefix
added to indicate a woman's name, and the "a" is a joiner. So Nomathemba is a
woman's name and means one who hopes and continues hoping regardless of events
and circumstances. I felt very honored and included as one of the community,
which is what they intended. My proper African name then expanded to become
Ewuradjoa Nomathemba Peggy Kay.

After I returned to the States, I corresponded for a time with a South African
alum of the school where I did my Ph.D. He is part of a well-known Zulu family,
the Buthelezis. After a time he told me he would give me the honorary last name of
Buthelezi, saying I would be the second white person to receive this name—the first
being a German student who had traveled to South Africa some years before. The
Buthelezi clan is so big that their family reunions are national events, and he told
me, "all Buthelezis are related." So, my full proper African name became Ewuradjoa
Nomathemba Peggy Kay Buthelezi. I have not yet figured out where Samyama fits
into that.

Unlike some of the mothers in the essays, Peggy's mother manages to prevail over the grandmother. Because her surname *Demarée,* "never meant anything," Peggy changes it legally to *Kay,* her mother's nickname, which gives her two first names like Francesca. After her mother discovers the French roots of *Demarée,* thus giving the name a story, Peggy would now like to reclaim it, which would be a return to the first name, a closing of the circle.

The French teacher's idea of creating a French persona is an excellent teaching strategy because the name change helps to free the student from her American identity and language inhibitions.

Whereas Elvira Kituyi's essay centers on her ancestors, Peggy's essay describes another African naming tradition that centers on time. In Ghana, Peggy notes that individuals receive a given name and a day name. Day names put the individual in a universal time family, rather than a single physical family or tribe. Peggy notes that Kofi Annan uses the name *Kofi,* meaning "boy born on a Friday," as his "public, international name," rather than his given birth name. His use of his day name, rather than his personal name, symbolizes his humility and his membership in the family of mankind.

Peggy's spiritual name, *Samyama,* given to her by her guru, reminds us of Shyama's essay and the spiritual renewal these names provide.

The Zulus give Peggy yet another name. When she goes to the hospital with life threatening injuries, they visit her and give her the name *Nomathemba,* based on "themba" (hope). By giving Peggy hope, the Zulus give her the courage to recover from a devastating accident. Here we find yet another rich African naming tradition—this one based on inspiring the individual with the meaning of her name. Although this is a belief the Zulus share with the Muslims, the Zulus are primarily animist, then Christian.

Another Zulu gives her the family name *Buthelezi,* telling her "all Buthelezis are related: "the family name thus designates not simply a familial relationship but also a spiritual one." Years ago in the South, I once heard the expression "an honorary family member" used to describe a neighbor's child who was a close friend. Have you ever heard the expression used? Where?

As opposed to Western thought, which has centered on the individual for centuries as exemplified by "I think, therefore, I am" (Descartes), Black Africans emphasize belonging and connectedness with one another. The Zulus have a saying, "I am related, therefore, I am"—relationships are key in determining who they are and what is of primary importance in life. John Donne mirrored the sentiment in his famous line: "No man is an island."[103] Our most ancient naming traditions, both Native American and African, emphasize the importance of giving a name that links the individual to others.

• • •

International Connections
Lucy Larkin
(by her mom: Tricia Larkin)

(...) So she is an American baby with Brazilian roots who lives in Switzerland with an English name!

In this era of globalization, it is no longer possible to judge where a woman is from by her name.

• • •

An International Name
Nada Giuffrida

My name means "hope" in Russian, "water that generates life" in Greek, "dew" in Arabic, "music" in Thai, and "nothing" in Spanish.
I think that's enough mixture in there.

In an e-mail discussion with young adults in their 20s and 30s, the dominant theme of the conversation was the international dimensions of their names—an indication that younger generations have more of a global view of the world than past generations. Because of global pressures affecting the planet's well-being, young people are deeply aware of the concept of a "global village" whose members will have to work together to save the earth. Destiny is no longer that of East or West but Global. Even the word *international,* which suggests a union of parts, has given way to *global,* which suggests an indivisible whole. As Benjamin Franklin put it so aptly, "We must, indeed, all hang together, or assuredly we shall all hang separately."[104]

・ ・ ・
International Ties
Adele Waugaman

I got my name because my parents wanted to give a nod to my francophone heritage—my mother's mother emigrated from Belgium to the U.S.—and they wanted to pick a name that was somewhat unusual in the U.S.

(I've since come to realize that Adel is not so unusual in Egypt and other Arab-speaking countries, where it is a man's name. And I met lots of women with my name when in South Africa.)

At an international conference a few years ago, I found myself talking to a guy from Jordan and a guy from India. Somehow we got to talking about names; and the Arabic speaking guy from Jordan told me my name was close to the Arab word for justice or "one who is just." The Hindi-speaking guy from India then told me that my name was close to the word for international. I was interested to hear both, particularly since we were having this conversation at a conference for the International Court—the first permanent international court charged with bringing the Pol Pots and Adolf Hitlers of the future to justice. I've also been told that Adele comes from the German name Adelheid, composed of "athala" (nobleness) and -"heid" (quality). I can't say that I'm descended from "noble quality," but I do like working for noble causes.

When a name is found in many different languages, it has ancient origins. Names found in different cultures remind us not only of the peregrinations of our ancient ancestors, but also that (with the exception of Hungarian and Finnish) Indo-European is the mother of all the European languages, Persian, and the Vedic (Indian) languages. A partial list of the European languages includes Germanic (Nordic languages, English, German, Dutch), Romance (French, Spanish, Portuguese, Italian, Romanian), Greek, Slavic, and Russian (including all of the northern Russian Federation extending to the Pacific Ocean). This linguistic family explains why some names are found in so many different languages: they all have the same origin.

My Daughter, Sophie
Yvonne Rollins

Her father and I chose the name Sophie for two reasons.

1) The name is the same in French and English, which allowed our daughter to feel at home in either the U.S. or France. The name was fashionable in France, but I discovered later that it was out of fashion in the U.S. I remember one day a colleague (10 years older than I) told me while I was talking to her about my daughter, "Oh, I had an Aunt Sophie!"—a statement that made me immediately realize that the name was old-fashioned. None of that ever bothered Sophie. She did not like her friends to call her "Soph" or even worse, "Sofa." In France, we don't use nicknames like here in America.

2) I liked the meaning of the name—the Greek word for wisdom.

I think my daughter likes her name.

Because *Sophie* stems from ancient Greek, it is a name like *Adele* that is found all over the world in many different cultures.

We sometimes forget that our ancient ancestors traveled great distances. The Celts traveled as far as China by 2000 BCE and left their genetic footprint with the blonds found among Mongolians today. Elizabeth Wayland Barber writes about the ancient Celtic inhabitants of China in *Mummies of Urumchi.* Alexander the Great traveled with his Greek soldiers as far as India in the 4th century BCE. The Vikings sailed to North America and were in Baghdad by the 10th century. Marco Polo went to China in the 13th century.

Native Americans immigrated to North America from Siberia 12,000 years ago. The migration of our ancestors was not limited to land, however. With *Kon-Tiki* and *Ra II,* Thor Heyerdahl proved that ancient South Americans could have sailed across the Pacific, and the ancient Egyptians could have sailed across the Atlantic. Recent discoveries suggest the Chinese mapped the world and settled the Americas as early as 2200 BCE, long before Columbus arrived in 1492.[105] Given names, found across the globe, in different languages and cultures, are a testament to the international travels of our ancestors in both ancient and medieval times.

Chapter 27
NAMES AND RELIGION

Many women's names are drawn from the Bible or the Qur'an. The Catholic Church dictates that children have a Christian name, or at least a name that is not offensive to Christians.[106] At confirmation, Catholic girls pick a saint's name, which becomes their middle name or an additional middle name. Historically, to avoid common Catholic names that were drawn primarily from the New Testament, Protestants picked Old Testament biblical names, Christian virtues, and even family surnames for given names.[107] The Muslim tradition dictates that a name should have a meaning that inspires the individual throughout life.

– A –
CHRISTIAN

– 1 –
Different Ways to Choose a Christian Name

Catholic mothers are encouraged to pick a saint's name for their children. As we heard from Bonnie and Bo, this can sometimes require some extra searching if the chosen given name is not a saint's name. Bonnie's parents (pp.16–17) and Bonita's parents (pp.36–38) both found St. Bonaventura as a patron saint for their given names.

• • •

The Catholic Calendar
Gloria a Velasco

I'm originally from the Philippines, a predominately Catholic country. My parents told me they picked my given name from the Catholic calendar, which provides a saint for each day. I was named for the saint designated for the day I was born.

• • •

Randomly Finding the Name in the Bible
Veronica Li

Veronica is my baptismal name. When I was a week old, my mother brought me to a church in Bangkok, my birthplace, to be baptized. My mom is a devout Catholic who attended a convent school in Hong Kong. Because all her classmates had Christian names, she had a rich roster to pick from. However, for her fourth child, she had run out of ideas. She asked the Italian priest to pick a name. He opened the

Bible to a page and read the first female name he saw: Veronica, the woman who wiped Jesus' face.

· · ·

Different Names for the Virgin:
Our Lady of Sorrows: The Power of a Name
Dolores Rice

Dolores is a family name, goes back for generations. Represents the Mother of God, the Lady of Sorrows. (…) I've wrestled with pain throughout my adult life and attribute the addiction to my name. I don't seek to alleviate pain but seem to dwell in it, a strange perversion to being named for pain and sorrow.

Some call me empathetic, others say I'm very serious, spiritual, a wise woman, an elder and have been older than my years since the day I was born.

· · ·

Christ: A Spiritual Dimension
Christina Keunen

My first name is Christina. I was raised in the Episcopal Church. I always felt an association with the "Christ" in my name, and felt that I had a spiritual side that came from that association. And also a responsibility to remember from whence I came. I never put a name to what I felt, but I felt a connection. I am still thankful to this day, for the man, whoever he was, who was willing to give up his life for what he believed in and for the welfare of others.

· · ·

Virtues: My Faith has Served Me Well
Faith Winters

My name is Faith and I am the second born in a family of four. My older sister is named Hope, then Faith but no Charity (we try hard!). Old joke. We are different from the proverbial song –"Faith, Hope and Charity" as the order is changed.

Faith—a most challenging name to live up to. In college I was forced to endure jokes such as "Keep the baby, Faith; keep the faith, baby; and you must have a lot of faith in that room!"

I roomed with another girl also named Faith and neither of us had ever encountered another with that name.

In concluding my faith has served me well in a life/death struggle I have with breast cancer.

Old Testament
Deborah Field Washburn

People didn't use full names much in the early Fifties: Judiths were Judy, Sarahs were Sally, etc. Old Testament names were popular among New England Protestants (though one of the Debbys was in fact Jewish).

Thanksgiving
Dorothy Kerr

(...) my parents were challenged with fertility issues for eight years before I came along, so "Gift of God" (Dorothy) seemed appropriate.

Faith and *Hope* are names heavily laden with meaning for Christians. I Corinthians 13:13 states, "And now abideth faith, hope, and love, these three; but the greatest of these is love." Faith, Hope and Love are considered to be the greatest Christian virtues.

Faith's and Chris's names make them an incarnation of their faith, giving them strength, spirituality, and responsibility. Dorothy's name reinforces her feeling of parental love and divine intervention. Beginning in the 17th century in Scotland and England, Protestants often picked names like *Faith, Hope, Charity, Grace,* or *Prudence* or Old Testament names—a tradition that still survives in the U.S. as Deborah points out. A saint's name, a biblical name, or that of a virtue attempts to center the child in a specific spiritual family or, more generally, in spirituality. Spiritual names can inspire an individual to live up to the name, to learn the story behind the name, and to seek for spiritual meaning through the name wherever it occurs, including in other religions.

A Spiritual Failing
Martha

I don't like to talk about the Bible story attached to my name because it's about a spiritual failing. It's the story about Jesus' visit to Mary and Martha. When He arrives, Martha sets about getting everything ready to serve Him. Mary sits at his feet and listens to everything He has to say. Finally Martha gets frustrated doing all the work alone and asks Jesus to tell Mary to come and help her. Jesus answers Martha by saying Mary made the right decision.

Martha was angry about doing all the work alone, so the story is interpreted as an illustration that good works are not enough if they are done with the wrong spirit, or in bad faith.

The story has always bothered me because I identify with Martha. She's trying to do the right thing, and Jesus is curt with her when she asks for help because she lost patience and should have been listening, instead of working "to serve" him.

I think it would have been a better story if Jesus had shown some sympathy, or if Mary had offered to help, or if they had just asked her to join them. Then maybe Martha would have had a chance to listen. Of course, then the parable wouldn't be the parable it is. The message would be lost – but all the Marthas of the world would not be burdened with a bad biblical reputation.

I guess people used to name their kids Martha to remind them to curb their anger and serve with the right spirit. I try to keep the positive aspects of the story in mind. In spite of the parable, I've always thought of my self as a "doer," trying to help people in any way I can.

It's not surprising that it's not a very popular name. And I have to confess, I've never liked the name.

– 2 –
Christmas

Several of our essayists have names associated with Christmas—Carol, Christine, and Holly.

• • •

Christmas Carols
Carol Armstrong

According to my mom, I was named Carol because I was born fairly close to the Christmas season, the season of Christmas carols. (Maybe she just made this up! Ha!) I don't use any other names or diminutives.

• • •

Christmas
Christine

Christine is like Christmas. I was born right before Christmas so my mom decided to name me Christine.

– 3 –
Confirmation Names

Picking a confirmation name provides Catholic adolescents with the opportunity to think about identity and spirituality.

A New Name
Dorothy Gonedridge

I was the only female baby to be baptized for many years. My dad wanted to name me Doris. They compromised and named me Dorothy Marion. At my confirmation, I began calling myself Dorothy Ann.

Sound Versus Meaning
Maryanne Genevieve

I didn't have a middle name. I only got one at confirmation when I was fourteen. You pick it yourself. I think most kids that age picks a name based on the sound rather than the meaning. I picked Genevieve, which is constantly misspelled. A lot of the girls picked pretty sounding names like Rosa, Cecelia, or family names

---

Since all confirmation names represent saints with outstanding spiritual qualities, picking a name for its sound is not as flighty as it might seem. Sound has a powerful subconscious impact.

Family names picked at confirmation suggest a desire to strengthen family ties by honoring family members with the choice of a confirmation name that is also family name.

These essayists describe a variety of ways for choosing a Christian name—according to the Catholic calendar, randomly opening the Bible to find the first female name, choosing a saint's name, one of the names for the Virgin, one of the Christian virtues, the name of Christ Himself, associations with Christmas, and biblical names.

Originally, all names had a meaning. Many of us may not be aware of the origins of our names or their spiritual meaning. As opposed to other Christian traditions, with confirmation, the Catholic Church has kept the ancient tradition of a spiritual name. Ideally, picking a saint's name at adolescence provides the opportunity for picking a spiritual archetype—a saint whose story is especially inspirational and compelling.

Researching the spiritual meaning of your name can inspire new ways of thinking about your identity. If your name doesn't have clear spiritual connections, you can create your very own with a bit of imagination.

"Jews living in gentile lands have historically taken local names to use when interacting with their gentile neighbors. The practice of taking local names became so common, in fact, that by the 12th century, the rabbis found it necessary to make a takkanah (rabbinical ruling) requiring Jews to have a Hebrew name."[108] Jews have a long history of persecution by Christians beginning with periodic localized exterminations or expulsions in medieval Europe, which culminated with their systematic extermination throughout Europe by the Nazis in the 20th century. The decision to assume a gentile name helps to protect them and allows them to assimilate more easily into their surrounding culture.

"The secular name usually corresponds in some way to the Hebrew name. Sometimes, the name is exactly the same or an Anglicized version of the same name: 'David,' 'Michael,' or 'Sarah' is as good in Hebrew as in English, though they are pronounced differently. A person with the Hebrew name 'Yosef' would probably have the English name 'Joseph' and 'Rivka' might become 'Rebecca.' Sometimes, the English name retains only part of the Hebrew name, for example, 'Aharon' might become 'Aaron' in English, but it might also become 'Harry' or 'Ronald.' Sometimes, the English name retains only the first letter of the Hebrew name: 'Pinchas' becomes 'Philip' or 'Nechama' becomes 'Natalie.' There are no hard-and-fast rules about how to translate Hebrew names into English, and indeed, there is no real reason why a person's secular name has to correspond to the Hebrew name at all."[109] In the Old Testament, names had an important spiritual dimension. Whether or not the Hebrew name is considered a spiritual name, or simply an ethnic name, depends on each Jewish individual's personal belief.

• • •

Displacing the First-born Male
Judith Eisenstadt Horwich

(...) Now, this naming business is quite different for a girl. (...) A blessing is said for her, wishing that she should grow to be like great Jewish women who have come before her. In the event she is a first born, no grand party is given for her. She does not have to be bought back from God. However, no "pit ni ha ben" for a brother born after her. She displaced him, now he cannot be called the family's first born. However, she has no special privileges as that first born. From the moment of birth as a woman, our human plumbing has a major importance starting with our naming ceremony.

Modern Jewish tradition is changing and parties are now given for first-born Jewish girls. It is called a *Brit Bat* and the baby girl is given her Hebrew name. Like the *Brit* in which the boy receives his Hebrew name following circumcision, the Brit Bat for girls follows the same ritual prayers. The girl receives her name at the synagogue when her father takes an *aliyah* (reading from the Torah). The Brit and the Brit Bat celebrate the birth of the child and entering into the covenant between God and the Jewish people. According to Genesis 17:11-12, the Brit is to be celebrated eight days after the birth of the boy, but many Jewish families schedule the Brit and the Brit Bat at the convenience of the parents, whether it's eight days or six months after the birth.[110] For Christians the naming ceremony takes place at baptism. Muslims say the *Shahadah* (profession of faith in one God, Allah, and his prophet, Muhammad) in the infant's ears to welcome her into Islam and name her much as Christians have baptism to welcome the baby into Christianity, name her, and promise to teach her to be a good person.[111] Hindus observe the *namakaran* ceremony either twelve days, one hundred and one days, or one year after the child's birth. Guests bring gifts and bless the child with the hope she will grow into a great person like her renowned ancestors. The purpose is to impress on the parents the responsibility they have for developing a worthy human being and for understanding the dignity and value of human life. [112] In all these different religious ceremonies, the child is named, welcomed into the faith, and the hope is expressed that she will grow into a worthy human being.

• • •

My Hebrew Name
Yonina

I am named after my maternal great-grandmother. My father, who was a lover of the Hebrew language and a fluent speaker, decided to translate her rather pedestrian Yiddish name into the Hebrew. Thus I was named Yonina with a choice of two meanings—little dove or the feminine for Jonah. I understand that it is either a family tradition or a Jewish tradition that the name of the firstborn is chosen by the mother and that of the second by the father. My maternal grandmother lived with us and was very happy that I (and another later-born granddaughter) were named after her mother. My little sister's name was chosen by my father.

My name, Yonina, is a name rarely heard in the U.S. and not a common one in Israel, where I now live. Growing up in Los Angeles, I was a one and only Yonina until my aunt, my grandmother's other daughter, and her family left Kentucky and joined the post-Second World War migration to California. They brought along a "little Yonina" with them. She is named after the same great-grandmother, and calls herself Yoni.

As a child, having an unusual name bothered me only the first day of a new semester, as the teacher would sometimes mispronounce it. But my family name was easy to read, and there were plenty of others who squirmed as the teachers struggled with their last names. But what could be sweeter than the diminutive and affectionate "Yoninale" which my close family would often call me. When I was in elementary school, we lived in a mixed neighborhood that was rapidly becoming Hispanic. My Hispanic friends thought that Yonina was a form of the Spanish name Nina. So I was an honorary Mexican.

As an adolescent, I joined a Zionist youth group. Everyone wanted to use his/her Hebrew name, if she/he had one, or selected a Hebrew name. I did not have to worry while some of my peers agitated, and Rosie became Shoshana and Larry turned into Aryeh. Now that I live in Israel, I count the Yoninas that I know or hear about; I can still number them on my fingers. Some are newly named Yoninas who were Janes, Janets, Janines, etc. A few are Israelis, and that is their given name.

There is no question in my mind that my Hebrew name shaped my life, values, and destiny. It is a good name and fits me like a skin.

"It is customary for Ashkenazi Jews (descendants of Eastern European, German, Polish, and Russian Jews) to name their babies after a deceased relative. However, for Sephardic Jews (of Northern Africa, including immigrants to Spain and Portugal), it is allowable and an honor to name a child after a living relative (of course, one would ask permission first). Either way, it is not necessary to use the exact name, a first initial will do."[113]

Yonina observes the similarity of her name with the Spanish *Nina*. Women's names ending in *-a* are universal: the *-a* ending links women's names subliminally to the maternal sound of *ma*.[114]

– C –
MUSLIM

• • •

The Influence of a Name: Tradition and Intuition
Salma

My father named me "Salma" because he loved the cadence of the word—soft and lyrical, simply rolling off the tongue without hesitation. He always considered it a beautiful name and knew that if he had a daughter, she would be "Salma."

In Muslim cultures, choosing a name for a child that is honorable and has some significance in Islam are important criteria. Parents often look for names from

256

the Quran, from the companions and family of the Prophet Muhammad, or from other venerable sources. While this was not what prompted my father to choose my name, luckily "Salma" also met these criteria. "Salma" was one of the first believers of Islam, and a wife of the Prophet Muhammad. She was known for her kindness, loyalty and affection, and scholars have called her learned and visionary.

The most common meaning of the name Salma is "peaceful," from the Arabic word salamah. It can also mean "safe," from the word salima or "perfection."

It's interesting how one's temperament comes to reflect the name one is given. In my case, it holds true—certainly for the first two meanings, if not for the third. Do we live up to our name, or is our name chosen because our parents have an intuitive sense of what our personalities may turn out to be?

I am definitely peaceful—reserved rather than boisterous; quiet, not loud or aggressive; soft-spoken, but not in a timid way; calm, and serene, and at peace (most of the time). Being peaceful is an attitude, an aura that surrounds you and an image that you project. Often people have expressed such sentiments to me—that I seem peaceful, content, quietly confident—and that they feel comfortable and calm in my company. I am often surprised by such comments, but always grateful.

In terms of the second definition—safe—that too fits. Safe means not involving danger or risk. I have never gone too far out on a limb, or put myself in situations that would cause harm to others or to me. I guess I tend to take the well-traveled path, the one that is reliable and tested and that will get me where I need to go, unscathed. I tend to "play it safe," but not in an unambitious way, just in a way that will not embarrass or hurt or inconvenience those close to me. I'm also a "safe bet"—reliable, trustworthy; I won't let you down. And I am definitely a safe: a strong lockable cabinet for valuables. People trust me with their secrets, and I guard them under lock and key.

But I am far from perfect. As I think about this third meaning of "Salma," I am reminded of a verse from a poem that my husband wrote to me over 20 years ago, during our courtship. He wrote on a scrap of paper tucked in my university locker: "Perfection is the province of dreams, of nyads and nymphs and fairy queens. Perfection is what you want it to be. For me it's you—my friend, my dream." So, perhaps at least in the eyes of one person, there may be something to that meaning too after all.

Salma was a common name when I grew up growing up in Pakistan, then in Saudi Arabia. Everyone could pronounce it. No one remarked on its originality or beauty. Everyone had at least one Salma in the family—an aunt, a sister, a cousin, or a grandmother.

But when we moved to New York City, my name became a novelty. "Salma" was new and unfamiliar. My older brother suggested I change it. He thought I could become a "Susan." But I didn't feel much like a Susan. His name was much more difficult to pronounce, "Shezad," which means "a prince." He ended up changing it when all his friends mispronounced it and called him "Shazam," the superhero, which I didn't think was so bad. His nickname had always been "Bubby," so he became "Bob" when we started school in the United States. Thirty years later his mail is still addressed "Mr. Robert Hasan."

I stuck with Salma. I loved my name and was proud of the culture and heritage it represented. I had no problem standing out in a field of Amys, Rachels, and Beths. The only issue was that people couldn't pronounce it correctly, which amazed me because it sounds exactly as it's written—S– A –L–M–A. There are no tricks, no silent letter, no letter that resembles one but sounds like another. You really can't go wrong. But people did. The most common mispronunciation was "Selma," like the town in Alabama. Americans had heard of Selma, and that's what they ended up calling me. I didn't really mind, nor did I correct them. It was close enough, and I had much bigger problems to worry about—like learning English and fending off mean, 8-year old bullies who loved harassing the new kid on the block. But then when I learned in 4th grade American History class that the city of Selma was the South's main military manufacturing center, producing tons of supplies and munitions during the Civil War, I wasn't so keen on that association. I was consoled the following year when I learned that Selma also played a pivotal role in the Civil Rights movement as the site of three important civil rights marches.

Today, it's much easier. Now, there's Salma Hayek. Everyone seems to know her. So when I introduce myself, people often say, "Oh, like Salma Hayek!" Yes, like Salma Hayek. I don't mind so much—after all, she is beautiful, smart and talented. And at least I'm not being confused with a small town in Alabama.

When it came to naming my own children, I let my father choose the name of our daughter, just as he had chosen mine. Again, he didn't search through baby books or pick a name based on its luminous history, but rather chose one that sounded beautiful to him. He was stationed in Qatar when I was pregnant in Geneva, and each night after a long day of work he would turn on the nightly news and be greeted by an eloquent, elegant, smart, and spirited young woman. Her name was "Saanya." And "Saanya" it was. When I later researched its meaning, my father couldn't have picked a better fitting name if he tried. The name comes from the Arabic word sani, which means "one of a kind." Saanya, our 11-year old, is truly unique—from her sparkling eyes to her effervescent personality to her boundless compassion. She fits her name to a tee. The name Saanya also comes from the Arabic word saniyaa, which means "radiant." Nail on the head again. While I only discovered this meaning when I googled her name for this essay, I have been calling my daughter "sunshine" from the moment she was born. She is a ball of energy, a bright shining star—radiant.

In naming our son, we let the nurses at Texas Children's Hospital have the final vote. We had our first two choices listed on a piece of paper. The first was

"Rayan." But when, in their Southern drawl, the nurses pronounced what would have been our son's name just like the name of a manufactured regenerated celluloid fiber (rayon), we quickly decided to go with choice number two. "Zayd." What a powerful name. Short. Monosyllabic. Strong. "Zayd" is the name of the orphan that Prophet Muhammad adopted and treated as his own good history. And it has a beautiful meaning in Arabic: "one who progresses and makes other people progress." A big name for our little five-year old to fill, but I have no doubt that he will.

Just as we saw in Native American and African naming traditions, Muslim names are meant to inspire the individual to think about herself in relationship to broader social and spiritual concepts.

If there is disagreement between the father and the mother as to what to name the child, the father's wishes prevail according to Islamic tradition.[115]

• • •

Meaning and Family
Seher Kul

Well, the deal was my dad chose my sister's name "Sahinaz," which is a combination of Sahi (really, truly) and naz (1. coyness, coquettishness. 2. feigned reluctance). This was his mother's name. "Sahinaz" is for my grandmother on my father's side. The deal was that my mother, therefore, could choose the name for the second girl in the family—me. So I'm named after my grandmother on my mother's side. "Seher" means: 1. the period just before dawn 2. daybreak, dawn.

Now to my last name Kul meaning: 1. slave. 2. mortal, human being, man (in relation to God). I'm actually really proud of my name. It is a Turkish name. My parents are both Turkish, but I grew up in Germany. All Muslim names have to have a meaning and I love that. Having my Grandma's name makes me also proud, of course. I'm her favorite grandchild. It is a connection of generations. Some people probably do not like to be named after someone in the family, but I think it is absolutely great. I love my grandma a lot. She is now 98 years old, and when she is gone her name will still be here. Turkish people do not have middle names, so I can skip that. I'm simply Seher. A lot of people cannot say my name but it is actually very easy to say, "Se Hair." That is how it sounds. I never wanted to change my last name. There is my feminist side. I was a Kul and I'm still no matter whom I married. Just to change my name because I married was never an option, although this is not traditionally Turkish. Usually the woman takes the man's last name as anywhere else.

Seher says that, "Muslim names have to have a meaning." Although she does not attribute a religious dimension to either her sister's or her given name, she does explain the spiritual dimension of her Turkish family name,

Kul, which means "mortal in relation to God," a reminder of man's humble position in the spiritual realm.

Like many women, Seher did not want to give up her maiden name, which she keeps after marriage despite the fact keeping the maiden name was not traditionally Turkish at that time. Mustafa Kema Atatürk, the founder of modern Turkey, passed many laws to modernize the country, including one in 1926 that required women to assume their husband's name upon marriage. Between 1926 and 1997, Turkey adopted the Western tradition of dropping the wife's maiden name upon marriage.[116] In 1997, a new law was passed: Turkish women could once again keep their maiden names, according to the original Muslim tradition.

– D –
BLACK AMERICAN MUSLIM

• • •

Roots
Mahasin

My name is Mahasin. It comes from an Arabic phrase "Oh, how beautiful!" Ma the Arabic word for "oh." Hasin the Arabic word for beautiful or good. Variations of Hasin may appear in male names like Hassan or Hussein, which mean handsome or even female names like Hasina, Husna, Husniyah all of which mean beautiful.

The thing about "Mahasin" is that the beauty that it is referring to is inner beauty like goodness or virtue. In recent years I have seen my name's meaning translated by European or Western writers to mean sometimes virtuous.

My parents were enthusiastic converts to Islam and I was the first girl child. Their conversion was actually a reconnection to their past as a people ethnically and also as a family historically with a Muslim ancestor. Many African Americans in the 60s were reconnecting with Africa. With my parents they were also Muslim and thus often said they wanted to make a stronger statement than just that they had returned to the land—but also to the religion of their ancestors as well. Many Muslims at that time used traditional names like Jamilah (pretty), Ayesha, Rasheeda, Malikah, etc. Since my father was one quarter Native American, he was drawn to the idea of a name that had some sort of "spiritual" connection in addition to its historical value.

At the earliest stages of my life, my parents were constantly telling me what my name meant, which was a subconscious way of telling me their expectations. So as I think about my life I realize that I lived up to those expectations by being a straight A student from elementary to college and volunteering for community work my whole life. Today as a writer and playwright, my work is usually described as mystic or esoteric even when I am producing sci-fi.

My husband of 20 years actually married me because he felt I had as he says, an inner beauty of a person trying to do the right thing.

I have always been particular about who may call me by my first name— meaning it was for friends only. I never let people mispronounce or shorten my name either. If you didn't, wouldn't or couldn't say it right then you lost the right to say it at all and would have to call me by my middle name or last name. Even in high school people called me by my last name Shamsid-Deen, which means— (Shams) Sun, (id) of, (deen) the religion or way of life. My original last name from my father was Sharrief, which means honorable, noble or distinguished. Political circumstances caused him to change his name when I was about 14.

Although Mahasin was unusual for an American Muslim when I was born, the next generation used it quite often. I have met a number of Mahasins a good 10 years or more younger than I. It is also very common I find when I travel to Egypt and the Sudan. The current generation of children (like my own daughter) actually ends up being named from variations of Hasin. Her name is Haseena. Islamic names are very entrenched in the African American community (although usually horribly mispronounced). Thus, the actual Muslims in the African American community nowadays seem to choose more unusual names than they did in my generation.

In the '60s Black Americans were trying to reconnect to their roots. Africans taken as slaves would have been primarily followers of animist religions, then Muslim (estimates vary between ten and thirty percent), and more rarely Christian (estimates range from three to five percent). Islam has a longer African history than Christianity. Islam was introduced into East Africa in the 7th century and into West Africa between the 11th and the 15th centuries. In the 15th century, Christianity was introduced in Central Africa by missionaries and in West Africa by Portuguese slave traders.[117]

For those too young to remember, Black Americans' search for their ancestors was epitomized by Alex Haley's *Roots, The Saga of an American Family*, 1976, which was awarded a Pulitzer Prize, and "spurred an interest in African or African sounding names."[118] This is why so many African American given names sound foreign, and why Malcolm X chose the last name of X: he didn't want a name that could have been a slave owner's. Today many websites give information about African traditional religions, African tribes, and African names: I have included web addresses for those who would like to do research into African names.[119]

The horrific history of slavery is as old as that of mankind. Members of every religion—pagan, Christian, Muslim, Jewish, Hindu, and Buddhist— have all been guilty of slavery at some point in their history. The charm against the evil eye is blue because so many slaves in the ancient Mediterranean world had blue eyes. The word *slave* comes from the word *Slav* because the Vikings sold so many Central European Slavs into slavery in the early Middle Ages. Entire sections of coastal Spain and Italy were abandoned from the 15th through the 19th centuries, with an estimated one million Christians captured by Muslim Barbary pirates.[120]

From the 16th to the 19th century between 9 and 12 million Africans were shipped to the New World as slaves with perhaps as many as another 19 million taken via the East Coast and the Red Sea for the Muslim slave trade. Africa was literally "bled of its human resources."[121] It is unimaginably horrific to discover that more slaves were exported out of Eastern Africa than out of Western Africa.

Having suffered oppression by white Christians in the U.S. for three centuries, from the 1700s to the 1900s, it is understandable that some Black Americans turned to Islam, another monotheistic religion also practiced in Africa and the original faith of some of the Africans first captured and sold into slavery in America. Slavery is a blot on human history that has tainted all religions. It has not been limited to one race, which might therefore be considered "inferior." All skin colors have suffered under the yoke of slavery. Unfortunately, millions of children and adults are still enslaved today. Even the U.S. continues to have problems with underground slavery. I have included web addresses of well established groups that help fight against slavery in our world today.[122]

– E –
RELIGIOUS UNITY

• • •

Maryanne

I was supposed to be named Bonnie (if a girl) or Michael (if a boy), but ended up being born on St. Anne's Feast Day (her birthday); so I was named Maryanne after Mary (Jesus' mother) and Ann (Mary's mother). Since these two women are so famous, especially Mary, her name is found in many different cultures, although spelled and pronounced differently. I work with a lot of different cultures, so I am called by the name used in different cultures. To the Central and South Americans, the Spanish speakers, I am "Maria." To the Arabs and Persians, I am "Maryam," and to the Africans who are Orthodox Christians, I am "Miriam."

Instead of being insulted by the misspelling or mispronunciation of my name, I feel honored to be called by the name used in these different cultures—it makes me feel accepted in their cultural family.

Most of the women who discuss the religious dimension of their names consider issues that lead them beyond the personal to spiritual and social concerns. The sense of being connected to something greater than the self is also paramount in the essays about ancient Native American and African naming traditions. Muslims, Jews, and Christians discuss the meaning and inspiration their names provide. Women with names drawn from mythology are also deeply inspired by their ancient names. Because of her desire for a more spiritual name, Shyama, a Hindu, changes her name to reflect the spiritual aura of Vishnu (p.103).

Because of mankind's migratory history, it is not surprising that the world's religions are all interconnected. At the World Council of Religious Leaders in 2009, his holiness Mahamandaleswar Sri Swami Gurusharananandaji Karsni Peeth, Matura noted the many similarities between Hindu and Jewish religious traditions. Rabbi Oded Weiner emphasized the linguistic link between *Hodim* (Hindu) and *Yehodim* (Jew). The first Christians were a melting pot of religious traditions—Jews, Arabs, Africans, Europeans, Hindus—that reflected the trade roads' culture of the Near East. The Saint Thomas Christians are an ancient Christian sect found in India.[123] There is mounting evidence Christ spent time in India before he started his ministry. [124] Deepak Chopra believes this and illuminates the links between Christianity and Eastern mysticism in *The Third Jesus: The Christ We Cannot Ignore*. Hinduism, the oldest of the world's written religions, is monotheistic with infinite representations of the divine. Like the Ba'há'is, Hindus believe in the legitimacy of all religions as different manifestations of the divine. Many American writers like Ralph Waldo Emerson, David Thoreau, Herman Melville, and William James were greatly inspired by Hindu writings.

A little Internet research can provide new, unifying, spiritual insights into our politically and economically polarized religions. Readers seeking further religious insights would enjoy Karen Armstrong's books: *The Great Transformation: The Beginning of Our Religious Traditions, The Battle for God: A History of Fundamentalism, The Bible: A Biography, In the Beginning: A New Interpretation of Genesis, Islam: A Short History*, and *Buddha*. Women who would like to start researching the spiritual dimensions of their names can start online with *Abarim Publications' Biblical Name Vault—Meaning of Bible Names*, the *Catholic Encyclopedia*, and multiple name sites obtainable by googling your given name + name, which will connect you to sites like *BabyNames, Baby Names World*, and *Behind the Name*. These sites provide stepping-stones for the beginning of your personal quest.

Chapter 28
CREATING MEANING FOR OUR NAMES: EXTERNAL ASSOCIATIONS

– A –
THE MEANING WE CREATE FOR OUR NAMES

Some women change the meaning of their names into something quite different from the traditional meaning, as Molly (p.23) and Meredith do (pp.160–161). In the following essays women create their own personal meaning for their given names, which helps to center them.

• • •

The Name is a Curse
Camille Mignolet
(by her granddaughter)

I will never forget my grandmother's admonition to me as a teenager: "Never name a girl Camille. The name brings back luck." In French, the idiomatic expression (porter malheur) is even stronger—the name "carries" bad luck, as if it is an intrinsic part of the name, not just an unfortunate circumstance. I remember being left speechless by her sadness and her desire to obliterate her name from our family history. My grandmother had a tragic life in many ways—living through two world wars in Belgium, suffering excommunication because of a divorce for which she was the wronged party, (My wealthy grandfather simply bought a dispensation.), laboring to save her only son, who returned a physical and mental wreck from Nazi camps after WWII, losing her other child to an American, who took her daughter far away when travel to and fro required more than a week and great expense.

Although I didn't understand it at the time, looking back now, I think she felt this way because if the name was a curse, she could blame her misfortune on something besides herself, her loved ones, society, or God. This projection of one's problems onto the name, which then assumes responsibility for the trials one suffers, is reminiscent of Beth's and Amy's essays in which both women humorously blame their names for their weight problem, but Camille carried the projection to the very different realm of fate and the loss of free will. "Camille" had reduced my grandmother to being a victim of forces beyond her control. Indeed, most of the events she survived were beyond her control, just as they were for most Europeans who survived two world wars.

Research on "Camille" doesn't turn up a series of disasters, but some very inspiring namesakes, male and female, because it is an androgynous name. If only I had thought about looking through the French encyclopedia to find other Camilles, perhaps I could have helped alleviate the sense of doom she felt surrounding her, the sense of rejection and humiliation she felt everyday for fifty years when she went to mass but was not allowed to take communion. Or perhaps, it is better that the encyclopedia was never opened: maybe "Camille" made the unbearable, bearable and the unexplainable, explainable. In a very paradoxical way, the cursed "Camille" protected her.

• • •

I Have Always Felt Like I Didn't Match My Name
Judy McGowan

I remember once, when I was young, looking up "Judy" in a baby name book. It said something about the typical Judy being bouncy and bubbly. I've never been either and have always felt like I didn't match my name, like people would expect someone different when they met someone named "Judy."

———————————

Baby name books are not always accurate. The meaning of the name *Judith (Judy)* has no connection with "bubbly" or "bouncy." Judy has been disassociated from her name with misinformation. Multiple sources should be consulted when doing name research.

Judy bears the exact same first and middle name as her mother (p.121), which may also play a part in her feeling that "people would expect someone different," because they expected her mother before Judy came along.

Judith is an Old Testament name made popular by Protestants, who preferred Old Testament names in order to avoid Catholic New Testament names. Judith is the heroine of the Apocryphal book of Judith. (The books of the Apocrypha are not contained in the Bible because the Church questions their reliability and accuracy.) Judith, a Jewish widow, murders the enemy general Holofernes by cutting off his head. In this way she saves the Jewish people from an Assyrian invasion.[125] In Renaissance Florence, she was considered a symbol of Sanctimony and Harmony over Lust and Pride, and briefly a symbol of the Republic's triumph over the Medicis. Her story was depicted in art by such great artists as Donatello, Boticelli, Mantegna, Luca Cranach the Elder, and especially by the female Renaissance artist Artemisia Gentileschi. Artemisia is also an inspiring heroine. Despite being raped, slandered, and tortured, she managed to become a popular Renaissance painter and the first woman accepted in the *Accademia delle Arti del Disegno* in Florence. Because she had been raped and abused, Artemisia did several paintings of Judith to illustrate that like the biblical Judith, she too could triumph in a male-dominated world.[126] Several novels have also been written about her, including recently *The Passion of Artemisia* by Susan

Vreeland. Another Judith, Judith Leyster, was one of only two women painters who gained membership in the Dutch Guild of Saint Luke of Haarlem in the seventeenth century. Judith Merril is the mother of science fiction, Judith Stafford is a well-known poet, and Anodea Judith is a therapist and specialist in the Chakras. *Judith* will also lead you into the realm of computer technology and new discoveries there.

If you have not researched your name, you will find namesakes who will inspire you in new ways and lead you into previously unknown realms. As a child, Frances did this kind of research with her name (pp.215–216). In undertaking this quest, we can ponder a brief dialogue from *Alice in Wonderland.*

Alice: "Would you tell me, please, which way I ought to go from here?"
Cheshire Cat: "That depends a good deal on where you want to get to."[127]

Following your personal interests on your name quest can enrich your life immeasurably: a surprise discovery will lead you in new directions you never contemplated.

• • •
A Mantra
Anakatarina Dervisevic

When I named my three daughters, it was important for the names to be mantras that they will grow into. Axelle Hannan: Axelle (French—peace from the father), Hannan (Arabic—compassion from the mother). Adrina Summar: Adrina (Italian—happiness), Summar (Arabic—a party that is so festive it lasts all night long). Angeline Noor: Angeline (after my mother—Angel), Noor (Arabic—light, the angel of light).

Anakatarina speaks of her daughters' names as mantras. A mantra is originally a Hindu term meaning "a religious or mystical syllable or poem."[128] Mantras are used in Eastern spiritual traditions to divert the mind from basic instinctual desires or material inclinations, by concentrating on a purely spiritual plane.[129] In naming her daughters, Anakatarina has surrounded herself and her family with peace, compassion, happiness, and light. She wants her children to grow into their names, which are meant to inspire them as they develop. Anakatarina creates a sound link between her children and between generations with the letter *a*. She also gives them names that reflect a wealth of different cultures—French, Italian, English, and Arabic—which provide the family with an international mindset.

True to Myself
Veronica

My name is Veronica. I have that name because my mom always liked it. See, when my youngest aunt was born, she was supposed to have that name, but for some reason, didn't get it. My grandma named her America (as in America Ferrera) instead. So when I was born, I got the name. It's Latin for "true image," which suits me well, I think, since I stay true to myself. From what I read, it was a popular name in Catholic families but spread beyond that eventually. But it's not very popular anymore. I never see it in "Most Popular Girls' Names" lists. And when I look at items personalized with people's names, I have a hard time finding "Veronica."

But I don't care if it's popular or not. It's my name and it makes me who I am. What I like about names, in general, is that it makes all of us who we are. They make us unique.

According to the Apocrypha, Veronica wiped the face of Jesus as He carried the cross. The cloth then bore the "true image" of the Savior's face. Research into this story, which seeks to determine what is true and what is not, will take you into the world of relics, art, history, Free Masonry, and scientific research.

Family, Roots, and Profession
Em Claire Knowles

I was named after my grandmothers: my father's mother's name was Emma and my mother's mother's name was Clara. My parents thought it necessary to honor their mothers with the name of EmClaire. Over time I changed the spelling to Em Claire. I often think that my mother being from Louisiana remembered the city of Eau Claire, which was originally a part of the Louisiana Purchase. Maybe not.

I am a librarian and the name of Em Claire seems to resonate with me when I consider the derivation of the parts of my names: Em, according to the OED, refers to a typing font and Claire is French for clear. When you merge the definitions, I think of clear print and clear thought, which are quite appropriate for a librarian.

Em Claire makes her name reflect multiple dimensions of her life—her origins, family, and profession—which remind us of the multiple facets of the Native American naming tradition.

. . .

I Have to Live Up to My Name
Sunny Cervantes

My grandmother wanted to name me Soledad. My mother found it old-fashioned. They compromised with Sunny. When you're named Sunny, it's quite difficult to be grumpy all the time. I find that I have to live up to my name because...well...I cannot imagine being named Stormy or Rainy. LOL!

Sunny lives up to her name signing off with an LOL (laugh out loud).

. . .

A Symbol
Holly Hoscheit

I was born in northern California—and my mother wanted to name me after Buffy St. Marie, the American Indian folk singer. My grandmother intervened and insisted that my mother not move into the hippie commune AND that I NOT be named Buffy. They settled on Holly. As far as I know, my dad didn't get any vote on the matter. I've often thought that my life would have been so different as a Buffy, especially since I ended up making my life on the east coast where everyone would have assumed a Waspy origin, not a hippie one.

There are aspects of my name that I like—that it is fairly unique, but not odd, that it is a symbol of Christmas, and that you can't really get it wrong. Conversely, I have always thought that it wasn't very feminine and "girlie." I also never really liked Holly Hobbie, kind of a homely sort![130]

Holly believes other people's associations to names have a profound influence on the person bearing the name.

The holly is an ancient symbol going back to Roman times. Many wonderful Christmas stories are associated with the tree, and the holly was thought to bring good luck.[131] "The Holly and the Ivy" is a lovely old Christmas carol. Hollies are among the most beautiful evergreens: they are hardy, carefree, perennials, which are all inspiring traits. Learning about the holly provides for a stroll through history, religion, and myth. For informative essays on the history of the holly, google: *Trees for Life—Mythology and Folklore of the Holly* or *Paghat's Garden: Holly Tree*, which describes Japanese mythology very similar to that of the West. Robert Graves discusses the Holly King in his book, *The White Goddess*.

268

. . .

Family and Meaning
Katherine Elizabeth Boyd
(Generation Y)

Katherine is my grandmother's name and it means "purity." I think it is Irish or English. Elizabeth Cecilia is my middle name. Elizabeth is my aunt, and Cecilia is for St. Cecilia, patron saint of music for Christians. I like my name!

Having both family ties and spiritual meaning for her names provides a double centering. It's not surprising that Katherine likes her name with its terrestrial and celestial reverberations.

. . .

Not Falling Below the Line
Bonnie Hill

My mother was twenty when I was born, and as a young woman with an already two-year-old, she had a lot on her mind and was still very young. So she decided some time around when I was born that she didn't want any of her children's names to fall below the line when writing their names. Hence my name Bonnie Linn, was spelled a bit differently. (Linn being my middle name.) I always loved my name; no one else had it, it was original and suited me just fine...until fourth grade when I desperately wanted to be more like the other girls. I decided to call myself Lynn (notice the spelling). That didn't last long, especially when my new fourth grade teacher (a man!) said how much he liked the name Bonnie.

Forward five years and new neighbors moved in next door and I began baby-sitting for them. To my shock and horror, the mom's name was also Bonnie Linn (spelled the "correct" way). And to increase the horror, I was then to find out that she was named after a candy (chocolate, I believe) called a "bonnie lynn" that her mother liked. I never got a chance to ask my mom if that's why she named me that too. Although I know I am named after my great-grandfather Boris.

I love my name, believe that it suits me well and feel honored that my mother gave me an uncommon name (despite the neighbor).

Oh, and I've dropped the Linn to keep my maiden name as my middle name which is Karmen (notice the spelling...not very common either!)

Thanks for the opportunity to share a beloved part of myself.

Bonnie Linn's mother has the marvelous and so far unique inspiration of giving her children names that "did not fall below the line." None of her names, maiden or married, fall below the line.

First, Middle, and Last Names: All with Meanings
Robin Michelle Tiberio
(Generation Y)

Robin means bright star in German. Michelle is the feminine form of Michael, my dad. Tiberio is from the river Tiber in Italy.

Robin's names have multidimensional facets, reminiscent of the Native American naming tradition. *Robin,* "bright star," inspires by its spiritual meaning. Her middle name links her to family, and her last name to her country of origin—a place name, one of the most ancient naming sources. All of us can search out these dimensions of our names.

. . .

What Responsibility!
Sandra Delgado

I was very pleased when I learned about the story of how my name was chosen, and although it is not a popular name anymore, I really like it. I like the way it sounds. A long time ago, when I was searching the origin of my name, I found out that Sandra is a short name for Alessandra, which is the feminine form of Alexander, which is the Latin form of a Greek name. The meaning of Alexander is "defender of mankind." What responsibility! But I think it suits me well and it meshes with my desire to become a psychologist. My name inspires me to always try to be my best in understanding and caring about people.

Sandra researches her name and discovers its ancient history and meaning, "defender of mankind," which inspires her to be an advocate for— i.e., a defender of—her patients.

. . .

No Wonder...
Ginta Romeikis

(...) as it became clear that I would be born on February 16th, Lithuanian Independence Day, they named me Gintar_. This is the female version of "gintaras," meaning amber, the national gem. (...) Amber carries the past within it. It should not be surprising that I became a psychoanalyst.

Like Sandra, Ginta finds inspiration in her name for her work with patients. Ginta's name means *amber*, a stone that reveals the past within it, which is what psychoanalysts strive to do in order to help patients understand how their psychology was formed.

Since ancient times, each month of the year has been assigned its own birthstones. On the Internet, the most complete and easily accessible information about birthstones, their history and mythology can be found by googling *Birthstones* or *Bernadine Gemstones*. The most ancient tradition is the Ayurvedic (from India), which dates back to at least 1500 BCE. Under "Birthstones," *Wikipedia* gives the poems originally published by Tiffany's in 1870, which are believed to date back to the Gregorian calendar of the 16th century. To find out more about stones and their various properties check out *Gems in Myth, Legend, and Lore* by Bruce Knuth or *Gem and Mineral Lore* by Paul Beyeri.

· · ·

Multiple Meanings
Miriam Weiss

Each year at Passover as we dipped spring greens in salt water, my father called attention to my name. Miriam comes from the Hebrew, Mar-bitter, and Yam-sea, a place at the bottom of the world-below sea level-where the Jordan evaporated leaving behind pillars of salt. Turning back, Lot's wife became one of these pillars. For my father a connection between my name and bitterness-of-character formed a chapter in his narrative of the Exodus—until the year that my husband defended me saying, "Miriam is the sweetest person I know."

The biblical Miriam transformed the world wherever it touched her life. As a young girl, she protected her baby brother in his basket in the Nile, watching until the Egyptian princess drew him out of the water and called him Moses. As a young woman, she led the people across the Sea of Reeds, and assuaged their fear by singing and dancing. Like her brothers, she saw visions. She spoke up when Moses neglected his wife Zipporah. She was punished with leprosy and isolation—though the people waited for her to heal before they continued wandering.

I am proud that my name links me to such evocative and powerful stories. However, I understand my name as metaphor, not prophecy. To my parents, my birth and my naming carried hope in a time of mourning. To my husband and children, my name identifies the still-point in the flurry of their comings and goings. I imagine myself as a catalyst in a complex chemical reaction-a seed-crystal condensing a tear-filled sea. When I call myself Miriam, I meet what changes and what stays the same in my life.

Miriam's essay is perfect for closing our consideration of the meaning we give our names because she so adeptly describes the multiple levels of meaning our names can have. Miriam analyzes her biblical namesake's story and finds many connotations—the protector, the leader, and the speaker of truth. She understands her name "as metaphor, not prophecy"—these stories serve to inspire her, not to predict what will happen to her. In other words, names are not destiny: names are what we make of them.

Miriam continues the search for meaning in her name by analyzing what it means in her personal life—for her parents, her family and for herself. "When I call myself Miriam, I meet what changes and what stays the same in my life." In this lovely paradox, Miriam expresses her awareness that our sense of identity should not be static, but changing and evolving—a concept which takes us back to our earliest naming traditions.

– B –
THE MEANING WE DENY OUR NAMES

In considering the meaning of names, there is a special category for independent women who insist that their name is only an external attribute.

• • •

I Want to Make a Difference.
Peggy Souza

My name is Peggy. Embarrassing as it is, I was named after the singer Peggy Lee. It is not Peggy Sue…save me; and it is not Margaret. Buddy Holly and Peggy Sue Got Married… I have heard it all. I am not the love interest on the Andy Griffith show whose daddy buys her a new convertible…well; actually, I am in a way. However, I always wanted to be the "cool, collected Margaret."

I did grow up in a privileged family. We belonged to a "hunting" country club that had horseback riding, swimming, and fishing on the lake, as well as dancing at the club on a Saturday night. This Peggy is also 5'4" and plays competitive tennis against men who are 6'2" and never considered me short.

I am also a woman who finished a bachelor's degree, cum laude, at the age of 46, while raising a blended family and having a child who is learning disabled. This Peggy is the Environmental Committee Chair for the neighborhood citizen's association, who has served in many volunteer positions, advocated for the learning disabled and believes in "paying it forward." So you ask, does your name influence you? No, I have had a privileged life and I have had a difficult life. Who is Peggy? I am a woman who wants to make a difference while I am here. That is my name….

Peggy may have developed a problematic relationship with her name because it is not a family name and she was teased about it. Her life is full of contradictions except for her desire to make a difference, which is what centers her and gives her life meaning. She maintains her name has not influenced her; it is only a moniker. Leslie Kent (p.95), Joan Hart (p.229), and Peggy Souza all negate the importance of their names—an interesting definition of identity by negation, representing, perhaps, a desire to transcend the name, to be known by deeds and emotional ties rather than merely a label—a desire we all share.

– C –
THE MEANING OTHERS BRING TO OUR NAMES

• • •

Etymology and a Love Story –
Bleuette
(by Yvonne Rollins)

Bleuette was my aunt by marriage, the wife of my favorite uncle Marcel. She was his second wife. Bleuette was not an ordinary woman. She was a very elegant Parisienne who had worked in the fashion industry in Paris. After marrying my uncle, she was content to sell clothes in a very nice shop in my provincial town.

Her name was totally new and unknown to us. She was born in Champagne and told us her father had given her name, but I can't remember why. I heard in "Bleuette" the adjective "blue," of course; but I had a vague notion the name meant something else. I discovered much later that "Bleuette" means "a posy"—in the sense of "giving posies" to a woman, that is "flirting" with her. Since my aunt was beautiful and my uncle was very much in love with her, her name (which existed as far back as the Middle Ages) seemed very romantic to me.

Since *bleuette* means a little blue flower, I have substituted *posy* to retain the poetic imagery of the story. Posy is a very old English word dating back to the 1500s meaning a small bouquet or short verse.[132] Like posy, bleuette is associated with poetry, dating back to a time when lovers sent each other "sweet nothings" *(billets doux)* on paper that was painted with little flowers or cut into flower shapes. At first the expression was to "send florets" *(envoyer des fleurettes)* but it evolved into "to tell florets" *(conter fleurettes)*, which, in turn, evolved simply into *fleureter* from which the English word *flirt* is derived.[133] Yvonne's essay illustrates how others find their own personal meanings in our names.

Women relate to their names in a variety of ways. They may identify with their names on a purely emotional basis, like the women who retain their nicknames throughout life because of the emotional oasis nicknames provide. External influences may play an important role with associations to family, culture, the fine arts, the performing arts, history, mythology, religion or nature. If explored and developed, these associations can provide many new ways of thinking about meanings and identity.

Names carry abundant associations, if not for the individual, then for others. These associations may be conscious or subconscious. We explored associations made to names in the chapter about unusual names and in the chapter about sound. We discovered that associations to names are so powerful they may subconsciously affect how people first react to us. In this chapter, we explored the associations we consciously give names.

Most of the essayists have stories or create stories for their names so that they feel their names represent something personal about them—something they created and identify with. Women may take an existentialist stand and maintain their names have no meaning. Even by rejecting a name as simply a moniker, essayists convey a deep sense of who they are. Essentially, women teach us a name is what you make of it. What you say about your name is a reflection of who you are and what matters most to you in life.

Chapter 29
HUMOR, PARADOX, AND IRONY: STEPPING OUTSIDE THE NAME

Humor requires incongruity—mismatched pieces, clashing perspectives that derail the anticipated. As observers, it's easy to laugh at others because we see them from the outside as they cannot see themselves. Laughing at ourselves is harder: stepping outside of the self to see ourselves as others do requires emotional detachment—a moment of impartiality—which necessitates at least two different viewpoints.

• • •
It's All Fun!
Donnetta Baker Mitchell

My name is Donnetta Baker Mitchell. I was born in Salt Lake City, Utah to parents of English/Irish/Scottish heritage and of the LDS (Mormon) faith. I was their first child and so they decided to be "creative" with my name. My Father's name was Donald and my Mother's name was Loretta...thus Donnetta. They were very proud to have invented this name.

When I was about 4 years old, we moved into a duplex. I was climbing on the iron railings on the porch and my Father yelled at me, "Donnetta, get off the porch!" A few minutes later, the neighbor next door (a big burly guy) came over and told my Dad "don't you ever tell my wife to get off the porch again!" Dad scrambled to explain my name and avoid getting punched...after that we knew that there were other Donnettas around.

As for having a somewhat unique name, I think that it's great and has given me a sense of being special. Of course, I usually have to spell my name for others; and it's kinda hard to have a nickname. Now that my married name is Mitchell, there are plenty of nicknames...Mitch, witch, bitch, etc. It's all fun!

Donnetta suggests we may first learn to detach from our names when we are children and discover that others have the same name. Because of this childhood lesson, Donna can laugh at all the teasing that she endures as an adult. She has developed such a healthy detachment from her name she can join in the fun. She understands that people can make fun of her name without making fun of her.

A Lovely Story
Lovely Ulmer-Sottong

My mother was in the hospital getting ready to have me, and she was reading an article in the Topeka Capital Newspaper about a Mr. and Mrs. Choosey who had named their daughter Pretty—for Pretty Choosey (get it?). She thought that was great and was going to name me Pretty. When she went to write it on the birth certificate, she realized my initials would be P.U. as my last name was Ulmer. She chose the next synonym that came to her mind, which was Lovely. My family proceeded to call me Love, and she embroidered Love U on many of my first grade clothes for ID purposes. (As an aside, I was the last of six children—one boy followed by five girls.)

My mother was bleeding very badly during her delivery and the doctor ordered blood, but they didn't have any of her type (small Kansas town). There were only two people in the county who had her type. The hospital called both: one was not home (out of town). The other had just returned from a short trip to Minnesota and had just walked into the house when the phone rang. He came immediately to the hospital. They did a transfusion in the delivery room directly from him to my mother, which saved her life and mine. So she wholly believed Lovely to be appropriate.

My name affected me greatly—as when I went to college, there were classes that were larger than my hometown! The professor couldn't remember names, but he always remembered mine and where I sat. This was common. If I wasn't prepared, I didn't go to class. (I missed very few.) As an aside, I was the first female Ph.D. from my hometown – that I got a 4.0 was less important than that the folks who knew me all my life could call me Doctor. Although I haven't been back to my hometown since my mother died in 2001, I smile every time at the memory.

Lovely's wry humor derives from her sensitivity to incongruities, which requires different viewpoints. Her story echoes Dorothy's adventures in *The Wizard of Oz:* both are from a small town in Kansas, both survive life-threatening disaster, find themselves in a strange new world, and become known for their determination and brains.

• • •

Weathering the Storm
Debby Taylor

"Naming is the most important thing in the world." -Confucius

On my tenth birthday I should have been the happiest of youngsters. Yes, my parents had given me the longed for gold monogram ring I'd campaigned for all year. But to my horror my proud parents had persuaded the jeweler to etch all FIVE initials onto the ring's plateau. Finally as the youngest member of my class I, too, was au fait, but what a fate. No one of the chic set had more than 3 initials on their ring and here was I needing to explain what DAVNK stood for (should I have the moxie to wear and show the ring).

Honoring my paternal grandfather's pastorhood, my parents had him christen me Deborah Ann Van Ness Kretschmann. The K on my ring, of course, was my surname. But whence the Deborah? The Ann? The Van Ness?

My father had already been teaching philosophy at Brooklyn College for six years when I was born. He loved all his students, but perhaps especially the girls! He was struck that at a college whose population was perhaps 80% Jewish, he'd not yet met a Deborah, "a fine Old Testament name." My mother agreed that I should be Deborah were I a she-person and added the Ann since it seemed to go well and her own middle name, which was Anna.

I trust the reader is wondering: but why the Van Ness? That was to honor a family name on my mother's side, the more distinguished side, or so my father thought. Did he hope it would get me into the DAR? If so, he forgot that the meaning of Deborah is bee, wasp, or hornet and that I would be far too fiery for those ladies.

So here's the thing: I grew up with too long a moniker for my liking, with an unusual name meaning a nasty insect, and a brother who sang my name "Oh, De– A –bor– I –a" to the Toreador's tune in Carmen. And when they nicknamed me DebbY that, too, set me apart. (Indeed when I met all those other Deborahs my freshman year at college, they were all DebbIEs.)

One other thing was that my parents called me Black-eyed Susan because of my dark eyes. Surely, all this should spell some sort of identity crisis, but I seem to have weathered the storm and come to expect to be called many different names.

Those closest to me, i.e. family, don't use Deborah or Debby. On occasion my husband will use it, but he tends to call me Poochie or Roo (as do my offspring and grandchildren and their friends.)

But, do I like "Deborah" or think it suits me? I just don't know. Every other Deborah I have known has had a certain je ne sais quoi, an elegance, a sangfroid that I do not see in myself, which is possibly why I have stuck to Debby.

Debby reminds us of the essays by women with multiple nicknames in Chapter IV; however, Debbie views all of her names with humor, pointing out their incongruities or juxtaposing them ironically. Irony presents us with the opposite of what we expect, which leads us to question our assumptions and our expectations, as well as those of others. Debby's different names and her humorous detachment from all of them bestow multiple perspectives, which provide flexibility and creativity in how she views herself.

Irony
Amy Moore

*Amy Rae Gaston was my given name. I grew up in Iowa. My father and mother
wanted a short name for the first name as they said it would be easier to call my
sister and me. My older sister is named Jill, which was a perfect one-syllable
name. They stepped out of the box a bit and went for the two syllable "Amy" when
I was born. My mother told me she had to fight for my name as my dad was
insistent on the rule. Looking back it was as if we were dogs...typical dog names
are quick---"Jack", "Bud", etc. Growing up in Iowa, I attended a small public
school. There was one other Amy at my school and one Amy who attended my
Sunday school class. They were both rather obese children and my sister, Jill, used
to say to me "Amy, you're getting kind of heavy. You don't want to be like those
other Amys!" It seemed every time I met an Amy I would check to see how they
were built---and very rarely it seemed that I met a thin and beautiful "Amy."
I ended up being a little pudgy in 4th and 5th grade and always had a complex
that maybe it was the "Amy" curse. Had I been named "Jan" like my mother
had considered, I'd be tall and thin and have more friends. Most Jans seemed
studious and fit and had lots of friends. Also, The Brady Bunch was a big show
and one of the characters was named Jan---I so wished I had been given that
name. Although, the cutest girl on the show was named Marcia, and that name
would've been like winning the lottery. During my baby fat days at elementary
school the kids would say "Amy Gaston...she's full of GAS and weighs a TON!"
Then I had my first and last name working against me. I decided to go as "Amy
Rae" for a while...maybe that would change the image. That didn't stick and so I
went back to plain old Amy.*

*When we moved to Florida I was 12 years old and entering the seventh grade.
The summer before that grade I lost all of my baby fat and had started looking more
like a "Jan." I was glad to leave the other two Amys back in Iowa to continue to
carry on the Amy Iowa image. After I was getting more secure in my own skin I
didn't mind Amy so much but didn't care for my last name. Still though, I would
dream of a name like Veronica, Vanessa, Nicolette ...those all sounded so fun and
exciting. Those names would've been too long for my family. I would sit and wonder
why my mom didn't fight for a long name...why did she give in to my dad who
wanted a boy, anyway? My father left my mother and my sister and me when I was
12 and has limited contact with us.*

*When I got married in 1996 I was so happy to put the last name Gaston aside
and adopt the new name, "Moore." What a better name that was! People would ask,
"Are you going to keep your name?" I would always laugh inside. I became pregnant
in 1998 and had so much fun looking through baby name books. I decided that our*

rule was no one-syllable names. We welcomed Alexandra Keller Moore. She's eight years old now and guess what? She wants a name with one syllable.

By ironically juxtaposing the names of little girls and dogs, Amy dehumanizes her name. She uses irony again describing "the Amy curse," which places the blame for her weight problem on her name just as Beth does (p.78). The implication is that the fault is not theirs: it is the destiny of their name tribe. This escapist projection allows Amy and Beth to see themselves as part of a group that bears the responsibility for their problems. Ironically, the group is both a solace and a menace.

In yet another irony, Amy's one-syllable married name provides some redemption for monosyllabic names. By ending her essay with a final irony— her daughter's rejection of a long name like she always wanted—Amy gives us the sense that we are observers who are never really in control of what happens to us, a useful observation as we go through life; to accept with a smile, when possible, what we cannot always control despite our best efforts.

• • •

Family Sagas
Kate Ribeiro

When I became pregnant with our second daughter, we decided we wanted to name her for her two grandmothers—Ema and Judith. I was named after my two grandmothers—Kathleen and Mae, and I always loved that I had and always would have this connection to two wonderful women. So when our second daughter was almost ready to enter this world, we announced to my mother-in-law and my mother that she would be named after the two of them. My mother-in-law, who doesn't speak a word of English, made it perfectly clear to me that she did not want her granddaughter named after her. Puzzled, I asked why. She simply said she did not want to hear the maid walking around the house saying in a cooing voice, "Oh, Emma.... You're so cute, Emma!" Fine. Ema was no longer an option. So back to the drawing board. Pretty quickly my husband and I decided on Elizabeth Hazel. Elizabeth, because I always loved the name and my favorite literary character is Elizabeth Bennett from Pride and Prejudice and Hazel for my great aunt Hazel, who passed away during my pregnancy.

Well if anyone thought that my mother-in-law had a problem with "Ema," s(he) would soon see she had a bigger problem with Eizabeth. Apparently my husband's ex-girlfriend (from years ago) was named Elizabeth; and Ema thought this was a great offense. Honestly, I could care less what his old girlfriend's name was; I simply liked the name. So Elizabeth Hazel was born. My mother, who never really liked her own name, was secretly overjoyed because years ago she had bought this beautiful doll named Elizabeth in hopes that one day she would have a granddaughter to give it to. Ema, on the other hand, still after nine years, calls her Hazel. I can even remember my older daughter when she was 4 or 5 calling her sister Hazel when she would speak Portuguese. I asked her why she called her Hazel. She said that was how you say Lissy in Portuguese. As if that isn't enough, for the past nine years, I have had to hear my husband sarcastically refer to our daughter (in the presence of his mother) as "Elizabeth, better known as Hazel."

If you're ever at the pool and hear someone cheering on a little swimmer shouting "Go Lizzi," and a Portuguese lady yelling, "Go, Hazel," you'll know we are cheering one and the same child!

Because Kate tells the story from multiple viewpoints, humor prevails in the constant clash of perspectives. These dueling realities provide detachment from the problem rather than identity with it, which makes the story amusing rather than irritating. One wonders how Lizzy/ Hazel feels about her dual identities and the added dimensions they will bring to her life. Vera's essay, which follows, offers some possible answers.

• • •

Vera Constance Vaughn

I'm an only child, the last descendant on either side of the family, and my parents couldn't agree on what to name me. I was born three and a half months early so they had longer to think about it, I guess. My mother, though she was not a conventional person, assumed I should be named after her Russian mother, Vera, and my other grandmother, Mary, which was submitted to the hospital and officially recorded. But my father who was a teacher of Spanish and scholar of Spanish literature had read a novel that included a character called Constancia—and before I was brought home from the hospital, without telling my mother, went to the city hall and changed my name. Finally, though I'm not sure how the compromise was reached, I became Vera Constance Chadwick. My first name alone was used by everyone in my life and still is, with the exception of my father and his family. Until he died at 85, I was Connie to him, and when we visited his hometown in Indiana, I became Vera-Constance, spoken almost as one name in the Southern way. The funny thing, as I look back on it, is that I had no particular objection to being called two different names by my parents—nor did I, I hope, suffer any dire ramifications psychologically such as becoming what was called then a split personality.

I wonder if other women frequently dislike their names. I do know I hated mine as a child. No one I knew was named Vera, and I thought it sounded silly with Chadwick. My mother's friends called me by my Russian nickname, Vyrachka, which I loved, but during my childhood in the McCarthy era nothing Russian-

sounding would not be welcome nor was Vyarachka any more harmonious with my Angelo-Saxon surname. After my marriage and for the past 40 years I have been Vera Sky and it seems as though the anomaly has sorted itself out. I finally like Vera with my last name. On a recent trip to Russia I realized that Vera is quite popular there and sounds very nice in Russian. What a shame I didn't think of changing the spelling when it mattered more! A closing thought: As I write this I realize that the mismatched names I lived with reflect deeper differences in my parents' backgrounds and personalities—that the name controversy is just the tip of the iceberg. For much of my life I struggled with differing parts of my heritage until I realized that the contrasts I've inherited have actually offered a diverse identity, which is not so bad—and which can actually be interesting and fun! But that's for another essay.

Vera's essay mirrors Kate's and offers both amusing and serious insights into how to handle dual cultures. She learns to celebrate them as an opportunity to enrich identity: the key is to have "fun." She makes an endearing typo about her surname *Chadwick,* which she refers to as "Angelo-Saxon." I think the typo refers to how she feels subconsciously about her name—an added letter, revealing positive associations to a well-loved name. She's in good company: when referring to Anglo-Saxon children being sold as slaves in a market in Rome, Pope Gregory I (7th century) said, "Non Angli, sed angeli" (not Angles, but angels), because he thought the children were so beautiful.

· · ·

An Ability to Laugh at Myself
Randi Finger

My name is certainly one that has some stories to go with it. (My husband says "Randi Finger" is an ideal name for a porn star!)

I was named for my great grandmother Rose and my great aunt Anna. In Jewish my name is Riva Chana, which means Rose Ann. My father, however, didn't like the name Rosie and, as many Jewish families do, he and my mother looked for an American name that started with an "R."

My mother saw a character in a (third rate) melodrama, "King's Row," which starred Ronald Reagan, Bob Cummings, and Ann Sheridan as "Randy Mahoney." I had always winced at the idea of having my name come from such a soap opera, but never saw the movie until after graduate school. When I did see it, I was delighted because "Randy" was this wonderful character: beautiful, kind, loyal, assertive but feminine, and a bit sassy.

Randy was the way my name had been spelled but I changed it informally for my business cards so that I would be identifiable as a woman. When Wil and

I got married and I changed my name, I made it official that now I am "Randi Finger Strathmann." I never had a middle name except for my Jewish name, so now I have one.

I've always felt that I developed the ability to laugh at myself because it helped me survive a name about which everyone always had some crack to make—and always as if they were the first to have thought of it.

Growing up, Randi survives constant teasing, which provides her with additional viewpoints of both herself and others. She notices that people don't realize they aren't as funny or as clever as they think they are. We may not know as much as we think we do, others may not know as much as they think they do, and it may be better "to look before you leap," i.e., to think before you speak, because your judgments may be based on a limited perspective.

For a long time she defines herself in opposition to her name, rather than with it, as most women do. Ironically, she discovers her assumptions about her name are inaccurate: the film character she is named for is actually very engaging. A fictional character helps make her name "real." Her "sassy" namesake also has an ironic sense of detachment. All of these opposing viewpoints open up new perspectives on identity, reality, and understanding, which are the great gifts of humor, irony, and paradox.

• • •

One Long Identity Crisis
Jane

I was born in 1938 to middle-class whites from Baltimore. My parents were Jane and Bill. They called their children Jane and Bill. I have never gotten over their complete lack of imagination. I went ten days unnamed and left the hospital without a first name on my birth certificate. At the time I applied for my passport, I discovered that my first name was Baby Girl and I had to supply the U.S. government with an affidavit saying I really was Jane.

Being Jane Junior had its frustrations. At first my mother was Big Jane and I was Little Jane. When I began to tower over my five-foot-two parent, I should have been Big Jane, but not everyone went along with the obvious. To some I was Janie, to others my mother was Janie. I could have been Young Jane, but Mom was not too eager to be Old Jane. Among our friends and relations, and even strangers, there was often confusion about who was being discussed or called. Later in life I received some of Big Jane's Social Security checks. You can imagine the mess trying to straighten out that bureaucracy.

Jane rhymes with plain and brain, and I am both; so I was unable to escape rather painful ostracism during my childhood and adolescence. Jane Doe, let Jane do it, Calamity Jane—the name is a magnet for cliché. Guess how many guys have uttered "Me Tarzan" and thought they were so witty. Most of my school days I was the only Jane in the class. Lately I have run into more Janes, although some of them have turned out to be Jeans. At least fifty percent of the people hear my name as Jean, even though I take great care to emphasize the long "a." On joining a recent tour group, I introduced myself as Jane. One of the women smiled and said, "I'm Jane too." Days later I found out her name was Jean. My life has been one long identity crisis. I'm not crazy about my name, but I don't have any idea what I would like to be called instead. Come to think of it, I hate my name.

Jane illustrates the paradox of naming—that, simultaneously, we are and are not our names. Our names may require us to deal with "a lot of baggage" simply because of what our names are (or are not) culturally, as opposed to who we are individually. In this respect, our names can teach us lessons about life and identity: things are rarely as simple as they seem. We are inextricably linked to others, their associations and preconceptions. Much as we might wish it otherwise, our name is never a *tabula rasa* for others.

• • •

Lost in Translation:
A Bad Joke

Since puns can be very difficult to translate, I am giving both the original French version as well as my English translation of Yvonne Rollins' essay.

• • •

Ma cousine Anne-Marie
Yvonne Rollins

Ma tante Marie avait appelé son aînée "Anne-Marie" en l'honneur de Sainte Anne d'Auray, une sainte célébrée en Bretagne. Peu de temps après la naissance du bébé, ma tante se trouvait chez nous et regardait par la fenêtre le bébé qui était dans son landau dans la cour. Tata Marie, penchée par la fenêtre, répétait sans cesse: petite Anne, petite Anne! Ma mère, qui était pince sans rire, s'est approchée en lui disant: Arrête, ton enfant n'est pas un âne! Honnêtement, c'était une blague de très mauvais goût et ma tante Marie en voulut longtemps à ma mère d'avoir fait cette remarque. Je crois que ma mère voulait surtout souligner que le nom de ma cousine (dont elle était la marraine) n'était pas "Anne" mais "Anne-Marie".

• • •
My Cousin Jenny-Marie
Yvonne Rollins

My aunt Marie named her first-born daughter, "Jenny-Marie" in honor of St. Geneviève, a famous French saint. Shortly after the birth, my aunt was visiting with her new baby. As she leaned out the window, looking at little Jenny who was in her bassinet in the courtyard, Aunt Marie repeated endlessly, "Little Jenny, Little Jenny!" With a straight face, my mother, approached Aunt Marie and said, "Stop. Your daughter is not a jenny*!" It was a very bad joke, and my aunt held a grudge for a long time. I think my mother (who was the child's godmother) wanted to emphasize that the child's name was not Jenny, but Jenny-Marie.

(*jenny—female donkey)

Because individuals often identify with names, it is difficult to tell a joke about a name that will not be taken personally.

• • •
My Mother's Names: Désirée-Emma-Gabrielle
Yvonne Rollins

Her name "Désirée" made me dream. I didn't know whether to laugh or to be jealous. I loved the sound of her three names—especially Gabrielle. Those closest to her called her "Dédé"; but her brothers always called her Désirée. My uncles made me realize Désirée was a respectable name.

Of course, Napoleon's mistress was named Désirée. That gave an imperial history to that name so heavily laden with the meaning of longing and desire. I think my mother didn't like her name too much but didn't want to say anything about it because it was also her mother's name. My mother became good friends with a woman named Aimée (the One Loved). We would always tease them when they arrived: "It's not Aimée (the One Loved) but Désirée (the One Desired)," or "It's Désirée followed, of course, by Aimée," etc.

• • •
What's in a Name?
Nancy Scott

Andy enrolled in the telephone poetry class I was taking. After class, I called him to find out more about his work. During that first chat, he said, "I know another Nancy Scott. She lives in New York City. She's a psychologist with a Ph.D."

I know there are lots of Nancy Scotts. That's fine, as long as none of them are famous authors. That's my spot. Let those others be abstract painters or astronauts.

I married my concise but common name. No one could ever pronounce my maiden Mullowney. It might be fun now to have an odd Irish variant name, but I like my impossible to mispronounce syllable.

But I don't like my middle name. I try never to use it now that I'm a grown-up. Except that, sometimes, there are too many Nancy Scott listings, or I run into someone who knew me as a kid and I'm forced to expose my redneck middle name, which actually came from my very not-redneck grandmother Josephine.

But I would hate a pen-name. I want bragging rights with no confusion. When I win the Grand Writing Award, I want people to be able to know and to pronounce my name.

Through Google, I've found another Nancy Scott who's a New Jersey poet. I bet that's her real name because who would choose such a non-poetic pen name. And she doesn't list a middle name—not even a wonderful middle name that's long and starts with a vowel. I bet I know why.

––––––

Nancy creates humor with a series of paradoxes. She turns our assumptions upside down, making a common name unique and a redneck name sophisticated. Alliteration, meter, and rhyme make the prose poetic.

• • •
The Multiple Dimensions of Names
Hope Hare

Hope was my mother's maiden name. My mother and aunt used to call me Hopey. My husband and sister are the only ones to do that now; and then, out of the blue, my new son-in-law called me Hopey in an email. I was charmed, and told him so.

I never thought about whether or not my name suited me, but yes, it does. I am an optimistic person, and can never believe that the worst will happen.

Hope is of course a word that everybody likes. Maybe that made a difference to me when I was growing up. When I was little, other children teased me about my name—it was not a common one, and children are notoriously conservative in such things. But I have always been happy with my name, pleased to be Hope—and if I had the time, I would think about the importance of names, the meanings of names, even the sounds of names. About the rhymes of names, the elusive colors of names, the memories connected with names. But that is your task, Elisabeth.

––––––

These essayists depict a progression in their detachment from their names. As a child Donetta learns there are other Donettas so she cannot claim an exclusive identity with her name, which provides her with emotional detachment and allows her to laugh at disparaging names: she is not simply a name. In childhood, Lovely's name is shortened to Love, which has a universal meaning but, paradoxically, makes her a unique individual. Deborah's humor centers on excess and Amy's on deficiency. Kate, Randy, Jane, and Yvonne discuss associations to names, which determine issues we have to deal with, even if they have nothing to do with us. Four of these six essays concern women who were teased about their names, which suggests that teasing can lead an individual to detach from her name as a means of self-defense. The essayists also discuss the associations people have to their names that have nothing to do with them but affect their identity. These erroneous associations automatically make these women observers and provide emotional detachment from the name.

Humor gives these women the ability to step out of the "name box"—out of the self. As observers, they glimpse not only how they look to others but also how others think. When Debbie is ashamed of her ring because it has five letters instead of three, we smile not only at her horror of being different but also at the idea that a ring has to have three letters. With their humor, these essayists are not isolated by their perceived limitations because they come to realize we all have them. The laughter is no longer directed at one isolated individual, but at all of us: the humor becomes inclusive rather than exclusive, therapeutic rather than harmful. The individual can then reintegrate with society. Humor provides different perspectives, which reveal incongruities and allow catharsis—a therapeutic, liberating vacation from the self[134]—and social reintegration.

If you wish to pursue humor in depth, check out Prof. Don Nilsen's *Encyclopedia of 20th Century American Humor* and Victor Raskin's *Primer of Humor Research*.

In the interest of energizing the immune system with a few laughs, google the *Internet Anagram Server* (http://wordsmith.org/anagram/index.html) where you can type in your given name and discover all of its anagrams. If you click on "Advanced," you can do your full name. You're undoubtedly in for some surprises. You will find both new ways to think about your name and new ways to detach yourself from it.

Chapter 30

NONVERBAL ASSOCIATIONS: LIBERATING THE IMAGINATION

In the preceding chapter, Hope invites us to continue our name quest by considering nonverbal associations to names. Nonverbal associations are like walking through the looking glass: bypassing words and reason, they liberate the imagination.

– A –
NAMES AND COLORS

Hope mentions the "elusive colors of names." Individuals with synesthesia are able to see numbers, letters, and even music in color. Synesthesia is a cross wiring of the senses: they are not separate from one another.[135] There is disagreement as to whether all infants are born with this ability. The condition seems to be especially prevalent among highly talented individuals like Russian composer Alexander Scriabin, French poets Rimbaud and Baudelaire, novelist Vladimir Nobokov, painters Kandinsky and Klee, and the physicist Richard Feinman. People with synesthesia can see letters, numbers, words, and music in distinct colors, and can even taste shapes.[136] Check out synesthete Cassidy Curtis' website, *otherthings.com,* and click on "synaesthesia" to see what your name looks like in color to him. Every synesthete sees the alphabet in slightly different colors, however. As Cassidy explains, this ability helps with memory as well as creativity.

Envision your name in color. Create a palette using your name as inspiration for new ways to think about your identity. On days you feel "down," picture your name in color and then consciously brighten the tint for a psychological lift. When thinking about your name and color, consider the ancient associations to colors. Blue is associated with the sky (divinity/spirituality) and water (life/fertility): the Virigin is always depicted wearing blue. Red is the color of blood, a symbol of life and prosperity. Throughout the Middle Ages, God was often painted wearing red and blue. Yellow, the color of the sun, is associated with splendor/the spirit, wisdom, constancy, and faith; therefore, we tie a yellow ribbon around the old oak tree. Yellow was reserved for the Chinese emperors. Green is a symbol for new life and renewal: Osiris, the Egyptian god of death and rebirth, is painted with green features. Muhammad's cloak is green, the most important color in Islam. Because purple dye was difficult to make, it was restricted to the wealthiest and most powerful for millennia. The imperial palace in China was inside the Forbidden

(Purple) City. Because of the impressionists, we now think of shadows as being blue and purple rather than black.

If you want to concentrate on your personality and color, try *What Color Is Your Personality: Red, Orange, Yellow, Green…* by Carol Ritberger or *Showing Our True Colors (True Success Book)* by Mary Miscisin. You can determine your personal color type with the help of the old standby *Color Me Beautiful,* which designates spring, summer, autumn, or winter palettes. *Life in Color* provides the latest spin on personal color selection.

To branch out and learn about the emotional impact of colors and their history consider any of Leatrice Eiseman's books, such as *Color: Messages and Meanings,* which discusses the emotional impact of colors. Jeanne Heifetz discusses their history in *When Blue Meant Yellow: How Colors Got Their Names,* and Victoria Finlay's *Color: A Natural History of the Palette* is a travelogue about colors. There are also histories of specific colors.

– B –
NAMES AND MUSIC

Like synesthetes, play with linking your name not only to color but also to sound. Think of your names, rhyming words, or words that reflect your innermost needs—create a mantra of your own. A little research about mantras, meditation, and consciousness will introduce you to Eastern thought.

Josquin des Prez, one of the most famous composers of the high Renaissance style of polyphonic music, was the first to put names to music using the innovative technique of *soggetto cavato*[137] which is based on *solfège,* a system for assigning syllables to notes.[138] You can figure out your musical signature, compose a ditty for your name, or you can have a composer create one for you.[139] *Soggetto cavato* translates the vowel *a* as the musical notes *f* or *a;* the vowel *e* as the note *d;* the vowel *i* as the note *g;* and the vowel *u* as the note *c.* You could, however, develop your own musical notation for your name. J.S. Bach frequently put his name in his music: "Johann Sebastian Bach loved to put unexpected themes and obscure references in his music. He often put his name in his music: B–A–C–H (in Germany B = B♭ and H = B, which translates to B–A–C–B♭. In the last page of *The Art of Fugue,* Bach brought in his name as a counterpoint."[140]

You can also use music to color your name with the Pythagorean scale for music and color: *do* = red, *re* = orange, *mi* = yellow, *fa* = green, *sol* = blue, *la* = indigo, and *si* = violet. The colors get brighter as you go up the octaves and darker as you go down. Because of his ability to synthesize, one wonders if Pythagoras was a synesthete.

– C –
NUMEROLOGY: ANCIENT AND MODERN

Because Hope's essay brings up a number of esoteric and artistic considerations about names, we should mention other esoteric arts. Numerology has been associated with names since ancient times and still plays an important role in many cultures. You can get a free, sample numerological reading for your name by googling *What Your Name Means (Numerology)*, *Sun-Angel* (and select "Free Name Meaning"), or *Ex Soul Name Numerology* and decide whether the numerological evaluation describes you accurately or not, which will provide another means for thinking about who you are.

Western thought was heavily influenced by Pythagoras, who believed that numbers are basic to the formation of the universe, that everything has a mathematical structure behind it. Pythagoras' beliefs were proven correct by the discovery of the Fibonacci numbers, an Eastern discovery, revealed to the West in 1202 by the Italian scholar Leonardo of Pisa, known as Fibonacci. Each number is the sum of the two preceding numbers: 0, 1, 1, 2, 3, 5, 8, 13, 21, 34, etc. These numbers form the very structure of the natural world like the branching of tree limbs, the curve of waves and seashells, and the florets of flowers.[141] Scientists can now activate computers using human thought, which means that computers are translating our thoughts into numbers. This new technology has great possibilities for the handicapped and for controlling instruments such as robots. In addition, computer usage provides researchers with vast quantities of numerical data about individuals, which are used to create personal profiles useful for marketing. Companies like Netflix can very effectively determine an individual's likes and dislikes using complex logarithms. DNA sequencing, a mapping of our genetic identity using numbers, opens up the possibility that science may one day be able to recreate a human being from a DNA sample, like a tooth or a hair. Of course, even if this becomes possible, a human being can never be exactly replicated because the life experiences will be different.

Only one essay mentioned a numerical link to a name—a lucky number, which was that of her saint's day, an "intuitive" feeling about a number as opposed to a philosophical or mathematical understanding. The various possible links between numbers and individuals have been, and still are, debated by numerologists, astrologists, mathematicians, and philosophers. Most of these fascinating concepts require an advanced understanding of mathematics and philosophy. Web articles by specialists like Prof. Karlis Podnieks of the University of Latvia Institute of Mathematics and Computer Science can be enlightening for understanding how the mind works[142]— numerology for the 21st century.

Douglas Hofstadter's Pulitzer Prize winning book *Godel, Escher, Bach: An Eternal Golden Braid* is an entertaining book about the mind, artificial intelligence, creativity, the interrelationships of math, philosophy, art, and music written in a style inspired by Lewis Carroll's *Alice in Wonderland*. To investigate the esoteric dimensions of names try *The Hidden Truth of Your Name*, which explores names, the kabbalah, runes, and numerology: nomenology attempts to study personality based on names.

– D –
ASTROLOGY

• • •

Taurus
Fanny Krieger

My mother who came to France from Bessarabia (a province between Romania and Russia and which was part of one or the other depending on the outcomes of wars) came to France in 1927, met my father and they married. She always said that she named me Fanny after 2 of her aunts who lived to be 100 and over. She was bestowing upon me a long life. I am now 79. I am under the sign of the Taurus and have probably most of the qualities and faults of the bull.

When I first arrived in the States after the war, the people I met all thought that I should change my name as Fanny had another meaning. So we tried Florence for a while and I could not get used to it, then we tried Frances, but again it was not me.

I saw a psychic a while back. The psychic who absolutely did not know me said upon meeting me and I'll paraphrase: "Your name is Fanny. A very interesting name, very appropriate for you and anyone in a very large circle of people know immediately whom Fanny refers to. And....you will live a long life!" In fact, I am fairly well known in the fly fishing community, especially with the influence I have had through the 2 organizations I founded for women fly fishers.

I am engaged now in a new project: doing a DVD teaching kids how to fly fish, using my 4 grand children. This will take place this summer and I hope to have that DVD available for distribution by the fall.

My best friend is a well-known children book writer, Marilyn Sachs. She has written 2 books based on my life. The first one "A Pocketful of Seeds" tells my story during my childhood in France till the end of the war. The second one "Lost in America" tells the story of the last year in France and the first year in America. Both books have done very well.

To come back to the name of Fanny, there were and probably are still very few girls named Fanny in France, despite the well-known book and movie of that name by Marcel Pagnol. I always felt a little special being the only one in all my school years with that name. My mother also said that she had read "Back Streets" an English book where the heroine was named Fanny. Often my mother called me by the Russian diminutive affectionate "Fanuska."

Only two of the essays mention astrology. Both essayists feel they "fit" their astrological sign. Contemporary astrology is described as "psychological" and is directed towards self-improvement: "...it involves prolonged periods of self-analysis, the courage to confront and integrate our own hidden darkness, to recognize our self-righteousness, defensiveness and deepest fears, and the decision to take personal responsibility for ourselves, rather than being content to live as passive victims."[143]

Peggy Kay, a certified astrologer, explains that astrology is simply a tool to help the individual better understand herself, to make her more conscious of how she relates to the world, and to think about the choices she makes. The planets and zodiac signs are symbolic of characteristics, qualities, types of energy and personality: through them we can expand our consciousness and our awareness of our strengths and weaknesses. Peggy emphasizes that astrology analyzes possible influences and outcomes, but free will negates destiny. You can get a free starter horoscope by googling *Astrodienst* (http://www.astro.com/cgi/awd.cgi?lang=e).

The awe and longing we feel looking at the stars is deep seated. Because of the big bang, scientists note that the earth was created with stardust. Gazing wistfully at the sky, we sense both our spiritual and physical origins. "Every atom in our bodies, other than hydrogen, was forged in the fiery belly of a star that lived and died before our own star, the sun, was born. (...) As Carl Sagan said, "...(We) are starstuff pondering the stars."[144] The ancients understood this intuitively by putting their heroes and gods in the constellations.

Readers who would like to learn more about new age astrology can consult *The Astrological History of the World* by Marjorie Orr or *Cosmos and Psyche: Intimations of a New World View* by Richard Tarnas.

Chapter 31
UNLOCKING THE SECRETS OF THE PAST:
LIBERATING MIND AND SOUL

Finally, Hope suggests we ponder the memories associated with names. Memories are found in every essay in this book. We are a collection of memories, thoughts, and sensations in the present and dreams for the future. Of these, memories fill the most chapters of our lives. But as Shakespeare says in *The Tempest*, "What's past is prologue": to understand the present we have to understand the past. We can gain greater insight into ourselves by going back through our past to see how we have woven together the psychological and spiritual threads of our lives. "Know thyself" is carved on the temple of Apollo at Delphi. "Seek" is repeated constantly throughout the Bible.

Today there are many avenues for developing psychological self-understanding by contemplating how our minds work and could, perhaps, work better. Sigmund Freud developed the field of psychoanalysis to provide insight into how our personality was gradually formed. Understanding this process allows the individual to make the most of her strengths, to recognize her weaknesses, and to compensate for them, if not eliminate them. You can begin your own personal investigation with Freud's *Interpretation of Dreams*, an ancient art, or Jung's *Psychology of the Unconscious*, or *Psychological Types*. For a feminine archetypal perspective, try Dr. Jean Shinoda Bolen's *Goddesses in Everywoman*.

Psychiatry has shifted more and more towards medications, but the euphoric hope that medications can solve all our problems is fading. It is worth pondering the World Health Organization's "remarkable and consistent finding" that without drugs, schizophrenics in the developing world do better than in the West with drugs because of better social tolerance and support.[145] The American Psychiatric Association is revising its Diagnostic Manual to include "risk syndromes." According to the *Washington Post's* article, "Psychiatry's bible to undergo a revision, DSM, could introduce new mental disorders" (2/10/2010), many specialists worry that as opposed to specific diagnoses, these revisions into broad categories, i.e., "risk syndromes," will lead to over diagnosis and over medication.[146] The *Consumer Reports* survey (July 2010) agrees with recent studies that indicate that the best results for psychological issues come from a combination of medication and therapy, rather than medications alone. There are many different kinds of therapy that can help us explore, enrich, and improve, if not perfect, ourselves. *Wikipedia* gives partial listings, which offer almost a hundred different types. There is something for everybody.

Because of our dual nature, we seek to understand not only our psychology but also our spirituality. Since ancient times, human beings have sought spiritual enlightenment with religious mentors—gurus, rabbis, imams, priests, and preachers. Tara, Shyama, and Peggy Kay discuss their spiritual growth with the aid of a guru. Exploring different religious traditions leads to a deeper appreciation of your own faith as well as that of others. The world's religions teach us that each one of us has a divine spark given to us by the Creator. How differently we would treat one another and even ourselves if we looked at another human being and thought, "There is a divine spirit standing before me. Her life and my life are sacred." With that realization, we could no longer hurt or disrespect ourselves or one another.

Harvard professor Huston Smith's *The Illustrated World Religions: A Guide to Our Wisdom Traditions* is a pleasant introduction to the world's diverse religious traditions. For a comprehensive guide to spirituality consult a list of the best spiritual books of the 20th century compiled by Philip Zaleski, editor of the annual *The Best Spiritual Writing* series. The list is available by googling *100 Best Spiritual Books*. The list includes works of literature, philosophy, spiritual journeys from the world's different faiths, as well as works that unite the different religious traditions.

The stories of our names remind us that without understanding the past, we cannot understand the present or the future. The pieces fit together although we may not yet know how they were assembled, either on an individual, historical, or a spiritual level. The challenge and the fun lie in trying to put the pieces of the puzzle together.

Chapter 32
INITIALS OR A SINGLE LETTER

New trends indicate an increasing shortening of our names to initials and even single letters.

* * *

"BAR"
Barbara Ann Ripley

Before I got married my maiden name was Barbara Ann Thompson: my initials spelled BAT. After I got married my initials spelled BAR.

Barbara's initials before and after marriage are acronyms—her initials spell words.

* * *

"KC"
Karen Lee Bieber

(...)My initials were KC or KLC if one included the middle name. My best friend from kindergarten days, Virginia, called me "KC," which evolved into "Casey" and "Kelsey." I used these nicknames in junior high to sign my secret notes to friends to keep my identity hidden from anyone who might come across our silly letters to one another. As an adult, this "KC" was taken up by my husband, Michael, who added a "B" for our last name of "Bieber." I loved it when he called me "KCB."

* * *

"Miss T"
Tarpley Long

"We can't call this teeny baby, Tarpley!" declared my 6'5" father, as he cradled me in his arms shortly after birth. "How about Miss T?"

* * *

"Miss T"
Tana Sommer-Belin

I also had a brief period in High School of using the name "Misty" that was derived from friends who started calling me "Miss T" and that morphed into "Misty."

As we saw with double and composite names, people prefer a single name and will associate familiar sounding names to names they already know. Because they are homonyms, it is not surprising that "Miss T" becomes "Misty."

• • •

"KT"
Kathleen T. M.

My initials, K.T., turned into my nickname, Katie, which I have been called since the week after my birth.

• • •

"K" / "M&M"
Kelly Williams
(Generation Y)

I actually don't know how my parents picked out my name. I go by my first name, Kelly, although I have had a couple different nicknames, my friends and parents sometimes call me Kel, or K. I do like my name. I think that I have the most common spelling of it. My Sigma Alpha Iota sisters have nicknamed me M&M, after something funny that had happened last year, and I have that written on the back of my Greek letters, and no one calls me that on a regular basis, but sometimes my sister sand the other Greek members on campus talk to me about it, or make jokes about my nickname.

• • •

"MB"
Marybeth Gaul

My name is Marybeth (one word!!!). I was born in 1968. My mom's godmother's daughter was named Marybeth and she loved the name, which was why it is mine now.

I was Marybeth exclusively until college—at some point in time during my freshman year, someone started calling me MB and that caught on and lives on until today—sort of. Here is the run down: my family and friends from high school and younger call me Marybeth, my college friends call me MB, my husband (whom I met in college) refers to me exclusively as MB (he introduces me to people as MB— it sounds weird to me when he says Marybeth which he sometimes does around my parents!!), and my husband's family calls me MB (though sometimes they will call me Marybeth around my family, I guess because they think that is what they should do, but it sounds strange and unnatural to me coming from their mouths!).

I was called both MB and Marybeth in law school (depending on whether the friends had a connection to my college friends or my now husband or not) but in my professional life, I was mostly Marybeth, probably because that is how I introduced myself. HOWEVER! I found that as some people got to know me well around the office, they would start to call me MB even though I never asked them to or told them that some people called me that! Funny how that happens. In my mom life

295

here in River Falls (a suburban development), I am called both. The likely reason for that, now that I think of it, is that I often sign my e-mails as MB, though some people started calling me that on their own.

I am equally comfortable with both names and as I said, it feels unnatural when someone who knows me as MB calls me Marybeth and vice versa. The funny thing about all of this is that Marybeth is ONE WORD so I am really not technically an MB at all!!!!

———————

Marybeth's metamorphosis into MB is an example of how technology is changing the way we think about names. Marybeth's concerns mirror those of women with double names. If she were to sign *Mb*, would that be a solution or would she feel that the signature is unbalanced with part of her name slighted?

• • •

"J"
J Heaton Helene Talcott
(by her mother Lisa Talcott)

My daughter's first name is J Heaton with no period after the J. Heaton is my husband's father's middle name (Worthington Heaton Talcott) and Heaton was a surname at one point in the family tree. The J represents many other important members of both sides of our family. (My mother Janet, mother-in-law Jacqueline, sister-in-law Judi, brother and father, John.) J seems to really like her name. The J does not have a period because it is not short for or representative of "one" thing. Instead it is just "J" for J's sake...may not make perfect sense but it did to us at the time. My Dad is an attorney and laughed about it when we put the J Heaton as her first name on her birth certificate.

• • •

"J Heaton"
(Generation Z)
(by herself)

My name is J Heaton Talcott! Sometimes my friends call me J or JDOG, but most of the time I just go by Heaton. I always thought the J in the beginning of my name fit my personality because I am really spazzy, and the J just reminds me of being spastic! And as for the Heaton, I always thought that it is sort of "unique." I LOVE the name, but sometimes people think that it is a boy's name, when it could be both. I still enjoy the family name as much as anyone else!

• • •
"JET"
(by her mother Lisa Barton)

My poor baby girl was named Johanna Eija Tamara ...plus last name. My dad wanted me to name my child for my mother...Josephine Johanna. I really hate the name Josephine (as did my mother), so Johanna it was. (Four grandchildren and all four have first names which begin with the letter J...for my mother...dad bullied all of us!) Her father liked the name Tamara, a character from a Robert Heinlein novel. This was supposed to be her middle name. One month before my daughter was born, a very dear friend (who was from Finland) passed away suddenly and unexpectedly at the ripe old age of 32. Her name was Eija Lisa. In honor of her, Eija was added to my daughter's name and on January 16, 1988, JET was born. Four pounds 12 ounces... and I gave her a name three times bigger than she was. I saddled her with 3 names, but I don't use any of them. To me, my friends and my family, she is JET. Her grandfather called her baby Jo. Teachers, of course, called her Johanna (or Joanna)...this really confused her at first because no one had ever called her Johanna before! Her friends use JET, Johanna, JoJo, MoJo, or just Jo. Eija's mom called her Eija, but JET never got the chance to know her, either.

I have no clue as to how much she hates me for what I did to her name wise... but I meant well. Hope she responds to you, I'd love to know what she thinks! I also wonder what she wishes I had named her. She's my JET...forever and always.

She at least knows why she has the names she has...I never will.

• • •
"Q"
Norquata Allen

My name is Norquata. My mother got my name from a friend of hers that was named Laquata. She liked that name so she changed it a bit and came up with Norquata. I go by Norquata and Quata. People call me many other things as well such as Quater, Qua, and Q. I think my name does suit me because it's unique. I am not your average person at all. When I meet someone they have a hard time learning my name especially if they have never heard it before. They say it with a long "a" rather than a short "a."

• • •
"T"
Taylor C. Boyd
(Generation Y)

My name is Taylor. It has become a quite popular name. I think the popularity of my name has made me become unique in personality. (You could ask any of the people that know me, and they will tell you I'm a very unique person.) My parents gave me the name Taylor because at the time it was a very unique name. However, there are many "Taylors" in my school.

I use Taylor although some people call me by my middle name (Cora). I think Taylor suits me because it somehow has a uniqueness and yet a very common feel about it. Taylor suits me also because I can't see myself as anything but a Taylor. Of course, that is true about most people and their names. I tell my friends all the time that since I have a common name, I must be unique in what I do and who I am.

Taylor Cora Boyd- my name being completely Scottish does make for an interesting conversation topic. Most of my family is Scottish so I guess that is part of the uniqueness of my name. I even met a person who had studied Scottish heritage and their only response was "Text book Scottish." I know it might have sounded like I don't like my name, don't get me wrong I love my name. It has given me a few nicknames, among them the typical Tay; Tay Tay; and T.

A search for initials that are names turned up Bat (Barbara Ann Thompson), Kaycee (KC) and Katie (KT). The essays indicate a growing trend in the use of initials or just a single letter for names. Many of the essays are about initials that are either acronyms (they spell a word) or homonyms (they sound like a name, e.g., *Miss T* becomes *Misty*). The homonyms suggest that people naturally make a name out of initials: people still think in terms of names. One wonders what the psychological ramifications of initials that are acronyms or homonyms may be: these women have identities hidden within their initials. The younger generation shows a tendency to shorten names and to reduce names to a single initial letter. The tendency to shorten names is inevitably due to rapid communication and limited space for texting. This shortening is an ironic move away from the trend towards longer given names. Perhaps our subconscious is moving us towards longer names on paper to counterweigh their truncation on the Internet. Paradoxically, essayists identified by a single letter describe a great sense of freedom about their identity and feel unique. Looking at a name reduced to a letter inevitably raises questions about the essence of identity, even if only on a subconscious level.

Chapter 33
NAME CYCLES
. . .
Something Unique...
Amy Bell

I spent two days running through names. Family names were overused. We wanted something unique but not difficult. We decided on Emily. A month after our daughter's birth (April 1995) we heard that Emily was the most popular girls' name and continued to be for the next ten years! If I could change her name I would. It is exactly what we were trying to avoid. We knew of NO Emilys. The spelling was chosen, to be unique, the French way and an older sibling is Jennie, NOT Jenny. Ironically, the same thing happened to my mother. In 1964 she named me Amy. She knew of no other Amys and wanted an old-fashioned, not popular name. In my fourth grade class there were three Amys.

. . .
A Younger Generation
Brenda Black

My Mom says that she named me for a movie star who was featured in the old Tarzan films (I haven't researched this): Brenda Joyce. During my youthful years, I never met another Brenda until in high school. There was a young black woman my own age in California who was named Brenda. As I grew into my adult years, there came a time when I would hear the name Brenda used in stores, and I would immediately react thinking that I was the one being called. It became clear to me that a young generation of girls was being named Brenda in apparently greater frequency. Now I have noticed that Brenda is often the name used in books and soap operas for the vixen. When I am introduced to people, they seldom remember my name and will call me Bonnie or Beverly or something similar. I presume this is because the name Brenda is not usual for someone in her 60s and I hardly ever meet a Brenda my age. Also, I think that the name is, generally speaking, a name used for the "lower classes." My family was salt of the earth rural from Kentucky and Indiana. A college education for a female was not expected in my family but I married an intelligent, ambitious lower class guy and got my education (bachelors and masters) after marriage and birthing two children. I became a Speech-language Pathologist and am now retired.

Despite the work of onomasticians—specialists in the study of names—who demonstrate that popular names come into fashion at a slow but steady pace,[147] names seem to suddenly appear out of the ether as Amy's essay suggests. Inevitably, the subconscious must be playing a role—possibly a Jungian universal subconscious guiding a kind of "harmonic convergence" of names. Brenda, who had an unusual name growing up, sees this cycle at work. Her name is no longer unusual in the younger generation. Human beings learn by copying. An entire scientific field, mimetics, has developed to study this human trait, which is used to explain fads.

Another unexpected paradox of our interconnected world noted in the *Economist* is that electronic communication is shrinking rather than expanding the number of baby names because people tend to communicate with others in a fairly restricted geographical area. They therefore model their name choices on that of their friends, rather than on national trends as used to be the case.[148] Who would have thought that, in some respects, the Internet may make us more, rather than less, provincial.

Chapter 34
GENERATIONS X, Y, AND Z

Because of their books, *Generations, The Fourth Turning,* and *Millennials Turning: The Next Great Generation,* William Strauss and Neil Howe have lead to us to think about generations with names. Their ongoing study is a fascinating consideration of how generations respond to one another, thereby creating patterns repeated throughout history. Tom Brokaw named the generation (1902–24) that survived the Great Depression and WWII, the *Greatest Generation.* Their offspring (1943–63) are referred to as the *Baby Boomers.* History has to establish a generation's identity: naming them at the outset is impossible. Since the Baby Boomers, we have had *Generation X* (approx.1960–1980), a name assigned because Generation X was an unknown quantity. *Gen Xers* are the children of the Baby Boomers. *Generation Y* (approx.1980–2000) is also known as the *Millennials* or the *Net Generation.* Until they name themselves, or a historic event provides a name for them, the next generation will probably be referred to as *Generation Z.* Naming the generation after Z poses intriguing problems and possibilities since we've reached the end of the alphabet.

· · ·
Multiple Names
Lisa Lake

Do you know why your parents chose your first name?

My mom named me Lisa Anne Lake. She chose simple, common names, with a middle name that we could use if we hated our first. Although not confirmed, I believe I was named after the "Lisa" computer, an early Mac. This is because my brother is named "Adam," also an early kind of Mac. My father wanted to name my sister Elizabeth, but it ended up as her middle name. I think this reflective of the "E II," another kind of Mac. I don't think he realized he was naming us after computers at the time, but it's a pretty big coincidence.

Do you have a nickname?

This is a weird question for me. Everyone I know in the real world calls me Lisa, but I went by the name "Domus" for a long time on the Internet. I pronounce it Dah-muss. I made the name up when I was 11 or 12. I use it whenever I need a username for something electronic.

I also play lots of games like Dungeons and Dragons, where you play a character. So in those games, I go by the character's name. I've made up at least a dozen of those. Right now I go by "Templetina" in one, and "Argi" in another.

Does your name suit you?

I guess. I must have felt it didn't suit me when I was 11 or 12, to make up "Domus." I'm just used to it now.

Anecdotes?

I hate the fact that Lisa sounds like half a dozen other names. Alicia, Alisa, etc. It used to drive me crazy in school, because I never knew if someone was calling my name or another person's.

The younger generation readily shortens names to nicknames, initials, and even a single letter. They also create new names for themselves on the Internet. One can only speculate about the possible creativity these alter egos may provide for those who will no longer identify uniquely with a single name. This is the positive aspect of multiple names. Like in the Native American tradition, names can become symbols that help identify different aspects of the self and provide immediate access to that part of the personality.

The Computer Age raises many questions about the development of a personal sense of identity in younger generations. The web offers immediate gratification for adolescent impulsivity, which provides both opportunity and risk. Will the Millenials, born into a total digital world of computers, webphones, and Blackberries be less credulous than previous generations? Will they develop a less individualistic, more social sense of self? Or will ever-increasing means of instantaneous communication catch them in a web of shallow self-centeredness? As usual, technological developments offer enormous potential for both positive and negative developments.

In *Hamlet's Blackberry*, William Powers takes a philosophical trip through the historical changes in the way mankind has communicated and provides sage advice about controlling the technology, rather than being controlled by it.

Chapter 35
RECENT NAMING PHENOMENA
– A –
NAMES AND DAEMONS

Daemons have become popular on the web due to the popularity of Philip Pullman's trilogy, *His Dark Materials*,[149] and the 2007 release of the movie *The Golden Compass,* based on the first of the three novels. In ancient Greece, daemons were considered to be "supernatural beings between mortals and gods."[150] The concept of spiritual links to the animal world is tied to shamanism—ancient animistic religions found all over the world. Pullman manifests each character's spirit with an animal daemon that has a given name. The daemon becomes a means of communicating with the self via a visualized animal companion, who should be of the opposite sex to provide a broader perspective—a concept developed by Jung as the *animus/anima.* On the website *Find Your Daemon* (http://findyourdaemon.googlepages. com/), Joy says her daemon, "Cen (a black panther) is the more sensible half of me. If something isn't going to work, he's the one to point it out. He's more pessimistic than I am, and more cautious as well."[151]

One of the potential results of imagining an animal soul mate is a renewed respect for nature, not seen in the West since the introduction of Christianity. This phenomenon calls to mind the Native American naming tradition, which often bestows an animal name that symbolizes a social or psychological aspect of the individual's identity and links the individual to the natural world.

Many websites provide quizzes to help you pick out a daemon spirit: e.g., *What Is Your Daemon* (http://www.gotoquiz.com/what_is_your_daemon). Sites on Shamanism, such as *Shamanism: Working with Animal Spirits* (http:// www.animalspirits.com/index1.html) are also helpful. Other sources are *The Way of the Shaman,* by anthropologist Michael Harner, one of the early texts of New Age Shamanism, and *Animal-Wise: The Spirit Language and Signs of Nature* by Ted Andrews.

As individuals in the developed world have become more and more isolated from nature, we have lost our sensitivity to its sanctity, and our connection with it, which has led us to an unconscionable and untenable exploitation of the natural world. Only the Native American and African essayists mention animal spirits or guardian spirits. The concept of guardian spirits is found in ancient Greek, Assyrian, and Roman religions. The Old Testament and the New Testament have passages describing guardian angels, which accompany the individual throughout life and even after death.[152] While still present in the essays, the spirit world is only a shadow of what it once was. We need to re-establish our ties to the natural world, and nurture and respect its sanctity once again.

– B –
NAMES AND AVATARS

In the ever-evolving world of the web, users may not only have different names, they may even create avatars to go with the names. "An avatar is a computer user's representation of himself/herself or an alter ego, whether in the form of a three-dimensional model used in computer games, a two-dimensional icon (picture) used on Internet forums and other communities, or a text construct found on early systems such as MUDs. (MUDs are computer programs that allow multiple users to participate in virtual reality games.) An *avatar* is an image that embodies the user. The term avatar can also refer to the personality connected with the screen name, or handle, of an Internet user."[153] *Avatar* comes from Sanskrit and means *descent:* it is used specifically to describe the various incarnations of Hindu deities, especially Vishnu—when they appear on earth. It has come to mean "an embodiment, a bodily manifestation of the divine."[154] The first computer representation of a user-named "Avatar" goes back to 1985 to a player represented in a computer game.

Avatars and virtual worlds are used for entertainment, teaching, advertising, e-commerce, and even for therapy.[155] Some avatars, such as those found in the virtual world of *Second Life,* are amazingly lifelike. Their uses are just beginning to be explored. Avatars may enhance creativity because people are not constrained by their real selves or the real world. "O brave new world! That has such people in't," Miranda exclaims in *The Tempest* (V, i, 186). One wonders what may be the psychological ramifications of a computer self that is linked to an incarnation of the divine?

On the negative side, according to stories out of Japan, which leads the rest of the world in computer technology, it is possible to live one's life entirely in a virtual world, even earning a living for virtual services—which creates a parallel universe. This is now also happening in the U.S. This is not a bad idea for escapists, and a parallel universe could possibly create jobs with minimal environmental impact. Virtual sex, a thriving business on *Second Life,* could possibly help with overpopulation. Creating a beautiful computer image of oneself living in a virtual world full of beautiful avatars is, indeed, like living among incarnations of the divine. The imperfections of the real world can be left behind.

What are the dangers of living in a parallel universe? Japan has a generation of lost youth, especially males, who became computer game addicts. With the help of social workers, they can be slowly integrated into the real world, but this has proven to be a difficult and expensive process. The same problems of computer addiction and isolation are now found in the U.S., even among girls. According to a recent study, "8.5% of American youth ages 8 to 18 who play video games show multiple signs of behavioral addiction."[156] This means three million children are affected. There is disagreement among specialists about all this, but Japan serves as a warning.

With the creation of virtual worlds like *Second Life,* adults as well as teenagers are now choosing to spend more and more time as avatars in virtual worlds rather than as themselves in the real world. The more life-like virtual worlds become, the more enticing they will be. It is much easier to be beautiful in a perfect virtual world than it is to be imperfect while struggling with the seemingly insurmountable problems of the real world.

The sirens are singing again. Now who will lash us to the mast so that we can hear their beautiful song without losing our way? As always, the future holds immense possibilities and risks. The ancients can provide the answers we have forgotten.

Chapter 36
NAMES AND WRITING

– A –
NAMES AND IMAGINATION:
INSPIRING CREATIVITY

Several essayists submitted writing they have done about names and identity. The first essay is about an alter. Writing about an alter offers the possibility of fantasizing about who you are, who you are not, or who you could be. Ultimately, every author assumes different names and different characters in writing fiction. Assuming a different name is like assuming a different identity that frees us, thus allowing us to see the world with different eyes.

• • •

Annabella
by Tessa Cochran

Let's start with what I wasn't named: Annabella. My parents had narrowed the choices down to two. Annabella was the one not taken. I don't know where that name came from but I can't think of one that would suit me less.

Annabella emits an aura of deep raspberry: sweetness and femininity. She wears hats a lot framing her round face and clear complexion and enhancing her naturally curly brown eyelashes. Dressing is a creative act for her. She assembles fluid, sensuous combinations of her clothes, as if each day were an opportunity to express herself creatively, making outer visage coincide with inner mood.

She's soft and round (but not weighty) as a result of her love of baking. She's definitely a comfort food kind of person: chocolate chip cookies, warm stews in winter, and fresh vegetables eaten cooked, not raw. The necessary ingredients seem always to be magically in her kitchen. She cooks intuitively, rarely consulting a recipe, as if she and food have a dynamic relationship. Knowing her flair for cooking, neighbors make up excuses to drop by her house just in case something good is coming out of the oven. They know she'll offer them more than just a taste.

Annabella breezes through life socially. Where she is, criticism isn't. And, people naturally want to take care of her. When she's traveling, always with oversized suitcases, she never lifts her own luggage off the carousel. Instead, she lingers, not expectantly but sure that some man will offer to lift them off for her. She met her husband, who holds an endowed chair in English Literature at a major university, when he insisted on delivering her luggage to the taxi stand.

Annabella sleeps like a baby, wakes up refreshed, and lounges languorously in bed before getting up. She seems to have a different relationship to time. She always seems to have read the latest books to come out in the Sunday book review.

Annabella doesn't have agendas because she doesn't need them. But she doesn't lack substance either. It's more like she was born happy and remained that way. Because of this people tend to listen to her, fascinated that she seems to occupy her place on earth without needing to justify herself or to try to impress other people. Well, maybe some are slightly skeptical or envious of the way life seems so effortless for her.

Yes, that's Annabella, my alter.

––––––––––

In her essay, Tessa defines herself by negation, by considering what she is not. This exercise clarifies who we are by defining what we are not interested in and may, simultaneously, inspire us to cultivate traits we wish we had.

• • •

My Christening
1984. V. Ginta Romeikis

At my christening
the priest anointed me with oil
sprinkled me with water
and blessed me with the sign of the cross.
That day I swallowed a grain of amber –
the gift of my parents.
The grain is planted in my blood.

Since my christening the priest has told me
to build bridges and cross them
wash wounds and caress them
to teach children to play
sing cry work and pray.
No, I will not cause a famine.
And, no, I will not feed the Earth.

But a grain of amber is planted in my blood.
I can harvest.

––––––––––

Ginta's poem encourages us to consider the earliest influences that shape our lives. The poem is full of symbols: the spiritual symbolism of her christening, the cultural symbolism of amber, and the therapeutic symbolism of building bridges—of healing wounds and teaching.

Stop and ask yourself what are the important symbols in your life. Work on a list: add to the list little by little. Write your poem using your own images.

• • •

ISLETA WOMAN
by Dolores Rice

Isleta woman
Red clay sculpted in sorrow
Imprisoned artifact of the Southwest.
Adobe lies crumbled at your feet.
Your children, fragile tumbleweeds,
Adrift on the desert sand.
Adorned in silver and turquoise
You sell your sacred traditions
Along the white man's road.

Although most readers have not suffered traumatic losses like Dolores describes, all of us have had losses in our lives. Assessing our losses and how we can compensate for, overcome, or adjust to them can help all of us determine what is important in our lives and what we are doing to foster what matters most. Judith Viorst's *Necessary Losses* explains how growth and development are not possible without loss.

• • •

Time Out (of Time)
Peggy Heller

Where did I leave that girl
  You know the one I mean
I mean the one who danced
  and sang and giggled through her days

Misplaced her, I guess, like that scarf
  of yellow silk or the extra camp trunk key

Where can she be
  that girl who could dress in Grandma's
  old curtains and become
  Scarlet O'Hara or Catherine the Great
  or a tight-rope walker

Left her, I guess, somewhere along the way
  to grown-up, sensible, on time

Do you think I'll someday find her again
    some time out of time
    like this lovely day
    carved from a schedule
    to sing and dance and giggle
a poem

Peggy Heller reminds us that we all have an inner child, made of our childhood memories. This inner child may be forgotten; but she is not lost. Something will awaken old memories and we will find her again. When we find her, she will present us with the almost forgotten world of our childhood. You can still find your inner child. What do you remember about her? What message would she bring to you?

• • •

For My Daughter, Meredith, with Love and a Hat
Peggy Heller

My relationship with Merry is like a hat,
a hat that declares to the world, "This is who I am,"
defining for us both that heady bond,
eloquent with individuality
humming with connection:

A hat that protects from the weather
when all else is stormy, we know
of our affinity and the safe haven
of its being.

A hat that keeps the lid on –
her wild excesses of headstrong experimentation
    and discovery
mine of frantic worry—headache

The hat I crocheted to cover her dear curious head
too lively to nap on stroller trips
in Brooklyn years ago

The hat she pulled from her sleeping bag
to cover my cold head in that cold house
in Boulder last month

309

We walk with heads up
(just because
just because)
with feathers in our caps

_____

Peggy's poem invites us to consider our relationships and to find symbols in our own lives. What symbols would you choose?

• • •
We are angels
Peggy Heller

We are angels
Briefly fleshed in human form
Free to love, to grow, to learn, to give
But we forget

Just as we forget
The angels we knew as certainly as playmates
Guiding, befriending us
Through sometimes perilous childhood

When we're teens
They go into hiding
Teasing us into thinking we're on our own
As we need to be

Reminding us that we are they
And the work and play lie ahead
When life—merely human—is done

_____

The circular construction of this poem reminds us of the circular name evolution we saw in the essays, which suggests this pattern may be closely linked to an intuitive sense of the nature of our existence. Can you find any circular patterns in your life?

– B –
QUOTATIONS

The following quotations were gathered from *The Quotations Page* (http://www.quotationspage.com) unless otherwise indicated.

Every human being has hundreds of separate people living under his skin. The talent of a writer is his ability to give them their separate names, identities, personalities and have them relate to other characters living with him.

~ Mel Brooks

Man knows that there are in the soul tints more bewildering, more numberless, and more nameless that the colors of an autumn forest...
I suppose that everyone of us hopes secretly for immortality; to leave, I mean, a name behind him which will live forever in this world, whatever he may be doing, himself, in the next.

~ G.K. Chesterton

They go too far because they do not reflect what personality is. Just as words have two functions—information and creation—so each human mind has two personalities, one on the surface, one deeper down. The upper personality has a name. . . . It is conscious and alert, it does things like dining out, answering letters, etc., and it differs vividly and amusingly from other personalities. The lower personality is a very queer affair. In many ways it is a perfect fool, but without it there is no literature, because unless a man dips a bucket down into it occasionally he cannot produce first-class work. There is something general about it. Although it is inside S. T. Coleridge, it cannot be labeled with his name. It has something in common with all other deeper personalities, and the mystic will assert that the common quality is God, and that here, in the obscure recesses of our being, we near the gates of the Divine. It is in any case the force that makes for anonymity. As it came from the depths, so it soars to the heights, out of local questionings; as it is general to all men, so the works it inspires have something general about them, namely beauty. The poet wrote the poem no doubt, but he forgot himself while he wrote it, and we forget him while we read. What is so wonderful about great literature is that it transforms the man who reads it towards the condition of the man who wrote, and brings to birth in us also the creative impulse. Lost in the beauty where he was lost, we find more than we ever threw away, we reach what seems to be our spiritual home, and remember that it was not the speaker who was in the beginning but the Word.

~ E. M. Forster, *Anonymity: an Enquiry,* 1925

Perhaps we should comprehend these things better were it not for the persistence of the superstition that human beings habitually think. There is no more persistent superstition than this. Linnæus helped it on to an undeserved permanence when he devised the name Homo sapiens for the highest species of the order primates. That was the quintessence of complimentary nomenclature. Of course human beings as such do not think. A real thinker is one of the rarest things in nature. He comes only at long intervals in human history, and when he does come, he is often astonishingly unwelcome. Indeed, he is sometimes speedily sent the way of the unfit and unprotesting earthworm. Emerson understood this, as he understood so many other of the deep things of life. For he wrote: "Beware when the great God lets loose a thinker on this planet. Then all things are at risk." The plain fact is that man is not ruled by thinking. When man thinks he thinks, he usually merely feels; and his instincts and feelings are powerful precisely in proportion as they are irrational. Reason reveals the other side, and a knowledge of the other side is fatal to the driving power of a prejudice. Prejudices have their important uses, but it is well to try not to mix them up with principles. The underlying principle in the widespread and ominous revolt of the unfit is that moral considerations must outweigh the mere blind struggle for existence in human affairs.
~ Nicholas Murray Butler, "The Revolt of the Unfit" from *Why Should We Change Our Form of Government* (Charles Scribner and Sons, 1912)

A good character is the best tombstone. Those who loved you, and were helped by you, will remember you when forget-me-nots are withered. Carve your name on hearts, and not on marble.
~ C. H. (Charles Haddon) Spurgeon

Life's splendor forever lies in wait about each one of us in all its fullness, but veiled from view, deep down, invisible, far off. It is there, though, not hostile, not reluctant, not deaf. If you summon it by the right word, by its right name, it will come.
~ Franz Kafka

As the only begotten of civilization and even of our humanity, language must be taken very seriously. Seriously, too, as an instrument (when used with due caution) for thinking about the relationships between phenomena. But it must never be taken seriously when it is used, as in the old creedal religions and their modern political counterparts, as being in any way the equivalents of immediate experience or as being a source of true knowledge about the nature of things.
~ Aldous Huxley

If then the power of speech is as great as any that can be named,—if the origin of language is by many philosophers considered nothing short of divine—if by means of words the secrets of the heart are brought to light, pain of soul is relieved, hidden grief is carried off, sympathy conveyed, experience recorded, and wisdom perpetuated,(...)—it will not answer to make light of Literature or to neglect its study: rather we may be sure that, in proportion as we master it in whatever language, and imbibe its spirit, we shall ourselves become in our own measure the ministers of like benefits to others (....)

~ *Idea of a University,* John Henry Newman, 1852

Death is nothing at all,
I have only slipped away into the next room,
I am I and you are you;
Whatever we were to each other, That we still are.
Call me by my old familiar name,
Speak to me in the easy way which you always used,
Put no difference in your tone,
Wear no forced air of solemnity or sorrow.
Laugh as we always laughed at the little jokes we shared together.
Let my name ever be the household word that it always was.
Let it be spoken without effect, without the trace of a shadow on it.
Life means all that it ever meant,
It is the same as it ever was, there is unbroken continuity.
Why should I be out of mind because I am out of sight?
I am waiting for you, for an interval, somewhere very near, just around the corner.
All is well.

~ Henry Scott Holland, Canon of St. Paul's Cathedral, London
Delivered for funeral of King Edward VII, 1910

I think I understand what military fame is; to be killed on the field of battle and have your name misspelled in the newspapers.

~ Gen. William Tecumseh Sherman

Vain ambition of kings
Who seek by trophies and dead things
To leave a living name behind,
And weave but nets to catch the wind.

~ *Vanitas Vanitatum,* John Webster

We begin life with the world presenting itself to us as it is. Someone – our parents, teachers, analysts – hypnotizes us to "see" the world and construe it in the "right" way. These others label the world, attach names and give voices to the beings and events in it, so that thereafter, we cannot read the world in any other language or hear it saying other things to us. The task is to break the hypnotic spell, so that we become undeaf, unblind and multilingual, thereby letting the world speak to us in new voices and write all its possible meanings in the new book of our existence. Be careful in your choice of hypnotists.

~ Sidney Jourard

Marriage has for women many equivalents of joining a mass movement. It offers them a new purpose in life, a new future and a new identity (a new name).
~ Eric Hoffer, *The True Believer* (Part II—The Potential Converts; ch.10)

mutato nomine, de te fabula narratur: (Change the name, and the story is about you.)
~ *Fabula narratur,* Satires by Horace, bk I, no. I, 69

The name of a man is a numbing blow from which he never recovers.
~ Marshall McLuhan (askoxford.com)

With a name like yours you might be any shape, almost.
~ Charles Ludwidge Dodgson, *Through the Looking Glass*
(London: Macmillan,1872) p.34.

A good name, like good will, is got by many actions and lost by one.
~ Lord Jeffery

He that hath an ill name is half hanged.
~ *Oxford Dictionary of Quotations,* p. 621, #49

Fear of a name increases fear of the thing itself.
~ J. K. Rowling, *Harry Potter and the Sorcerer's Stone,* 1997

A signature always reveals a man's character—and sometimes even his name.
~ Evan Esar, American Humorist (1899–1995)

You don't get to pick your own nickname. They've gotta give you one. It's like we're all tryin' to make pets out of each other and we're not comfortable unless we get to name 'em.

~ Laura Moncur Merriton, 03-26-08

If you want to win friends, make it a point to remember them. If you remember my name, you pay me a subtle compliment; you indicate that I have made an impression on you. Remember my name and you add to my feeling of importance.

~ Dale Carnegie

The name that can be named is not the eternal name.
The Nameless is the Origin of Heaven and Earth,
The Named is the Mother of All Things.

> ~ Tao-te Ching ch.2
> (*Oxford Dictionary of Quotations*, p.467)

My name is Legion.

> ~ *The Holy Bible*, Mark 5:9

A sign of celebrity is that his name is often worth more than his services.

> ~ Daniel J. Boorstin, U.S. historian (1914–)

For when the One Great Scorer comes
To write against your name,
He marks—not that you won or lost—
But how you played the game.

> ~ Grantland Rice, "Alumunus Football,"
> *Only the Brave and Other Poems*, p. 144 (1941)

I don't remember anybody's name. How do you think the "dahling" thing got started?

> ~ Zsa Zsa Gabor (1919 -)

The glory and the nothing of a name.

> ~ Churchill's Grave (1816)

Wife and servant are the same.
But only differ in the name.

> ~ Charles Churchill, "To the Ladies," Poems (1703)

A self-made man may prefer a self-made name.

> ~ on Samuel Goldfish's changing his name to Samuel Goldwyn,
> Bosley Crowther Lion's Share (1957)
> (*Oxford Dictionary of Quotations*, p. 359, #7)

The problem that has no name being the fact that American women are kept from growing to their full human capacities.

> ~ *The Feminine Mystique* (1963), Betty Friedan
> (*Oxford Dictionary of Quotations*, p.334, #10)

Today the problem that has no name is how to juggle work, love, home, and children.

> ~ *The Second Stage* (1987), Betty Friedan
> (Oxford Dictionary of Quotations, p.334, #12)

I don't care what you say about me, as long as you say something about me, and as long as you spell my name right.

~ George M.Cohan, 1912
(*Oxford Dictionary of Quotations*, p.230, #9)

Kathy is who I really am—for friends and family, you know—and Kat Von D if, for lack of a better term, a product.

~ Katherine Von Drachenberg (Tatoo Artist, TV Star-Author).(Neely Tucker,"Kat Von D, Stretching Her Canvas," The *Washington Post*, 16 Mar. 2009: Style Section C, p. C2.)

There is a real sense in which we are what we are called, at least from the Old Testament onward, when God renamed Jacob Israel, which means that he struggled with God. (…) After all, in life people seem uncannily to have become the names they have or to be the opposite of those names (but still in some strange relation ot the import of their names.

~ James, Wood, *How Fiction Works*
(New York: Picador/ Farrar, Strauss, and Giroux, 2008) p.115

– C –
NAMES AND LITERATURE

Je confondis les choses avec leurs noms: c'est croire
(I confused things with their names: that's belief.)

~ Jean-Paul Sartre, *Les Mots* (1964)
(*Thinkexist.com*)

I have fallen in love with American names
The sharp gaunt names that never get fat,
(…)

~ Stephen Vincent Benét,
American Names, 1927, (Ox. Dict. of Q. p.64, #23)

The naming of cats is a difficult matter,
It isn't just one of your holiday games;
You may think at first I'm as mad as a hatter
when I tell you, a cat must have THREE DIFFERENT names.

~ T.S. Elliot, *Old Possum's Book of Practical Cats*, (1939) "The Naming of Cats," (*Oxford Dictionary of Quotations*, p.295, #17)

JULIET

'Tis but thy name that is my enemy;

Thou art thyself, though not a Montague.

What's Montague? it is nor hand, nor foot,

Nor arm, nor face, nor any other part

Belonging to a man. O, be some other name!

What's in a name? that which we call a rose

By any other name would smell as sweet;

So Romeo would, were he not Romeo call'd,

Retain that dear perfection which he owes

Without that title. Romeo, doff thy name,

And for that name which is no part of thee

Take all myself.

ROMEO

I take thee at thy word:

Call me but love, and I'll be new baptized;

Henceforth I never will be Romeo.

JULIET

What man art thou that thus bescreen'd in night

So stumblest on my counsel?

ROMEO

By a name

I know not how to tell thee who I am:

My name, dear saint, is hateful to myself,

Because it is an enemy to thee;

Had I it written, I would tear the word.

~ Shakespeare, Romeo and Juliet: Act II, ii, 38-57
(Philadelphia: Lippincott, 1916): Googlebooks

When I don't like the name of a place or a person I always imagine a new one and always think of them so. (p. 26)

"Yes, that is the right name for it. I know because of the thrill. When I hit on a name that suits exactly it gives me a thrill. ... (p. 28)

"Will you please call me Cordelia? She said eagerly.

"*Call* you Cordelia? Is that your name?"

"No-o-o, it's not exactly my name, but I would love to be called Cordelia. It's such a perfectly elegant name."

"I don't know what on earth you mean. If Cordelia isn't your name, what is?"

"Anne Shirley," reluctantly faltered forth the owner of that name, "but oh, please do call me Cordelia. It can't matter so much to you what you call me if I'm only going to be here a little while, can it? And Anne is such an unromantic name."

"Unromantic fiddlesticks!" said the unsympathetic Marilla. "Anne is a real good plain sensible name. You've no need to be ashamed of it." (p. 35)

(…)

"I've always imagined that my name was Cordelia—at least, I always have of late years. When I was young I used to imagine it was Geraldine, but I like Cordelia better now. But if you call me Anne please call me Anne spelled with an *e*." (p. 35)

"But where on earth is the sense of naming a geranium?"

"Oh, I like things to have handles even if they are only geraniums. It makes them seem more like people. How do you know but that it hurts a geranium's feelings just to be called a geranium and nothing else? You wouldn't like to be called nothing but a woman all the time." (p. 50)

"…'Our Father who art in heaven hallowed be Thy name.' That is just like a line of music. …" (p. 82)

~ Lucy Maud Montgomery, *Anne of Green Gables*
(New York: Grosset & Dunlop, 1908): Googlebooks

I gave an involuntary half-start at hearing the alias: I had forgotten my new name.

~ Charlotte Brontë, *Jane Eyre,*
(London: Dutton, 1922) p. 349: Googlebooks

Jaques: I do not like her name.
Orlando: There was no thought of pleasing you when she was christened.

~ Shakespeare, *As You Like It,* III, ii, 276
(*Oxford Dictionary of Quotations,* p. 681, #22)

"He was just a word for me. I did not see the man in the name any more than you do. Do you see him? Do you see the story?"

~ Joseph Conrad, *Heart of Darkness*
(Plain Label Books, p. 71): Googlebooks

In vapid listlessness I leant my head against the window, and continued spelling over Catherine Earnshaw-Heathcliff-Linton, til my eyes closed; but they had not rested five minutes when a glare of white letters started from the dark, as vivid as specters—the air swarmed with Catherines …. (p.17)

Heathcliff—I shudder to name him! (p. 151)

He often asked about the infant, when he saw me; and on hearing its name, smiled grimly, and observed: "They wish me to hate it too, do they?" (p.159)

~ Emily Bronte, *Wuthering Heights*
(New York: Harper, 1858): Googlebooks

"You want nothing but patience—or give it a more fascinating name, call it hope."

~ Jane Austen, *Sense and Sensibility*
(Manor Classics: Rockville, MD, 2008) p. 67: Googlebooks

"The name referred to no one. (...) When asked who I am, the only answer possible is: I am the infinite, the vastness that is the substance of all things. I am no one and everyone, nothing and everything—just as you are."

~ Suzanne Segal, *Collision with the Infinite*, Blue Door Press, 1966
http://www.nonduality.com/suzanne.htm

Algernon: (...) I have introduced you to everyone as Ernest. You answer to the name of Ernest. You look as if your name was Ernest. You are the most Ernest looking person I ever saw in my life. It's perfectly absurd your saying that your name isn't Ernest. It's on your cards. (...)

Jack: Well, my name is Ernest in town and Jack in the country (....)(p. 5)

Jack: (...) I don't much care about the name of Ernest. I don't think the name suits me at all. (p.10)

~ Oscar Wilde, *The Importance of Being Ernest* (Mineola, NY:
Dover Thrift Editions, 1990): Googlebooks

To speak her name was to call up pictures of people and places, to set a quiet drama going in one's brain." (p. xii)

I simply wrote down what of herself and myself and other people Antonia's name recalls to me." (p. 2)

~ Willa Cather, *My Antonia*,
(Houghton Mifflin: Boston, 1918) Googlebooks

We do what we must, and call it by the best names....

~ *Essays and Lectures, Literary Classics of the United States*,
New York, NY, p. 477
Ralph Waldo Emerson (1803 - 1882)

Take not God's name in vain; select
A time when it will have effect.

~ Ambrose Pierce, *The Unabridged Devil's Dictionary*
(Athens: University of Georgia, 2002) p.50: Googlebooks

There exists a false aristocracy based on family name, property, and inherited wealth. But there likewise exists a true aristocracy based on intelligence, talent and virtue. (p. 61)

~ Tom Robbins, *Fierce Invalids Home from Hot Climates,*
(Bantam Dell, division of Random House, New York, NY, 2000): Googlebooks

Mother is the name for God in the lips and hearts of little children

~ William Thackeray, *Vanity Fair,*
(London: Thomas, Nelson and Sons, London,1906), p. 426:
Googlebooks

and thou shalt be called by a new name.

~ *The Bible,* Isaiah 62:2

Naming my Daughter
By Patricia Fargnoli
In the Uruba tribe of Africa, children are named not only at birth but throughout their lives by their characteristics and the events that befall them.

The one who took hold in the cold night
The one who kicked loudly
The one who slid down quickly in the ice storm
She who came while the doctor was eating dessert
New one held up by heels in the glare
The river between two brothers
Second pot on the stove
Princess of a hundred dolls
Hair like water falling beneath moonlight
Strides into the day
She who runs away with motorcycle club president
Daughter kicked with a boot
Daughter blizzard in the sky
Daughter night-pocket
She who sells sports club memberships
One who loves over and over
She who wants child but lost one.
She who wants marriage but has none
She who never gives up
Diana (Goddess of the Chase)
Doris (for the carrot-top grandmother she never knew)
Fargnoli (for the father who drank and left and died)
Peter Pan, Iron Pumper
Tumbleweed who goes months without calling

Daughter who is a pillar of light
Daughter mirror,
Daughter stands alone
Daughter boomerang who always comes back
Daughter who flies forward into the day where I will be nameless.
~ *Necessary Light*. Utah State University Press, 1999.
Reprinted with permission.

In English my name means hope. In Spanish it means too many letters. It means sadness, it means waiting. (…)

It was my great-grandmother's name and now it is mine. (…) Esperanza. I have inherited her name, but I don't want to inherit her place by the window.

At school they say my name funny as if the syllables were made out of tin and hurt the roof of your mouth. But in Spanish my name is made out of a softer something, like silver, not quite as thick as sister's name. Magdalena who at least can come home and become Nenny. But I am always Esperanza.

I would like to baptize myself under a new name, a name more like the real me, the one nobody sees. Esperanza as Lisandra or Maritza or Zeze the X. Yes. Something like Zeze the X will do.
~ Sandra Cisneros, *The House on Mango Street*,
(New York: Knopf Doubleday, 1991), pp.10-11

"I hate my name, too—so sentimental! I wish everyone would say 'Jo,' instead of 'Josephine.' How did you make the boys stop calling you 'Dora?'"

"I thrashed 'em." (p. 22)
~ Louisa May Alcott, *Little Women*, (Boston: Little, Brown, and Co., 1922): Googlebooks

"Ah, heaven, she gifs me the name that no one speaks since Minna died!" cried the Professor, pausing in a puddle to regard her with grateful delight. (p. 288)
~ Louisa M. Alcott, *Good Wives*,
(Montana: Kessinger Publishing, LLC, 2004): Googlebooks

What a vague name! She repeated it in a low voice, for the mere pleasure of it; it rang in her ears like a great cathedral bell; it shone before her eyes, even on the labels of her pomade-pots. (p. 44)

"Ah, you see," he said in a weary voice, "that I was right not to come back; this name (Emma), this name that fills my whole soul, and that escaped me, you forbid me to use! Madame Bovary, the whole world calls you thus! Besides it is not your name; it is the name of another." (p. 118)

And at this name, that carried her back to the memory of her adulteries and her calamities, Madame Bovary turned away her head, as at the loathing of another bitterer poison that rose to her mouth." (p. 349)
~ Gustave Flaubert, *Madame Bovary*,
(London: W.W.Gibbings, 1901): Googlebooks

A last discovery. I write all of my novels and stories as you have seen, in a great surge of delightful passion. Only recently, glancing at the novel, I realized that Montag is named after a paper manufacturing company. And Faber, of course, is a maker of pencils! What a sly thing my subconscious was, to name them thus.

And not tell me!

~ Ray Bradbury, *Farenheit 451*
(USA: Delray Books, 1950), Afterword, p. 173: Googlebooks

- OVERVIEW -
PART TWO
THE NAME FROM THE OUTSIDE IN

In Part II, women discuss how they get their names, specifically, the external influences that shape the meaning of names and identity. According to ancient African naming traditions, ancestors are key in naming and provide the sense of belonging to a great chain of being. Time takes on a totally different aspect from that of the West: past, present, and future coincide. Because we think so much about the past and the future, we often fail to appreciate the present, the only time we inhabit even in our hopes, dreams, and memories. The African naming tradition reminds us of the important truth of the eternal present.

The tradition of giving family names is still dominant in the U.S. The African naming tradition has a very different concept of family from ours, however, which includes a spiritual dimension not found in Western culture. Africans pray to deceased namesakes just as Catholics pray to the saints: the links to the spiritual world can be found within the family. In the West, with its emphasis on the present, we may forget family links can be a great source of strength and inspiration. Story telling, which is key to keeping memories of deceased family members alive, is becoming a lost art in the Western world, perhaps, because of the omnipresence of technology and the hectic lives we lead.

African day names create temporal relatives who reach beyond physical ties to create a universal family. In ancient traditions, family names have spiritual and universal dimensions no longer found in the West. Considering the complexity of the self found in the naming traditions of ancient cultures like those of the Native Americans and the Africans, one wonders if monotheism did not influence our understanding of the self in a very profound way—leading monotheists to think in a singular way not only about spirituality but also about identity.

By bestowing the family name on individuals who are not part of the family, Africans and Native Americans add yet another spiritual dimension to the concept of family. This tradition evidently survives in the West, but I have only heard it mentioned once years ago in the South, which may have been influenced by African traditions as Southern language, food, music, literature, and worship have been.

When namesakes do not skip a generation, children face challenges for establishing an identity separate from that of their parental namesake. When names skip a generation or reach back beyond living memory to become part of family history, they are less problematic for children as they seek to establish their own personal identity. Nicknames or a middle name can help distinguish direct generational namesakes.

The link between grandparent and grandchild namesakes is especially important. Grandparents introduce grandchildren to a lost past they will never know, so that grandchildren can appreciate both what they have and what they have lost. Ideally, this glimpse into the past can help children redirect the future as they grow into adults if they feel changes are either excessive or errant. In turn, grandchildren help grandparents understand the future. Although the differences between past and future have always existed, they are accelerating rapidly due to technological developments. Together, grandparents and grandchildren make time whole by uniting past, present, and future.

Essayists discuss names that honor two or more relatives, which include double names, middle names, and composite names created out of two or more relatives' names. Given names that are family surnames automatically provide a name tribe—an entire lineage, male and female—which can be very empowering. The theme of loss appears throughout the essays about family names. Names are frequently given to honor a deceased family member. Family names keep the memory of the deceased alive and make loss less painful. Some essayists describe the discovery of their physical links to a deceased relative, which make them feel they are part of a chain of being that does not end with the death of a loved one. Physical links help reinforce spiritual links. Although we may not often think about it in the West, we are physically linked to ancestors we do not even know: we carry them within us and they make us who we are. Thinking about our physical links to the past and the future can be a great source of spiritual renewal.

Although most names are still family names, women discuss many other sources for their given names: a friend, a godmother, the performing arts (film, music, ballet), literature, folklore, places, and mythology. Women whose names are connected to literature have stories about history and culture—a connection to the world of the mind. Names based on places go back to our earliest naming traditions and are full of stories and history. The symbolism of mythology provides complex layers of meaning and diverse cultural ties for names and identity. If women do not have a family name and the stories that go with it, it is important for them to know why their name was chosen so that they have a family story for their name. When these stories are missing, women can subconsciously feel left out. Delving into the stories attached to one's name provides unending ways for enriching identity and inspiring spiritual regeneration.

With the repetition of given names, middle names, nicknames, and initials, naming patterns are formed within families, which add visual and oral dimensions to names and belonging. When given names are repeated generationally within a family, the repetition makes determining individual identities difficult, but creates a time continuum in which one generation flows seamlessly into another. Most cultures do not link direct generations with given names, which helps lessen the feelings of competition between fathers and sons and mothers and daughters.

Maintaining the sibling-naming pattern is very important: problems result when it is broken, or when one child is given the worst of the possible naming options. Chinese naming traditions help siblings bond. Each child has two names: one is part of a proverb. The children literally make more sense when they are together and complete the proverb—a powerful subconscious message for family unity. Middle names provide multiple links—to parents, siblings, grandparents, and families. So many different aspects of middle names were discussed that, as Joanne Goldman points out, they must represent a centering for the individual. Family names can create special bonds between family members.

Women discuss double naming patterns. Double names derive from European naming traditions: the Scotch-Irish, English, French, and German all brought double naming traditions to America. Double names have been especially important in the South because of these immigrants. Besides double given names, there are other double naming patterns that may have been influenced by the Puritan and Mormon double naming traditions, which use "Brother" and "Sister" plus a given name. Southern women also have a tradition of unusual names. After the Civil War, women in the South bonded together to face devastation—a twenty-five percent drop in the white male population and veterans suffering from PTSD, a condition not yet diagnosed or understood. Southern women bonded during these difficult times and have been called paradoxically "Steel Magnolias" because of their femininity and determination. They bonded in a sorority like atmosphere as they worked together in a world filled with shattered men. As a group, they have nicknames for one another that are playfully idiosyncratic, which reflect this world in which men do not play a role. One essayist described the Southern tendency to use initials for women's names, which may be another legacy from the Civil War when women were stepping into roles formerly held by men. In the North, women entered a male-dominated work force, a very different environment for women's names and for femininity, which had to be tailored to fit into the male-dominated workplace. These radically contrasting environments help explain the differences in naming traditions for women in the North and South as well as differences in ideals of femininity. As the U.S. becomes more homogeneous, these differences between Southern and Northern women are disappearing.

Because we are drowning in sound, we take it for granted and forget its profound impact. The sound of our names is not only key to our personal sense of identity but also to the creation of the universe according to religion and science: the one mirrors the other. Sound involves touch as well as hearing. Scientists are making important strides with the deaf by giving them hand held devices that translate sound into vibrations. Sound is also important for healing, not only with words and music, but also with sound waves. Language and music are intertwined in the essence of our being and are reflected even in our speech. The power of the sound of a name is described in literature and song, as in *Maria* from *West Side Story*. In Eastern cultures, the name can serve as a mantra and, paradoxically, a means of liberation from the self. Sound is key not only to our identity, but also to our well-being.

The evolution in the sound of names provides insights into cultural changes. Since the U.S. Census has been keeping records, women's names have been getting longer; and men's names have gradually followed suit. The increasing length of our names may be a response to the increasing complexity of the technological world we live in as well as the ongoing desire to pick names that are different, which necessitates longer names. Because of the Internet and texting, shorter names will probably reappear in the continuing evolution of our names both for practical reasons and because the name pendulum is in constant motion.

The evolving sound of our names provides subtle indications of social changes. There is a surprising lack of names beginning with a vowel in the top ten for both males and females from 1880s, when the U.S. Census is first taken, until the 21st century. The adjustment in male names to female names both in the length of the names and in the increasing number of names beginning with a vowel represents a harmonic convergence: male names adjust to female names with a bit of a lag. The sudden leap in the number of names in the top ten beginning with a vowel for both men and women suggests a new sensitivity—a gentler projection of the self with a vowel as opposed to a consonant. Women's names in the top ten with the feminine, soft -*a* ending are also increasing. The decline in women's names beginning with *M* (subliminally associated with mother), as well as the fall of *Mary* from first place (from the 1880s through the 1950s) to #102 in 2009, suggests a relinquishing of old-fashioned stereotypes. After disappearing completely in the 1990s, a female name beginning with an *M* reappears in the top ten in 2000s—but it is an androgynous name, *Meredith*, which represents a dramatic cultural change. Women's names drawn from nature, dropped as old-fashioned or too feminine, are reappearing and may increase as we become more sensitive to the environment. Both the appearance of *Isabella*, as the most popular girl's name in 2009, and the increase in the girls' names ending in *–a* in the top ten names, are indications of the increasing Hispanic influence, which may repopularize *Mary* as *Maria*.

Some women pick names for their children based solely on sound. Siblings can be linked by the sound of their names, either by picking the first syllable, the last syllable, or by initials. Women discuss one-syllable names and three-syllable double names. One-syllable names are problematic for some women because they have no true diminutives and seem, literally, to lack substance. Three-syllable double names are mostly light-hearted anapests, a meter associated with light verse since antiquity. Some women are unhappy with these double names because of stereotypes and their "lilt," which are felt to convey a lack of seriousness. Sound provides a means for measuring an individual's sensitivity by how she listens, or fails to listen, to names when being introduced. One essayist has even determined that you can gauge another individual's adaptability by their ability or inability to respond to the sound of an unusual name. Sound has powerful subconscious ramifications, which can affect how we feel about ourselves and others.

Unusual spelling of a name allows women to maintain cultural ties as well as to create a more personal identity. Spelling also reflects changing fashion trends. If spelling is not consistent, due to either the individual or to a computer glitch, the discrepancy can cause difficult-to-correct bureaucratic problems.

Children are named by a surprising array of nomenclators. The father, the mother, both parents together, grandmothers, the extended family, friends, or younger siblings can provide names. Traditionally, girls have been and are still often named for their grandmothers. Grandmothers are the keepers of the family legacy, so it is not surprising that some grandmothers may insist on their preference for naming the child. Younger siblings can inadvertently provide names for their older sibling through mispronunciation or shortening of the name; and the older sibling may keep that resulting nickname. Physical appearance can also play a role in naming: sometimes a baby just does not seem to fit the chosen name.

Grandmothers expressed their preferences for a variety of nicknames other than grandmother, grandma, or granny. These nicknames (e.g., *Nana, Mima, Mémé*) do away with *grand,* which may make the grandmother feel younger. The nicknames also drop *mother,* which may help both to decrease competitiveness with the mother and to allow the grandmother to be more lenient with her grandchildren than she was with her own children.

Most of the essayists with androgynous names (either surnames or sexually ambiguous given names) are happy with their names and feel that these names have been helpful for opening doors that might otherwise have stayed closed. They grow to appreciate the uniqueness of their names and feel their names energize them. They are a very lively group of essayists.

Adopted women had a great interest in names and family history because adoption involves two families and questions about origins. Researching ancestry provides links and stories that nurture a sense of belonging. Essayists who were adopted helped others discover more about their families and identity. This need to know one's origins is a universal theme in our most ancient myths.

Assimilation is an important topic for many women. Native Americans have heart-wrenching stories about the suppression of names, language, tribes, and even family. Jewish women tell stories of families barely escaping from Europe in WWII and then facing discrimination again in the U.S. Some of the Jewish essayists explain that their families gave them names that would allow them to assimilate easily into American culture. If an essayist has no stories to go with her American given name, she has difficulty relating to it. To fully assimilate, the woman's different cultures have to be acknowledged. If one culture is suppressed, it will eventually assert itself. Children do as they are taught: suppression breeds suppression. Happily assimilated essayists were free to enjoy their entire cultural heritage and they represent the best of America—a diverse society that respects all cultures and religions.

Black Americans describe a long, painful process of integration reflected by their constantly changing name description—Negro, Colored, Black, African American, Black Americans (to distinguish them from newly arrived Black Africans)—none of which identify Blacks from the Caribbean and South America, who are sometimes designated as Haitians, Dominicans, etc.; but of course, not all Haitians or Dominicans are black. There could even be another category for Black American Latinas. According to geneticists, virtually all American Blacks have white ancestors. All of this nomenclature highlights the pitfalls of trying to categorize women according to race. If we did the same thing for Caucasians, they could be listed as White-Indian-Brazilian, or White-Swedish-Arab or any other combination of ethnic groups. If applied equally to everyone, this fragmentation of individuals into various ethnic groups would make us realize we are all of mixed ethnicity, which is the very essence of what it is to be human because of our ancient migratory history that continues to this day. There is no such thing as a "pure" race.

Race is gradually breaking down as a concept. Scientists have proven recently that there is only one human race. The biological differences among the races represent .1%, or less, of our genetic makeup. In other words, we are all 99.9% alike. Ancient creation myths tell stories of the first man and the first woman, the parents of all of mankind. Science has discovered we are all related: anthropology, history, linguistics, and genetics emphasize our complex interrelated story. Names that are found across the globe in different cultures and different languages are a testimony to the very ancient ties between diverse civilizations.

The religious dimensions of names are important for many women. Native Americans have secret spiritual names. Jewish women have Hebrew names as well as American given names, and Catholics pick a saint's name for a middle name at confirmation. Muslims and Zulus believe that given names should inspire, so the meaning of the name is very important. In the Old Testament, an important change in an individual's life may be acknowledged by a changed name. A spiritual name allows the individual to immediately access that part of her identity as opposed to the everyday given name that is associated with worldly activities and relationships. Sacred names are an ancient naming tradition that offers the possibility of spiritual renewal.

Women create personal meanings for their names. Finding meaning in a name involves interpreting the name's story to find its personal meaning as Veronica does, or creating a unique story for the name as Em Claire does (p.267). Women also create their own meaning for their names based on emotions as Molly Hart (p.23) and Tracy do (p.216). Other women have names whose meaning is simple, but inspiring—like Sunny's and Holly's. Women like Meredith, Sandra, Ginta, and Miriam think carefully about the meaning of their names and how they apply to their lives: they interpret the meanings of their names to fit into what they do. Even when women consider names to be a simple moniker, or reject any significance of the name, they reveal what is the most important to them. Creating a personal meaning for one's name is a creative act that allows the individual to define and center herself: every woman can do this for her name.

Women use humor throughout the essays. The more humor women exhibit in their essays, the more they are able to look at themselves with detachment, which broadens their perspective. Not all women survive teasing unscathed, but many of the women who wrote the most humorous essays were teased about their names, which suggests that the teasing may have taught them not only to see themselves as others do, but also to perceive how others think. Their irony and paradox provide surprising juxtapositions that lead us to reflect about things differently and echo Zen Buddhist practices which seek to free the individual from self-absorption and to reach beyond preconceptions by considering paradox. Clashing perspectives can awaken the individual to new possibilities and provide the opportunity for growth. Because humor provides different viewpoints, the more women use it, the more complex their understanding of identity and reality tends to be.

There is only one reference to numerology—a lucky number. Numerology, which represents a greatly simplified ancient concept, is considered to be a pseudo-science discerning certain traits based on numerical symbolism and formulas. The ancients had a very complex understanding of numbers and creation, which we are only now beginning to prove scientifically. Pythagoras believed that numbers were the foundation for everything in nature. The Fibonacci numbers proved this, and science is continuously refining this principle with the most recent effort being computer technology, which translates human thought into numbers. Complex logarithms enable businesses, such as Netflix, to determine what an individual's likes and dislikes are. Creation is not limited to numbers, however, just because numbers are basic to its construction: numbers simply reflect one of the means of creation, which science continues to study. We are beginning to understand the importance of numbers in creation and identity in totally new ways—numerology for the twenty-first century.

There were very few references to astrology. Two women referred to their astrological signs. One was a Gemini and the other a Taurus. Both women felt their personalities reflected their astrological signs. Today, astrology describes itself as psychological and attempts to help the individual understand how she may respond to different situations and character types.

Women discuss many current naming phenomena. Initials and single letters are playing more and more of a role in women's names, most probably due to signing emails and texting—which is counterbalancing the movement towards longer given names. The younger generations readily shorten names and nicknames to initials, or to single letters. Many of them also use a variety of names due to Internet usage—e.g., to play games or to post comments. Throughout the essays we see younger women who exhibit more flexibility with their names than the previous generation. The freedom of the younger generation to use multiple names could foster greater creativity—a more complex understanding of reality that is not limited by one static identity. The younger generations also talk more of their global identity in discussing their names. Their awareness of multiple identities and their sense of a global identity mirrors the complexity of our ancient Native American and African naming traditions. Ego-state therapy—transactional analysis, founded by Eric Berne *(The Games People Play)*—recognizes and continues to refine our understanding of the complexity, the multiplicity, of the self.

Other recent naming phenomena include daemons and avatars. Contemporary daemons are descendants of shamanism (the ancient animist religions of the world) and their spiritual links to the natural world, specifically through animals. Daemons could assist reintegration with the natural world from which most Western women remain almost totally isolated. Avatars, originally incarnations of the Hindu Vishnu, the Preserver, now also describe computer alters—graphic creations that can represent a virtual self freed from any of the imperfections of the physical self. The possibilities and dangers of virtual worlds are still being discovered. Ancient naming traditions, which recognize the need for a multi-dimensional self, can serve as a guide and an inspiration for the new age of identity we are entering.

———————————

As the ancients knew, and as science is now beginning to prove, everything is interrelated. The universe is complex beyond our ability to comprehend with string theory, multiple universes, wormholes, and black holes. String theory is searching for the ultimate equation that unites everything in the universe. These multiple dimensions and myriad connections are mirrors of our own complex identity. Our histories, races, and religions are all interconnected, chapters in a single story—that of mankind. Although we have forgotten those links, linguists, historians, archaeologists, and scientists are gradually rediscovering them. The more connections we develop, the more dimensions we can relate to, the richer our lives will be, as we find meaning everywhere, rather than in just one place, in all of mankind rather than in just one family or "race," in the sanctity of all religions rather than just one, in universal time rather than just a life span. Our identity is not singular, but a crazy quilt of colors, shapes, and sizes whose disparate pieces create an intricate whole. We need to consider all the pieces, where they came from, and how they were put together to attain our full potential.

Scientists have discovered a universal paradox, which mirrors that of our own existence: there are two major forces in the universe—one that is pulling it apart and one that is keeping it together. It is this tension, this instability that keeps life evolving just as it is uncertainty that nurtures creativity. Uncertainty inspires us to imagine, makes us think, helps us change, and keeps life interesting. If we knew all the answers, there would be nothing to learn, nothing to hope for, nothing to dream about. Paradoxically, uncertainty is a great gift. The stories about our given names are full of paradoxes and uncertainties. Given names are no longer an immediate key to ethnicity. Our given names are also getting longer, more complex, with gentler beginnings; but simultaneously, they are getting shorter with email and texting—reduced to single letters or initials, reminding us of, but hopefully not reducing us to, the elemental—reminding us to balance the short and the long, the essential and the nonessential. In yet another paradox, in our search for self-identity, it is only through others that we can find ourselves. Paradoxes bring together disparate truths, which offer us the possibility of reaching beyond our preconceptions: paradoxes are keys for liberating the heart and mind.

Our names are what we make of them, which is an invitation to find as many connections with our names as possible. These links will make us wiser, more compassionate human beings. Seek out your archetypal namesakes in social, intellectual, artistic, natural, and spiritual domains. Find new names, new symbols, new ways to enrich and renew your creativity and self-understanding. As Harvard professor Howard Gardner explains in *Multiple Intelligences,* our brains are like interconnected computers, each with a different expertise: the very structure of our brain mirrors the diversity of the self.

As the ancients taught us so long ago, the self has many dimensions. Family, culture, society, nature, science, art, and spirit are all part of what creates an individual. In the Western world we have centered identity so much on the individual self, we have lost touch with other aspects necessary for a sense of meaning and fulfillment. The younger generations suggest the identity pendulum is beginning to swing back to a much broader sense of the self that encompasses many dimensions—with an understanding that we can only find meaning outside the self. As our ancient naming traditions—the Native American and the African—explain in the essays, we must be "good" in the natural and social dimensions of our existence. In this time of a changing sense of self from a singular to a multiple identity, our most ancient naming traditions can serve as a guide so we do not lose our way: they will tie us to the mast so the sirens do not lure us to drown in the sea of a singular, dissociated self.

According to the Native Americans, we can relate to four dimensions with our names—the Personal, the Social, the Natural (Nature), and the Spiritual. All of us can do this for our names by finding meanings for different letters. After pondering the qualities you aspire to and the dimensions you need to relate to, start searching for associations. For example, *E* could stand for the four elements—Nature. *A* suggests azure/sky—Spirit. *J* might be joy, Jesus, or Jewish—all relating to the Spirit. *N* brings to mind neighbor/family/Mankind—the Social dimension. Your imagination will provide wonderful surprises in this game of associations. You may recognize this technique as a reflection of the ancient art of allegory.

You will even discover that one letter will suffice to incarnate all four dimensions. For example, I'll take *E* for *Elisabeth* –1) for the flawed me/the Personal, 2) for all the other Elisabeths/Mankind/the Social, 3) for the elements/Nature, and 4) for the ethereal/the Spiritual. Thinking abut these dimensions will help you maintain balance in your life.

To find fulfillment, let your identity reflect the wonderful, multidimensional world we live in: revel in and give thanks for all it has to offer.

NAME TERMINOLOGY

First name, given name, Christian name, personal name, and forename are all synonyms. Given names are names other than the family name, nickname, or middle name. Given names may be compound.

acronym—an abbreviation formed from the initial letters of a series of words and pronounced as a word (e.g., NATO, NASA). L.J. is an initialism and K.C. is an acronym (for Casey).

androgynous or unisex names—names appropriate for both males and females (e.g., *Pat, Jamie, Jackie, Tracy*)

anthroponymy—the study of human beings' names

bacronym—a word created by Meredith Williams of Potomac, MD in the 1983 edition of the *Washington Post* neologism contest to define the use of a word that already exists to create a phrase: e.g., GOD - Guaranteed Overnight Delivery.

eponym—something named for a person: e.g., Achilles' heel, Alzheimer's, bloomers (for Amelia Bloomer). "There are almost no eponyms based on women's names." (*Sexism in English*, Aileen Pace Nilsen, http://faculty.ed.umuc.edu/~jmatthew/articles/sexinEnglish.html)

ethnonym—name of an ethnic group (e.g., Jew), including slang (e.g., Wasp), puberty names, baptismal names, confirmation names

heteronyms—words with the same sound but spelled differently with different meanings [e.g., aye, eye, I; Jacky, Jackie—usually referring to male ("y") and female ("ie")]

matronym—name derived from the maternal lineage, a naming tradition still in use in Iceland (Minervudottir = Minerva's daughter, http://en.wikipedia.org/wiki/Icelandic_name).

nickname—informal name bestowed by family or friends or created by the individual herself. Nicknames may be given based on the individual's traits or as a sign of affection.

nom de plume—a name a writer assumes to hide his real identity

onomastics (or onomatology)—the study of proper names (i.e., the names of people, places, or things)

onomastician—someone who studies onomastics

patronym—a surname based on the male lineage (e.g., Jackson)

pseudonym—an assumed name

puberty names, baptismal names, confirmation names—are all names acquired after a religious rite of passage

surname—family name

teknonym—name based on that of the child, usually the oldest (e.g., The Mother of Jesus, Susan's mom, etc.)

ENDNOTES

1. Native American Women

1. "Popular Baby Names in the UK," *BabyCenter.co.uk,* http://www.babycentre.co.uk/pregnancy/naming/popularbabynames/?_requestid=6646702 (2/1/2010).

2. "Top Ten Names 2008," *Social Security Administration,* http://www.ssa.gov/OACT/babynames/ (12/16/2009).

3. Ray Cook, "Behind the Name: Hailey," *Helium,* http://www.helium.com/items/819456-behind-the-name-hailey (7/23/2009).

2. Nicknames

4. Elsdon C. Smith, *The Story of Our Names* (Detroit, Harper & Brothers, 1950) 76.
John Nisbet, "Simply ask for Goup-the-Lift," *Leopard: The Magazine for North-East Scotland,* August 2006, http://www.leopardmag.co.uk/feats/124/goup-the-lift (1/04/2010).
"tee-name," "to-name," "nickname": *Complete Unabridged Oxford English Dictionary* (Oxford, Oxford University Press, 1989).
Ray Hennessy, "Frequently Asked Questions for What's in a Name," *What's in a Name?,* http://www.whatsinaname.net/faq.html#13.

5. Sigmund Freud, *The Standard Edition of The Complete Psychological Works of Sigmund Freud* (London: The Hogarth Press and the Institute of Psychoanalysis, 1959) vol. 9, 237-241 (5/5/2009).

6. Vladimir Nabokov, *Pnin* (New York, Random House, 2004) 76.

7. "Matty Mattel," *Wikipedia,* http://en.wikipedia.org/wiki/Matty_Mattel. For a picture see, "Mattel Dolls, 1945-1960s," http://www.dollreference.com/mattel_dolls1960s.html

7. Common Given Names

8. The Fabulous Four refers to the Beatles. Cf. The "Absolutely Fabulous" is a British sitcom, which is being remade for American TV, 2009. Two of the stars are Eddy and Patsy. "Absolutely Fabulous," *Wikipedia,* http://en.wikipedia.org/wiki/Absolutely_Fabulous

12. The Missing Middle Name

9. "Names for Children—Surnames," http://family.jrank.org/pages/1196/Names-Children-Surnames.html (5/5/2009).

10. "Dutch name," *Wikipedia,* http://en.wikipedia.org/wiki/Dutch_name (5/5/2009).

11. For example, place names in England have Celtic (London), Anglo-Saxon (Hastings, Reading, Birmingham, Buckingham, Norwich, Sandwich, Gainsborough, Scarborough), Roman (Manchester, Worchester), Viking (Faceby, Kexby, Mablethorpe, Thorpe) and French (Beaumont, Beaulieu, Egremont, Richmond) towns, which reveal the cultural history of England. Consult: "Language," *Regia Anglorum—The Languae of the Anglo-Saxons and Vikings,* http://www.regia.org/languag.htm (7/20/2009), and "List of towns in England," *Wikipedia,* http://en.wikipedia.org/wiki/List_of_towns_in_England (7/20/2009).

A similar consideration of U.S. state names reveals that more than half are of Native American origin, seven are derived from French, five from Spanish, thirteen from British/English, one (Rhode Island) was named by the Italian explorer Verrazano, and only one that can be considered "Caucasian American"—Washington state, named for George Washington. U.S. state names reveal the earliest history of the country. In addition, there are place names that reflect Dutch, German, and Scandinavian settlers, among many others. Consult: "The Origins of U.S. State Names," *AlphaDictionary.com,* http://www.alphadictionary.com/articles/index.html.

13. Women's Liberation and Name Consciousness

12. "Married and maiden names," *Wikipedia*,* http://en.wikipedia.org/wiki/Married_and_maiden_names (5/5/2009).

*All references from *Wikipedia* have been checked for accuracy against other sources. I am using *Wikepedia* because I believe strongly in the importance of making knowledge accessible to all.

13. Marriage in the West has been a constantly evolving process, even in the Christian church. In ancient times, brides were protected from whimsical divorces or the death of the husband by the payment of a bride price (bride wealth) by the groom to the father and/or by the payment of a dowry by the bride's family to the groom. If the marriage ended in divorce, the husband did not get to keep the bride price or he had to repay the dowry—whichever applied. (In some cultures, both were paid). In addition, if the divorce was frivolous, the husband might also have to pay a substantial fine. The bride price and the dowry protected the bride against an unwarranted divorce and provided for her and her children should the husband divorce or die. The bride price is described in the code of Hammurabi, the Old Testament, and Greek literature. The tradition of the bride price is carried on in a token form in Muslim, Far Eastern, and in some Jewish marriages. ["The Evolution of Marriage Ancient," *My Jewish Learning,* http://www.myjewishlearning.com/life/Relationships/Spouses_and_Partners/About_Marriage/Ancient_Jewish_Marriage.shtml; "Dowry," *Wikipedia,* http://en.wikipedia.org/wiki/Dowry; Stephanie Coontz, *Marriage: A History* (New York: Viking, 2005) 81-82].

Throughout history, marriage was an important political tool. Women from wealthy families traditionally had no say in their marriages: the more wealth that was involved, the less say they had. Theoretically, according to cannon (church) law, a woman could not be forced to marry against her will. (Prof. Kenneth R. Bartlett, Univ. of Toronto, "Renaissance Women: The Italian Renaissance, course #3970"). A few clever women did manage to gain great power, an especially tricky endeavor for women in a male-dominated society.

In ancient times, polygamy restricted women's marital influence. Polygamy continued to be practiced even into the early Middle Ages—at least for men wealthy enough to support several wives and their children. Not choosing one wife and her children over another could have benefits. If there was no specified heir, a nobleman could actually feel less threatened: competition was between siblings, rather than between fathers and sons. (Charlemagne had several concubines and his daughters did not legally marry—his grandchildren had no legitimate claim to the throne and, therefore, posed less of a danger.) The nobility eventually realized marriage established one legitimate hereditary line, which was more orderly, and involved less mayhem than competing lineages. However, ever fearful of not having enough legitimate heirs, aristocratic males regularly sired illegitimate children to insure the survival of the lineage in some form, if not through direct inheritance: bastards were only forbidden the crown.

To help maintain its power, the Catholic Church developed a complicated system of relationships to the seventh degree, along with a host of others, so that, when necessary, any inconvenient royal marriage could be declared "incestuous," (Coontz, 98-100). This complicated system of relationships had some unintended benefits: it forced more far-flung marriages, thus creating widespread alliances. "This system marks a transition from archaic societies" with a limited choice of wives "to that of modern society with a wide range of choices." [Philippe Arlès, *Revelations of the Medieval World*, vol. 2, p.119 in Georges Dubuy, ed., *A History of Private Life* (Boston: Belknap Press, 1993)]. In the thirteenth century, because of the problem of easy divorces, the church dropped down to four degrees of relationship (as opposed to seven) and did away with even more esoteric relationships—such as relationships to godparents.

Surprisingly, "For the first eight centuries of its existence, the church showed little interest in marriage or divorce of the lower classes," (Coontz, 104). Marriages involving property continued to follow ancient patterns involving family negotiations. All that was necessary for most marriages, however, was mutual consent—a promise made by the couple to one another, with or without witnesses. For centuries, no church ceremony was required for a marriage. Beginning in the 12th century, marriages took place at the church door. The priest was only a witness. By the 13th century, after exchanging vows and the ring, the wedding party could come inside the church for Mass. (The tradition of the ring goes back at least to the Romans. Men did not start receiving rings before the 16th century.) In 1215, the Fourth Lateran Council tried, but failed, to institute church marriages, (Coontz, 105-107). By the 13th to 14th centuries, the presence of clergy for weddings became standard, [Kirsti S. Thomas, "Medieval and Renaissance Marriage: Theory and Customs," http://www.drizzle.com/~celyn/mrwp/mrwed.html (8/7/2010)].

Among the peasantry, having a child before marriage was not unusual and served as proof of the woman's fertility. Peasants depended heavily on their children for labor. Feudal lords could arrange the marriages of serfs. This power to pick the serf's spouse may explain the confusion surrounding *le droit de seigneur* (the lord's right), which may refer to the right of the lord to pick his serf's wife, rather than to the lord's right to spend the wedding night with his serf's bride. However, le droit de seigneur is debated among scholars. (Le droit de seigneur is at the heart of Beaumarchais' opera, *Le Mariage de Figaro*.) A payment of some sort was also usually made to the feudal lord [mariage, *Grande Larousse* (Paris: Librarie Larousse, 1963)]. A couple could ride through the village in a wagon in which villagers would place necessities to help the newlyweds start their household.

It was only in 1545 with the Catholic Council of Trent that a marriage had to be witnessed by a priest (and two other witnesses) to be officially recognized. *The Book of Common Prayer* (1559) notes, perhaps the first time, that marriage could take place inside the church. As the population grew and young people left for cities to find work, marriages could no longer be strictly monitored. Many marriages were simply by mutual consent. These marriages were referred to as *Fleet Street marriages*, because so many were performed on this street in London. In 1566, the Catholic Church authorized a catechism for marriage, but this did not apply to Protestants, who continued with marriage by consent. ("Marriage," *Wikipedia*, http://en.wikipedia.org/wiki/Marriage). Martin Luther insisted on civil wedding contracts. It was only in 1753 with the Marriage Act, that marriages in England and Wales required an Anglican priest recognized by the church. The Council of Trent (1545) and the Marriage Act of 1753 were passed in order to stop couples from marrying without parental approval and to solidify the power of the church. The necessity of being married by a priest is a tradition that is less than five hundred years old for Catholics and less than three hundred for Protestants.

Another surprising fact is that "...people in north-western Europe generally married later than elsewhere in the world. Between 1500 and 1700 the median age of first marriage for women was twenty-six, which is higher than the median age of first marriage for American women at any point during the twentieth century" (Coontz, 125). Only the wealthy could marry at a young age. Most women had to work to fund their own dowries; and apprentices had to become masters of their trades before they could marry. Marriages were "working partnerships." More than in other parts of the world, women helped build north-western Europe, which explains, in part, why it grew so fast" (Coontz, 128-130).

This marital "working partnership" changed dramatically when the husband became the primary provider for the family with the advent of technology and the market economy beginning in the 18th century (Coontz, 146). With the blossoming of the Romantic Era and the rejection of Enlightenment's Reason, the concept of women and marriage changed dramatically. Emotions ruled both men and women: women were considered especially frail and vulnerable. This view of women continued through the Victorian era (1837-1901), was modified briefly during WWI and WWII, only to be domesticated, once again, in the 1950s. The sexual revolution of the 1960s led to the ongoing reevaluation of women and their role in society that mirrors that of the "working relationship" Coontz describes in Europe when commerce and towns were beginning to flourish between 1500 and 1700. Now, as back then, women are marrying later in life— not to establish their own dowries as in the past—but to establish their careers before having children.

So how do names fit into all of this? Noble women have always kept their names and titles, even if they added new ones with marriage. Marriage registers give both the maiden and married names. In Europe, women kept (and still keep) their maiden names. The married woman's legal name is her maiden name. (In Spain, both men and women have two surnames, the paternal followed by the maternal. Women do not change their names upon marriage. The Spanish tradition of double surnames is attributable to the Moorish influence. Arab women keep their maiden names: they do not take on their husband's surname.)

The history of *madame* has an interesting evolution. Madame was first used by the courtly love poets of 12th century France, who introduced the idea of romantic love to Western civilization. Madame means "my lady" and was used to address women of noble rank, married or not ("madame," *Grande Larousse*). In England, servants addressed their mistress or any lady of rank as "madam" (1300). By the Renaissance, madam(e) could be used derisively with lewd undertones (1598). (This usage was inevitable in that it enables double entendres: gentlemen could discuss their amorous escapes while seemingly discussing their wives. Madam(e) warded off suspicion if anyone overheard the conversation.) By the end of the 17th century, there were complaints that the term was being used too broadly to refer to almost any woman. During the 18th century, with the enlightenment, the birth of universal ideas of liberty and equality, the usage of madam continued to spread throughout the population: every woman thereby gained a title. It was contracted to "Ma'am" in English—and is still used in the South and also by sales personnel who may still address their female clients as "Madam." Madame was also used to refer to nuns of a certain rank in France and, especially, older nuns in England until the Reformation ("madame," *Oxford English Dictionary*).

The earliest uses of *mistress* were associated with women who had power or knowledge—a female teacher (1340), a woman who headed a family or establishment (1375), who had authority over a child (1400), who ruled, had authority and servants (1426), who governed a state or people (1450), who had mastered any branch of study (1484). By 1430, mistress could refer to a woman in a sexual relationship without being married while simultaneously being used as a term of respect added to the surname of a married woman (1430) or to the surname of an unmarried woman (1474). Like madam, mistress could be used as a double entendre. Madam and mistress were originally used to denote status and power and were used to address either married or unmarried women ("mistress," *Oxford English Dictionary*).

Mrs. appeared as an abbreviation (1485) much earlier than *Miss* (1606). Miss was gradually associated with unmarried women most probably because one of its meanings was sweetheart (1425). It was also used to refer to a concubine or whore by 1439, despite the fact it was also used to address unmarried women. Madam(e), Mistress, Mrs., and Miss, gradually became more and more generic and finally served as titles to indicate the marital status for any woman, not just one highly placed or highly educated. All these English terms derive from the French, which derives, in turn, from Latin.

The *Oxford Dictionary* reveals that the earliest written terms used to describe marital relationships are *husband* (Old English with Old Norse roots, 1000), *wife* (Old English, with Dutch, Germanic, and Norse roots, 1000), *spouse* (from Old French, 1200, with much older Latin roots), *wedding* (from Old English with Dutch, Germanic, and Norse roots, 1000) and *marriage* (from Old French, 1300). The etymologies of these words reveal the mixed cultural heritage that has helped to create our marriages as well as the variety of words we use for these relationships. (5/5/2009)

14. "History of Bar/Bat Mitzvah and Confirmation," *My Jewish Learning.com*, http://www.myjewishlearning.com/life/Life_Events/BarBat_Mitzvah/History.shtml (5/5/2009).

339

15. "The First American Bat Mitzvah," *Jewish Virtual Library.org* (A Division of the American-Israeli Cooperative Enterprise), http://www.jewishvirtuallibrary.org/jsource/Judaism/firstbat.html (5/5/2009).

14. Women and Their Titles

16. "Oberlin College," *Wikipedia,* http://en.wikipedia.org/wiki/Oberlin_College (5/5/2009).

17. "Firsts for U.S. Women," *Catalyst.org,* http://www.catalyst.org/publication/211/firsts-for-us-women (5/5/2009).

15. Choosing a New Given Name

18. "Tara (Buddhism)," *Wikipedia,* http://en.wikipedia.org/wiki/Tara_%28Buddhism%29 (5/5/2009).

19. "REL-TIB-012 Mask of the Goddess Tara," *Pestalozzi.org.uk,* http://www.pestalozzi.org.uk/PIDEC+Library/library/Religion/ReligionTibet/reltib012.htm (5/5/2009).

20. "Tara (Buddhism), Contents # 2: 'Origin as a Buddhist bodhisattva,'" *Wikipedia,* http://en.wikipedia.org/wiki/Tara_%28Buddhism%29 (5/5/2009).

21. Prof. Emeritus Thomas F. McDaniel, *Name Changes in the Bible,* http://www.docstoc.com/docs/3285387/NAME-CHANGES-IN-THE-BIBLE-Thomas– F –McDaniel-Professor-Emeritus (3/5/2009).

22. Jeff Jonson, *Diving Promise of Fame in Bible Names,* https://www.amazines.com/Christian/article_detail.cfm/614468?articleid=614468 (3/5/2009).

16. Family Names

23. "A Brief Lesson in Jewish and Yiddish Names and How They are Chosen," *Jewish Baby Naming Traditions,* http://collegeuniversity.suite101.com/article.cfm/jewish_baby_girl_names (3/5/2009).

24. "Scotch-Irish American," *Wikipedia,* http://en.wikipedia.org/wiki/Scotch-Irish_American (4/5/2009). The English attempt to eliminate Irish names is one of the earliest examples of a governmental effort to obliterate a culture by eradicating its names. Native Americans and Native Australians were also robbed of their names and languages. Hitler robbed the Jews of their given names and labeled them all with a "J" in order to dehumanize them. Dehumanization makes terrible things possible. Erasing names is one of the first steps in that process.

25. "Irish Naming Patterns," *RootsWeb.com,* http://www.rootsweb.ancestry.com/~irlcor2/Naming.html (4/5/2009).

26. "Scottish Naming Traditions - Carr/Leith Family History," *RootsWeb.com*, http://freepages.genealogy.rootsweb.ancestry.com/~carrleith/namingtraditions.html (4/5/2009).

27. "Names for Children—Surnames," http://family.jrank.org/pages/1196/Names-Children-Surnames.html (4/5/2009).

28. "Names for Children—Surnames," http://family.jrank.org/pages/1196/Names-Children-Surnames.htm (4/5/2008), Justin Kaplan and Anne Bernays, *The Language of Names* (New York, Simon & Schuster: 1997). The authors point out that boys who have the same name as their father and are referred to as Junior appear more likely to end up in mental institutions than those not named for their fathers, which suggests that a boy named for a father may feel more stress than a daughter named for a mother.

29. "Edith," *Wikipedia*, http://en.wikipedia.org/wiki/Edith. "Meaning, Origin and History of the Name Edith," *Behind the Name*, http://www.behindthename.com/name/edith (4/5/2009).

30. Natalie Angier, "Do Races Differ? Not Really, DNA Shows," *New York Times*, August 22, 2000, http://astro.temple.edu/~ruby/opp/racesnyt.html (4/5/2009).

31. Natalie Angier, "Do Races Differ? Not Really, DNA Shows," *New York Times*, August 22, 2000, http://partners.nytimes.com/library/national/science/082200sci-genetics-race.html (4/5/08/2009).

32. "Genetics and the Meaning of Race," *Genetics and Identity*, http://www.ahc.umn.edu/bioethics/genetics_and_identity/case.html#top (4/5/2009).

33. Alan R. Templeton, "Human Races: A Genetic and Evolutionary Perspective" fall 1998 issue, *American Anthropologist*, quoted from "Biological Differences Among Races do not Exist, WU research shows," http://record.wustl.edu/archive/1998/10-15-98/articles/races.html (4/13/2009).

34. "Irish Ancestors: Origins of surnames," *IrishTimes.com*, April 28, 2009, http://www.irishtimes.com/ancestor/magazine/surname/index.htm (4/5/2009).

35. "Irish clans," *Wikipedia*, http://en.wikipedia.org/wiki/Irish_clans (5/5/2009).
"Surnames," *Baby Names.org*, http://www.babynames.org.uk/surnames.htm (5/5/2009).
"Surnames," *Online Etymology Dictionary*, http://www.etymonline.com/index.php?search=surname&searchmode=none (5/5/2009).

36. "England's historical roots 'found' in surnames," *Telegraph.co.uk.*, Nov. 21, 2007, http://www.telegraph.co.uk/news/uknews/1570057/Englands-historical-roots-found-in-surnames.
"Surname," *Online Etymology Dictionary*, http://www.etymonline.com/index.php?search=surname&searchmode=none (5/5/2009).

37. "Surnames-as-First-Names," *Edgar's Name Pages*, http://www.geocities.com/edgarbook/names/other/surnames.html (5/5/2009).

38. "Surnames-as-First-Names," *Edgar's Name Pages,* http://www.geocities.com/edgarbook/names/other/surnames.html (5/5/2009).

39. "What is Yizkor," *About.com: Judaism,* http://judaism.about.com/od/deathandmournin1/f/yizkor.htm (4/5/2009).

40. "Day of the Dead," *Wikipedia,* http://en.wikipedia.org/wiki/Day_of_the_Dead (4/5/2009).

41. "Importance of Rituals Dedicated to the Dead in Hinduism," *Audarya Fellowship,* http://www.indiadivine.org/audarya/hinduism/448385-importance-rituals-dedicated-dead-hinduism.html (12/14/ 09).

42. "Ghost Festival," *Wikipedia,* http://en.wikipedia.org/wiki/Ghost_Festival (12/14/2009).
"Chinese Ghost Festival—Religion Facts," http://www.religionfacts.com/chinese_religion/holidays/ghost_festival.htm (12/14/2009).
"The Hungry Ghost Festival," http://www.essortment.com/all/hungryghostfes_rjkb.htm (12/14/2009).

43. "Obon," japan-guide.com, http://www.japan-guide.com/e/e2286.html (4/5/2008).
"Obon Festival," *Wikipedia,* http://en.wikipedia.org/wiki/Bon_Festival (4/5/2009).
Adam "Omega" Arnold, "Obon Week: Japan's Festival to Honor the Dead," *Animefringe,* http://www.animefringe.com/magazine/01.08/feature/3/index.php3 (4/5/2009).

44. "Butterfly effect," *Wikipedia,* http://en.wikipedia.org/wiki/Butterfly_effect (7/29/2009). "The butterfly effect was first described in 1890. In essence, the butterfly effect, a term popularized by Edward Lorenz in the 1960s, proves that seemingly inconsequential physical events, such as the fluttering of a butterfly's wing, can have far-reaching consequences."

45. "Transpersonal psychology," *Wikipedia,* http://en.wikipedia.org/wiki/Transpersonal_psychology (12/14/2009).
"What is Transpersonal Psychology?" *The Institute of Transpersonal Psychology,* http://www.itp.edu/about/transpersonal.php (12/14/09).

17. Names Other Than Family Names

46. "Godparent," *Wikipedia,* http://en.wikipedia.org/wiki/Godparent (5/5/2009).

47. "Quincy Market, Boston," http://www.aviewoncities.com/boston/quincymarket.htm (7/29/2009).

48. "Cynthia—meaning of Cynthia name," *Think Baby Names,* http://www.thinkbabynames.com/meaning/0/Cynthia (5/5/2009).

49. "Meredith," *Wikipedia,* http://en.wikipedia.org/wiki/Meredith (8/17/2009).

50. "Names for Children—Surnames," http://family.jrank.org/pages/1196/Names-Children-Surnames.html (5/5/2009).

18. Naming Patterns

51. "This Name's For You," Beth Boswell Jacks, http://www.USADeepSouth.com./article1300.html (5/6/2009).

52. "awefully," *The American Heritage Dictionary of the English Language,* http://www.bartleby.com/61/28/A0552800.html (5/5/2009).

53. "French Names," *Wikipedia,* http://en.wikipedia.org/wiki/French_names (5/6/2009).

54. Shannon Mullen, "Fitting in takes a toll on tradition," *The Asbury Park Sunday Press,* Oct.12, 2008: A1, A15 (5/6/2009), http://www.buffalo.edu/news/pdf/October08/AsburyPPBuscagliaTwoSurnames.pdf (5/6/2009).

55. "Southern United States," *Wikipedia,* http://en.wikipedia.org/wiki/Southern_United_States (5/6/2009).

56. "Irish Name," *Wikipedia,* http://en.wikipedia.org/wiki/Irish_name (8/7/2010)

57. "Southern Baby Names," *Professor's House.com,* http://www.professorshouse.com/family/baby-names/southern-baby-names.aspx (5/5/2009).

58. "Southern Female Names Beginning with 'C,'" *Unique Baby Gear Ideas.com,* http://www.unique-baby-gear-ideas.com/southern-female-names-c.html (5/6/2009).

59. "Central African Names and African American Naming Patterns," John Norton, *The William and Mary Quarterly,* 3rd series, vol. 50, #4, Oct. 1993, pp.727-742.

60. Donald Wright, "Slavery in Africa," http://autocww.colorado.edu/~blackmon/E64ContentFiles/AfricanHistory/SlaveryInAfrica.html.

61. "The Fourth Sin in Double Barreled Names," *Appellation Mountain.net,* http://appellationmountain.net/2008/02/29/the-fourth-sin-in-double-barreled-names (5/6/2009).

62. John Spur, "English Puritanism, 1603-1689," *Social History in Perspective,* ed. Jeremy Black (New York: Palgrave Macmillan, 1998) 41.

63. "Reuben—meaning of Reuben name," *Think Baby Names,* http://www.thinkbabynames.com/meaning/1/Reuben (5/6/2009).

64. Cole C. Kingsees, *The American Civil War, Greenwood Guides to Historic Events, 1500-1900* (Santa Barbara: Greenwood Press, 2004)
Amazon Digital Press, 91, http://books.google.com/books?id=Z9DQkJgKlAsC (5/6/2009).
John Spur, "English Puritanism, 1603-1689," *Social History in Perspective,* ed. Jeremy Black (New York: Palgrave Macmillan,1998) 41.

65. "Social Register," *Wikipdia,* http://en.wikipedia.org/wiki/Social_Register (5/6/2009).

66. "Boston Brahmin," *Wikipedia,* http://en.wikipedia.org/wiki/Boston_Brahmin (5/6/2009).

19. Sound

67. According to Pythagoras all things in the universe are interrelated, and this can be proven mathematically. John Newlands proved this in chemistry with the law of octaves in 1865 ("John. A. R. Newlands," *Wikipedia,* http://en.wikipedia.org/wiki/ John_Alexander_Reina_Newlands). In 1202 Fibonacci brought India's discovery of the mathematical structure of nature to the West. ["Fibonacci number," *Wikipedia,* http:// en.wikipedia.org/wiki/Fibonacci_number (5/6/2009)]. For a more detailed discussion of Pythagorean thought, consult Manly Hall, *The Secret Teachings of All Ages* (New York: Tascher/Penguin, 2003); see also "Pythagoras," *Wikipedia* http://en.wikipedia.org/wiki/ Pythagoras (5/6/2009).

68. "Understanding How Earthquakes Make Buildings Vibrate," *WISER: Women's Institutes and Seismic Engineering Research,* http://www.ideers.bris.ac.uk/meta/ WISERScienceKit.pdf (5/6/2009).

69. Manly P. Hall, *The Secret Teachings of All Ages* (New York: Tascher/Penguin, 2003) 256.
Elizabeth Hare and Don Campbell, *Sacred Space, Sacred Sound* (Adyar, India: Quest Books, 2007) 14-15: "Resonance is the frequency at which an object starts to vibrate. Everything has a frequency that sets it in motion, from a bridge over a river, to a rock, to a crystal goblet. Our entire body is a symphony of sound, made of different resonant frequencies of every organ, bone, and tissue. We each have a sound signature, or personal vibratory rate, that is made up of the composite frequency of all our bodily systems."

70. "What is Sound Healing?" *The College of Sound Healing,* http://www. collegeofsoundhealing.co.uk/pages/about.html (5/7/2009).

71. "Harmony of the Spheres," *YouTube,* http://www.youtube.com/ watch?v=1EFZuzgcIzY (5/6/2009).

72. "112 Meditations from Shiva to Parvati," *totallyok.com,* http://www.totallyok. com/secret/047m.htm (5/6/2009).
"Mantra," *Wikipedia,* http://en.wikipedia.org/wiki/Mantra (5/6/2009).
"Mantra: What is a Mantra and How Does it Work?" http://www.sanskritmantra. com/what.htm (5/6/2009), quoting from *Healing Mantras* by Thomas Ashley-Ford (Louisville, CO: Sounds True, 2000).

73. Susan Kruglinski, "Musical Scales Mimic the Sound of Language," *Discover Magazine* (published online Jan.14, 2008), http://discovermagazine.com/2008/jan/ musical-scales-mimic-sound-of-language (5/7/2009).

74. Deborah Ross, et al., "Musical intervals in speech," Center for Cognitive Neuroscience and Department of Neurobiology (Durham, NC: Duke University, Durham, April 2007), http://www.ncbi.nlm.nih.gov/pmc/articles/PMC1876656/ (5/7/2009).

75. Henry Fountain, "For Mating Mosquitoes, 'Harmonic Convergence,'" *New York Times* (Science section. January 9, 2009) Online: http://www.nytimes.com/2009/01/13/science/13obwhine.html?fta=y.
Lauren Cator, et al.,"Harmonic Convergence in the Love Songs of the Dengue Vector Mosquito," *Science Magazine*, (Feb.20, 2009 Vol. 323. no. 5917, pp.1077-1079. DOI: 10.1126/science.1166541). Originally published in *Science Express*, Jan. 8, 2009 http://www.sciencemag.org/cgi/content/abstract/1166541 (5/7/2009).

76. Analysis of American men and women's names is based on data posted by the Social Security Administration's, *Popular Baby Names*, http://www.ssa.gov/OACT/babynames/ (5/7/2009).

77. Roy Feinson, *The Secret Universe of Names; The Dynamic Interplay of Names and Destiny* (New York, Overlook Duckworth, 2004) 526.

78. "Behind the Name: Name Element," *Behind the Name*, http://www.behindthename.com/glossary/view/name_element (7/31/2009).

79. Beth Jacks, "Double Names from the U.S. Deep South," USADeepSouth.com., http://usads.ms11.net/namelist3.html.
Lonneye Sue Sims Pearson, "What's in a (Southern) Name?" *USADeepSouth.com.* http://usads.ms11.net/name.html (5/7/2009).

80. "Lilt," *Miriam-Webster Online Dictionary*, http://www.merriam-webster.com/dictionary/LILT (2/2/2010).

81. "Lilt," *The Free Dictionary* by Farlex, http://www.thefreedictionary.com/lilt (5/7/2009).

82. "Amphimacer," *Wikipedia*, http://en.wikipedia.org/wiki/Cretic (5/7/2009).

83. "Anapest," *Wikipedia*, http://www.google.com/search?client=safari&rls=en&q=anapaest&ie=UTF-8&oe=UTF-8) (5/7/2009).

84. "Anapest," *The Online Encyclopedia*, http://encyclopedia.jrank.org/articles/pages/4660/anapaest.html (5/7/2009).

85. "Anapest," *Wikipedia*, http://www.google.com/search?client=safari&rls=en&q=anapaest&ie=UTF-8&oe=UTF-8 (5/7/2009).

86. "Southern American English," *Wikipedia*, http://en.wikipedia.org/wiki/Southern_American_English (5/7/2009).

87. Kathryn Woodcock, Ph.D., O.M.C., P.Eng., "Consonant Confusion with Sloping Audiogram," http://www.deafened.org/consconf.htm (7/31/2009), based on research by G. A. Miller and P.E. Nicely, is an analysis of auditory confusion among some English consonants. *Journal of the Acoustical Society of America*, vol. 27: 338–352, 1955.

20. Spelling

88. Glyndon, Howard, "Women's Names," *New York Times*, Jan. 10, 1869. http://query.nytimes.com/mem/archivefree/pdf?_r=1&res=9F05E5D7113AEF34BC4852DFB7668382679FDE (5/7/2009).

21. Who Names the Child

89. "Nomenclator," *Oxford English Dictionary* (Oxford: Oxford University Press, 2009).

90. "Grandparents Nicknames—List of Grandma & Grandpa Nicknames," *The New Parents Guide*, http://www.thenewparentsguide.com/grandparents-nicknames.htm (5/7/2009).

91. I still remember discovering Queen Elizabeth I as a child and being inspired by her amazing intelligence and survival in that treacherous, male-dominated era. Her courage remained a subtle inspiration, as her story would resurface from time to time in my life and thoughts.

92. "Moniker," *Wikipedia*, http://en.wikipedia.org/wiki/Moniker (5/7/2009).

24. Names and Adoption

93. Kathryn Thomas, "Pope Benedict XVI Changes Catholic Church's Stance on Unbaptized Babies and Limbo," April 20, 2007, *Associated Content.com*, http://www.associatedcontent.com/article/221601/pope_benedict_xvi_changes_catholic.html?cat=7 (5/7/2009).

25. Assimilation

94. Persian Language, *Wikipedia*, http://en.wikipedia.org/wiki/Persian_language

95. "Persian alphabet, pronunciation and language," *Omniglot: writing systems and languages of the world*, http://www.omniglot.com/writing/persian.htm (5/7/2009).

96. "Chamber Judgment in the Case of Unal v. Turkey," *Registry of the European Court of Human Rights* 571/ 16.11.2004, http://www.echr.coe.int/eng/Press/2004/Nov/ChamberjudgmentUnalTekeli161104.htm (5/7/2009).

97. "Niger River," *Wikipedia*, http://en.wikipedia.org/wiki/Niger_River (5/7/2009).

98. "Pan-African flag," *Wikipedia*, http://en.wikipedia.org/wiki/Pan-African_flag (5/7/2009).

99. "Every Race has a Flag but the Coon," *Wikipedia*, http://en.wikipedia.org/wiki/Every_Race_Has_a_Flag_but_the_Coon (5/7/2009).

100. "Pan-African flag," *Wikipedia*, http://en.wikipedia.org/wiki/Pan-African_flag

"The History of the Red, Black, and Green Flag," http://en.wikipedia.org/wiki/Pan-African_flag (5/7/2009).

101. "History of slavery," *Wikipedia*, http://en.wikipedia.org/wiki/Slave_trade#North_America (5/7/2009).
The first Black African slaves were brought to North America by the Spanish in a failed attempt to colonize North Carolina in 1526. The slaves revolted and fled into the wilderness. The Dutch brought slaves to Virginia in 1619. The Emancipation Proclamation (1863) only freed slaves in the Confederacy. The Thirteenth Amendment put an official end to slavery in 1865. Discrimination and Jim Crow laws severely restricted Black Americans rights to work, to education, and to health care. Discrimination was only officially ended in 1964 with the Civil Rights Act. Considering how recent this legislation is, the election of a Black American president in 2009, only 45 years later, is a testament to the vitality of both Black Americans and American society in general.

102. A. Portes, R. Rumbaut, *The Story of the Immigrant Second Generation* (Berkley: University of California Press, 2001), http://www.ucpress.edu/books/pages/9357.php (1/21/2010).

26. The Shrinking Planet

103. John Donne, "Devotions Upon Emergent Occasions: Meditation XVII," *The Phrase Finder* (www.phrases.org.uk), copyright Gary Martin, http://www.phrases.org.uk/meanings/257100.html (5/7/2009).

104. "Benjamin Franklin," *Wikiquote*, http://en.wikiquote.org/wiki/Benjamin_Franklin (5/7/2009).

105. Dr. Herndon M. Harris, Jr. and Charlotte Harris Rees, *The Asiatic Fathers of America - Chinese Discovery and Colonization of Ancient America* (Lynchburg, VA: Warwick House Publishing, 2006).
Paul Rozario, *Zheng He and the Treasure Fleet*, 1405—1433 (Singapore: SNP International, 2005).
Gavin Menzies, *1421, The Year China Discovered America* (New York: William Morrow, 2003), http://www.gavinmenzies.net/media.asp (5/7/2009).

27. Names and Religion

106. "Must a child have a saint's name to be baptized?" *Catholic Answers Forums*, http://forums.catholic.com/showthread.php?t=198327 (5/7/2009).

107. "The Protestant Reformation," *Behind the Name.com*, http://www.behindthename.com/glossary/view/protestant_reformation (5/7/2009).

108. Tracey R. Rich, "Jewish Names," *Judaism 101*, http://www.jewfaq.org/jnames. htm (5/7/2009).

109. Tracey R. Rich, "Jewish Names," *Judaism 101*, http://www.jewfaq.org/jnames. htm (5/7/2009).

110. Jane Moritz, "New Jewish Baby: Rituals, Traditions, and Gifts," copyright 2007, Challah Connection, *searchwarp.com*, http://searchwarp.com/swa234143.htm (5/7/2009).

"Do Muslims Celebrate Baptism?" *Reading Islam.com—Ask About Islam*, http:// www.readingislam.com/servlet/Satellite?cid=1123996016334&pagename=IslamOnline-English-AAbout_Islam/AskAboutIslamE/AskAboutIslamE (5/7/2009).

"Are Muslims Baptised?" *Reading Islam.com*, http://www.readingislam.com/ servlet/Satellite?cid=1123996015860&pagename=IslamOnline-English-AAbout_Islam/ AskAboutIslamE/AskAboutIslamE (5/7/2009).

"Religion in the Workplace: Destination: Islam," *Tanenbaum, Moving Beyond Differences*, http://www.tanenbaum.org/toolkit_islam4.html (5/7/2009).

111. "Baptism," *Catholic Encyclopedia, New Advent.com*, http://www.newadvent.org/ cathen/02258b.htm (8/7/2010).

"Baptism," *Wikipedia*, http://wikipedia.org/wiki/Baptism (8/7/2010).

112. Email response from *Hinduismnet.com*, http://www.hinduismnet.com/ (9/29/2009).

Another interesting website on Hinduism is *Hindu Wisdom*, http://www. hinduwisdom.info/contents.htm (9/29/2009).

113. Jane Moritz, "New Jewish Baby. Rituals, Traditions, and Gifts," copyright 2007, Challah Connection, *searchwarp.com*, http://searchwarp.com/swa234143.htm (5/8/2009).

114. "Mother in Different Languages," *SCFI* (Society for the Confluence of Festivals in India), http://www.mothersdaycelebration.com/mother-in-different-languages.html (5/8/2009).

Stanley Lieberson, *A Matter of Taste: How Names, Fashions, and Culture Change* (New Haven: Yale University Press, 2000). Lieberson observes that women's names ending in -a were very fashionable from the 1700s through 1850, then drop. They begin another upward cycle through the 20th century.

115. Christine Huda Dodge, "Muslim Baby Names," *About.com: Islam*, http://islam. about.com/od/babynames/tp/babynames.htm (5/8/2009).

116. Margot Badron, "Turkey - Women: Two Heads are Better Than One" (Originally published by *Al-Ahram Weekly Online*, 7 - 13 March 2002, Issue No. 576) *bianet (Istanbul International Independent Media Forum)*, http://www.bianet.org/english/ kategori/english/9362/turkey-women-two-heads-are-better-than-one (5/82009).

117. "Islam and the African Slave Trade," http://www.h-net.org/~africa/threads/islamslavery.html. Scholars discuss and debate what percentage of slaves were Muslim. The numbers are not known and work still needs to be done on this subject. This site is part of the H–Africa Discussion Network (http://www.h-net.org/~africa/), where scholars exchange ideas about Africa studies (5/8/2009).

A map showing the spread of Islam in Africa is available at http://exploringafrica.matrix.msu.edu/images/islam_spread.jpg (5/8/2009).

118. "Roots (TV miniseries)," *Wikipedia,* http://en.wikipedia.org/wiki/Roots_(mini-series) (5/8/2009).

119. Chidi Denis Isizoh, "African Traditional Religion," http://www.afrikaworld.net/afrel/. This is an excellent site for research into African religions (5/8/2009).

"African traditional religion," *Wikipedia,* http://en.wikipedia.org/wiki/African_traditional_religion.

Information on the different tribes is available at *The Africa Guide,* http://www.africaguide.com/culture/tribes/index.htm (5/8/2009)

120. Robert C. Davis, *Christian Slaves, Muslim Masters: White Slavery in the Mediterranean, the Barbary Coast, and Italy, 1500- 1800* (New York: Palgrave Macmillan, 2003), http://www.thebirdman.org/Index/Others/Others-Doc-Race&Groups-General/+Doc-Race&Groups-General WhiteSlavery/UntoldStoryOfWhiteSlavery.htm (5/8/2009).

121. Elikia M'bokolo, "The Impact of the Slave Trade on Africa—Le Monde Diplomatique—English Edition," translated by Barry Smerin, *Le Monde Diplomatique: English Edition,* April 2, 1998, http://mondediplo.com/1998/04/02africa (5/8/2009).

122. "Contemporary Slavery (section in article on Slavery)," *Wikipedia,* http://en.wikipedia.org/wiki/Slavery#Contemporary_slavery (5/8/2009).

Ricco Villanueva Siasco, "Modern Slavery," *info.please.com,* http://www.infoplease.com/spot/slavery1.html (5/8/2009).

For detailed information about worldwide slavery, check out *Free the Slaves,* headed by human rights' activist and scholar Kevin Bales. http://www.freetheslaves.net/Page.aspx?pid=183&srcid=-2 (8/7/2010).

See also *Anti-Slavery,* the oldest international human rights organization, founded in 1787 in Britain, http://www.antislavery.org/english/what_we_do/antislavery_international_today/frequently_asked_questions.aspx (2/19/2010).

123. "St. Thomas Christian tradition," *Wikipedia,* http://en.wikipedia.org/wiki/Seven_Churches_of_Saint_Thomas (5/8/2009)

124. Nicolas Notovitch, *The Unknown Life of Christ* (Chicago: Rand McNally, 1894). "Nicolas Notovitch," *Wikipedia,* http://en.wikipedia.org/wiki/Nicolas_Notovitch (5/8/2009).

Stephen Knapp, "Christianity's Similarities with Hinduism," http://www.scribd.com/doc/2022948/Christianitys-Similarities-with-Hinduism-by-Stephen-Knapp. This site is an excerpt from Stephen Knapp's *Proof of Vedic Culture's Global Existence* (Detroit: World Relief Network, 2000). (5/8/2009)

Holger Kersten, *Jesus Lived in India* (New York: Penguin, 2001).

James W. Deardorff, *Jesus Lived in India* (Lanham, MD: International Scholars Press, 2002).

Paul David, *Jesus in India—The Movie* (2008). http://www.jesus-in-india-the-movie.com/html/home.html (5/8/2009).

125. "Judith - Origin and meaning of the name Judith," *Baby Names World,* http://babynamesworld.parentsconnect.com/meaning_of_Judith.html (5/8/2009).

126. "Artemisia Gentileschi," *Wikipedia,* http://en.wikipedia.org/wiki/Artemisia_Gentileschi ((8/7/2010).

Christine Parker, *The Life and Art of Artemisia Gentileschi,* http://www.artemisia-gentileschi.com/index.shtml (5/8/2009).

127. Lewis Caroll, *Alice in Wonderland and Through the Looking Glass* (New York: Barnes and Noble, 2004) 73.

128. "Mantra," *Wikipedia,* http://en.wikipedia.org/wiki/Mantra (5/8/2009).

129. "Mantra," *Wikipedia,* http://en.wikipedia.org/wiki/Mantra (5/8/2009).

130. "Holly Hobby," *Wikipedia,* http://en.wikipedia.org/wiki/Toot_and_Puddle. This *Wikipedia* article gives the history of Holly Hobbie along with illustrations and other web links for the character, movie, books, and cards (5/8/2009).

131. "Holly," *Gardenline Online* (University of Saskatchewan and the Provincial gov.), http://gardenline.usask.ca/misc/holly.html (2/2/2010).

Suzetta Tucker, "ChristStory Christmas Holly Page," *ChristStory Christian Legends and Symbols,* http://ww2.netnitco.net/users/legend01/holly.htm (5/7/ 2009).

132. "Posy," *OnLine Etymology Dictionary,* http://www.etymonline.com/index.php?search=posy&searchmode=none (5/8/2009).

"Posy," *The Free Dictionary* by Farlex, http://www.thefreedictionary.com/posy (5/8/2009).

133. Olivier Schopfer, "Conter fleurette," *24 heures,* http://salem.blog.24heures.ch/archive/2007/10/30/conter-fleurette.html (2/2/2010).

29. Humor, Paradox, and Irony

134. Prof. James R. Kincaid, *Dickens and the Rhetoric of Laughter: a Victorian Web Book,* http://www.victorianweb.org/authors/dickens/kincaid2/intro2.html (2/2/2010).

Prof. Kincaid notes that Freud says humor enables us to deal with pain and helps make us empathic. Freud believed that laughter relieved "psychic tension." The therapeutic sense of distance from the self which humor provides is described adeptly by the Yiddish proverb, "What soap is to the body, laughter is to the soul," (http://www.quotegarden.com/laughter.html). Scientists have now proven that laughter helps lower blood pressure and helps with pain, the heart, and the immune system. "Scientists Discover New Health Benefits with Laughter," *KUTV-Utah News-2News* (4/11/08) http://www.kutv.com/content/news/topnews/story/Scientists-Discover-New-Health-Benefits-With/rKF6LfGfLU2F-PfEQQj0PA.cspx (5/8/2009). The *Wikipedia* article on laughter, http://en.wikipedia.org/wiki/Laughter#Laughter_and_Health, lists the physical benefits of laughter, which include raising levels of disease-fighting cells and the release of endorphins. So along with the apple a day, add a good laugh.

30. Nonverbal Associations

135. "Synesthesia," *Medical Dictionary definitions of popular medical terms,* http://www.medterms.com/script/main/art.asp?articlekey=8445 (5/8/2009).

136. Lee Dye, "Why Some People See Numbers, Letters in Colors," *abc NEWS,* (March 2, 2008), http://abcnews.go.com/Technology/Story?id=98039&page=1 (5/8/2009).

Richard Cytowic, *The Man Who Tasted Shapes* (New York: J.P. Tarcher/Putnam, 1993).

137. "Soggetto cavato," *Wikipedia,* http://en.wikipedia.org/wiki/Soggetto_cavato (5/8/2009).

138. "Solfège," *Wikipedia,* http://en.wikipedia.org/wiki/Solfege (5/8/2009).

139. Jeff Whitmill, *The Music of Your Name,* http://www.moyn.org/ (5/8/2009).

140. "Johann Sebastian Bach," *Everything2.com* (7/12/2000), http://everything2.com/node/36696 (2/2/20010).

141. "Fibonacci number," *Wikipedia,* http://en.wikipedia.org/wiki/Fibonacci_number (5/8/2009).

142. Prof. K. Podnieks, *Platonism, Intuition and the Nature of Mathematics, Part 2,* http://www.ltn.lv/~podnieks/gt1a.html#BM1_3 (5/8/2009) Prof. Podnieks' website is the winner of an Academics Award and an Internet Guide Award by Britannica.

143. Claire Martin, "An Introduction to Psychological Astrology" (London: CPA Press, 2005), *astro.com,* http://www.astro.com/mtp/mtp0_e.htm (2/2/2010).

For a concise introduction to Astrology see: *An Introduction to Astrology,* http://www.faainc.org.au/pdf/Intro2Astrology.pdf (5/8/2009).

144. Connie Barlow, "We are made of Stardust," *Stardust: Toward a New Periodic Table of Elements,* http://www.alphadictionary.com/articles/index.html (2/2/2010).

31. Unlocking the Secrets of the Past

145. "Schizophrenia: Youth's Greatest Disabler—Course and outcome of schizophrenia," *World Health Organization,* http://www.searo.who.int/en/Section1174/Section1199/Section1567/Section1827_8055.htm (2/2/2010).

146. Rob Stein, "The Next Generation of Mental Disorders," The *Washington Post* (2/10/2010).

34. Generations X, Y, and Z

147. Alex Madrigal, "Why Your Baby's Name Will Sound Like Everyone Else's," *Wired Science,* http://www.wired.com/wiredscience/2009/05/babynames/ (5/8/2009).

148. Jacob Goldenberg and Moshe Levy, "Local Yokels, Babies' Names and the Internet," The *Economist,* 7/06/2009, http://www.economist.com/displayStory.cfm?story_id=13940652 (2/2/2010).

35. Recent Naming Phenomena

149. "His Dark Materials," *Wikipedia,* http://en.wikipedia.org/wiki/His_Dark_Materials (5/8/2009).

150. "Daemon," *Wikipedia,* http://en.wikipedia.org/wiki/Daemon_(mythology) (5/8/ 2009).

151. "Joy's Daemon," *Daemon Page, page 2,* http://daemonpage.com/yourdaemons2.php (5/8/2009).

152. "Guardian Angels," *Catholic Encyclopedia,* http://www.newadvent.org/cathen/07049c.htm (5/8/2009).

153. "Avatar (computing)," *Wikipedia,* http://en.wikipedia.org/wiki/Avatar_(computing) (5/8/2009).

154. "Avatar (computing)," *Wikipedia* http://en.wikipedia.org/wiki/Avatar_(computing) (5/8/2009).

155. Steve Mollman, "Avatars in rehab: Getting therapy in virtual worlds," (7/11/2008), *CNN.com/technology,* http://www.cnn.com/2008/TECH/07/16/db.secondlifetherapy/index.html (5/8/2009).

156. Donna St. George, "Study Finds Some Youths 'Addicted' to Video Games," *Washington Post* (4/20/2009), http://www.commercialfreechildhood.org/news/2009/04/youthsaddicted.html (8/22/2009).

BIBLIOGRAPHY

"Absolutely Fabulous." *Wikipedia, the free encyclopeida.org*. Web. 18 Feb. 2010. http://en.wikipedia.org/wiki/Absolutely_Fabulous.

Adam, Arnold. "Animefringe: Features: Obon Week: Japan's Festival to Honor the Dead." *Animefringe.on line magazine*. Web. 18 Feb. 2010. http://www.animefringe.com/magazine/01.08/feature/3/index.php3.

The Africa Guide.com. Web. 19 Feb. 2010. http://www.africaguide.com/culture/tribes/index.htm.

"African traditional religion." *Wikipedia, the free encyclopedia*. Web. 19 Feb. 2010. http://en.wikipedia.org/wiki/African_traditional_religion.

"Anapaest," *Britannica Online Encyclopedia*. Web. 8 Aug. 2010. http://www.britannica.com/EBchecked/topic/22718/anapest.

"Anapaest," *Wikipedia, the free encyclopedia*. Web. 8 Aug. 2010. http://en.wikipedia.org/wiki/Anapaest.

Angier, Natalie, "Do Races Differ? Not Really, DNA Shows." Science: *New York Times*. Web. 8 Aug. 201. http://partners.nytimes.com/library/national/science/082200sci-genetics-race.html.

"Anti-Slavery - Frequently Asked Questions." *Anti-Slavery.org*. Web. 19 Feb. 2010. http://www.antislavery.org/english/what_we_do/antislavery_international_today/frequently_asked_questions.aspx.

"Are Muslims Baptized?" *Reading Islam.com*. Web. 20 April 2008. http://www.readingislam.com/servlet/Satellite?cid=1123996015860&pagename=IslamOnline-English-AAbout_Islam/AskAboutIslamE/AskAboutIslamE.

Arlès, Philippe. *A History of Private Life, vol.2 of Revelations of the Medieval World*, ed. Georges du Buy. Boston: Belknap, 1993. Print. 119.

"Artemisia Gentileschi." *Wikipedia, the free encyclopedia*. Web. 19 Feb. 2010. http://en.wikipedia.org/wiki/Artemisia_Gentileschi.

Badron, Margot. "Turkey - Women: Two Heads are Better Than One." *English-Bianet.org*. Web. 19 Feb. 2010. http://www.bianet.org/english/kategori/english/9362/turkey-women-two-heads-are-better-than-one.

Barlow, Connie. "We are made of Stardust." *alphaDictionary.com*. Web. 20 Feb. 2010. http://www.alphadictionary.com/articles/index.html.

Bartleby.com: Great Books Online -- Quotes, Poems, Novels, Classics and hundreds more. Web. 18 Feb. 2010. http://www.bartleby.com/61/28/A0552800.html.

Bartlett, Prof., Kenneth R. *Renaissance Women: The Italian Renaissance, course #3970*, Teaching Company. CD.

"Baptism." *Catholic Encyclopedia. New Advent.org.* Web. 19 Feb. 2010. http://www.newadvent.org/cathen/02258b.htm.

"Baptism." *Wikipedia, the free encyclopedia.* Web. 8 Aug. 2010 http://en.wikipedia.org/wiki/Baptism.

Beard, Robert, Ph.D., *alphaDictionary.com.* Web. 17 Feb. 2010. http://www.alphadictionary.com/articles/index.html.

"Behind the Name: Name Element." *Behind the Name: the Etymology and History of First Names.* Web. 19 Feb. 2010. http://www.behindthename.com/glossary/view/name_element.

"Behind the Name: Protestant Reformation." *Behind the Name: the Etymology and History of First Names.* Web. 19 Feb. 2010. http://www.behindthename.com/glossary/view/protestant_reformation.

"Benjamin Franklin." *Wikiquote.* Web. 19 Feb. 2010. http://en.wikiquote.org/wiki/Benjamin_Franklin.

"Bon Festival." *Wikipedia, the free encyclopedia.* Web. 18 Feb. 2010. http://en.wikipedia.org/wiki/Bon_Festival.

"Boston Brahmin." *Wikipedia, the free encyclopedia.* Web. 18 Feb. 2010. http://en.wikipedia.org/wiki/Boston_Brahmin.

"A Brief Lesson in Hebrew and Yiddish names and how they are chosen." Suite101.com. Web. 18 Feb.2010. http://collegeuniversity.suite101.com/article.cfm/jewish_baby_girl_names.

"Butterfly effect." *Wikipedia, the free encyclopedia.* Web. 18 Feb. 2010. http://en.wikipedia.org/wiki/Butterfly_effect.

Caroll, Lewis. *Through the Looking Glass.* New York: Barnes and Noble, 2004. Print.

Cator, Lauren, Ben J. Arthur, Laura Harrington, and Ronald Hoy. "Harmonic Convergence in the Love Songs of the Dengue Vector Mosquito." (Originally published in Science Express on 8 January 2009 Science 20 February 2009: vol. 323. no. 5917, pp. 1077 - 1079 DOI: 10.1126/science.1166541) *ScienceMagazine.org.* Web. 19 Feb. 2010. http://www.sciencemag.org/cgi/content/abstract/1166541.

"Chamber Judgement in the Case of Unal Tekeli v. Turkey." *European Court of Human Rights.* Web. 7 May 2009. http://www.echr.coe.int/eng/Press/2004/Nov/ChamberjudgmentÜnalTekeli161104.htm.

"Chinese Ghost Festival - ReligionFacts." *ReligionFacts.com.* Web. 18 Feb. 2010. http://www.religionfacts.com/chinese_religion/holidays/ghost_festival.htm.

The Complete Unabridged Oxford Dictionary. Oxford: Oxford UP, 1989. Print.

"Contents." *Hindu Wisdom.* Web. 19 Feb. 2010. http://www.hinduwisdom.info/contents.htm.

Cook, Ray. "Behind the name: Hailey." *Helium - Where Knowledge Rules. com*. Web. 17 Feb. 2010. http://www.helium.com/items/819456-behind-the-name-hailey.

Coontz, Stephanie. *Marriage: A History*. New York: Viking, 2005. Print.

"Cretic." *Wikipedia, the free encyclopedia*. Web. 19 Feb. 2010. http://en.wikipedia.org/wiki/Cretic.

"Cynthia - meaning of Cynthia name." *Think Baby Names.com*. Web. 18 Feb. 2010. http://www.thinkbabynames.com/meaning/0/Cynthia.

Cytowic, Richard. *The Man Who Tasted Shapes*. New York: Tarcher/Putnam, 1993. Print.

"Daemon (classical mythology)." *Wikipedia.org*. Web. 19 Feb. 2010. http://en.wikipedia.org/wiki/Daemon_(mythology).

Davis, Robert C. *Christian Slaves, Muslim Masters: White Slavery in the Meditarranean, the Barbwry Coast, and Italy, 1500-1800*. New York: Palgrave/MacMillan, 2003. Print.

"Day of the Dead." *Wikipedia, the free encyclopedia*. Web. 18 Feb. 2010. http://en.wikipedia.org/wiki/Day_of_the_Dead.

Deardorff, James W. *Jesus Lived in India*. Lanham, MD: International Scholars, 2002. Print.

"Do Muslims Celebrate Baptism?" *Reading Islam.com*. Web. 19 Feb. 2010. http://www.readingislam.com/servlet/Satellite?cid=1123996016334&pagename=IslamOnline-English-AAbout_Islam/AskAboutIslamE/AskAboutIslamE.

Donne, John. "No man is an island." *The Phrase Finder.org*. Web. 19 Feb. 2010. http://www.phrases.org.uk/meanings/257100.html.

"Dowry." *Wikipedia, the free encyclopedia*. Web. 18 Feb. 2010. http://en.wikipedia.org/wiki/Dowry.

"Dutch name." *Wikipedia, the free encyclopedia*. Web. 17 Feb. 2010. http://en.wikipedia.org/wiki/Dutch_name.

Dye, Lee. "Why Some People See Numbers, Letters in Color - ABC News." *ABCNews.com*. Web. 19 Feb. 2010. http://abcnews.go.com/Technology/Story?id=98039&page=1.

"EasyBib: Website form for your bibliography or works cited list." *EasyBib: Free Bibliography Maker - MLA, APA, Chicago citation styles*. Web. 18 Feb. 2010. http://easybib.com/cite/form/website.

"Every Race Has a Flag but the Coon." *Wikipedia, the free encyclopedia*. Web. 19 Feb. 2010. http://en.wikipedia.org/wiki/Every_Race_Has_a_Flag_but_the_Coon.

"The Evolution of Marriage: Ancient - My Jewish Learning." *My Jewish Learning.com*. Web.17 Feb.2010. http://www.myjewishlearning.com/life/Relationships/Spouses_and_Partners/About_Marriage/Ancient_Jewish_Marriage.shtml.

Feinson, Roy. *The Secret Universe of Names: The Dynamic Interplay of Names and Destiny.* New York: Overlook Duckworth, 2004. Print.

"Female Southern Female Names - Southern Girls' Names Starting with C." *Unique Baby Gear Ideas.com.* Web. 18 Feb. 2010. http://www.unique-baby-gear-ideas.com/southern-female-names-c.html.

"Fibonacci number." *Wikipedia, the free encyclopedia.* Web. 18 Feb. 2010. http://en.wikipedia.org/wiki/Fibonacci_number.

"The First American Bat Mitvah." *Jewish Virtual Library.org.* Web. 18 Feb. 2010. http://www.jewishvirtuallibrary.org/jsource/Judaism/firstbat.html.

"Firsts for U.S. Women." *Catalyst.org.* Web. 17 Feb. 2010. http://www.catalyst.org/publication/211/firsts-for-us-women.

Fitzpatrick, Tony. "Biological differences among races do not exist, WU research shows." *Washington University in Saint Louis.* Web. 18 Feb. 2010. http://record.wustl.edu/archive/1998/10-15-98/articles/races.html.

Fountain, Henry. "For Mating Mosquitoes, 'Harmonic Convergence.'" *New York Times.* Web. 9 Jan. 2009. Web. 9 Jan. 2009. http://www.nytimes.com/2009/01/13/science/13obwhine.html?_r=1&emc=eta1.

Free the Slaves. Web. 19 Feb. 2010. http://www.freetheslaves.net/Page.aspx?pid=183&srcid=-2.

"French name." *Wikipedia, the free encyclopedia.* Web. 18 Feb. 2010. http://en.wikipedia.org/wiki/French_names.

"Frequently Asked Questions for What's in a Name." *What's in a Name.net.* Web. 18 Feb. 2010. http://www.whatsinaname.net/faq.html#13.

Freud, Sigmund. *The Standard Edition of the Complete Psychological Works of Sigmund Freud.* Vol. 9. London: Hogarth and the Institute of Psychoanalysis, 1959. Print. 235.

"Genetics and Identity." *Academic Health Center - University of Minnesota.* Web. 18 Feb. 2010. http://www.ahc.umn.edu/bioethics/genetics_and_identity/case.html#top.

"German name." *Wikipedia, the free encyclopedia.* Web. 18 Feb. 2010. http://en.wikipedia.org/wiki/German_names.

"Ghost Festival." *Wikipedia, the free encyclopedia.* Web. 18 Feb. 2010. http://en.wikipedia.org/wiki/Ghost_Festival.

"Godparent." *Wikipedia, the free encyclopedia.* Web. 18 Feb. 2010. http://en.wikipedia.org/wiki/Godparent.

Goldenberg, Jacob, and Moshe Levy. "Local Yokels, Babies' Names, and the Internet." *The Economist.com.* Web. 19 Feb. 2010. http://www.economist.com/displayStory.cfm?story_id=13940652.

"Grandparents Nicknames - List of Grandma & Grandpa Nicknames." *The New Parents Guide.com.* Web. 19 Feb. 2010. http://www.thenewparentsguide.com/grandparents-nicknames.htm.

"Guardian Angels." *Catholic Encyclopeida. NewAdvent.org.* Web. 20 Feb. 2010. http://www.newadvent.org/cathen/07049c.htm.

Hall, Manly. *The Secret Teachings of the Ages.* New York: Tarcher/Penguin, 2003. Print.

Hare, Elizabeth, and Don Campbell. *Sacred Space, Sacred Sound.* Aydar, India: Quest, 2007. Print.

"Harmony of the Spheres." *Princeton University. YouTube.* Web. 18 Feb. 2010. http://www.youtube.com/watch?v=1EFZuzgcIzY.

Harris, Herndon M., Ph.D., and Charlotte Harris Reese. *The Asiatic Fathers of America: Chinese Dicovery and Colonization of Ancient America.* Lynchberg: Warwick House, 2006. Print.

Heather, Simon. "What is Sound Healing?" *The College of Sound Healing Home Page.* Web. 18 Feb. 2010. http://www.collegeofsoundhealing.co.uk/pages/about.html.

Hinduismnet.com. Web. 19 Feb. 2010. http://www.hinduismnet.com/.

"History of slavery." *Wikipedia, the free encyclopedia.* Web. 19 Feb. 2010. http://en.wikipedia.org/wiki/Slave_trade#North_America.

"Holly Hobbie." *Wikipedia, the free encyclopedia.* Web. 19 Feb. 2010. http://en.wikipedia.org/wiki/Toot_and_Puddle.

Howard, Glyndon. "Women's Names." *New York Times,* 10 Jan. 1869. Web. 7 May 2009. http://query.nytimes.com/mem/archivefree/pdf?_r=1&res=9F05E5D7113AEF34BC4852DFB7668382679FDE.

Huda Dodge, Christine. "Muslim Baby Names - Name Your Muslim Baby." *About.com: Islam.* Web. 19 Feb. 2010. http://islam.about.com/od/babynames/tp/babynames.htm.

"Importance of Rituals Dedicated to the Dead in Hinduism - Audarya Fellowship." *IndiaDivine.org.* Web. 18 Feb. 2010. http://www.indiadivine.org/audarya/hinduism/448385-importance-rituals-dedicated-dead-hinduism.html.

"Irish Ancestors /Origins of surnames." *The Irish Times.com.* Web. 18 Feb. 2010. http://www.irishtimes.com/ancestor/magazine/surname/index.htm.

"Irish clans." *Wikipedia, the free encyclopedia.* Web. 18 Feb. 2010. http://en.wikipedia.org/wiki/Irish_clans.

"Irish Naming Patterns." *RootsWeb.com.* Web. 18 Feb. 2010. http://www.rootsweb.ancestry.com/~irlcor2/Naming.html.

Isizoh, Chici D. "African Traditional Religion." *AfrikaWorld.net.* Web. 19 Feb. 2010. http://www.afrikaworld.net/afrel/.

"Islam and the African Slave Trade." *H–Net: Humanities and Social Sciences Online*. Web. 19 Feb. 2010. http://www.h-net.org/~africa/threads/islamslavery.html.

Jacks, Beth. "Double Names from the U.S. Deep South." *USADeepSouth.com.*. Web. 5 July 2007. http://usads.ms11.net/namelist3.html.

Jesus in India. Dir. Paul Davids. Universal Studios Productions LLLP, Los Angeles. DVD.

"Jewish Names." *Judaism 101*. Web. 19 Feb. 2010. http://www.jewfaq.org/jnames.htm.

"Johann Sebastian Bach@Everything2.com." *Welcome to Everything@Everything2.com*. Web. 19 Feb. 2010. http://everything2.com/node/36696.

"John Alexander Reina Newlands." *Wikipedia, the free encyclopedia*. Web. 18 Feb. 2010. http://en.wikipedia.org/wiki/John_Alexander_Reina_Newlands.

Jonson, Jeff. "Diving Promise of Fame In Bible Names." *Amazines.com, Free Articles at Amazines.Com - Author Publishing and Free Article Database*. Web. 18 Feb. 2010. http://www.amazines.com/Christian/article_detail.cfm/614468?articleid=614468

"Joy's Daemon." *The Daemon Page*. Web. 19 Feb. 2010. http://daemonpage.com/yourdaemons2.php.

"Judith," *BabyNamesWorld.ParentsConnect.com*. Web. 19 Feb. 2010. http://babynamesworld.parentsconnect.com/meaning_of_Judith.html.

Kaplan, Justin, and Anne Bernays. *The Language of Names*. New York: Simon & Schuster, 1997. Print.

Kersten, Holger. *Jesus Lived in India*. New York: Penguin, 2001. Print.

Kincaid, Prof., James. "Introduction --The Nature of Laughter." *The Victorian Web: An Overview*. Web. 19 Feb. 2010. http://www.victorianweb.org/authors/dickens/kincaid2/intro2.html.

Kingseed, Cole Christian. "The American Civil War." *Google Books*. Web. 19 Feb. 2010. http://books.google.com/books?id=Z9DQkJgKlAsC.

Knapp, Stephen. "Christianity's Similarities with Hinduism." *Scribd.com*. Web. 19 Feb. 2010. http://www.scribd.com/doc/2022948/Christianitys-Similarities-with-Hinduism-by-Stephen-Knapp.

Knapp, Stephen. *Proof of Vedic Culture's Global Existence*. Detroit: World Relief Network, 2000. Print.

Kruglinski, Susan. "Musical Scales Mimic the Sound of Language." (originally published *Discover Magazine*. Jan. 2008). *Discovermagazine.com*. (July 14, 2008). Web. 7 July 2009. http://discovermagazine.com/2008/jan/musical-scales-mimic-sound-of-language.

"Laughter." *Wikipedia, the free encyclopedia*. Web. 19 Feb. 2010. http://en.wikipedia.org/wiki/Laughter#Laughter_and_Health.

Lieberson, Stanley. *A Matter of Taste: How Names, Fashions, and Culture Chsnge.* Yale University Press: New Haven, 2000. Print.

"Lilt - Definition and More from the Free Merriam-Webster Dictionary." *Dictionary and Thesaurus - Merriam-Webster Online.* Web. 19 Feb. 2010. http://www.merriam-webster.com/dictionary/LILT.

"List of towns in England." *Wikipedia, the free encyclopedia.* Web. 18 Feb. 2010. http://en.wikipedia.org/wiki/List_of_towns_in_England.

Madrigal, Alex. "Why Your Baby's Name Will Sound Like Everyone Else's." *Wired Science.* Web. 20 Feb. 2010. http://www.wired.com/wiredscience/2009/05/babynames/.

"Mantra." *Wikipedia, the free encyclopedia.* Web. 18 Feb. 2010. http://en.wikipedia.org/wiki/Mantra.

"Mariage." *Grande Larousse.* Vol. 7. Paris: Librarie Larousse, 1963. Print.

"Marriage." *Wikipedia, the free encyclopedia.* Web. 17 Feb. 2010. http://en.wikipedia.org/wiki/Marriage.

"Married and maiden names." *Wikipedia, the free encyclopedia.* Web. 18 Feb. 2010. http://en.wikipedia.org/wiki/Married_and_maiden_names.

Martin, Claire. "An Introduction to Psychological Astrology." *Astrology and Horoscope Homepage - Astrodienst.* Web. 20 Feb. 2010. http://www.astro.com/mtp/mtp0_e.htm.

"Mattel Dolls 1945-1960s." *Doll Reference: Antique to Vintage Dolls 1800-1970s.* Web. 17 Feb. 2010. http://www.dollreference.com/mattel_dolls1960s.html.

M'bokolo, Elikia. "The Impact of the Slave Trade on Africa." *Le Monde Diplomatique.* Web. 5 Aug. 2009. http://mondediplo.com/1998/04/02africa.

McDaniel, Thomas F., Prof. Emeritus. "Name Changes in the Bible." *Docstoc.* Web. 18 Feb. 2010. http://www.docstoc.com/docs/3285387/NAME-CHANGES-IN-THE-BIBLE-Thomas– F –McDaniel-Professor-Emeritus.

"Medieval and Renaissance Marriage." *Welcome to Drizzle - The Pacific Northwest's Best Little Online Community!* Web. 18 Feb. 2010. http://www.drizzle.com/~celyn/mrwp/mrwed.html.

Menzies, Gavin. *1421 The Year China Discovered America.* New York: William Morrow, 2009. Print.

Menzies, Gavin. *1434 How China Changed the World 1421.* Web. 19 Feb. 2010. http://www.gavinmenzies.net/media.asp.

"Meredith." *Wikipedia, the free encyclopedia.* Web. 18 Feb. 2010. http://en.wikipedia.org/wiki/Meredith.

Miller, G.A., and P.E. Nicely. "An analysis of perceptual confusion among some English consonants." *Journal of the Acoustical Society of America,* 27 (1955): 338-52. Print.

Mollman, Steve. "Avatars in rehab: Getting therapy in virtual worlds." *CNN.com.*Web. 20 Feb. 2010. http://www.cnn.com/2008/TECH/07/16/db.secondlifetherapy/index. html.

"Moniker." *Wikipedia, the free encyclopedia.* Web. 19 Feb. 2010. http://en.wikipedia.org/ wiki/Moniker.

"Mother in Different Languages: Ways of Saying Mother,Mom in Different Languages." Mother's Day-Mother's Day Celebration 2010. *SCFI* (Society for the Confluence of Festivals in India). Web. 19 Feb. 2010. http://www.mothersdaycelebration.com/ mother-in-different-languages.html.

Mullen, Shannon. "Fitting in takes a toll on tradition Latinos often drop mother's name." *The Asbury Park Sunday Press* (12 Oct. 2008).

"Musical intervals in speech." *National Center for Biotechnology Information.* Web. 19 Feb. 2010. http://www.ncbi.nlm.nih.gov/pmc/articles/PMC1876656/.

"Must a child have a saint's name to be baptized?" *Catholic Answers Forums.* Web. 19 Feb. 2010. http://forums.catholic.com/showthread.php?t=198327.

Nabokov, Vladimir. *Pnin.* New York: Random House, 2004. Print.

"Names for Children - Surnames." *Marriage and Family Encyclopedia.* Web. 17 Feb. 2010. http://family.jrank.org/pages/1196/Names-Children-Surnames.html.

Nesbit, John. "Simply ask for Goup-the-Lift." *Leopard magazine.* Web. 18 Feb. 2010. http://www.leopardmag.co.uk/feats/124/goup-the-lift.

"New Jewish Baby: Rituals, Traditions, and Gifts by Jane Moritz Challah Connection." *SearchWarp Writers' Community for Do It Yourself and Current Events Commentary.* Web. 19 Feb. 2010. http://searchwarp.com/swa234143.htm.

"Nicolas Notovitch." *Wikipedia, the free encyclopedia.* Web. 19 Feb. 2010. http:// en.wikipedia.org/wiki/Nicolas_Notovitch.

"Niger River." *Wikipedia, the free encyclopedia.* Web. 19 Feb. 2010. http://en.wikipedia.org/ wiki/Niger_River.

Norah. "Question: Double Names in the South." *www.namenerds.com.* Personal e-mail correspondence with the author. 23 Nov. 2008.

Norton, John. "Central African Names and African American Naming Patterns." *The William and Mary Quarterly* 3rd ser. 50.4 (1993): 727-42. Print.

Notovitch, Nicolas. *The Unknown Life of Jesus Christ.* Chicago: Rand McNally, 1894. Print.

"Oberlin College." *Wikipedia, the free encyclopedia.* Web. 18 Feb. 2010. http://en.wikipedia. org/wiki/Oberlin_College.

"Obon." *Japan-guide.com - Japan Travel and Living Guide.* Web. 18 Feb. 2010. http://www. japan-guide.com/e/e2286.html.

Online Etymology Dictionary. Web. 18 Feb. 2010. http://www.etymonline.com/index. php?search=surname&searchmode=none.

"Overview: History of Bar/Bat Mitzvah and Confirmation - My Jewish Learning." *Jewish Life & Judaism - My Jewish Learning.* Web. 18 Feb. 2010. http://www. myjewishlearning.com/life/Life_Events/BarBat_Mitzvah/History.shtml.

Oxford Dictionary of Quotations. 6th ed. Oxford: Oxford UP, 2004. Print.

"Pan-African flag." *Wikipedia, the free encyclopedia.* Web. 19 Feb. 2010. http:// en.wikipedia.org/wiki/Pan-African_flag.

"Pan-African flag." *Wikipedia, the free encyclopedia.* Web. 19 Feb. 2010. http:// en.wikipedia.org/wiki/Pan-African_flag.

Pearson, Lonneye Sue Sims. "What's in a (Southern) Name?" *USADeepSouth.com.* Web. 5 July 2009. http://usads.ms11.net/name.html.

"Persian language." *Wikipedia, the free encyclopedia.* Web. 19 Feb. 2010. http://en.wikipedia. org/wiki/Persian_language.

Podnieks, Prof., K. "Platonism, Intuition and the Nature of Mathematics. Part 2. By K.Podnieks." *LTN - SigmaNet klientu m.* Web. 19 Feb. 2010. http://www.ltn. lv/~podnieks/gt1a.html#BM1_3.

"Pope Benedict XVI Changes Catholic Church's Stance on Unbaptized Babies and Limbo." *Associated Content.* Web. 18 Feb. 2010. http://www.associatedcontent.com/ article/221601/pope_benedict_xvi_changes_catholic.html?cat=7.

"Popular baby names in the UK." *Pregnancy, baby and toddler health information at BabyCentre UK.* Web. 17 Feb. 2010. http://www.babycentre.co.uk/pregnancy/ naming/popularbabynames/?_requestid=6646702.

"Popular baby names." *Social Security Online - The Official Website of the U.S. Social Security Administration.* Web. 17 Feb. 2010. http://www.ssa.gov/OACT/babynames/.

Portes, Alejandro, and Ruben G. Rumbaut. Legacies: The Story of the Immigrant Second Generation. *University of California Press.* Web. 19 Feb. 2010. http://www.ucpress. edu/books/pages/9357.php.

"Posy - definition of posy by the Free Online Dictionary, Thesaurus and Encyclopedia." *Dictionary, Encyclopedia and Thesaurus - The Free Dictionary.* Web. 19 Feb. 2010. http://www.thefreedictionary.com/posy.

"Posy." *Online Etymology Dictionary.* Web. 19 Feb. 2010. http://www.etymonline.com/ index.php?search=posy&searchmode=none.

Prophet, Elizabeth Clare. *The Lost Years of Jesus.* Livingston, MT: Summit University Press, 1984.

"Pythagoras." *Wikipedia, the free encyclopedia*. Web. 18 Feb. 2010. http://en.wikipedia.org/wiki/Pythagoras.

"Quincy Market, Boston." *A View On Cities*. Web. 18 Feb. 2010. http://www.aviewoncities.com/boston/quincymarket.htm.

"Reuben - meaning of Reuben name." *Think Baby Names.com*. Web. 18 Feb. 2010. http://www.thinkbabynames.com/meaning/1/Reuben.

"Roots (TV miniseries)." *Wikipedia, the free encyclopedia*. Web. 19 Feb. 2010. http://en.wikipedia.org/wiki/Roots_(mini-series).

Rosario, Paul. *Zheng He and the Treasure Fleet, 1405-1433*. Singapore: SNP International, 2005. Print.

"Saint Thomas Christians." *Wikipedia, the free encyclopedia*. Web. 19 Feb. 2010. http://en.wikipedia.org/wiki/Seven_Churches_of_Saint_Thomas.

Sarahh, "Is There Baptism in Islam?" *Yahoo! Answers.com*. Web. 8 Aug. 2010. http://answers.yahoo.com/question/index?qid=20091230042819AApwS76>

"Schizophrenia : Youth." *SEARO World Health Organization Report, Who Publications, UN Specialized*. Web. 19 Feb. 2010. http://www.searo.who.int/en/Section1174/Section1199/Section1567/Section1827_8055.htm.

Schopher, Olivier. "Conter fleurette." *24 heures*. Web. 19 Feb. 2010. http://salem.blog.24heures.ch/archive/2007/10/30/conter-fleurette.html.

"Scotch-Irish American." *Wikipedia, the free encyclopedia*. Web. 18 Feb. 2010. http://en.wikipedia.org/wiki/Scotch-Irish_American.

"Scottish Naming Traditions - Carr / Leith Family History." *RootsWeb: Freepages*. Web. 18 Feb. 2010. http://freepages.genealogy.rootsweb.ancestry.com/~carrleith/namingtraditions.html.

Siasco, Villanueva, Ricco. "Slavery in Africa." *Info.please.com*. Web. 18 Feb. 2010. http://autocww.colorado.edu/~blackmon/E64ContentFiles/AfricanHistory/SlaveryInAfrica.html.

"Slavery." *Wikipedia, the free encyclopedia*. Web. 19 Feb. 2010. http://en.wikipedia.org/wiki/Slavery#Contemporary_slavery.

"Slavery in the Modern World." *Infoplease: Encyclopedia, Almanac, Atlas, Biographies, Dictionary, Thesaurus. Free online reference, research & homework help*. Web. 19 Feb. 2010. http://www.infoplease.com/spot/slavery1.html.

Smith, Elsdon C. *The Story of Our Names*. Detroit: Harper & Brothers, 1950. Print.

"Social Register." *Wikipedia, the free encyclopedia*. Web. 18 Feb. 2010. http://en.wikipedia.org/wiki/Social_Register.

"Solfège." *Wikipedia, the free encyclopedia*. Web. 19 Feb. 2010. http://en.wikipedia.org/wiki/Solfege.

"Southern American English." *Wikipedia, the free encyclopedia*. Web. 19 Feb. 2010. http://en.wikipedia.org/wiki/Southern_American_English.

"Southern baby names - Beth Boswell Jacks - naming babies." *USADS index page*. Web. 18 Feb. 2010. http://www.USADeepSouth.com./article1300.html.

"Southern Baby Names," *Professor's House*. Web. 18 Feb. 2010. http://www.professorshouse.com/family/baby-names/southern-baby-names.aspx.

"Southern United States." *Wikipedia, the free encyclopedia*. Web. 18 Feb. 2010. http://en.wikipedia.org/wiki/Southern_United_States.

Spur, John. *English Puritanism 1603-1689*. New York: Palgrave Macmillan, 1998. Print.

St. George, Donna. "Study Finds Some Youths 'Addicted' to Video Games." *Campaign for a Commercial-Free Childhood Home*. Web. 20 Feb. 2010. http://www.commercialfreechildhood.org/news/2009/04/youthsaddicted.html.

Stein, Rob. "The Next Generation of Mental Disorders." *The Washington Post*. 10 Feb. 2010: 1-A2. Print.

"Synesthesia definition - Medical Dictionary definitions of popular medical terms easily defined on MedTerms." *MedicineNet.com*. Web. 19 Feb. 2010. http://www.medterms.com/script/main/art.asp?articlekey=8445.

"Tara (Buddhism)." *Wikipedia, the free encyclopedia*. Web. 18 Feb. 2010. http://en.wikipedia.org/wiki/Tara_%28Buddhism%29.

"Transpersonal psychology." *Wikipedia, the free encyclopedia*. Web. 18 Feb. 2010. http://en.wikipedia.org/wiki/Transpersonal_psychology.

Tucker, Suzetta. "ChristStory Christmas Holly Page." *ChristStory Christian Legends and Symbols*. Web. 19 Feb. 2010. http://ww2.netnitco.net/users/legend01/holly.htm.

"Understanding How Earthquakes Make Buildings Vibrate." *WISER: Women's Institutes and Seismic Engineering Research Workshops*. Web. 8 Aug. 2010 www.ideers.bris.ac.uk/meta/WISERScienceKit.pdf.

"What is a Mantra and How Does It Work?" *Sanskrit Mantras and Spiritual Power*. Web. 18 Feb. 2010. http://www.sanskritmantra.com/what.htm.

"What is Transpersonal Psychology? | Institute of Transpersonal Psychology." *The Institute of Transpersonal Psychology | Graduate Education at the Frontier of Psychology and Spirituality since 1975*. Web. 18 Feb. 2010. www.ideers.bris.ac.uk/meta/WISERScienceKit.pdf.

"What is Yizkor?" *About Judaism*. Web. 18 Feb. 2010. http://judaism.about.com/od/deathandmournin1/f/yizkor.htm.

Whitmill, Jeff. *The Music of Your Name*. Web. 19 Feb. 2010. http://www.moyn.org/.

Williams, Sara. "Holly." *Gardenline Online*. Web. 19 Feb. 2010. http://gardenline.usask.ca/misc/holly.html.

Woodcock, Kathryn, Ph.D., O.M.C., P. Eng., "Consonant Confusion with Sloping Audiogram," (based on research by G.A. Miller and P.E. Nicely in *The Journal of the Acoustical Society of America,* vol. 27: 338-352, 1955) Web. 31 July 2009. http://www.deafened.org/consconf.htm>

Wright, Donald R., Ph.D., "Slavery in Africa," *Microsoft® Encarta® Online Encyclopedia 2000.*

CPSIA information can be obtained at www.ICGtesting.com
260801BV00004B/128/P

9 780615 382265